LIVING LANGUAGE®

ULTIMATE

RUSSIAN

ADVANCED

Available from LIVING LANGUAGE®

ULTIMATE COURSES. This comprehensive program covers conversation, grammar, reading, writing, and culture. Each of the 40 lessons begins with a dialogue and includes explanations of grammar and usage, vocabulary, and notes on customs and culture. Unique to this course are two sets of recordings: four hours in the target language only for use with the manual, and four bilingual recordings, ideal for learning on the go. Basic-Intermediate. French, German, Inglés, Italian, Japanese, Russian, Spanish, and Chinese (1999).

ULTIMATE ADVANCED COURSES. Sequels to the Basic-Intermediate program, these courses include sections on business vocabulary and etiquette, in addition to the dialogue-based lessons. Advanced. French, German, Inglés, Italian, Japanese, Russian, and Spanish.

COMPLETE BASIC COURSES (Level 1). The original, best-selling Living Language program developed by U.S. government experts in 1946, revised and updated in 1993, includes three hours of recordings on cassette or compact disc, a manual, and a two-way 20,000-word dictionary. Featuring a proven speed-learning method, the course progresses from words to phrases to complete sentences and dialogues. Recordings are all in the target language. Beginner-Intermediate. French, German, Inglés, Italian, Japanese, Portuguese, Russian, and Spanish.

INTERMEDIATE COURSES (Level 2): A Conversational Approach to Verbs. This course teaches more than 150 conjugations through practical phrases and dialogues. Four 60-minute bilingual cassettes and a 384-page text with 40 dialogues, exercises, and verb charts. Intermediate. French, German, Italian, and Spanish.

ADVANCED CONVERSATION COURSES (Level 3). Four 60-minute cassettes, all in the target language, feature more sophisticated dialogues, idiomatic expressions, and grammar. The accompanying 350-page conversation manual also includes the transcript with English translations, plus verb charts, culture notes, and exercises to check's one's progress. Advanced. French and Spanish.

Books also available separately.

At bookstores everywhere, or call 1-800-733-3000 for additional information. Please refer to code 71071B when calling.

You can also reach us on the web at: livinglanguage.com

ULTIMATE

RUSSIAN

ADVANCED

WRITTEN BY

JACK BLANSHEI,

DEPARTMENT OF RUSSIAN, EURASIAN

AND EAST ASIAN LANGUAGES AND CULTURES

EMORY UNIVERSITY

EDITED BY

ANA SUFFREDINI

LIVING LANGUAGE®
A Random House Company

Copyright © 1998 by Living Language, A Random House Company

All rights reserved. No part of this book may be reproduced or transmitted in any form or by any means, electronic or mechanical, including photocopying, recording, or by any information storage and retrieval system, without permission in writing from the publisher.

Published by Living Language, A Random House Company, 201 East 50th Street, New York, New York 10022. Member of the Crown Publishing Group.

Random House, Inc. New York, Toronto, London, Sydney, Auckland

www.livinglanguage.com

Living Language and colophon are registered trademarks of Crown Publishers, Inc.

Printed in the United States of America

Library of Congress Cataloging-in-Publication Data is available upon request.

ISBN 0-517-88505-0

10 9 8 7 6 5 4 3 2 1

First Edition

ACKNOWLEDGMENTS

Thanks to the Living Language staff: Kathryn Mintz, Helga Schier, Lisa Alpert, Christopher Warnasch, Olivia Varela, Germaine Ma, Jim Walsh, Lenny Henderson, and Erin Bekowies. Thanks also to: Sergei Mihailov, Galina Samoukova, Dr. Richard Schupbach, Alexandre Slavashevich, and Dr. Nyusya Millman.

Special thanks to Sergey Pilyugin and Vladislav Kostiuchenko for their invaluable counsel and proofreading, Charles Vitek of the CDC for providing epidemiological information, Ellen Mickiewicz for information about Russian telecommunications, Igor Savilyev for materials on hiring practices in Russia, Aleksey Kistyenov for information about real estate rentals, Shannon Mudd and Alan Clack for their information about economic conditions, and the U.S. Department of Commerce *BISNIS* bulletin for essential materials about business opportunities

To my wife, Sarah, without whose encouragement and support this book would not have been possible

CONTENTS

Contents   ix

LIVING LANGUAGE®
ULTIMATE

RUSSIAN

ADVANCED

INTRODUCTION

Living Language® Ultimate Russian: Advanced is a continuation of the beginner-intermediate *Ultimate Russian* program. If you have already mastered the basics of Russian in school, while traveling abroad, or with other Living Language courses, then this program is right for you.

The complete course includes this text, along with eight hours of recordings. However, if you are confident of your pronunciation, you can use the manual on its own.

With *Ultimate Russian: Advanced* you'll continue to learn how to speak, understand, read, and write idiomatic Russian. The program will also introduce you to some of the more interesting aspects of Russian culture and business. You'll be able to participate in engaging conversations about a variety of topics, as well as recognize and respond to several styles of formal and informal speech.

The course will take you everywhere, from a picnic at a dacha, to a tour of St. Petersburg, to a job interview, while teaching useful vocabulary and expressions. You'll also learn about subtle cultural distinctions in personal interaction, such as the Russian style of giving or receiving compliments, that will help smooth your way abroad.

COURSE MATERIALS

THE MANUAL

Living Language Ultimate Russian: Advanced consists of twenty lessons. It is best to read and study each lesson in the manual before listening to it on the recordings.

ДИАЛОГ (DIALOGUE): Each lesson begins with a dialogue in standard, idiomatic Russian presenting a realistic situation—a job interview, a report on the news, a meeting with a health care professional—set in various Russian locales. All dialogues are translated into colloquial English.

ПРИМЕЧАНИЯ (NOTES): The notes in this section refer to specific expressions and phrases in the dialogue. They'll introduce you to the cultural and historical background relevant to a particular expression, and allow you to see grammar rules and vocabulary in action.

1

ГРАММАТИКА И СЛОВОУПОТРЕБЛЕНИЕ (GRAMMAR AND USAGE): After a brief review of basic Russian grammar, you'll concentrate on the more advanced grammatical forms and their usages. This section will help you integrate what you already know and enable you to express yourself more accurately and appropriately by using idiomatic Russian. The heading of each topic corresponds to its listing in the table of contents.

ИДИОМАТИКА (IDIOMATIC USAGE): This section focuses on idiomatic expressions. You'll learn how to make complaints, what to say at the dinner table, how to discuss politics, and even how to propose marriage! You'll also learn that "you can't spoil kasha with butter" really means "you can't have too much of a good thing," and that in Russian you cry into someone's vest, not on their shoulder.

СТРОГО ПО ДЕЛУ (STRICTLY BUSINESS): In this section you'll explore different areas of the Russian economy, as well as cultural and historical information relevant to business etiquette and procedures. Covering topics such as dress codes, import and export, and contract negotiations, this section will enable you to do business in Russia with confidence.

УПРАЖНЕНИЯ (EXERCISES): This section allows you to review the grammar and vocabulary covered in the lessons. You can check your answers in the КЛОЧ К УПРАЖНЕНИЯМ (Answer Key), which appears after Lesson 20.

ПРЕДЛАГАЕМЫЕ ЗАНЯТИЯ (SUGGESTED ACTIVITY): This section offers suggestions for practical applications of what you've just studied as well as activities to expand your knowledge.

ПРИЛОЖЕНИЯ (APPENDIX): There are eight sections in the appendix: tables for the declension of nouns and adjectives; spelling rules; verb classification and conjugation; a list of prepositions and cases they govern; irregular comparative adjectives; a list of common consonant mutations; declension of numerals; and a letter-writing section.

СЛОВАРЬ (GLOSSARY): The extensive two-way glossary will prove an invaluable reference as you work through this program and as you apply your knowledge when dealing with the Russians and traveling abroad.

INDEX: The manual ends with an index of the major grammar points and business topics covered in the lessons.

The appendix, glossary, and index make this manual an excellent source for future reference and study.

RECORDINGS (SETS A & B)

This program provides you with eight hours of audio instruction and practice. There are two sets of recordings: the first is designed for use with the manual, while the second may be used independently. By listening to and imitating the native speakers, you'll improve your pronunciation and comprehension, while learning to use new phrases and structures.

RECORDINGS FOR USE WITH THE MANUAL (SET A)

This set of recordings gives you four hours of audio practice in Russian only, featuring the complete dialogues of all 20 lessons. The recorded material in each dialogue appears in **boldface type** in your manual. You'll first hear native Russian speakers read the complete dialogue without interruption, at normal conversational speed. Then you'll have a chance to listen to the dialogue a second time and repeat each phrase in the pauses provided. The last five dialogues are recorded at normal conversational speed only.

If you wish to practice your comprehension, first listen to the recordings of the dialogue without consulting the translations in the manual. Write down a summary of what you think the dialogue is about, and then listen to the recordings a second time, checking how much you understood against the translations in the manual. After you study each lesson in the manual and practice with Set A, go on to the second set of recordings (Set B), which can be used on the go—while driving, jogging, traveling on a plane, or doing housework.

RECORDINGS FOR USE ON THE GO (SET B)

This set of recordings gives you four hours of audio instruction and practice in Russian and English. Because they are bilingual, these recordings may be used on the go, without the manual, wherever it is convenient to learn.

The 20 lessons on Set B correspond to those in the manual. A bilingual narrator guides you through the four sections of each lesson.

The first section presents the most important phrases from the original dialogue. You will first hear the abridged dialogue without interruption, at normal conversational speed. You'll then hear it again, phrase by phrase, with English translations and pauses that allow you to repeat each phrase after the native Russian speakers.

The second section reviews and expands upon the most important vocabulary introduced in the lesson. You will practice words and phrases collected from the Диалóг (Dialogue), Примечáния (Notes), Идиомáтика (Idiomatic Usage), and Стрóго по дéлу (Strictly Business) sections. Additional expressions show how the words may be used in other contexts. Again, you are given time to repeat each Russian phrase after the native speakers.

In the third section you will explore the lesson's most important grammatical structures. After a quick review of the rules, you can practice with illustrative phrases and sentences.

The conversational exercises in the last section integrate what you've learned and help you generate sentences in Russian on your own. You'll take part in brief conversations, ask and respond to questions, transform sentences, and occasionally translate from English into Russian. After you respond, you'll hear the correct answer from a native speaker.

The interactive approach on this set of recordings focuses on the idiomatic spoken word and will teach you to speak, understand, and think in Russian.

Now let's begin.

УРОК 1

A. ДИАЛОГ (Dialogue)

В аэропорту́.

На борту́ самолёта, соверша́ющего рейс[1] из Атла́нты в Москву́ че́рез Фра́нкфурт. До поса́дки в аэропорту́ Шереме́тьево[2] оста́лось приме́рно полчаса́.

ГО́ЛОС БОРТПРОВОДНИЦЫ ПО ДИНА́МИКУ: **Да́мы и господа́! Через мину́т два́дцать пять мы соверши́м поса́дку в аэропорту́ Шереме́тьево го́рода Москвы́. Сейча́с по моско́вскому вре́мени 21[3] час. Температу́ра 12 гра́дусов по Це́льсию,[4] или 54 гра́дуса по Фаренге́йту. Не забу́дьте, пожа́луйста, запо́лнить тамо́женные деклара́ции, кото́рые вам разда́ли ра́ньше. Это значи́тельно уско́рит прохожде́ние тамо́женного досмо́тра. Через не́сколько минут самолёт пойдёт на поса́дку и поэ́тому про́сим вас заня́ть свои́ места́ и пристегну́ться.[5]**

ДАВИД: **Мне ка́жется, что нам доста́точно запо́лнить одну́ деклара́цию на двои́х.[6]**

ЕЛЕ́НА: **Наве́рное, ты прав, но я всё же спрошу́ стюардéссу... Прости́те, де́вушка![7] Мы с му́жем должны́ запо́лнить отде́льные деклара́ции?**

СТЮ́РАРДЕ́ССА: **Нет, так как вы путеше́ствуете вме́сте, хва́тит[8] одно́й.**

ЕЛЕ́НА: **Спаси́бо.**

Пройдя́ па́спортный контро́ль, супру́ги[9] Моран собира́ют свои́ ве́щи и гото́вятся к тамо́женному досмо́тру.

ТАМОЖЕННИК: **Ва́ши деклара́ции, пожа́луйста.**

ДАВИД: **Вот, одна́ на двои́х. Мы путеше́ствуем вме́сте.**

ТАМОЖЕННИК: **Это ва́ши чемода́ны?**

ЕЛЕ́НА: **Да. Вот э́ти два больши́х чемода́на и две су́мки.**

ТАМОЖЕННИК: Вы везёте алкого́льные напи́тки, ору́жие или нарко́тики?

ДАВИД: Нет, то́лько лека́рство по реце́пту для себя́.

ТАМОЖЕННИК: В деклара́ции ука́зано, что у вас нали́чными[10] то́лько 150 до́лларов. Это так?

ДАВИД: Пра́вильно. И ещё есть 600 до́лларов доро́жными че́ками.

ТАМОЖЕННИК: Хорошо́. Вот, бери́те деклара́цию. Не потеря́йте её. Её бу́дет необходи́мо предста́вить ещё при вы́езде. А сейча́с откро́йте, пожа́луйста, этот чемода́н.

ДАВИД: Ле́на, дай мне ключ от чемода́на.

ЕЛЕНА: Вот он.

ТАМОЖЕННИК: Что вы бу́дете де́лать с этой те́хникой?[11]

ДАВИД: Магнитофо́н, кассе́ты и прои́грыватель компа́кт-ди́сков—это пода́рки друзья́м.

ТАМОЖЕННИК: А радиоприёмник и компью́тер?

ДАВИД: Это для со́бственного по́льзования.

ТАМОЖЕННИК: Поня́тно. Закро́йте чемода́н. Всё в поря́дке. Проходи́те.

Давид и Елена прохо́дят в гла́вный зал ожида́ния аэропо́рта.

ЕЛЕНА: Я[12] сейча́с волну́юсь то́лько об одно́м: лишь бы нашёлся Бори́с!

ДАВИД: Смотри́! Вот он!

БОРИС: С прие́здом![13] Добро́ пожа́ловать в Москву́! Очень рад вас ви́деть! Ну, как долете́ли?

ДАВИД: Очень до́лгий и утоми́тельный рейс, зато́ сам полёт был дово́льно споко́йным, хотя подлета́я к Фра́нкфурту, мы попа́ли в лёгкую болта́нку.

БОРИС: Ничего́, ско́ро вы бу́дете в гости́нице и хорошо́ отдохнёте. К сожале́нию, свою́ маши́ну мы отда́ли[14] в ремо́нт. Поэ́тому нам придётся взять такси́.

ЕЛЕНА: А ско́лько ехать в гости́ницу?

БОРИС: Вы остано́витесь[15] в Радиссон-Славя́нской, не так ли? Зна́чит, ехать нам туда́ приме́рно час, если не бу́дет большо́го движе́ния.

ДАВИД: Это бы́ло очень любе́зно с ва́шей сто́роны встре́тить нас. Жаль, что рейс при́был с опозда́нием.

БОРИС: Ничего́.

ДАВИД: Кака́я у вас пого́да в после́днее время?[16]

БОРИС: На са́мом деле вам повезло́.[17] В после́днее вре́мя пого́да у нас стои́т очень мя́гкая, тёплая.

ДАВИД: А раз мы прие́хали, за́втра она, наве́рное, испо́ртится.

ЕЛЕНА: Ну, заче́м, Давид, не на́до быть таки́м пессими́стом!

БОРИС: Елена права́. По сего́дняшнему прогно́зу тёплая пого́да должна́ бу́дет продолжа́ться. А вот свобо́дное такси́. Так как мы еди́нственные пассажи́ры,[18] то за час мы доберёмся до гости́ницы.

At the airport.

On board a flight from Atlanta to Moscow, via Frankfurt. About half an hour from landing at Sheremetyevo Airport.

VOICE ON THE INTERCOM: Ladies and gentlemen! We will be landing at Moscow's Sheremetyevo Airport in approximately twenty-five minutes. The local time in Moscow is 9:00 P.M. and the temperature is 12° Celsius, or 54° Fahrenheit. Please be sure that you have completed the declaration forms distributed earlier. Please return to your seats and fasten your seat belts as we prepare for landing.

DAVID: Elena, I think we just need to fill out one form for both of us.

ELENA: I think you're right, but I'd better ask the flight attendant. . . . Excuse me, Miss. Do my husband and I have to fill out separate declaration forms?

ATTENDANT: No, as long as you're traveling together, you only need one form.

ELENA: Thank you.

After having their passports and visas checked, the Morans collect their luggage and enter the customs area.

CUSTOMS OFFICIAL: Your declaration forms, please.

DAVID: Here's one form for both of us. We're traveling together.

CUSTOMS OFFICIAL: Are these your suitcases?

ELENA: Yes, these two big ones and two carry-on bags.

CUSTOMS OFFICIAL: Are you bringing in any alcohol, firearms, or drugs?

DAVID: No, only some prescription medicine for myself.

CUSTOMS OFFICIAL: According to this declaration you have only $150 in cash. Is that correct?

DAVID: That's right, and we also have $600 in traveler's checks.

CUSTOMS OFFICIAL: That's okay. Here's your declaration. Don't lose it. You'll have to show it again when you leave the country. Now, please open this suitcase.

DAVID: Elena, hand me the key to this suitcase.

ELENA: Here it is.

CUSTOMS OFFICIAL: What will you be doing with this electronic equipment?

ELENA: The tape recorder and CD player are gifts for friends.

CUSTOMS OFFICIAL: And what about the radio and computer?

DAVID: That's for our own use.

CUSTOMS OFFICIAL: Okay. You can close the suitcase now. Everything seems to be in order. Proceed.

David and Elena enter the waiting room of the main terminal.

ELENA: Now, if only we could find Boris!

DAVID: Look! There he is!

BORIS: Welcome to Moscow! It's great to see you! How was your trip?

DAVID: Very long and tiring, but the flight was pretty smooth. We just ran into a little turbulence as we approached Frankfurt.

SASHA: Well, you'll be at your hotel very soon, and you'll be able to get some rest. Unfortunately, our car is in the shop, so we'll have to take a taxi to town.

ELENA: How long will it take to get to our hotel?

BORIS: You're staying a the Radisson-Slavyanskaya, right? It'll be about an hour if the traffic's not too heavy.

DAVID: You were very kind to meet us. Sorry our flight was late.

BORIS: Oh, that's nothing.

DAVID: So, what's the weather been like here?

BORIS: Actually, you're in luck. We've been having very mild weather.

DAVID: But now that we're here, it'll probably turn bad.

ELENA: Oh, David, don't be such a pessimist!

BORIS: Elena is right. The forecast this morning predicted continued good weather. Ah, here's a free taxi, and we have it to ourselves so we should be at the hotel within an hour.

B. ПРИМЕЧАНИЯ (Notes)

1. Рейс refers to a particular flight number or path. Полёт is used to indicate any trip by air. Начинáется посáдка на рейс № 549 Москвá-Нью Йорк. (Flight No. 549 to New York is now boarding.) Наш полёт был спокóйным и удóбным. (Our flight was smooth and comfortable.)

2. Шеремéтьево-2 is Moscow's international airport. It is located about twenty miles north of Moscow, and it takes approximately one hour to reach the airport from the center of Moscow by taxi or car. Shuttle bus service to the center of town is also available. There are three other airports (Шереметьево-1, Домодéдово, and Внýково) in Moscow, and travelers with connecting flights should always verify from which airport they will be leaving.

3. In Russia, the 24-hour clock is used for all official schedules, such as transportation and theater, and for all official appointments, such as business meetings and doctor's visits. The 12-hour clock is used in an informal setting and casual conversation.

4. Temperature in Russia, as in most of Europe, is measured in degrees Celsius (по Це́льсию). 0° C is equal to 32° F. To convert Celsius to Fahrenheit, multiply the Celsius figure by 9/5 (1.8) and add 32. To get Celsius values from Fahrenheit, subtract 32 from the Fahrenheit figure and divide by 9/5 (1.8).

5. The verb пристёгивать/пристегну́ть means "to fasten" or "to button up." The reflexive form, престегну́ться, can also mean "to fasten one's seat belt," in which case it is used alone, without explicitly stating the word реме́нь (belt). Расстёгиваться/расстегну́ться refers to unfastening one's belt or unbuttoning a coat or a jacket.

6. На двои́х also appears in the phrase Ко́мната на двои́х (a room for two).

7. Де́вушка (Miss) is the common form of address for a woman of any age who is working in some service capacity, such as a flight attendant, salesperson, hotel floor attendant, or waitress.

8. The verb хвата́ть/хвати́ть denotes sufficiency or insufficiency. The object is in the genitive case. У меня́ не хвата́ет де́нег. (I don't have enough money.) Не хва́тит вре́мени. (There won't be enough time.) Де́нег нам хва́тит на все расхо́ды. (We'll have enough money to cover all the expenses.) This verb is also used in the idiomatic expression Э́того мне ещё не хвата́ло! (That was the last straw!)

9. Супру́г/а (male/female) means "spouse"; the plural супру́ги refers to a married couple. Вчера́ в аэропорту́ я встре́тил его́ супру́гу. (I met his spouse [wife] at the airport yesterday.) Разреши́те предста́вить моего́ супру́га. (Allow me to introduce my spouse [husband].)

10. Note: нали́чные (де́ньги) (cash on hand), плати́ть нали́чными (to pay in cash), and нали́чность ("dough," money). За э́ти биле́ты обяза́тельно плати́ть нали́чными. (You have to pay for these tickets in cash.) К сожале́нию, сейча́с у меня́ нет нали́чных. (Unfortunately, I don't have any cash on me now.)

11. Те́хника can refer to any type of technical equipment or gadgetry. It can also mean "engineering," "technology," and "technique," depending on the context: строи́тельная те́хника (civil engineering), вычисли́тельная те́хника (computer science), те́хника безопа́сности (safety devices). Э́то де́ло те́хники. (It's a matter of technique.)

12. Remember that the pronoun я (I) is capitalized only at the beginning of a sentence.

13. С прие́здом! (Welcome!) is the colloquial, shortened form of Поздравля́ю вас с прие́здом! (lit: I congratulate you on your arrival!) It is commonly used to greet arriving friends and relatives. Добро́

пожа́ловать! (lit. It is good that you have come to see us!) is a somewhat more formal welcome, used when someone is arriving to a place for the first time.

14. The verb отдава́ть/отда́ть (to give) has several different meanings, depending on context. Here it means "to hand or turn something in," but it can also be used in the expressions отда́ть себе́ отчёт (to realize), отдава́ть жизнь нау́ке (to devote one's life to science); отда́ть под суд (to prosecute); отдава́ть честь (to salute); and отдава́ть до́лжное (to give someone credit, to give someone his/her due).

15. The verb остана́вливаться/останови́ться (lit., to stop oneself) is commonly used with reference to hotel accommodations. It can also be used when staying at a friend's house or stopping over in a city. Где вы остано́витесь в Москве́? (Where you will be staying in Moscow?) Он ча́сто остана́вливается у нас по пути́ в Петербу́рг. (He often stops over at our place on his way to St. Petersburg.)

16. В после́днее вре́мя or за после́днее время both mean "recently." In colloquial speech the preposition is omitted. После́днее вре́мя, пого́да у нас была́ о́чень холо́дная. (Lately, the weather's been very cold.)

17. The verb везти́, conjugated in the third person, is used to indicate that fortune is or is not going one's way. The person affected is in the dative case. Ему́ всегда́ везёт. (He is always lucky.) Нам о́чень повезло́. (We were very lucky.) Им совсе́м не везёт. (They're just not having any luck at all.)

18. Passengers arriving in Moscow often have to share taxis from the airport.

C. ГРАММАТИКА И СЛОВОУПОТРЕБЛЕНИЕ (Grammar and Usage)

1. ГЛАГОЛЫ В НАСТОЯЩЕМ ВРЕМЕНИ (VERBS IN THE PRESENT TENSE)

Most Russian verbs fall into one of two groups: 1st Conjugation or 2nd Conjugation. First Conjugation verbs include most verbs ending in -ать and many that end in -еть. The Second Conjugation verbs include most verbs ending in -ить.* The following model illustrates the conjugation of Russian verbs in the present tense:

	FIRST CONJUGATION		SECOND CONJUGATION		
	Жела́ть (to wish)	Ждать (to wait)	Идти́ (to go)	Говори́ть (to speak)	Проси́ть (to request)
я	жела́ю	жду	иду́	говорю́	прошу́
ты	жела́ешь	ждёшь	идёшь	говори́шь	про́сишь
он/она́/оно́	жела́ет	ждёт	идёт	говори́т	про́сит
мы	жела́ем	ждём	идём	говори́м	про́сим
вы	жела́ете	ждёте	идёте	говори́те	про́сите
они́	жела́ют	ждут	иду́т	говоря́т	про́сят

The present tense is used to describe ongoing or habitual actions or to make simple statements of fact. It translates into English as "I speak" or "I am speaking."

Что они́ сейча́с де́лают?
What are they doing now?

Они́ сейча́с получа́ют бага́ж.
They're getting their luggage.

Что они́ обы́чно де́лают по суббо́там?
What do they usually do on Saturdays?

Они́ быва́ют у сестры́ Еле́ны.
They visit Elena's sister.

Они́ ча́сто лета́ют в Москву́ че́рез Фра́нкфурт.
They often fly to Moscow via Frankfurt.

Они́ ре́дко е́здят в дере́вню.
They seldom go (drive) to the countryside.

The present tense of a motion verb may be used to indicate an action that is likely to take place in the immediate future.

Вы сего́дня ве́чером идёте в кино́?
Are you going to the movies tonight?

*See the Appendix for a more detailed classification of verbs and their conjugation.

Пе́рвый уро́к

The present tense in Russian is also used to denote an action that was begun in the past and continues in the present. This construction is usually translated in English as "has/have . . . been + -ing."

Ско́лько лет вы уже́ живёте в Москве́?
How long have you been living in Moscow?

Они́ уже́ давно́ рабо́тают на по́чте.
They have been working at the post office for a long time (and still are).

Он уже́ шесть лет рабо́тает на тамо́жне.
He has been working at Customs for six years (and still is).

Remember that быть (to be) is omitted in the present tense.

Я тури́ст(ка).
I am a tourist.

Это мой чемода́н.
This is my suitcase.

2. ИМЕНИ́ТЕЛЬНЫЙ ПАДЕ́Ж (THE NOMINATIVE CASE)

The nominative case* in Russian denotes the subject of a sentence or the agent of an action. It answers the questions Кто? (Who?) and Что? (What?).

Самолёт прилете́л во́время.
The plane arrived on time.

На́ши го́сти прохо́дят тамо́женный контро́ль.
Our guests are going through customs control.

Remember that, where English uses word order to establish the function of a word, Russian uses case. Therefore, the subject of a Russian sentence (i.e., the noun or pronoun in the nominative case) does not necessarily precede the verb.

*See the Appendix for a table of noun declensions.

В этой гости́нице остана́вливались и мои́ <u>роди́тели</u>.

My parents also stayed at this hotel.

Ра́ньше, по прие́зде нас всегда́ встреча́ли <u>сотру́дники</u> из институ́та.

The associates from the institute always used to meet us upon our arrival.

3. ИМЕНИ́ТЕЛЬНЫЙ ПАДЕ́Ж СУЩЕСТВИ́ТЕЛЬНЫХ (THE NOMINATIVE CASE OF NOUNS—GENDER AND NUMBER)

Russian nouns can be masculine, feminine, or neuter. These are merely grammatical categories and are seldom a reflection of physical reality, unless they refer to people. The gender of most nouns can often be identified by the ending. Following are the nominative noun endings, organized according to gender and number:

	SINGULAR	PLURAL
MASCULINE	consonant	-ы (after hard consonants)
	-й	-и (after г, ж, ч, х, щ, or ь)
FEMININE	-а	-ы/-и (after г, ж, ч, х, щ)
	-я	-и
	-ь	-и
NEUTER	-о	-а
	-е	-я
	-ё, -мя	irregular

Following are some examples:

airplane	самолёт	самолёты	airplanes
museum	музе́й	музе́и	museums
hotel	гости́ница	гости́ницы	hotels
declaration	деклара́ция	деклара́ции	declarations
door	дверь	две́ри	doors
window	окно́	о́кна	windows
building	зда́ние	зда́ния	buildings
raw material(s)	сырьё	(no plural)	
time	вре́мя	времена́	times

Note that the soft sign (-ь), -а, and -я are typically feminine, singular endings. However, a small number of masculine, singular nouns also have these endings. These must be memorized as exceptions. Following are the most common:

teacher	учи́тель	учителя́	teachers
father-in-law	тесть	те́сти	fathers-in-law
tsar	царь	цари́	tsars
guest	гость	го́сти	guests
grandfather	де́душка	де́душки	grandfathers
uncle	дя́дя	дя́ди	uncles
man	мужчи́на	мужчи́ны	men

There are also some nouns that end in a stressed á in the plural form. A few of them are listed below:

city	го́род	города́	cities
train	по́езд	поезда́	trains
passport	па́спорт	паспорта́	passports
professor	профе́ссор	профессора́	professors
house	дом	дома́	houses
mister, gentleman	господи́н	господа́	sirs, gentlemen

The following are examples of irregular plural endings of masculine nouns:

brother	брат	бра́тья	brothers
husband	муж	мужья́	husbands
citizen	граждани́н	гра́ждане	citizens
friend	друг	друзья́	friends

There are a number of "common gender" nouns that can denote a male or female person; e.g., глава́ (head, chief), пья́ница (drunkard), колле́га (colleague), судья́ (judge). In addition, some grammatically masculine nouns denoting various professions are now commonly applied to both men and women, e.g., писа́тель* (writer), журнали́ст (journalist, reporter), адвока́т (attorney), секрета́рь (secretary), библиоте́карь (librarian), врач (physician), инжене́р (engineer).

---

*The feminine forms писа́тельница, журнали́стка, and to a lesser extent, секрета́рша, are considered less prestigious.

Я врач, а моя́ жена́ инжене́р.
I'm a physician, and my wife is an engineer.

Finally, a small number of nouns, primarily of foreign origin, do not decline, e.g., интервью, меню́, кафе́, кака́о, такси́. However, they are technically neuter, and any adjectives that describe them take the neuter ending.

Возьмём пе́рвое свобо́дное такси́.
We'll take the first available taxi.

Some common nouns are used only in the singular. These include the names of certain fruits and vegetables; e.g., виногра́д (grapes), морко́вь (carrots), изю́м (raisins), капу́ста (cabbage), карто́фель (potatoes), лук (onions). A whole species of plants or trees is also rendered by singular-only nouns; e.g., сосна́ (pine trees), ви́шня (cherry trees), берёза (birch trees), клубни́ка (strawberries).

Мы всегда́ еди́м карто́фель с больши́м удово́льствием.
We always eat potatoes with great pleasure.

У нас на се́вере мо́жно ви́деть берёзу везде́.
You can see birch trees everywhere in the north of our country.

Наша семья́ лю́бит собира́ть клубни́ку.
Our family loves to pick strawberries.

Likewise, a large number of nouns are used only in the plural. These often denote objects with more than one component; e.g., джи́нсы (jeans), очки́ (glasses, spectacles), брю́ки (trousers), но́жницы (scissors), тру́сики (briefs), консе́рвы (preserves), духи́ (perfume), де́ньги (money), во́лосы (hair), бу́дни (weekdays).

Хочу́ купи́ть ей хоро́шие духи́.
I want to buy her some nice perfume at the duty free shop.

Куда́ вы положи́ли мои́ но́жницы?
Where did you put my scissors?

У этой де́вушки очень краси́вые во́лосы.
This girl has very beautiful hair.

Finally, a few neuter nouns, particularly those ending in -мя, have irregular plural endings

time, season	вре́мя	времена́	times, seasons
name	и́мя	имена́	names

D. ИДИОМАТИКА (Idiomatic Usage)

HELLOS AND GOOD-BYES.

Aside from the conventional greetings, such as здра́вствуйте (hello), до́брый день (good day), and до свида́ния (good-bye), there are less formal ways of saying "Hello."

Приве́т!
   Hi!; Hello there!

Салю́т!*
   Hi!

Ско́лько лет, ско́лько зим!
   Long time no see! (lit., How many summers, how many winters!)

С прие́здом!
   Welcome!

And here are a few ways to say "good-bye":

Счастли́во!†
   Take care!

Счастли́вого пути́!
   Bon voyage!

До встре́чи!
   See you later!

---

*This greeting is similar to the Italian *Ciao* in that it can mean both "Hello" and "'Bye."
†This is a shortened form of the full expression "счастли́во остава́ться" (lit., Stay lucky.).

Пока!
So long!

До ско́рого!*
See you soon!

E. СТРОГО ПО ДЕЛУ
(Strictly Business)

ГЕОГРАФИЯ И ЭКОНОМИКА (GEOGRAPHY AND ECONOMY)

Russia, or more officially, the Russian Federation (Росси́йская Федера́ция), occupies a landmass of aproximately 17 million square kilometers (65 million square miles, or about twice the size of the United States). It extends across ten time zones, from the Baltic Sea (Балти́йское мо́ре) to the Pacific Ocean (Ти́хий океа́н) and from the Arctic Ocean (Ледови́тый океа́н) in the north to the Black Sea (Чёрное мо́ре) in the south. Countries that border Russia range from Norway and Finland in the north, the former Soviet republics of Kazakhstan, Georgia, and Armenia in the south, to Mongolia, China, and North Korea in the east. A distance of less than 50 miles across the Bering Strait (Бе́рингов проли́в) separates the northeastern tip of Siberia from the western edge of Alaska.

Most of the European segment of Russia up to the Urals (Ура́л) constitutes a broad plain with low hills. The region east of the Urals is dominated by a vast coniferous forest (тайга́) that lies between the tundra (ту́ндра) with its permafrost soil (ве́чная мерзлота́) and the Siberian steppe (сиби́рская степь). Despite its immense size, Russia has limited access to major sea lanes, with only three major ports open year-round: Vladivostok (Владивосто́к) in the Far East (Да́льний Восто́к), which is kept open in the winter by ice-breakers (ледоко́лы); Rostov-on-the-Don (Росто́в-на-Дону́); and Murmansk (Му́рманск) on the northern Arctic Circle (Се́верный поля́рный круг). Its major navigable rivers, the Volga (Во́лга), Dniepr (Лнелр), Оь (Обь), and Yenisey (Енисе́й), have limited use due to long periods of freezing temperatures. Extreme temperatures have also made the construction of national roadways difficult. Rail and air are, therefore, the principal means of year-round passenger and freight

*A shortened form of до ско́рого свида́ния (lit., until we meet again soon).

transportation. Temperatures in Moscow and St. Petersburg, for example, remain at or below freezing between November and early April. Summer temperatures in those cities average about 21° Celsius (70° Fahrenheit).

Russia is rich in natural resources (приро́дные ресу́рсы), with immense deposits of minerals, particularly iron ore, nickel, cobalt, lead, copper, and gold, most of which is found in Siberia. Siberia is also the principal source of the country's coal supply. The least inhabited areas of Russia, such as eastern Siberia, also contain the largest reserves of other energy sources, such as hydrocarbons and hydroelectric power, and vast amounts of unexploited natural gas and oil reserves. Despite these reserves and significant progress in privatizing state assets in moving to a modern market economy (совреме́нная ры́ночная эконо́мика), real financial stabilization remains elusive, partially due to the scarcity of investment funds (фо́нды капиталовложе́ний) and the failure of industry managers to make difficult cost-cutting decisions (реше́ния по сниже́нию себесто́имости проду́кции). Financial stability has also been hindered by the government's inability to collect all assessed taxes (неспосо́бность по собира́емости нало́гов), particularly corporate taxes (нало́ги с дохо́дов предприя́тий). On the more positive side, tighter budgetary policies have managed to avoid runaway inflation (гиперинфля́ция) and real capital income of Russians has been increasing, although this is in part due to the fact that many Russians are taking second jobs. Capital flight abroad (уте́чка капита́ла заграни́цу) and deterioration of physical plants (ухудше́ние состоя́ния зда́ний и обору́дования), however, remain serious problems.

Despite these formidable difficulties, given its wealth of natural resources and a well-educated population (Russia boasts a literacy rate of 98 percent), Russia's economic potential is very promising.

УПРАЖНЕНИЯ (Exercises)

Всегда указывайте, куда падает ударе́ние. (Always indicate stress marks.)

A. Впиши́те глаго́лы, ука́занные в ско́бках, в настоя́щем вре́мени. (Insert the present tense forms of the verbs in parentheses.)

    1. Они́, наве́рное, _____(ждать) их в аэропорту́.

    2. Мы о́чень _____(жела́ть) встре́титься с ва́ми.

    3. Я _____(про́сит) вас заня́ть свои́ места́.

    4. Она́ о́чень _____(боя́ться), что на́ши го́сти опозда́ют.

    5. Мы всегда́_____(проверя́ть) вре́мя прилёта.

    6. Что вы сейча́с_____(де́лать)?

    7. Ка́жется, что они́ сейча́с_____(идти́) в библиоте́ку.

    8. О чём она́_____(говори́ть)?

    9. Ему́ всегда́_____(везти́)!

    10. Мы _____(наде́яться), что вам понра́вился полёт.

B. Напиши́те мно́жественное число́ сле́дующих существи́тельных в имени́тельном падеже́ и переведи́те их на англи́йский. (Give the nominative plural forms of the following nouns and their English meaning.)

    1. брат

    2. гости́ница

    3. полёт

    4. муж

    5. деклара́ция

    6. ключ

    7. ме́сто

    8. вре́мя

    9. супру́г

    10. го́род

C. Переведи́те сле́ующие предложе́ния с англи́йского на ру́сский. (Translate the following sentences into Russian.)

    1. They have been working here for a long time.

    2. Are they still waiting at the airport?

    3. Where are our suitcases?

4. This computer is for my own use.
5. How long does it take to get to the hotel?
6. This is a very long and tiring flight.
7. What kind of weather have you been having lately?
8. Oh good! Here's a free taxi!
9. This passenger is my father-in-law.
10. They are now going through Customs Control.

ПРЕДЛАГАЕМЫЕ ЗАНЯТИЯ
(Suggested Activity)

Consult an atlas of the Russian Federation and locate the major cities and sites mentioned in the cultural notes and dialogue.

УРОК 2

A. ДИАЛОГ (Dialogue)

В гости́нице.

Америка́нские супру́ги Марк и Ли́дия Го́рдины регистри́руются в центра́льной гости́нице[1] в Москве́, гото́вясь к сбо́ру семьи́.

ДЕЖУ́РНЫЙ АДМИНИСТРА́ТОР: До́брый день. Чем могу́ быть поле́зен?

МАРК: Мы с жено́й[2] заброни́ровали но́мер на пять су́ток.[3]

АДМИНИСТРА́ТОР: Ва́ши паспорта́, пожа́луйста....(проверя́ет бронь). **Ах да, супру́ги Го́рдины. Вы бу́дете у нас по 25-ое ма́рта,[4] не пра́вда ли?**

ЛИ́ДИЯ: Пра́вильно, но мы та́кже хоти́м заброни́ровать ко́мнату для осо́бого приёма. Понима́ете, мы устра́иваем[5] встре́чу семьи́.

АДМИНИСТРА́ТОР: Поня́тно! Я ду́маю, что это мо́жно реши́ть по́сле того́, как вы устро́итесь в ва́шем но́мере.[6] Ваш но́мер 706-о́й, на седьмо́м этаже́. Лифт в конце́ коридо́ра ря́дом с магази́ном сувени́ров. Вот вам ключи́ от но́мера и гости́ничная ка́рточка.[7]

МАРК: Гости́ничная ка́рточка? Что это тако́е?

АДМИНИСТРА́ТОР: Это ваш про́пуск в гости́ницу. Пожа́луйста, не отдава́йте её посторо́нним[8] ли́цам.

МАРК: Поня́тно. Ну, пойдём в но́мер.

АДМИНИСТРА́ТОР: Вам на́до помо́чь с веща́ми?

МАРК: Нет, спаси́бо. Мы са́ми спра́вимся. Кста́ти, в но́мере есть телефо́н?

АДМИНИСТРА́ТОР: Да, разуме́ется. Номера́ у нас со все́ми удо́бствами: душ, туале́т, и, коне́чно телеви́зор, телефо́н.

МАРК: Вы зна́ете, нам ну́жно бу́дет позвони́ть за грани́цу. Это мо́жно сде́лать из но́мера?

АДМИНИСТРАТОР: Да, коне́чно, то́лько снача́ла позвони́ть на междунаро́дную ста́нцию. Но сове́тую вам заказа́ть разгово́р[9] зара́нее.

ЛИДИЯ: Так и сде́лаем. Ещё одно́. Мо́жно ли из гости́ницы посла́ть сообще́ние по фа́ксу на́шим деловы́м партнёрам в Санкт-Петербу́рг?

АДМИНИСТРАТОР: Очень про́сто. У нас на второ́м этаже́ име́ется би́знес центр, где вы найдёте фа́ксы,[10] ксе́роксы, а та́кже[11] компью́теры для свя́зи по электро́нной по́чте.

МАРК: Отли́чно! С кото́рого часа́ рабо́тает це́нтр?

АДМИНИСТРАТОР: С семи́ утра́ до десяти́ ве́чера.

ЛИДИЯ: И после́дний вопро́с. Когда́ у вас расчётный[12] час?

АДМИНИСТРАТОР: Расчётный час в на́шей гости́нице—по́лдень.

ЛИДИЯ: Спаси́бо.

АДМИНИСТРАТОР: Пожа́луйста.

Через час Марк и Лидия ещё раз обраща́ются к администра́тору, что́бы организова́ть приём.

АДМИНИСТРА́ТОР: Ну как, понра́вился вам ваш но́мер?

ЛИДИЯ: Но́мер хоро́ший. И с таки́м краси́вым ви́дом на Кра́сную пло́щадь! Тем не ме́нее, есть и жа́лобы.

АДМИНИСТРАТОР: А именно?

МАРК: Де́ло в том, что туале́т пло́хо рабо́тает. Почему́-то вода́ там постоя́нно течёт. Это, наве́рное, не даст нам спать.

ЛИДИЯ: Да, и на крова́ти лишь одна́ поду́шка. Нельзя́ ли ещё одну́?

АДМИНИСТРАТОР: Ох, прошу́ извине́ния! Я сейча́с же вы́зову на́шего водопрово́дчика. А что каса́ется поду́шки, ли́шние поду́шки и одея́ла должны́ быть в ни́жнем ящике комо́да.

ЛИДИЯ: Хорошо́, посмо́трим.

АДМИНИСТРАТОР: Так, вы сказа́ли, что вы жела́ете забронировать номер для приёма. Какого числа будет приём и сколько примерно человек будет присутствовать?

МАРК: Мы бы хотели провести встречу 24-го, то есть в пятницу. Лидия, как считаешь, сколько будет на приёме?

ЛИДИЯ: Ну, если все приглашённые придут, тогда будет около двадцати пяти, хотя, наверное, твоего дяди Володи не будет.

МАРК: Да, ты, наверное, права. Последнее время он плохо себя чувствует, ведь ему же восемьдесят лет. Причём он живёт в Екатеринбурге.

АДМИНИСТРАТОР: Это довольно длинная поездка. А вашим остальным родственникам надо будет переночевать у нас?

МАРК: Думаю, что нет. Если не считать дядю Володю, они все живут в московской области.[13]

АДМИНИСТРАТОР: Так, если вам нужна будет только одна большая комната в пятницу, то можем предоставить вам просторный зал на пятом этаже, тоже с хорошим видом на Красную площадь. По-моему, там достаточно места для 25 человек.

ЛИДИЯ: Вы сможете подать обед в том же самом зале?

АДМИНИСТРАТОР: Да, конечно. Всё это можно устроить с нашей кухней.

МАРК: А сколько это будет стоить?

АДМИНИСТРАТОР: Мы предлагаем вам стандартный тариф[14]— 200 долларов за день. Однако из-за большого спроса на помещения,[15] с вас заранее потребуют половину в виде задатка.

МАРК: Ладно. Кредитные карты вы принимаете?

АДМИНИСТРАТОР: Мы принимаем все наиболее распространённые карты.[16]

ЛИДИЯ: Будем надеяться, что всё хорошо получится.

АДМИНИСТРАТОР: Не надо беспокоиться. Я уверен, что ваша встреча пройдёт отлично.

At the hotel.

An American couple, Mark and Lydia Gordin, check into a central hotel in Moscow for a reunion with Russian relatives.

CLERK: Hello. How may I help you?

MARK: My wife and I have reservations for five nights.

CLERK: May I have your passports, please? (*checks the register*) Ah yes, Mr. and Mrs. Gordin. You will be staying with us until the 25th of March, right?

LYDIA: That's correct, but we would also like to reserve a room for a special reception. You see, we'll be having a family reunion.

CLERK: That's wonderful, but I think we can take care of that after you get settled into your room. Your room number is 706. That's on the seventh floor. The elevator is at the end of the hall near the souvenir shop. Here is your key and hotel identification card.

MARK: Hotel identification card? What is that?

CLERK: That is your entry pass into the hotel. Please do not give it to any strangers.

MARK: I understand. Okay, let's go to the room.

CLERK: Will you be needing any help with your baggage?

MARK: No, thanks, we can manage. By the way, is there a telephone in the room?

CLERK: Yes, of course. All rooms are fully equipped with a shower, a toilet, and, of course, a TV, and a telephone.

MARK: We're going to have to make an overseas call. Can we do that from our room?

CLERK: Of course, just call the international operator first. I would advise you to order your call beforehand.

LYDIA: Oh yes, one other thing. Would it be possible to send a fax from the hotel to some of our business associates in St. Petersburg?

CLERK: Certainly. We have a business center on the second floor where you'll find fax machines, photocopiers, and computers for sending E-mail.

MARK: That's wonderful! What are the hours of the center?

CLERK: It's open from seven in the morning to ten at night.

LYDIA: One last question. What time is check-out?

CLERK: Check-out at our hotel is twelve noon.

LYDIA: Thank you.

CLERK: Not at all.

The Gordins return one hour later to make arrangements for the reception.

CLERK: So, how do you like your room?

LYDIA: It's a nice room with a lovely view of Red Square! But we do have some complaints.

CLERK: What sort of complaints?

MARK: The fact is, the toilet's not working right. The water's constantly dripping for some reason, and that probably won't let us sleep.

LYDIA: Yes, and there's only one pillow on the bed. Can we get another one?

CLERK: Oh, I'm very sorry! I'll call our plumber right away. As to the pillow, there should be extra pillows and blankets in the bottom drawer of the dresser.

LYDIA: Okay, we'll take a look.

CLERK: Now, you said you wanted to reserve a room for a reception? For what day and how large a room will you need?

MARK: We would like to have the reception on the 24th, which is Friday. Lydia, how many people do you think will be there?

LYDIA: Well, if everyone who was invited comes, there should be about twenty-five, although I think that Uncle Vladimir probably won't be able to make it.

MARK: Yes, you're probably right. He hasn't been feeling too well lately, and he's eighty-seven. Besides, he lives in Ekaterinburg.

CLERK: That is quite a way to travel. Will any of your relatives need overnight accommodations?

MARK: I don't think so. Except for Uncle Vladimir, they all live in the Moscow area.

CLERK: So, if you just need one large room for Friday, we have a very nice suite on the fifth floor that also has a nice view of Red Square. I believe it could easily accommodate twenty-five guests.

LYDIA: Can we arrange to have a meal served in that room?

CLERK: Of course. All those arrangements can be made with our kitchen.

MARK: Now, how much will that cost?

CLERK: We will charge you the regular daily rate for that room, which is $200. Because of the heavy demand for rooms, however, we will require a fifty percent deposit.

MARK: That's fine. Do you accept credit cards?

CLERK: All major credit cards are accepted.

LYDIA: Well, I hope everything works out okay.

CLERK: There's no need to worry. I'm certain your reception will be quite a success.

B. ПРИМЕЧАНИЯ (Notes)

1. Most of the centrally located hotels in Moscow are on and around Тверска́я у́лица and Мане́жная пло́щадь, all very near Кра́сная пло́щадь (Red Square). The most famous and traditional in the grand style are the "five-star" Метропо́ль and Национа́ль hotels. A much more modern hotel in the central area is the Бальтшуг-Кемпинская, located across the Moscow River, almost directly opposite the Kremlin. About one mile from the Kremlin, farther up Тверска́я у́лица, is another superior class modern hotel, the Пала́с. Other less expensive hotels on Тверска́я include the Интури́ст (about four blocks from Red Square), Центра́льная, and Минск. The latter two do not offer any business services.

2. A plural personal pronoun + c + a noun in the instrumental case is often used to link nouns and pronouns in an inclusive sense. Мы с Оле́гом купи́ли все ну́жные проду́кты. (Oleg and I bought all the necessary groceries.) Они с сестро́й пригото́вили прекра́сный обе́д. (He and his sister prepared a wonderful dinner.)

3. Су́тки is a plural noun that refers to a 24-hour period. Two days, i.e., two 24-hour periods, would be дво́е* су́ток; three days, тро́е су́ток;

*Note that the collective numerals двое, трое, четверо, etc., are followed by the genitive plural.

etc. Note also кру́глые су́тки (around the clock) and це́лые су́тки (for days). Буфе́т на шесто́м этаже́ рабо́тает кру́глые су́тки. (The buffet on the sixth floor is open around the clock.) Они́ путеше́ствовали це́лые су́тки, не отправля́я нам не одну́ телегра́мму. (They were traveling for days without sending us a single postcard.)

4. Remember that the days of the week and the months of the year are not capitalized in Russian, unless they begin a sentence.

5. The Russian verb устра́ивать/устро́ить and its reflexive form устра́иваться/устро́иться have a number of meanings that can be applied to arranging events, getting settled in a place of work or residence, or conveying suitability. Дава́йте обсуди́м эти вопро́сы за́втра в де́вять часо́в, если это вам бу́дет удо́бно. —Хорошо́. Это меня́ вполне́ устра́ивает. (Let's discuss these questions tomorrow at nine if that's convenient for you. —Good. That suits me fine.) Ну как, вы уже́ устро́ились на но́вую рабо́ту? (Well then, did you get settled into your new job?) Она́ устро́илась в, большо́м кре́сле и начала́ чита́ть газе́ту. (She settled into the big easy chair and began to read the newspaper.) Я уве́рен, что всё устро́ится. (I am convinced that everything will work out.) На сле́дующей неде́ле мы устро́им большой прие́м. (Next week we'll arrange a big reception.) Мы попроси́ли наших сотру́дников устро́ить нам хоро́ший номер в новой гости́нице. (We asked our associates to get us a good room in the new hotel.)

In addition, устра́ивать/устро́ить has the colloquial meaning of creating some unusual situation: Пожа́луйста, дава́йте не бу́дем устра́ивать сканда́л по этому по́воду! (Please, let's not make a big scene out of this!)

6. Here но́мер (number) refers to a hotel room. It can also be used to refer to an issue of a magazine or newspaper (но́мер журна́ла; номер газе́ты), a telephone number (телефо́нный номер), the number of a building in a street address (Улица Пу́шкина, дом номер 2), or the number of a bus or streetcar line (авто́бус номер 5).

7. Although a hotel pass (гости́ничная ка́рточка) is theoretically checked by security personnel at the entrance of most major hotels in Moscow and St. Petersburg, in practice foreign guests are not asked to show their pass. When guests depart from a hotel, however, they must present their paid hotel bill before being allowed to leave the hotel with their luggage.

8. Посторо́нний (lit. one who is outside) is generally used to refer to an outsider, stranger, or foreigner. As an adjective, it can refer to something extraneous or out of place: Посторо́нним вход воспрещён. (Unauthorized Persons Not Admitted). Дежу́рный администра́тор почему́-то на́чал разгово́р с совсе́м посторо́нних вопро́сов. (For some reason or other, the hotel clerk started the conversation with

questions that were quite extraneous.) Изредка в хо́лле гости́ницы собира́лись каки́е-то посторо́нние мужчи́ны. (Every once in a while some strangers would gather in the hotel lobby.)

9. International calls can be dialed directly from major hotels and most residential apartments. Dial 8, wait for the dial tone, then 10, the country code, the area code, and then the local number. The country code for the US is 1. If you have trouble getting through, you can book a call with an international operator. This should be done several hours in advance. To book a call from Moscow or St. Petersburg dial 8, wait for a dial tone, then dial 194 or 196. If you are dialing from a hotel, dial 333-4101 in Moscow and 315-0012 in St. Petersburg.

10. As in English, the abbreviated form факс(ы) is generally used to refer to fax machines instead of the more formal факси́мильный аппара́т.

11. Ксе́рокс-маши́на and копи́р are also widely used to refer to copiers.

12. Расчётный час here means "check-out time." Выпи́сываться из гости́ницы means "to check out of a hotel." The same verb can also be used to mean "to be discharged from a hospital": Через три дня по́сле опера́ции он вы́писался из больни́цы. (He was discharged from the hospital three days after his operation.)

13. О́бласть is an administrative territorial subdivision in Russia, equivalent to a state in the United States.

14. Тари́ф can be translated as "rate," "tariff," or "charges," depending upon context. Вы не зна́ете, почто́вый тари́ф на посы́лки заграни́цу? (Do you know what the postal rate is for overseas packages?) Тари́ф на номера́ в на́ших гости́ницах повыша́ется ежего́дно. (Our hotel rates have been going up every year.) Наконе́ц, они́ при́няли Генера́льное соглаше́ние по тари́фам и торго́вле. (They finally accepted the General Agreement on Tariff and Trade.)

15. Помеще́ния is used to refer to any type of living or working space: rooms, premises, housing, or accommodations; e.g., служе́бные помеще́ния (business offices). These words also appear in the door sign Служе́бные помеще́ния (Authorized Persons Only). Все расхо́ды на помеще́ние бу́дут на́ми покры́ты. (All expenses for accommodations will be covered by us.) Матч бу́дет в помеще́нии под кры́шей. (The game will be played indoors.)

16. Наибо́лее распространённые ка́рты literally means "the most prevalent cards." In practice, such cards include American Express, Visa, and MasterCard. These credit cards are generally accepted by all major hotels and principal restaurants in Moscow, St. Petersburg, and other large cities within the Russian Federation.

C. ГРАММАТИКА И СЛОВОУПОТРЕБЛЕНИЕ
(Grammar and Usage)

1. РОДИТЕЛЬНЫЙ ПАДЕЖ (THE GENITIVE CASE)

The genitive case is used primarily to express possession. It answers the questions Кого? (Of whom?) and Чего? (Of what?), and it generally corresponds to the possessive s or prepositional phrases beginning with "of" in English.

Пáспорт моéй женьı́.
My wife's passport

Телефóнный нóмер гост́иницы.
The telephone number of the hotel

Лифт в концé коридóра.
The elevator is at the end of the corridor

Following are the genitive case endings for nouns and adjectives according to gender and number:

	NOUNS		
	NOMINATIVE SINGULAR	GENITIVE SINGULAR	GENITIVE PLURAL
MASCULINE	нóмер (number)	нóмер-а	номер-óв
	портфéль (briefcase)	портфéл-я	портфéл-ей
	музéй (museum)	музé-я	музé-ев
NEUTER	письмó (letter)	письмá	пи́сем
	состоя́ние (condition)	состоя́ни-я	состоя́н-ий
	врéмя (time)	врéмен-и	времён
FEMININE	квартúра (apartment)	квартúр-ы	квартúр
	торгóвля (commerce)	торгóвл-и	торгóвл-ей
	истóрия (history)	истóри-и	истóри-й
	плóщадь (square)	плóщад-и	площад-éй

	NOMINATIVE SINGULAR	GENITIVE SINGULAR	GENITIVE PLURAL
MASCULINE/ NEUTER	но́вый/но́вое (new)	но́в-ого	но́в-ых
	большо́й/большо́е (big)	больш-о́го	больш-и́х
	хоро́ший/хоро́шее (good)	хоро́ш-его	хоро́ш-их
	тре́тий (third)	тре́ть-его	тре́ть-их
FEMININE	но́вая	но́в-ой	но́в-ых
	больша́я	больш-о́й	больш-и́х
	хоро́шая	хоро́ш-ей	хоро́ш-их
	тре́тья	тре́ть-ей	тре́ть-их

The genitive case is also used:

a) after words expressing measure and quantity, such as ско́лько (how much, how many), ма́ло (a few), мно́го (many, much), не́сколько (a few, several). Note that the genitive plural is used with objects that can be counted and the singular is used for substances.

Ско́лько дней вы бу́дете у нас?
How many days will you be staying with us?

Ско́лько челове́к будет на приёме?
How many people will be at the reception?

Он жа́ловлся на то, что у них оста́лось ма́ло хле́ба.
He complained that they had little bread left.

Он вы́пил не́сколько стака́нов во́дки и ушёл.
He drank several glasses of vodka and left.

b) after cardinal numbers, except оди́н (one). The genitive singular follows 2, 3, and 4. The genitive plural follows 5–9, 0, as well as 11–19.

Я рабо́тал в гости́нице то́лько три ме́сяца, а мой брат рабо́тал там восемна́дцать ме́сяцев.
I worked in the hotel for only three months, but my brother worked there for eighteen months.

Вчера́ на приёме бы́ло два́дцать но́вых госте́й, и почти́ все из них ворча́ли на ску́дное угоще́ние.
There were twenty new guests at the reception yesterday, and almost all of them griped about the skimpy refreshments.

Note that the last digit of a compound number determines whether the singular or plural genitive should be used.

В собрáнии учáствовали сóрок три студéнта.
Forty-three students took part in the meeting.

В этой гостúнице имéется сто одúн нóмер.
This hotel has a hundred and one rooms.

   c) after certain prepositions.* The most commonly used prepositions governing the genitive case are без (without), до (up to, prior to), из (from, out of), от (from, away from), с (from), and у (at, in the possession of).

В гостúнице вы мóжете обмéнивать дóллары на рублú без пáспорта.
You can change dollars to rubles at the hotel without a passport.

Ресторáн рабóтает с шестú утрá до десятú вéчера.
The restaurant is open from six in the morning to ten in the evening.

Вчерá утром нáши гóсти вýписались из гостúницы.
Our guests checked out of the hotel yesterday morning.

У нас на вторóм этажé есть бúзнес цéнтр.
We have a business center on the second floor.

Я встрéчу вас у вхóда в метрó.
I'll meet you at the entrance to the subway.

2. НАЗВАНИЕ ВРЕМЕНИ (TELLING TIME)

To express the current hour, the number should be in the nominative case and the time unit, i.e., "hour" should be in the genitive singular for 2–4, and in the genitive plural for 5 and up. Note that "one o'clock" is simply час (without the number).

Скóлько сейчáс врéмени? —Сейчас час.
What time is it now? —It's one o'clock.

*See Appendix for a complete list of prepositions governing the genitive case.

Сейча́с три часа́.
It's three o'clock.

Сейча́с шесть часо́в.
It's six o'clock.

The hour and minutes can be expressed by:
    a) stating the current hour plus the number of minutes elapsed (with both numbers in the nominative case), or
    b) stating the number of minutes elapsed (in the nominative case) followed by the coming hour (expressed as an ordinal number).

Сейча́с шесть два́дцать.
Сейча́с 20 мину́т седьмо́го (lit., 20 minutes of the seventh hour)
It is now 6:20.

Сейчас три пятна́дцать.
Сейчас пятнадцать минут четвёртого.
It is now 3:15.

Сейча́с час де́сять.
Сейча́с де́сять мину́т второ́го.
It's now 1:10.

When the time is 30 minutes or more past the hour, it is common practice to use the following formula: the preposition без + the number of minutes remaining (in the genitive) + the coming hour (in the nominative).

Сейча́с без двадцати́ пяти́ четы́ре.
It's twenty-five minutes to four. (lit., without twenty five minutes—four)

Сейча́с без десяти́ шесть.
It's ten minutes to six. (lit., without ten minutes—six)

Сейчас без пяти́ де́вять.
It's five to nine.

As in English, there are a few special time-related terms: че́тверть (quarter), пол (half), по́лдень (noon), and по́лночь (midnight).

Сейча́с без че́тверти де́сять.
It's now a quarter to ten.

Сейча́с че́тверть седьмо́го.
    It's a quarter after six.

Сейча́с полдевя́того.
    It's half-past eight.

Сейча́с по́лдень.
    It's now noon.

As you know, the 24-hour clock is widely used throughout Russia for all official schedules and appointments. When using the 12-hour clock in colloquial speech, the time of day is specified using утра (usually from 5 A.M. to noon), дня (from 12:01 to 5 P.M.), ве́чера (from 6 P.M. to midnight), or но́чи (from midnight to 4 A.M.). Note that the word часо́в ("hours" in the genitive) is optional.

Сейча́с два́дцать три часа́/оди́ннадцать часо́в ве́чера.
    It is now 23:00/11:00 P.M.

When responding to the questions Когда́? (When?), Во ско́лько? (At what time?), or В кото́ром часу́? (At what hour?), the time unit (hour, minute) should be in the accusative case preceded by the preposition в.

Во ско́лько они́ прие́хали? —В четы́ре часа́.
    (At) what time did they arrive? —At four o'clock.

Во ско́лько открыва́ется рестора́н? —В семь часо́в утра́.
    At what time does the restaurant open? —At 7 A.M.

Я вам позвоню́ в во́семь (часо́в) ве́чера.
    I'll call you at eight in the evening.

To indicate that something will occur by a specified time, the time should be in the dative case, preceded by the preposition к.

За́втрак принесу́т вам в но́мер к восьми́ (часа́м).*
    Breakfast will be brought to your room by eight.

*Note that час must be in the dative plural.

Нам обязáтельно нáдо вы́писаться из гости́ницы к двенáдцати (часáм).
We must check out of the hotel by twelve.

To specify an interval of time, use the prepositions с (from) and до (to), with the time in the genitive case.

Обед подаю́т с пяти́ до десяти́.
Supper is served from five to ten.

Посети́телей в нóмере мóжно принимáть с восьми́ до оди́ннадцати.
Visitors to your room can be received from 8 A.M. to 11 P.M.

3. НАЗВАНИЕ ЧИСЛА (CALENDAR TIME)

To respond to the question Какóе числó? (What's the date?) and express the current date or identify a particular date, use an ordinal number in the nominative case.

Какóе сегóдня числó? —Сегóдня пятнáдцатое (апрéля).
What is today's date? —Today is the fifteenth (of April).

Какóе числó бы́ло вчерá? —Вчерá бы́ло четы́рнадцатое.
What was yesterday's date? —Yesterday was the fourteenth.

To respond to the questions Какóго числá? (On what date?) or Когдá? (When?), or to express a date on which something occurred or will occur, use an ordinal number in the genitive case.

Мы бы хотéли провести́ приём трéтьего мáя.
We would like to hold our reception on the third of May.

Пéрвого мáрта мы получи́ли нáши паспортá.
We received our passports on March first.

To indicate a date before which some event will or did occur, the ordinal number should be in the dative case, preceded by the preposition к.

Я увéрен, что мои́ роди́тели приéдут к семнáдцатому этого мéсяца.
I am sure that my parents will arrive by the seventeenth of this month.

Если не получу́ ви́зу к два́дцать девя́тому* сле́дующего ме́сяца, то пода́м жа́лобу в ко́нсульство.

If I don't get a visa by the twenty-ninth of next month, I'm going to lodge a complaint with the consulate.

Remember that, as with time, "from" and "to" are expressed by the prepositions с and до, respectively, and that the date should be in the genitive case.

Мы пробу́дем в ва́шей гости́нице с четвёртого до семна́дцатого э́того ме́сяца.

We will be staying at your hotel from the fourth to the seventeenth of this month.

Note that до means "up to but not including" a period of time. To indicate "through"—i.e., "up to and including"—use the preposition по plus the accusative case of a date.

Я понима́ю, что вы бу́дете у нас с пя́того по шестна́дцатое.

I understand that you will be with us from the fifth through the sixteenth.

D. ИДИОМАТИКА (Idiomatic Usage)

COMPLAINING.

Russians do not hesitate to complain about undesirable situations. Here are some commonly used expressions of dissatisfaction.

Жа́ловаться (TO COMPLAIN)

Я не понима́ю, почему́ она́ ещё жа́луется на обслу́живание у нас. По-мо́ему, оно значи́тельно улу́чшилось.

I don't understand why she's still complaining about our service. I think it's improved significantly.

Пода́ть жа́лобу (TO FILE A COMPLAINT)

Если мы не полу́чим лу́чший но́мер, нам на́до бу́дет пода́ть жа́лобу в дире́кцию гости́ницы.

If we don't get a better room, we'll have to lodge a complaint with the hotel management.

*Note that only the final component of a compound ordinal number is declined.

Быть в претéнзии (TO HOLD A GRUDGE)

Я надéюсь, что вы не в претéнзии на меня́ за нечáянный недосмóтр.
I hope you're not holding a grudge against me because of my inadvertent oversight.

Ворчáть (TO GRIPE)

Не удивúтельно, что онú ворчáт на своú услóвия трудá!
It's no suprise that they're griping about their working conditions!

Нытьё (WHINING)

Знáешь, мне ужé надоéло слýшать его постоя́нное нытьё!
You know, I'm tired of listening to his constant whining!

Кáпать на мозгú (TO PESTER; LIT., TO DRIP WATER ON ONE'S BRAINS)

Давáйте не бýдем встречáться с ним. Он весь вéчер бýдет нам кáпать на мозгú.
Let's not get together with him. He'll be bugging us all evening.

Плáкаться в жилéтку (TO CRY ON SOMEONE'S SHOULDER; LIT., TO CRY INTO SOMEONE'S VEST)

Если у них вознúкнут какúе-нибудь неприя́тности с бронúрованием нóмера в гостúнице, онú обязáтельно забегýт ко мне, чтобы поплáкаться в жилéтку.
If they have any trouble reserving a hotel room, I'm sure they'll come running to me to cry on my shoulder.

E. СТРОГО ПО ДЕЛУ
(Strictly Business)

ПОМЕЩЕНИЯ ДЛЯ БИЗНЕСА (BUSINESS FACILITIES)

Many major hotels in Russia's large cities now offer a variety of telecommunication services (услуги телесвя́зи), banking, and conference (конферéнц-залы) facilities. The special rooms housing such facilities are usually called business centers (бúзнес-цéнтры). Business centers are also available in several areas of Moscow, including the GUM department store adjacent to Red Square. The number of fax machines at such facilities and individual businesses is constantly growing. For extensive long-term needs, fax forwarding services can be obtained in Russia by subscribing to one of the major international carriers such as Sprint/Telnet, Moscow Infonet, Scitor, Geonet, and others. An account for transmissions from Russia can be obtained through the Infocom IV or Relcom, the largest Russian telecommunications network (e-mail address: postmaster@kiae.su).

Most major hotels have money exchange (обмéн валю́ты) desks that operate around the clock (кру́глые су́тки). Western currency can be exchanged at these points or at any one of the exchange offices located in the city without showing any official identification or completing any forms. Traveler's checks, however, must be exchanged at banks or hotel bank branches. This method requires the completion of a special certificate (спра́вка) and the payment of an exchange fee.

ТЕЛЕКОММУНИКАЦИИ (TELECOMMUNICATIONS)

Activity in the area of telecommunications in Russia is becoming increasingly more vigorous and attractive to Western companies as the Russian Ministry of Communications (Министéрство свя́зи) strives to improve all forms of communication services (срéдства коммуника́ции), particularly telephone service. Stimulated by the potential of a vast market, many Western communication companies have been investing considerable plant and much needed capital in the improvement and expansion of Russia's communications network. Although the immediate beneficiaries of high-tech development have primarily been the major Russian corporations (e.g., LUKoil, Gazprom), banks, and large jointly owned companies, it is hoped that with proper policy planning and implementation, high-quality telephone service will be available to the general public.

The decentralization of the Russian communication system in the 1990s resulted in an extremely fragmented infrastructure with regional monopolies controlling communication networks. The largest of these is the Moscow City Telephone Network (Моско́вская городска́я телефо́нная сеть or МГТС) with which US West formed a joint ven-ture (совмéстное предприя́тие) in 1993 to develop a cellular telephone network (со́товая связь). The state-owned and operated long-distance telecommunications provider, Rostelekom (Росси́йскя телекоммуникацио́нная компа́ния) has formed a consortium (консо́рциум) with the backing of Western investors to develop a fiber optical network (волоко́нно-опти́ческая сеть) providing 50,000 kilometers of cable hookup, the so-called 50/50 project (прое́кт "50X50"). AT&T formed a joint venture with the Russian Moscow-based company Rosnet (Russian Telecommunications Network/Росси́йская телекоммуникацио́нная сеть), called Rosnet International, which will provide TCP/IP, frame relay (протоко́л ка́дровой ретрансля́ции), e-mail (электро́нная по́чта), fax, and telex services. AT&T has several other joint ventures with Rosnet that provide supply data communications services to various regions of Russia. Other Western companies providing communication services include Sprint, Siemens, and Eicon Technology. The Motorola Company, in a joint venture with the Ostankino Broadcasting Tower in Moscow, provides paging (радиовы́зов)* services, which are becoming quite popular in the Russian business and professional community, as well as among security personnel. Dozens of companies in major Russian cities provide telecommunications equipment and services. Some of the companies in Moscow and St. Petersburg include Alcatal BSR, AT&T Network Systems International, Comstar, Moscow Cellular Communications (Моско́вская со́товая связь), Sovam Teleport, Sprint AOZT, and US West International, Inc. Most of these companies can install satellite-connected (спу́тниковые соедине́ния) phones that are independent of local networks and allow clients to circumvent the usual bottleneck of international dialing.

УПРАЖНЕНИЯ (Exercises)

A. Запо́лните про́пуски ну́жной фо́рмой ука́занных чисел. (Fill in the blanks with the required form of the indicated dates.)

1. На́ши го́сти прие́дут _____ (25th of May).
2. Ка́жется, её день рожде́ния _____ (January 31st).
3. _____(on July 5th) мы получи́ли письмо́ из Москвы.
4. Сего́дня _____(18th of August).
5. Они́, наве́рное, уезжа́ют _____(1st of December).

*устройство радивызова or пейджер = pager

B. Впишите нужные предлоги и формы указанного числа или времени. (Insert the required preposition and form of the indicated date or time.)

1. Я надеюсь, что мы получим документы _____(by the 10th of the month).
2. Они будут у нас_____(from the fifth) _____ (through the 10th).
3. Магазин сувениров работает_____(from 8 а.м.)_____(to 5 р.м.).
4. По расписанию, этот рейс должен прибыть_____(at 22:00).
5. Они обычно заканчивают работать_____(by 7 р.м.).

C. Переведите следующие предложения с английского на русский. (Translate the following sentences from English into Russian.)

1. I think she was born on April 4th.
2. What time is it, please? —It is now a quarter to five.
3. Is it already 4:20! I'll be late for the plane!
4. The hotel manager said supper would be brought to the room by six.
5. When is your mother's birthday? —She was born on October 3rd.
6. What time did the new students arrive yesterday?
7. I told her I would call by eleven in the morning.
8. I usually work from nine in the morning to four in the afternoon.
9. What time did they check out of the hotel? —I think they checked out at 9 а.м.
10. What was the date yesterday? —Yesterday was the 23rd.

УРОК 3

A. ДИАЛОГ (Dialogue)

В поисках квартиры.

Сюзан Дейвис, журналист, находящаяся в командировке[1] в Москве, должна снять квартиру в аренду сроком примерно на три месяца. Русский коллега порекомендовал ей обратиться в агентство недвижимости, куда она сейчас собирается позвонить. Найдя телефонный номер в записной книжке, она набирает[2] его.

ГОЛОС: Алло?

СЮЗАН: Алло? Агентство Пенни Лэйн Риалти?

ГОЛОС: Нет, здесь нет никакого агентства. По какому номеру вы звоните?

СЮЗАН: 237-3006.

ГОЛОС: Нет, вы не туда попали[3].

СЮЗАН: Ой, извините.

Сюзан вешает трубку[4], проверяет номер и набирает его заново.

СЕКРЕТАРША: Пенни Лэйн Риалти. Доброе утро.

СЮЗАН: Алло. Пенни Лэйн Риалти?

СЕКРЕТАРША: Да. Вас слушает[5] Пенни Лейн. Кто говорит?

СЮЗАН: Добрый день. Это говорит Сюзан Дейвис. Коллега из газеты Коммерсант дал мне ваш номер и порекомендовал поговорить с господином Сусловым насчёт аренды квартиры. Позовите его к телефону, пожалуйста.

СЕКРЕТАРША: Господина Суслова сейчас нет. Он должен прийти примерно через час. Ему что-нибудь передать?

СЮЗАН: Передайте ему, пожалуйста, что звонила Сюзан Дейвис по рекомендации Андрея Карпова насчёт аренды квартиры. Я ещё раз позвоню примерно через два часа.

СЕКРЕТАРША: Хорошо́. Если хоти́те, вы мо́жете дать мне ваш телефо́н и он перезвони́т вам, как то́лько придёт.

СЮЗАН: Да, коне́чно. Я пока́ останови́лась в гости́нице «Белгра́д»[6]. Но́мер гости́ницы 248-1643, а но́мер мое́й ко́мнаты 573.

СЕКРЕТАРША: Хорошо́. Я переда́м.

Приме́рно через два часа́ Сюзан ещё раз звони́т в аге́нтство.

СЕКРЕТАРША: До́брый лень. Пенни Лэйн Ри́алти.

СЮЗАН: Позови́те, пожа́луйста, господи́на Суслова.

СЕКРЕТАРША: Могу́ ли я узна́ть, кто звони́т?

СЮЗАН: Это говори́т Сюзан Дейвис, я уже́ звони́ла сего́дня. . .

СЕКРЕТАРША: Ах, да. одну́ мину́точку. (Секрета́рша зовёт господи́на Суслова.) Михаи́л Алексе́евич ! Возьми́те[7] тру́бку!

СУСЛОВ: Алло́, это Су́слов. Я слу́шаю.

СЮЗАН: Господи́н Су́слов. Это говори́т Сюзан Дейвис. Оди́н из ва́ших колле́г из газе́ты Коммерса́нт посове́товал мне—

СУСЛОВ: Ах, да. Вы знако́мая Андре́я Ка́рпова, не пра́вда ли?

СЮЗАН: Так то́чно. Не смогли́ бы вы помо́чь мне с аре́ндой кварти́ры?

СУСЛОВ: Коне́чно. Мы располага́ем[8] о́чень больши́м коли́чеством свобо́дных кварти́р. Кварти́ра какой пло́щади[9] вас интересу́ет и на какой срок вы жела́ете её снять?

СЮЗАН: Ну, небольша́я кварти́ра, может быть, из двух ко́мнат с ме́белью, и не сли́шком далеко́ от це́нтра.

СУСЛОВ: Ду́маю, что мы смо́жем найти́ вам не́что подходя́щее. Вы смогли́ бы зайти́ к нам за́втра, чтобы просмотре́ть спи́сок свобо́дных кварти́р?

СЮЗАН: Хорошо́. Как насчёт девяти́ часо́в?

СУСЛОВ: Отли́чно.

Тре́тий уро́к

СЮЗАН: Ещё одно. Примерно, во сколько это мне может обойтись?[10]

СУСЛОВ: Ну, это зависит от того, где находится квартира, в каком состоянии она, какие в ней есть удобства, и от ряда других факторов. Об этом можно поговорить завтра.

СЮЗАН: Хорошо. До завтра.

Примерно через 15 минут в номере Сюзан звонит телефон.

СЮЗАН: Алло.

СЕКРЕТАРША: Здравствуйте. Это говорит Агентство Пенни Лэйн. К сожалению, господин Суслов забыл, что на девять часов у него назначена встреча с другим клиентом. Вы не смогли бы прийти в десять?

СЮЗАН: Смогу. Кстати, ваше агентство всё ещё находится на Ленинградском проспекте?[11]

СЕКРЕТАРША: Совершенно верно. Номер дома 39. Наш офис на втором этаже.

Сюзан решила позвонить своему знакомому Карпову, чтобы сообщить ему о своём звонке[12] в агентство недвижимости. Она набирает номер его офиса.

СЕКРЕТАРША 2: Алло. Газета «Коммерсант».

СЮЗАН: Попросите, пожалуйста, господина Карпова. Это говорит Сюзан Дейвис.

СЕКРЕТАРША 2: Он сейчас занят, говорит по телефону. Вы сможете подождать?

СЮЗАН: Хорошо.

Спустя[13] две минуты.

КАРПОВ: Алло, Сюзан?

СЮЗАН: Здра́вствуй, Андре́й я про́сто хоте́ла поблагодари́ть тебя за то, что ты порекомендова́л мне аге́нтство Пенни Лэйн. Я зайду́ туда́ за́втра, просмотрю́, каки́е у них есть свобо́дные кварти́ры.

КАРПОВ: О́чень рад. Я уве́рен, что ты найдёшь что-нибудь подходя́щее. Михаи́л Су́слов хорошо́ осведомлён в э́тих дела́х и, без сомне́ния, бу́дет весьма́ поле́зен. Позвони́, когда́ найдёшь кварти́ру. Хоте́л бы узна́ть, где ты бу́дешь жить.

СЮЗАН: Коне́чно, позвоню́. Когда́ лу́чше всего́ звони́ть?

КАРПОВ: Я обы́чно у себя́ в о́фисе с восьми́ до двух, но мо́жно в любо́е вре́мя оста́вить сообще́ние[14] на автоотве́тчике.

СЮЗАН: Ла́дно.

Finding an apartment.

Susan Davis, a journalist, is on a newspaper assignment in Moscow and needs to find an apartment for about three months. A Russian colleague has given her the name of a rental agency that she decides to call from her hotel room. She checks her address book and dials.

VOICE: Hello?

SUSAN: Hello? Penney Lane Realty Agency?

VOICE: No. There's no agency here. What number are you calling?

SUSAN: 237-3006.

VOICE: No. You have the wrong number.

SUSAN: Oh, excuse me.

Susan hangs up, checks the number, and dials again.

SECRETARY: Penney Lane Realty. Good morning.

SUSAN: Hello? Penney Lane Realty?

SECRETARY: Yes. It's Penney Lane. Who's calling please?

SUSAN: Hello. This is Susan Davis. A colleague from *Kommersant* gave me your number and suggested I talk to Mr. Suslov about renting an apartment. May I speak to him, please?

SECRETARY: Mr. Suslov isn't in now. He should be here in about an hour. Would you like to leave a message for him?

SUSAN: Yes, please tell him that Susan Davis called at the suggestion of Andrey Karpov about renting an apartment. I will call back in about two hours.

SECRETARY: Fine. Do you want to leave your number in case he has a chance to call you back before then?

SUSAN: Sure. I am temporarily staying at the Belgrade Hotel. The hotel number is 248-1643, and I'm in room 573.

SECRETARY: I'll give him the message.

About two hours later, Susan calls the agency again.

SECRETARY: Good afternoon. Penney Lane Agency.

SUSAN: Mr. Suslov please.

SECRETARY: May I ask who's calling, please?

SUSAN: Susan Davis, I called earlier today . . .

SECRETARY: Oh, yes, one moment, please. (*The secretary calls to Mr. Suslov.*) Misha, pick up the phone!

SUSLOV: Hello. Suslov speaking.

SUSAN: Mr. Suslov, this is Susan Davis. One of your colleagues at *Kommersant* suggested that I—

SUSLOV. Oh, yes! You're a friend of Andrey Karpov, right?

SUSAN: That's right. Do you think you can help me find an apartment?

SUSLOV: Certainly. We have extensive listings of available apartments. How big an apartment will you need, and for how long?

SUSAN: Just a small, furnished studio apartment for about three months, and not too far from the center.

SUSLOV: I think we can find something suitable. Can you drop by our office tomorrow to look over our listings?

SUSAN: Yes, how about nine o'clock?

SUSLOV: That would be fine.

SUSAN: Oh, one more thing. Approximately how much would the rent be?

SUSLOV: Well, that would depend on the location, condition of the apartment, availability of utilities, and a number of other factors. We can discuss that tomorrow.

SUSAN: Okay. See you tomorrow.

About fifteen minutes later the phone rings in Susan's room.

SUSAN: Hello.

SECRETARY: Hello. This is Penney Lane Realty. Unfortunately, Mr. Suslov forgot that he has another appointment at 9:00. Can you make it at 10:00?

SUSAN: Yes, I can. Incidentally, are you still located on Leningradskiy Prospekt?

SECRETARY: That's right. Number 39. Our office is on the second floor.

Susan decides to call her friend Karpov to report on her progress. She dials his office number.

SECRETARY 2: Hello. *Kommersant.*

SUSAN: Excuse me, may I speak to Mr. Andrey Karpov, please. This is Susan Davis.

SECRETARY 2: Mr. Karpov is on another line. Will you hold?

SUSAN: Okay.

Two minutes later.

KARPOV: Hello, Susan?

SUSAN: Hi, Andrey. I just wanted to thank you for recommending Penney Lane. I'll be dropping by their offices tomorrow to look over some of the listings.

KARPOV: I'm glad to hear it. I'm sure you'll find something suitable. Mikhail Suslov is very knowledgeable about rentals, and I'm sure he'll be very helpful. Give me a ring when you find something. I'd like to know where you'll be living.

SUSAN: Of course. What is the best time to call you?

KARPOV: I'm usually in the office between eight and two, but you can always leave a message on my answering machine.

SUSAN: Okay.

B. ПРИМЕЧАНИЯ (Notes)

1. In the earlier days of the Soviet Union, командиро́вка referred to an official out-of-town Party assignment. It now refers to any out-of-town business trip. Журнали́ст получи́л командиро́вку заграни́цу. (The reporter received an overseas assignment.) Мой партнёр в командиро́вке. (My partner is away on business.)

2. The verb набира́ть has a number of different meanings, including "to dial": набира́ть ско́рость (to pick up speed), набира́ть высоту́ (to climb; i.e., to go to a higher altitude in a plane), набира́ть очки́ (to score points in some athletic event). Как то́лько мы дости́гли верши́ны холма́, колыма́га начала́ набира́ть ско́рость. (As soon as we got over the hill, the old jalopy began to pick up speed) Как то́лько мы на́чали набира́ть высоту́, мне ста́ло бо́льно в уша́х. (As soon as we started to gain altitude, my ears began to hurt.)

   The reflexive form of the verb, набра́ться, + genitive case can also be used in expressions conveying a need for renewed strength or wisdom. Он до́лго лежа́л в больни́це, а тепе́рь ему́ на́до набра́ться сил. (He was hospitalized for a long time, but now he has to get his strength back.) Он дово́льно образо́ванный челове́к, но всё же ему́ на́до ума́ набра́ться. (He's fairly well educated, but he's got to get some sense into his head.)

   Набра́ться also has the very colloquial meaning of "to become dead drunk." Ну, говори́ть с ним бесполе́зно, ведь он набра́лся! (Well, it's useless to talk to him, you can see he's sloshed!)

3. Вы не туда́ попа́ли literally means "You've stumbled into the wrong place." The verb попа́сть (to fall into, to hit upon) appears in other expressions: попа́сть на рабо́ту (to land a job), попа́сть на по́езд (to be on time for a train), попа́сть под дождь (to get caught in the rain), and попа́сть под суд (to be brought to trial). По́сле оконча́ния университе́та, она́ попа́ла на чуде́сную рабо́ту в Москве́. (After graduating from the university, she landed a great job in Moscow.)

4. Another way to say ве́шать тру́бку (to hang up the telephone receiver) is класть тру́бку. Броса́ть тру́бку is much stronger and means "to slam down the telephone receiver."

5. Я вас слу́шаю (lit., I am listening to you) is a typical phrase used over the telephone to invite a response after identifying oneself.

6. Although not among the more centrally located hotels near the Kremlin, the Belgrade is much less expensive, has adequate facilities, and is conveniently located near a major connecting subway station (Смоле́нская ста́нция) and the very popular Arbat shopping promenade.

7. "To pick up the phone" can also be expressed by the verb снима́ть/снять. Я не понима́ю, почему́ никто́ не снима́ет тру́бку! (I can't understand why no one is picking up the phone!)

8. The verb располага́ть (to have available) is used often in Russian. Наша гости́ница располага́ет больши́м выбором конференц-за́лов. (Our hotel has a large selection of conference rooms available.) Я не располага́ю вре́менем. (I have no time to spare.)

9. Russians talk about the size of an apartment in terms of square meters or the number of rooms, although the former is more common. When referring to the number of rooms, the kitchen or bathroom is not included. So a two-room apartment in Russia is the equivalent of a one-bedroom apartment in the United States.

10. The verb обходи́ться/обойти́сь (to manage) is often used colloquially to mean "to cost someone a quantity of money." Это ему́ обойдётся в 50 до́лларов. (That will cost him 50 dollars.) The verb can also mean "to get by" (with or without something) or "to work out." Ничего́, мы обойдёмся и без маши́ны. (That's okay, we'll get by without a car.) В конце́ концо́в, всё хорошо́ обошло́сь. (Everything worked out well in the end.)

11. Ленингра́дский проспе́кт is a major thoroughfare in Moscow that is actually a northward extension of Тверска́я у́лица, starting at Белору́сский вокза́л (the Byelorussian Railroad Station). Тверска́я у́лица was the road used by former tsars to travel between Moscow and St. Petersburg via the town of Тверь on the Во́лга river. Тверска́я у́лица is the "main drag" of downtown Moscow and the site of many hotels, restaurants, and department stores.

12. The noun звоно́к (lit., bell, ring) is commonly used in reference to a phone call. Она́ позвони́ла в дверь, но никто́ не отвеча́л. (She rang the doorbell, but no one answered.) Спаси́бо за звоно́к вчера́ ве́чером. (Thank you for your call last night.) Likewise, the verb звони́ть/позвони́ть is used when saying, "Give me a call." Позвони́ мне, когда́ у тебя́ бу́дет вре́мя. (Give me a call when you have time.)

13. Remember that the preposition спустя́ (after a period of time) is always followed by a time expression in the accusative case. Спустя́ три часа́, она́ сно́ва позвони́ла мне. (Three hours later, she called me again.)

14. Сообще́ние (communication, message, report) is also used in reference to transportation: пути́ сообще́ния (roadways), возду́шное сообще́ние (airways), железнодоро́жное сообще́ние (railways).

С. ГРАММАТИКА И СЛОВОУПОТРЕБЛЕНИЕ (Grammar and Usage)

1. ДАТЕЛЬНЫЙ ПАДЕЖ (THE DATIVE CASE)

The dative case is primarily used to denote an indirect object of a verb or the recipient or beneficiary of an action. In English, the indirect object is often introduced by "to."

Пожалуйста, переда́йте ва́шему бра́ту адрес на́шего аге́нтства.
Please give our agency's address to your brother.

Они́ купи́ли нам интере́сные кни́ги.
They bought us interesting books.

Мы уже́ заплати́ли официа́нту.
We already paid the waiter.

Почему́ вы не писа́ли пи́сьма ва́шей сестре́?
Why didn't you write letters to your sister?

The following are the Dative Case endings for nouns and adjectives according to gender and number:

	NOUNS		
	NOMINATIVE SINGULAR	DATIVE SINGULAR	DATIVE PLURAL
MASCULINE	клие́нт (client)	клие́нт-у	клие́нт-ам
	портфе́ль (briefcase)	портфе́л-ю	портфе́л-ям
	музе́й (museum)	музе́-ю	музе́-ям
NEUTER	письмо́ (letter)	письм-у́	пи́сьм-ам
	состоя́ние (condition)	сотоя́ни-ю	состоя́ни-ям
	вре́мя (time)	вре́мен-и	времен-а́м
FEMININE	кварти́ра (apartment)	кварти́р-е	кварти́р-ам
	торго́вля (commerce)	торго́вл-е	торго́вл-ям
	исто́рия (history)	исто́ри-и	исто́ри-ям
	пло́щадь (square, area)	пло́щад-и	площад-я́м

	ADJECTIVES		
	NOMINATIVE SINGULAR	DATIVE SINGULAR	DATIVE PLURAL
MASCULINE/ NEUTER	но́вый/но́вое (new)	но́в-ому	но́в-ым
	большо́й/большо́е (big)	больш-о́му	больш-и́м
	хоро́ший/хоро́шее (good)	хоро́ш-ему	хоро́ш-им
	тре́тий/тре́тье (third)	тре́ть-ему	тре́ть-им
FEMININE	но́вая	но́в-ой	но́вым
	больша́я	больш-о́й	больш-и́м
	хоро́шая	хоро́ш-ей	хоро́ш-им
	тре́тья	тре́ть-ей	тре́ть-им

Note that certain verbs require the dative case in Russian, but take a direct object in English. These verbs generally reflect activities that involve rendering assistance, advice, transmitting information, addressing and responding to people, or expressing an attitude such as belief, envy. The most common include:

помога́ть/помо́чь	to help
сове́товать/посове́товать	to advise
сообща́ть/сообщи́ть	to inform, to communicate
звони́ть/позвони́ть	to call on the telephone
рекомендова́ть/порекомендова́ть	to advise, to recommend
передава́ть/переда́ть	to transmit, to convey
сказа́ть	to tell
отвеча́ть/отве́тить	to answer
ве́рить/пове́рить	to believe, to trust
зави́довать	to envy

Он охо́тно помо́жет вам найти кварти́ру.
He will gladly help you find an apartment.

Она посове́товал мне поговори́ть с вами об аре́нде кварти́ры.
She advised me to talk to you about renting an apartment.

Я ему сообщи́л о нашем но́вом местонахожде́нии.
I informed him about our new location.

Позвони́те мне, когда́ у вас бу́дет вре́мя.
Call me when you have time.

Они ей порекомендова́ли останови́ться в нашей гости́нице.
They advised her to stay at our hotel.

Я им сказал, что я хочу снимать квартиру в центре.
I told them that I want to rent an apartment downtown.

Я не знаю, можно ли верить ему.
I don't know if you can believe him.

The dative case is also required following certain prepositions. The preposition к, for example, is always followed by the dative case. It is most commonly used to indicate movement, in space or time, toward someone (кому) or something (чему).

Позовите, пожалуйста, к телефону Ивана.
Please ask Ivan to come to the telephone.

Они подошли к молодому человеку и спросили, где находится агентство недвижимости.
They came up to the young man and asked him where the real estate agency was located.

Вы сможете зайти к нам к десяти часам завтра?
Can you drop by to see us by ten o' clock tomorrow?

Мне надо закончить доклад к концу этого месяца.
I need to complete the report by the end of this month.

К is also used alone with nouns in expressions relating an emotional reaction.

К сожалению, она не сможет встретиться с вами завтра.
Unfortunately, she won't be able to meet you tomorrow.

К счастью, она оставила мне сообщение на автоответчике.
Fortunately, she left me a message on the answering machine.

К нашему великому огорчению, свободных квартир не было.
To our great chagrin, there were no vacant apartments.

К моему удивлению, они уже переехали в новый дом.
To my suprise, they had already moved to a new house.

The preposition по is used with the dative case to mean "by," "according to," or "via some means of communication."

По како́му но́меру вы звони́те?
What number (lit., according to what number) are you calling?

По како́му а́дресу мне на́до отпра́вить докуме́нты?
To what address (lit., according to what address) do I need to send the documents?

Она́ мне позвони́ла по рекоменда́ции колле́ги из газе́ты «Коммерса́нт».
She called me at the recommdendation of a colleague at the *Kommersant* newspaper.

Она́ говори́ла со мно́й по телефо́ну вчера́ ве́чером.
She spoke with me by phone yesterday evening.

Поезда́ ре́дко прихо́дят по расписа́нию.
The trains seldom arrive on schedule (i.e., according to the schedule).

Я всегда́ слу́шаю но́вости по ра́дио.
I always listen to the news on the radio.

The preposition по is also used with the dative plural to indicate recurrent time.

По среда́м мы всегда́ хо́дим в парк.
On Wednesdays we always go to the park.

По утра́м они́ обы́чно бе́гают трусцо́й.
They usually jog in the mornings.

Other prepositions governing the dative case include: благодаря́ (thanks to, because of) and вопреки́ (in spite of).

Благодаря́ ва́шей по́мощи, я нашёл хоро́шую кварти́ру.
Thanks to your help I found a nice apartment.

Вопреки́ моему́ сове́ту, она́ не хоте́ла звони́ть в аге́нтство.
In spite of my advice, she didn't want to call the agency.

2. ОТРИЦАНИЕ (NEGATION)

To negate a statement, simply place не (not) before the verb. Negative responses often begin with the word нет (no).

Она́ не жела́ет снима́ть кварти́ру в це́нтре го́рода.
She doesn't want to rent an apartment in the center of town

Почему́ вы ра́ньше не звони́ли в аге́нтство?
Why didn't you call the agency sooner?

To say that something doesn't exist, use нет* plus the absent object in the genitive case.

На э́той у́лице нет никако́го аге́нтства недви́жимости.
There's no real estate agency whatever on this street.

В э́том жило́м до́ме нет свобо́дных кварти́р.
There are no vacant apartments in this building.

To say that something wasn't or won't be (i.e., did not exist or will not exist), use the particle не plus бы́ло or бу́дет for both singular and plural objects.

Они́ мне сказа́ли, что, наве́рное, свобо́дных кварти́р не бу́дет.
They told me that there probably won't be any vacant apartments.

К сожале́нию, сего́дня ве́чером не бу́дет конце́рта.
Unfortunately, there won't be a concert this evening.

Note that не́ is stressed in the past tense.

На про́шлой неде́ле не́ было свобо́дных малометра́жных кварти́р.
Last week there were no small vacant apartments.

To express a more specific negation, use a negative pronoun in the appropriate case, immediately followed by не. The most common negative pronouns include ничто́ (nothing), никто́ (no one), никако́й (none whatever), and ниче́й (nobody's). They decline like что, кто, какой, and чей:

*In this case нет is a contraction of "не есть."

	NOTHING	NO ONE	NONE	NOBODY'S
NOM.	ничто́	никто́	никако́й	ниче́й
GEN.	ничего́	никого́	никако́го	ничьего́
DAT.	ничему́	никому́	никако́му	ничьему́
ACC.	ничто́	никого́	никако́й/о́го	ниче́й/ьего́
INST.	ни с чём	ни с ке́м	ни с каки́м	ни с чьи́м
PREP.	ни о чём	ни о ком	ни о како́м	ни о чьём

Вас ничего́ не интересу́ет.
Nothing interests you.

Никто́ не говори́л мне об э́том.
No one told me about this.

Он никого́ не знает в том аге́нтстве недви́жимости.
He doesn't know anyone at that real estate agency.

Он никому́ не позвони́т сего́дня ве́чером. Он о́чень за́нят.
He won't call anyone this evening. He's very busy.

If the negative pronoun is the object of a preposition, the preposition is placed between the particle ни and the declined form of что or кто.

Мы не говори́ли ни о чьей кварти́ре.
We weren't talking about anybody's apartment.

Сего́дня ве́чером он ни с кем не бу́дет встреча́ться.
He won't be meeting with anyone this evening.

You will note that unlike in English, multiple negatives are common in Russian. Remember, the negative particle must precede each negated verb, except the infinitive.

Мы никогда́ нигде́ ни с кем не хоте́ли встреча́ться.
We never wanted to meet with anyone anywhere.

Они́ ничего́ ни о чём не говори́ли никому́.
They didn't say anything to anyone about anything.

D. ИДИОМАТИКА (Idiomatic Usage)

MAKING PHONE CALLS.

Despite the considerable progress made in recent years in the availability of modern telephone equipment and services, much of the domestic phone system in Russia still suffers from frequent disconnections (разъединéние свя́зи), delays, and poor sound quality. Therefore, persistence and patience are required. Placing calls from a phone booth (телефóнная бýдка) in Moscow or St. Petersburg requires a special token (жетóн), which can be purchased at newspaper stands (Совпечáть), some stores, and at most kiosks. Local and international calls can be dialed directly from your hotel room, business establishment, or residence.* Here are some commonly used phrases involving the telephone:

A person making a call may say:

Мне нýжно заказáть разговóр с Вéрой Попóвой с оплáтой абонéнта.
  I want to make a collect call to Vera Popova.

Снимúте закáз.
  Cancel the call.

Я хотéл бы поговорúть с господúном Кáрповым, пожáлуйста.
  I'd like to speak with Mr. Karpov, please.

Попросúте к телефóну Ольгу Петровну.
  May I speak to Olga Petrovna, please?

Попросúте к телефóну Николая Владúмировича.
  May I speak to Nikolay Vladimirovich.

Мне нýжен добáвочный нóмер 25.
  I need extension 25.

Передáйте емý/ей, что звонúл Пётр.
  Tell him/her that Peter called.

*See Note 8 in Lesson 2 for more on making telephone calls.

Попроси́те его́/её позвони́ть Дави́ду.
    Ask him/her to call David.

Я перезвоню́ че́рез час.
    I'll call back in an hour.

A person answering the telephone may say:

Сейча́с позову́.
    I'll get him/her.

Здесь таки́х нет.
    There's no one here by that name.

Вы непра́вильно набра́ли но́мер.
    You've got the wrong number.

Подожди́те мину́точку.
    Just a minute.

Не клади́те тру́бку.
    Hold the line./Don't hang up.

Вам не тру́дно позвони́ть ещё раз?
    Could you call again?

If there's a problem on the line you can say:

Пло́хо слы́шно. Я перезвоню́.
    We've got a bad connection. I'll redial.

Нас прерва́ли.
    We got cut off.

You can end your conversation by saying:

Ну, всё.
    Well, that's all.

Созвони́мся.
    We'll be in touch.

Я вы́нужден/а зако́нчить разгово́р.

I really have to go now. (lit., I must end the conversation)

E. СТРОГО ПО ДЕЛУ
(Strictly Business)

НЕДВИЖИМОСТЬ (REAL ESTATE)

In response to the increasing number of foreign firms and personnel, especially in Moscow and St. Petersburg, and as a result of property privatization, there has been a rise in the number of real estate and rental agencies, some of which also function as employment agencies for foreigners seeking jobs in both foreign and Russian companies. These agencies advertise their services in the local English-language newspapers (e.g., the *Moscow Times,* the *St. Petersburg Press*), the Russian-language daily version of the *Moscow Times* «Капита́л», and in many weekly magazines, such as «Коммерса́нт», «Де́ньги», «Деловы́е Лю́ди». Other good sources of information are the business telephone books that can be purchased in most large cities and the weekly tabloid «Из рук в ру́ки» (*From Hand to Hand*) which also includes personal ads.

A typical tenancy agreement (Догово́р об аре́нде жило́го помеще́ния) stipulates the obligations (обя́занности) and rights (права́) of the lessor (арендода́тель) and the lessee (аренда́тор), and the leasing conditions, such as the maximum number of occupants, the term of the lease (срок аре́нды), and subleasing (субаре́нда). Normally attached to the lease is a complete inventory of all furniture (ме́бель), electrical appliances (электроприбо́ры), and other miscellaneous items.

The privatization of housing has been proceeding at a somewhat slower pace than that of industries. Still, any property that has been privatized can be leased, rented, or purchased by foreign individuals or by properly registered foreign firms with investments in Russia. Agencies can arrange the purchase of an apartment on variable terms and interest rates, but since many laws and regulations governing the purchase of property are still in flux, you should consult an attorney (адвока́т) knowledgeable about current rules for private property acquisition (приобрете́ние ча́стной со́бственности).

A number of colloquial terms that have become standard for describing rental property structures and amenities. Following are a few of the more common ones:

1) Ста́линский дом (often abbreviated in real estate listings as Дом СТАЛИН) means rather spacious apartments with high ceilings that were built during the earlier Soviet period.

2) Хрущёвский дом (abbreviated Дом ХРУЩ) refers to a block of five-story buildings with each floor containing four apartments. These buildings usually are without elevators or garbage chutes.

3) Бло́чный дом (abb. Дом БЛОЧ) is an apartment complex or block of apartments.

4) Домофо́н is a video or audio intercom system.

5) An apartment with сове́тский ремо́нт (lit., Soviet finish) has wallpaper, as opposed to за́падный ремонт, which describes an apartment with painted walls.

6) Ко́довый подъе́зд (lit., coded entrance) means the door to the building entrance has a coded push-button panel.

7) Кухня гарниту́р is a furnished kitchen.

8) Сигнализа́ция is a burglar alarm system.

9) Разде́льный санита́рный узел (abbreviated с/у разд.) means that the commode and bathroom are separate.

10) СВЧ-печь (usually abbreviated СВЧ) is a microwave oven. Another slang expression for a microwave oven is микроволно́вка.

Also growing are suburban housing developments offering one- or two-story attached homes (котте́джи), somewhat similar to garden style townhouses. A typical cottage includes a utility area (вспомога́тельные помеще́ния), a ground-floor garage (цо́кольный гара́ж), a general family area (общесеме́йная зо́на), and a sleeping area (зо́на спа́лен), a total area of about 200 sq. meters. Many of these homes are equipped with satellite TV hookups (спу́тниковое телеви́дение), international telephone connections (междунаро́дная телефо́нная связь), and self-contained heating units (автоно́мный теплогенера́тор).

Although space in new office buildings (офисные зда́ния) is gradually increasing, most office facilities (офисные помещения) in Moscow and St. Petersburg are housed in either recently renovated commercial buildings or converted apartment houses. There are several well-established real estate agencies (фи́рмы по торго́вле недви́жимостью or риэлтеры) and construction firms (строи́тельные фи́рмы) in these cities that have completed the construction of modern facilities leased by such firms as Credit Suisse, Exxon Enterprises, the International Monetary Fund, Phillip Morris, and the First National Bank of Boston. In view of the ongoing process of privatization, before leasing (брать в аре́нду) any office space or building, it is important to establish clearly who the property owner (владе́ец со́бственности) is. The lease agreement (догово́р аре́нды) should be examined by an attorney (адвока́т) and notarized (засвиде́тельствование нотариа́льное). Inspection of leased property (обозре́ние аренду́емых помеще́ний) should always include an examination of the specifications certificate (прове́рка техни́ческого па́спорта), which stipulates zoning and use regulations (правила по зони́рованию и испо́льзованию со́бственности).

УПРАЖНЕНИЯ (Exercises)

A) Впиши́те слова́ в ну́жной фо́рме. (Insert the correct form of the required words.)

1. За́втра я_____ (вы) наш но́вый а́дрес.
   (will give)

2. _____, они́ уже́ получи́ли на́ше письмо́.
   (to my surprise)

3. Она́_____(я) _____ ва́шего колле́ги.
   (phoned)   (at the recommendation)

4. _____, у нас нет свобо́дных кварти́р.
   (unfortunately)

5. Они́, наве́рное, найду́т кварти́ру_____.
   (by the end of the month)

6. Вы слу́шали но́вости _____сего́дня у́тром?
   (on the radio)

7. Они́ вчера́_____(он) о но́вом расписа́нии.
   (informed)

8. Я о́чень_____(ты).
   (envy)

9. _____вы посла́ли письмо́?
   (to which address)

10. _____(аге́нт), в како́й гости́нице вы прожива́ете?
    (Did you tell)

B) Переведи́те сле́дующие предложе́ния на ру́сский язы́к. (Translate the following sentences into Russian.)

1. Please ask Mr. Petrov to come to the phone.
2. May I call you tomorrow at three o'clock?
3. I would like to rent a one-room apartment in the center of town.
4. We have a large selection of new apartments.

5. Mr. Suslov is on another line. Will you hold?

6. You've dialed the wrong number.

7. I advise you to call a real estate agency.

8. I left you a message on [your] answering machine.

9. I'm sure everything will turn out fine.

10. Unfortunately, Mr. Petrov has another appointment at ten.

11. He didn't speak to anyone on the phone.

12. They didn't know about anything.

13. She didn't like any apartment in that building.

14. He didn't recommend any real estate agencies.

15. There was no answering machine in her apartment.

ПРЕДЛАГАЕМЫЕ ЗАНЯТИЯ
(Suggested Activity)

Consult a recent Russian newspaper to find ads for apartment rentals. Note the description of the apartment, its location, and the price. Try to identify an apartment that you might like to rent or that is similar to your home. Compare rental costs with those in the United States.

УРОК 4

А. ДИАЛОГ (Dialogue)

Пикни́к на да́че.[1]

Олег и Марина пригласили своих американских знакомых, Роберта и Алису, провести у них выходные на своей даче. За своими знакомыми Олег и Марина заезжают в субботу утром.

ОЛЕГ: **Приве́т! Я ви́жу, вы уже́ гото́вы.**

АЛИСА: **Ждём не дождёмся. Я ду́маю, что нам сле́дует отдохну́ть от на́шей рути́ны, и мы призна́тельны вам за это любе́зное приглаше́ние.**

МАРИНА: **О, не сто́ит благода́рности.**

РОБЕРТ: **Вот это да!**[2] **Я смотрю́, что вы основа́тельно**[3] **подгото́вились к пикнику́!**

ОЛЕГ: **Это, по бо́льшей ча́сти, проду́кты**[4] **для пикника́. Вы попро́буете, что тако́е хоро́шая ру́сская ку́хня.**

АЛИСА: **Отли́чно! Наде́юсь, вы разреши́те помо́чь вам.**

МАРИНА: **Гото́вить мы бу́дем сами, но вы мо́жете помо́чь нам собра́ть грибы́ и ягоды.**

АЛИСА: **С удово́льствием!**

Че́рез час они добира́ются[5] до да́чи.

ОЛЕГ: **Ну вот мы и прие́хали!**

РОБЕРТ: **Отли́чное ме́сто, пря́мо ря́дом с ручьём.**

АЛИСА: **И лес так бли́зко!**

МАРИНА: **Смотри́те, там спра́ва нахо́дится земляни́чная**[6] **поля́на. А метра́х в трёхстах по тропи́нке нале́во, вы найдёте мно́го грибо́в. И не волну́йтесь, я покажу́ вам, какие из них съедо́бные, а каки́е—нет.**

ОЛЕГ: **Хорошо́, дава́йте заберём ве́щи из маши́ны и пойдём на прогу́лку.**

Вче́твером они бы́стро перено́сят су́мки из маши́ны в дом и направля́ются к ле́су. Не́сколько часо́в они гуля́ют по ле́су, собира́я я́годы, и зате́м возвраща́ются на да́чу.

АЛИСА: **Это бы́ло здо́рово. Так поле́зно было погуля́ть.**

МАРИНА: **Я наде́юсь, что ты доста́точно проголода́лась[7], так как у нас заплани́рован большо́й обед.**

РОБЕРТ: **Я уже́ умира́ю от го́лода.**

ОЛЕГ: **Вы вдвоём иди́те и отдохни́те немно́го, а мы с Мари́ной пока́ начнём гото́вить обе́д.**

АЛИСА: **Ты уве́рен, что вы спра́витесь без нас?**

МАРИНА: **Вы уже́ и так помогли́ нам — я́годы, кото́рые вы собра́ли, про́сто изуми́тельны.**

Че́рез час Алиса выхо́дит из спа́льни.

АЛИСА: **О, как вку́сно па́хнет[8]! Что ты гото́вишь? Мо́жно, я посмотрю́?**

МАРИНА: **Коне́чно! Это баклажа́нная икра́. Попро́буй сама́. Отломи́ кусо́чек чёрного хле́ба.**

АЛИСА: **О, очень вку́сно! Ты должна́ дать мне реце́пт.**

МАРИНА: **Коне́чно. Это не тру́дно делать. Ме́лко поруби́ть печёный баклажа́н и доба́вить немно́го ме́лкору́бленого[9] лу́ка, зелёного пе́рца, помидо́ров, немно́го дроблёного чеснока́, и ещё полча́шки или приме́рно че́тверть ли́тра[10] оли́вкового ма́сла, ча́йную ло́жку[11] мёда. Всё это довести́ до кипе́ния[12]. Ещё один час кипяти́ть на ме́дленном огне́.[13] Пото́м снять кры́шку со сковороды́ и кипяти́ть приме́рно ещё 30 мину́т. Наконе́ц, я добавля́ю лимо́нный сок, переношу́ икру́ в глубо́кую таре́лку и ста́влю её в холоди́льник на́ ночь.**

АЛИСА: **Я обяза́тельно постара́юсь пригото́вить это блю́до. Спаси́бо.**

МАРИНА: **Нé за что! Ну что-ж, всё почти готóво. Алиса, хóчешь позвáть Рóберта?**

РОБЕРТ: **В этом нет необходимости — этот превосхóдный зáпах и так разбудил меня.**

ОЛЕГ: **Отлично! Тогдá давáйте садиться.**

МАРИНА: **Мы начнём с маринóванных грибóв в сметáне, копчёного сигá, сёмги[14] и столичного салáта.**

АЛИСА: **Мммм. Этот салáт прóсто бесподóбен.**

РОБЕРТ: **Алиса, я дýмаю, что нам придётся перейти на диéту пóсле этого уик-энда!**

МАРИНА: **Это тóлько начáло, так что готóвьтесь!**

ОЛЕГ: **Вот это свекóльник.[15]**

АЛИСА: **Он так освежáет!**

ОЛЕГ: **Да, мы чáсто едим свекóльник или холóдный борщ лéтом.**

РОБЕРТ: **Марина, ты замечáтельно готóвишь!**

МАРИНА: **Нет, действительно, ничегó необычного.**

ОЛЕГ: **Вы тóлько дождитесь моегó пáлтуса, зажáренного в сметáне с хрéном! Вся семья знáет, как хорошó я готóвлю это блюдо.**

АЛИСА: **Жáреный пáлтус! Я не встáну после такóго обéда!**

ОЛЕГ: **Не волнýйся. Рыба не так уж тяжелá для желýдка, а крóме того, у нас впереди цéлая ночь! Я предлагáю тост за нáших друзéй и хорóшую едý!**

ВСЕ: **На здорóвье!**

A picnic at a dacha.

Oleg and Marina have invited their American friends, Robert and Alice to spend the weekend with them at their dacha. On Saturday morning they come by to pick up their friends.

OLEG: Hi! I see you're all ready.

ALICE: More than ready! We can certainly use a break in our routine, and we really appreciate your kind invitation.

MARINA: Our pleasure.

ROBERT: Boy, I see you have quite a few things packed in the car.

OLEG: Mostly groceries for our meals. You're going to get a taste of good Russian country cooking.

ALICE: That's sound great. I hope you'll let us help you.

MARINA: We'll do the cooking, of course, but you can help us pick berries and mushrooms, if you want.

ALICE: I'd love to.

An hour later, they reach the dacha.

OLEG: Well, here we are!

ROBERT: What a great spot, right near the stream!

ALICE: And so close to the woods!

MARINA: Yes, you see over there to the right is a big strawberry patch, and about 300 meters down the path to the left you'll find plenty of mushrooms. Don't worry, we'll show you which ones are safe to eat.

OLEG: Why don't we unload the car and go for a walk?

The two couples quickly carry the groceries and bags into the house and head for the woods. They spend a few hours hiking and berry picking and return to the dacha.

ALICE: That was wonderful! I really needed the exercise.

MARINA: Well, I hope you're hungry because we have a big dinner planned for tonight.

ROBERT: I'm starving already.

OLEG: Why don't you rest up for a little bit, and Marina and I will start dinner.

ALICE: Are you sure we can't help?

MARINA: You've already done your part—the berries you picked look great!

An hour or so later, Alice comes out of the bedroom.

ALICE: What a wonderful aroma! What are you making? Do you mind if I watch?

MARINA: Not at all. This is eggplant caviar. Why don't you try some? Break off a piece of that black bread over there.

ALICE: Oh, this is wonderful! You have to give me the recipe.

MARINA: No problem. It's not hard to make. Finely chop up some baked eggplant, add a little finely chopped onion, green pepper, tomatoes, a little crushed garlic, a half-cup or about a quarter liter of olive oil, and a teaspoon of honey. All of this is brought to a boil and then simmered for an hour. Then take the cover off the pan and simmer for about thirty minutes. Finally, add some lemon juice, transfer the caviar to a bowl, and leave it in the refrigerator overnight.

ALICE: I'll definitely try to make it. Thank you.

MARINA: Don't mention it. Well, everything's almost ready. Alice, do you want to get Robert?

ROBERT: No need—that beautiful aroma was enough to wake me up.

OLEG: Great! Let's all sit down.

MARINA: We'll start with some marinated mushrooms in sour cream, smoked whitefish and lox, and Russian salad.

ALICE: Mmmmm. This Russian salad is delicious!

ROBERT: Alice, I think we'll have to go on a diet after this weekend!

MARINA: There's plenty more to come, so be prepared!

OLEG: This is cold beet soup.

ALICE: It's so refreshing!

OLEG: Yes, we often eat cold beet soup or cold borscht in the summer.

ROBERT: Marina, you really are an excellent cook!

MARINA: This is nothing. Really.

OLEG: Well, just wait 'till you try my baked halibut with horseradish and sour cream! I'm renowned in the family for this dish.

ALICE: Baked halibut! I won't be able to move after this meal!

OLEG: Don't worry, the fish is light. And besides, we have all night! I propose a toast to our friends and to good food!

ALL: Cheers!

B. ПРИМЕЧАНИЯ (Notes)

1. A да́ча is a summer country cottage or home, most often located in the suburbs (за́город) of large cities. Dacha-owning Russians cherish the opportunity to get away from the city for weekends and summer vacations.

2. Вот э́то да! is a frequently used colloquial expression that generally conveys delight or admiration. Зна́ешь, я то́лько что узна́л, что меня́ назна́чат в Пари́ж! —Вот э́то да! (You know, I just found out that I'm getting assigned to Paris! —How about that!) За́втра ве́чером, ко дню рожде́ния отца́, мы устро́им импровизи́рованный ве́чер! —Вот э́то да! (We're giving a suprise birthday party for my father tomorrow evening! —That's great!)

3. In this context, основа́тельно has the colloquial meaning of "amply." It is more commonly used, however, to mean "thoroughly," "soundly." Адвока́т основа́тельно дока́зывал свои́ до́воды про́тив оправда́ния. (The lawyer thoroughly substantiated his arguments against acquittal.)

4. Проду́кты (products) here means "groceries." To go food shopping is ходи́ть за проду́ктами. Note also моло́чные проду́кты (dairy products), заморо́женные проду́кты (frozen foods). Проду́кты can also refer to nonfood items such as побо́чные проду́кты (by-products) or проду́кты сгора́ния (combustion products).

5. Добира́ться (imperfective)/добра́ться (perfective) means "to reach a place." This verb is frequently used in the expression Вы хорошо́ добра́лись домо́й? (Did you get home okay?)

6. Земляни́ка refers to wild strawberries. Cultivated strawberries, the kind we are used to in the United States, are клубни́ка from which the adjective клубни́чный (strawberry-flavored) is derived: e.g., клубни́чное моро́женое (strawberry ice cream).

7. Note that the reflexive form проголода́ться means "to grow hungry," whereas the nonreflexive form голода́ть means "to go hungry."

Эти бе́дные де́ти действи́тельно голода́ют. (These poor children are going hungry.) На́ши шко́льники действи́тельно проголода́лись. (Our pupils are really getting hungry.)

8. Remember that the verb па́хнет (to smell of) is always used with the instrumental case to indicate the type of smell. От рук па́хнет лу́ком. (My hands smell of onion.) От него́ па́хнет алкого́лем. (He smells of alcohol.) The verb can also be used this way in the figurative sense. Па́хнет весно́й. (Spring is in the air.) Па́хнет бедо́й. (This smacks of trouble.) Па́хнет can also be used to say that something smells good or bad without specifying the type of smell. На ку́хне хорошо́ па́хнет. (It smells nice in the kitchen.) От него́ пло́хо па́хнет. (He smells bad.)

9. Other related terms include: руби́ть (to chop or mince), наре́зать ку́биками (to dice), and наре́зать ло́мтиками (to slice thinly).

10. The metric system is standard in Russia. One ounce equals approximately 30 grams dry weight or 30 ml liquid. A quart (32 ounces) is approximately equal to 1 liter. One-half cup or four ounces would be about 1/8 liter (125 ml).

11. Another term for teaspoon is ло́жечка. Note also: столо́вая ло́жка (tablespoon), щепо́ть/щепо́тка (a pinch or dash).

12. The formula: Доводи́ть/довести́ до + a noun in the genitive case appears in many common expressions, such as: доводи́ть до све́дения (to inform), доводи́ть до слёз (to drive to tears), доводи́ть до кра́йности (to carry to an extreme), and доводи́ть до сумасше́ствия (to drive mad). Настоя́щим письмо́м, дово́дим до Ва́шего све́дения, что мы гото́вы подписа́ть контра́кт. (We herewith inform you that we are prepared to sign a contract.) Её расска́з довёл меня́ до слёз. (Her story drove me to tears.) По-мо́ему, она́ дово́дит свои́ аргуме́нты до кра́йности. (In my opinion, she carries her arguments to an extreme.) Их неразу́мное упо́рство дово́дит нас до сумасше́ствия. (Their unreasonable persistence is driving us insane.)

13. Кипяти́ть на ме́дленном огне́ (lit., to boil on a slow flame) is to simmer; which can also be expressed by слегка́ кипе́ть (lit., to boil lightly). Note also: печь (to bake), жа́рить на огне́ (to roast or broil), жа́рить на сковороде́ (to fry), and жа́рить на решётке (to grill).

14. Сёмга refers to smoked salmon (lox), while the generic word for salmon is лосо́сь.

15. Свеко́льник is a traditional chicken stock soup containing julienned strips of beets, parsnips, and carrots, crushed garlic, onion, lemon juice, and sugar. It is served chilled with a dollop of sour cream.

C. ГРАММАТИКА И СЛОВОУПОТРЕБЛЕНИЕ
(Grammar and Usage)

1. СОВЕРШЕННЫЙ И НЕСОВЕРШЕННЫЙ ВИДЫ ГЛАГОЛОВ (THE PERFECTIVE AND IMPERFECTIVE ASPECT OF VERBS)

Most Russian verbs have an imperfective and a perfective form. Known as aspects, these forms describe the nature of an action. In general, the imperfective aspect denotes a continuous or habitual action, while the perfective denotes a single, complete action. The perfective form is often derived by adding a prefix to the imperfective form. The most common of these prefixes include: при-, вы-, про-, по-, add на-.

IMPERFECTIVE	PERFECTIVE	
гото́вить	пригото́вить	to prepare, to cook
пить	вы́пить	to drink
чита́ть	прочита́ть	to read
гуля́ть	погуля́ть	to stroll
писа́ть	написа́ть	to write

Other perfective verbs are derived from their imperfective counterparts by either dropping the syllable -ва- preceding the ending, or changing the infinitive ending from -ать to -ить or -нуть.

IMPERFECTIVE	PERFECTIVE	
встава́ть	встать	to get up
забыва́ть	забы́ть	to forget
отдыха́ть	отдохну́ть	to rest
получа́ть	получи́ть	to receive

Finally, some perfective forms are irregular:

говори́ть	сказа́ть	to speak
брать	взять	to take
приглаша́ть	пригласи́ть	to invite
понима́ть	поня́ть	to understand
помога́ть	помо́чь	to help

Imperfective verbs can be used in the present, future, or past tense to denote ongoing, continuous, or repeated actions. They stress the process or action itself, rather than the result, and they are often translated into English with the progressive (-ing) tense, or in the past with "used to."

Он сейча́с гото́вит вку́сный обе́д.
He is in the process of preparing a very tasty dinner now.

Ка́ждое воскресе́нье Оле́г гото́вит обе́д.
Oleg makes dinner every Sunday.

Три часа́ по́вар гото́вил своё но́вое блю́до.
The chef worked on his new entrée for three hours.

The imperfective must be used following the adverbs of time ча́сто (often), ре́дко (seldom), иногда́ (sometimes), and всегда́ (always).

Мы ча́сто прово́дим выходны́е на да́че.
We often spend our weekends at the dacha.

Е́сли за э́тим сле́дует тако́й же обе́д, то мы всегда́ бу́дем помога́ть вам собира́ть грибы́!
We'll always help you pick mushrooms if a dinner like this follows!

The perfective aspect, on the other hand, can only be used in the past or future tense to denote an action that was or will be completed. The perfective aspect emphasizes the intention to achieve a result, and it is commonly used to describe a single action occurring at a specific moment of time.

Они́ наверняка́ при́мут на́ше приглаше́ние на обе́д в суббо́ту.
They will definitely accept our invitation for dinner on Saturday.

Они́ уже́ перенесли́ все свои́ ве́щи в дом и пошли́ собира́ть грибы́.
They already took all their things into the house, and they went mushroom picking.

2. ВОЗВРАТНЫЕ ГЛАГОЛЫ (REFLEXIVE VERBS)

Reflexive verbs end in -ся or -сь* in the infinitive. They are conjugated like regular verbs but retain the -ся/-сь ending in all forms.

готовиться (TO PREPARE ONESELF)

I prepare myself	я готóвлюсь	мы готóвимся	we prepare ourselves
you prepare yourself (fam.)	ты готóвишься	вы готóвитесь	you prepare yourselves/ yourself (polite)
he/she/it prepares him/her/itself	он/она/оно готóвится	они готóвятся	they prepare themselves

Reflexive verbs "reflect" the action back on the subject; i.e., the subject and the object of an action are the same. In English, this is expressed with pronouns like "oneself, yourself, themselves," etc. Many verbs that are reflexive in Russian, however, are not reflexive in English. Common verbs in this group include: готóвиться (to get ready), брúться (to shave), and купáться (to take a bath; to wade).

Студéнты готóвятся к экзáмену.
The students are getting (themselves) ready for an exam.

Кáждое утро он брéется.
He shaves (himself) every morning.

Лéтом они любят купáться в óзере вóзле дáчи.
They love to bathe in the lake near their dacha.

Note that reflexive verbs often have a nonreflexive counterpart that requires a direct object and whose meaning can sometimes be different. Compare:

Онú возращáют кнúги в библиотéку.
They are returning the books to the library.

Нáши друзья́ сейчáс возвращáются домóй.
Our friends are returning home now.

Они всегдá нахóдят приятное мéсто для пикникá.
They always find a good spot for a picnic.

*-ся follows a consonant, and -сь follows a vowel.

Их да́ча нахо́дится о́коло большо́го ле́са.
   Their dacha is located near a big forest.

На про́шлой неде́ле, мы спра́вили новосе́лье.
   We gave a house-warming party last week.

Я уве́рен, что вы спра́витесь и без нас.
   I'm sure you'll manage without us.

   The reflexive form can also be used to impart a passive meaning.* The
   agent of the action is then in the instrumental case.

Кни́ги возврща́ются мои́ми студе́нтами в библиоте́ку.
   The books are being returned to the library by my students.

Я́годы и грибы́ собира́ются на́шими друзья́ми.
   Berries and mushrooms are being gathered by our friends.

Пикни́ки ча́сто устра́иваются на́шими сосе́дями.
   Picnics are frequently arranged by our neighbors.

   A number of verbs that reflect feelings and attitudes appear only in the
   reflexive form, though the reflexive suffix has no overt function. The most
   common of these is нра́виться (to appeal to, to like).

Как вам понра́вилась их да́ча?
   How did you like their dacha?

   Remember that the object that is appealing is the subject of the Russian
   sentence, while the person to whom the object is appealing appears
   in the dative case: i.e., что/кто нра́вится кому́ (something is appealing
   to someone). Also note that the perfective aspect of нравиться
   (понра́виться) is used to describe an initial impression.

Я уве́рен, что ваш па́лтус нам понра́вится, Олег!
   I'm sure we'll like your halibut, Oleg!

Мари́на, мне действи́тельно понра́вилась баклажа́нная икра́. Как её
гото́вить?
   Marina, I really liked the eggplant caviar. How do you make it?

*For more on the passive voice, see Уро́к 10.

Нам о́чень нра́вится е́здить на на́шу да́чу по выходны́м.
We really like to go to our dacha on weekends.

Other verbs used like нра́виться include: боя́ться (to fear) and дожда́ться (to wait for).

Я бою́сь, что они́ отклоня́т на́ше приглаше́ние.
I'm afraid they will decline our invitation.

Ждём не дождёмся обе́да!
We can hardly wait for supper!

D. ИДИОМАТИКА (Idiomatic Usage)

SOUP'S ON!

Russians love to eat! Here are some expressions you're likely to hear around the table:

Ешь—не хочу́! (THERE'S FOOD GALORE! WHAT A FEAST!)

Они́ пригото́вили сто́лько блюд — ешь не хочу́!
They prepared so many dishes —what a feast!

Во́лчий аппети́т (BIG APPETITE; LIT., A WOLF'S APPETITE)

Я так проголода́лся, что у меня́ во́лчий аппети́т!
I'm so hungry I could eat a horse!

Пожа́луйста, угоща́йтесь! (PLEASE HELP YOURSELF!)

Не стесня́йтесь, угоща́йтесь, пожа́луйста!
Don't be bashful, please help yourself!

Прия́тного аппети́та! (ENJOY YOUR MEAL! BON APPÉTIT!)

Ну, господа́, сади́тесь. Жела́ю вам прия́тного аппети́та!
Well then, gentlemen. Take a seat. Enjoy your meal!*

*This expression could be used in company or by anyone who is serving a meal, such as a waiter.

Нагуля́ть аппети́т (TO WORK UP AN APPETITE)

Собира́я я́годы всё у́тро, го́сти нагуля́ли большо́й аппети́т.
While picking berries all morning, the guests worked up a big appetite.

Нае́сться (TO EAT TO ONE'S FILL)

Ну, как вам понра́вилась на́ша ру́сская ку́хня? —Замеча́тельно, я
действи́тельно нае́лся!
Well, how did you like our Russian cuisine? —Wonderful, I really
stuffed myself!

Па́льчики обли́жешь (FINGER-LICKIN' GOOD)

Всё бы́ло так вку́сно, что па́льчики обли́жешь!
Everything was finger-lickin' good!

The above expression could also be used to describe some tasty dish that
is about to be offered.

Попро́буй эти я́блочные ола́дьи—па́льчики обли́жешь!
Just taste these apple fritters—they'll make your mouth water!

Ку́шать на здоро́вье (TO EAT IN GOOD HEALTH)

Ку́шай, ку́шай на здоро́вье!
Eat, eat in good health!

Russians are also excellent hosts, and may take a lack of appetite as an
insult. So, if you're not hungry, you're likely to hear the following adage:

Аппети́т прихо́дит во вре́мя еды́.
The appetite grows with eating.

And of course, a good meal is always accompanied by good drink.

Пить на бру́дершафт (TO DRINK TO BROTHERHOOD, FRATERNITY)

This toast is made to express a newer, deeper feeling between individuals. Traditionally, the participants link arms, drink from each other's
glass, embrace, and kiss. The form of address between them then becomes "ты."

К концу́ обе́да го́сти и хозя́ева вы́пили на бру́дершафт.
Toward the end of the meal, the guests and hosts drank to brotherhood.

За ва́ше здоро́вье! (To your health!)

This is probably the most common toast proposed in both informal and formal settings. Be sure not to confuse за ваше здоровье with на здоровье ("bless you," after a sneeze).

Снача́ла я хочу́ предложи́ть тост за ва́ше здоро́вье!
First of all I want to make a toast to your health!

And when it's time to go. . .

Пить на посошо́к (to drink one for the road; lit., for the walking stick):

This toast is usually offered by a guest when she/he thinks it's time to leave a party. Russian hosts normally honor that suggestion, but the guest should not offer it too early, lest the host be offended.

Ну, мои́ друзья́, уже́ по́здно. Разреши́те вы́пить на посошо́к!
Well, my friends, it's getting late. Let's have one for the road!

E. СТРОГО ПО ДЕЛУ
(Strictly Business)

ОБЕД В РЕСТОРАНЕ И ПРИЁМ ГОСТЕЙ
(DINING OUT AND ENTERTAINING)

Visitors to Russia usually take advantage of the smorgasbord-type breakfasts that are included in many of the hotel room rates. The amount of food offered is ample and invariably includes блины́ (thin pancakes), jams, dark and white bread, coffee, tea, and rather watery juices, a variety of cheeses, marinated fish, and vegetables, sweet rolls (бу́лочки), кефи́р (a thin yogurt-like mixture), ри́совая, ма́нная or овся́ная ка́ша (rice, farina, or oatmeal hot cereal), milk, and я́йца вкруту́ю (hard-boiled eggs). This buffet is usually served between 7:00 and 10 a.m. Fortified with a meal of this kind, one can usually get along with a light midday lunch. In Moscow and St. Petersburg, an increasing number of small private restaurants offer "businessmen's lunches" at fairly reasonable prices. Such restaurants are very popular with expatriate Americans. Hotel fare other than breakfast can be quite expensive. Payment at restaurants can be made with either rubles or credit cards. There are also some Russian fast-food outlets (бистро) that are attempting to compete with the popular McDonald's and Pizza Hut. In contrast to the working breakfast, business lunch, or dinner common in the United States, conducting business in Russia outside working hours is still the exception rather than the rule. You should allow your Russian host to initiate such discussion if he or she so desires. Meals taken with potential or actual Russian business partners are primarily social occasions during which the participants have the opportunity to get to know each other better. The American participant in such initial meetings should show an interest in Russian culture, politics, history, or art.

A few precautions should be kept in mind when dining out. To be absolutely safe, you should drink only bottled water. Many varieties of bottled mineral and spring water are available at hotels, restaurants, food stores, and street vendor stands. Tea and coffee are safe if the water has been adequately boiled.

Patience is a virtue in Russian restaurants (with the exception of a few first-class hotel restaurants where prices are also first-class). Dining out in the evening is usually considered to be a complete evening of entertainment. Service will be slow. On the other hand, you will not be rushed to make room for other clients. Reservations are always a good idea. The host usually pays for the meal, in which case you should express your gratitude, Большое Вам спасибо, я очень признателен/на (Thank you very much, I'm very grateful), or you can offer to pay for the bill, Разрешите, это будет за мой счёт (Allow me to put this on my account). If you know that the Russian host's company is not footing the bill, you should at least offer to split it, Давайте поделим счёт пополам (Let's split the bill), or you can insist on paying it, Пожалуйста, я настаиваю на том, что в этот раз я угощаю (Please, I insist that the meal is on me this time). Tipping (чаевые) in addition to the included service charge is now expected at a rate of 10 to 15 percent.

Long-term expatriates find that frequent hosting of buffet suppers and receptions at home can be rewarding both professionally and personally. Many individuals and a few catering firms can provide excellent Russian-style meals if the American hosts have neither the time nor talent to do this themselves. These services are usually advertised in local newspapers. Recommendations for caterers can be obtained from Russian business or professional associates.

Foreign residents who entertain will find that reciprocal invitations (ответные приглашения) are quickly extended and may lead to mutually beneficial professional relationships that are often indispensable for establishing and expanding commercial interests. In addition, they afford opportunities to further one's command of the language and understanding of Russian culture and society.

Americans invited to a Russian home should bring wine or flowers. The flowers should always be an odd number, as even-numbered flowers are only presented at funerals.

УПРАЖНЕНИЯ (Exercises)

A. Заполните пропуски, пользуясь правильной формой и нужным видом глаголов, указанных в скобках. (Fill in the blanks using the correct form and required aspect of the verbs in parentheses.)

1. Завтра они нам наверняка_____(готовить/приготовить) вкусный обед.

2. Кого ещё они_____(приглашать/пригласить) на дачу?

3. Я всегда_____(помогать/помочь) ей готовить обед.

4. Мы_____направляться/направиться в лес, когда я_____(находить/найти) большую земляничную поляну.

5. Не_____(звонить/позвонить) ему сейчас! Он очень занят.

6. На прошлой неделе, они_____(собрать/собирать) ягоды каждый день.

7. Когда вы вчера_____(возвращаться/возвратиться) домой?

8. Как вам_____(нравиться/понравиться) наш обед вчера вечером?

9. Не_____(забывать/забыть) помогать ему готовить обед!

10. Я очень рад, что они уже_____(принимать/принять) наше приглашение.

B. Переведи́те сле́дующие предложе́ния с англи́йского на ру́сский. (Translate the following sentences from English to Russian.)

1. Did you return my books to the library?
2. When I called them [by phone] they were still preparing supper.
3. The mushrooms you picked are simply wonderful!
4. Their dacha is located near a very big forest.
5. I am sure they will accept our invitation.
6. Are they still preparing for the exam?
7. Try this eggplant caviar. I know you will like it.
8. We've grown so hungry, we just can't wait for supper.
9. Everything is ready now, so let's sit down.
10. Don't worry, this dish is very light.

ПРЕДЛАГАЕМЫЕ ЗАНЯТИЯ
(Suggested Activity)

Visit a Russian restaurant and try ordering your meal in Russian. Alternatively, find a recipe for a typical Russian dish (preferably written in Russian), and try preparing it.

УРОК 5

A. ДИАЛОГ (Dialogue)

Собеседование[1] в связи с новой работой.

Донна Льюис, недавно закончившая американский университет и получившая степень бакалавра[2] со специализацией по международным отношениям и русскому языку, получила приглашение на собеседование в одной западной фирме в Москве. Она входит в здание фирмы, где её встречает дежурный.[3]

ДЕЖУРНЫЙ: **Доброе утро. Вам к кому?**

ДОННА: **Здравствуйте, у меня назначена встреча с господином Судаковым из отдела кадров.**

ДЕЖУРНЫЙ: **Ваше имя?**

ДОННА: **Донна Льюис. Я разговаривала по телефону с его секретаршей вчера. Мне назначили собеседование на десять часов утра.**

ДЕЖУРНЫЙ: **Минуточку.** (Он набирает номер отдела кадров.) **Михаил Сергеевич, здесь у меня молодая девушка, у которой назначена с вами встреча . . . Хорошо, я пошлю её к вам.**

Дежурный вешает трубку и обращается[4] к Донне.

ДЕЖУРНЫЙ: **Господин Судаков ждёт вас. Вам надо подняться на лифте на третий этаж. Комната номер 350.**

ДОННА: **Спасибо.**

Донна находит нужную комнату и стучит в дверь.

СУДАКОВ: **Войдите. Добрый день! Донна Льюис?**

ДОННА: **Да. Добрый день.** (Пожимают руки.)

СУДАКОВ: **Михаил Судаков. Очень приятно. Садитесь, пожалуйста. Перейдём к делу. Значит, вы хотели бы работать в нашей фирме.**

ДОННА: **Совершéнно вéрно.**

СУДАКОВ: **Тогдá расскажúте мне немнóго о себé и объяснúте подрóбнее, почемý вы хотúте рабóтать у нас.**

ДОННА: **Три гóда томý назáд я закóнчила университéт в Питсбурге, штат Пеннсильвания. Моя́ основнáя специáльность былá междунарóдные отношéния, но я тáкже изучáла рýсский язы́к. Пóсле университéта я рабóтала нéсколько лет в óбласти мáркетинга, но я всегдá хотéла имéть[5] возмóжность испóльзовать знáни языкá. Поэ́тому я закóнчила интенсúвный курс рýсского языкá в Институ́те Пýшкина в Москвé.**

СУДАКОВ: **А когдá это было?**

ДОННА: **В этом годý, лéтом.**

СУДАКОВ: **Знáчит, вы тóлько что закóнчили заня́тия?**

ДОННА: **Да, сéссия у нас былá на прóшлой недéле.**

СУДАКОВ: **Поня́тно. Ну, сýдя по вáшему разговóру, вы, навéрное, сдáли экзáмены на отлúчно! По-рýсски вы говорúте достáточно бéгло. Это, без сомнéния, большóй плюс.**

ДОННА: **Спасúбо.**

СУДАКОВ: **Так, расскажúте мне, что вам извéстно о нáшей компáнии и тáкже, как вы дýмаете, какую робóту вы смоглú бы выполня́ть.**

ДОННА: **Я знáю, что вáша фúрма поставля́ет на россúйский[6] ры́нок большóе колúчество америкáнских товáров. Как мне кáжется, это óчень интерéсно и достáточно трýдно. Я бы хотéла проводúть исслéдования россúйского ры́нка, занимáться перевóдом, а тáкже имéть возмóжность рабóтать с людьмú и испóльзовать мой спосóбности в кáчестве мéнеджера.**

СУДАКОВ: **Да, вы действúтельно в э́том заинтересóваны.[7] В дáнное врéмя у нас есть вакáнсия на дóлжность ассистéнта в отдéле мáркетинга. Опя́ть-таки, вáше знáние рýсского языкá очень пригодúтся.**

Стук в дверь, в кабинéт вхóдит жéнщина.

СУДАКОВ: А вот Татья́на Воробьёва, помо́щник заве́дующего на́шим отде́лом ка́дров. Она́ даст вам не́сколько анке́т, кото́рые вы запо́лните.

ДОННА: Спаси́бо.

ТАТЬЯНА: Сюда́, пожа́луйста.

В кабине́те Татья́ны Воробьёвой.

ТАТЬЯНА: Вот два экземпля́ра анке́ты[8] о приёме на рабо́ту. Оди́н экземпля́р вы мо́жете оста́вить у себя́, а друго́й отдади́те нам. На ва́шем ме́сте, я бы занесла́ нам анке́ту ли́чно, так как на по́чту полага́ться[9] не сто́ит. Вы уже́ оста́вили нам ваш телефо́н и а́дрес, что́бы мы смогли́ связа́ться с ва́ми, е́сли вы нам сро́чно пона́добитесь?

ДОННА: С тех пор как я разгова́ривала с господи́ном Суда́ковым в про́шлый раз, я поменя́ла а́дрес. Сейча́с я живу́ иа Смоле́нской у́лице, дом 14/21, кварти́ра 205. Телефо́нниый но́мер 291-5702. Кста́ти, вы не зна́ете, когда́ приме́рно мне ждать результа́та собесе́дования?

ТАТЬЯНА: Я ду́маю, мы при́мем реше́ние в тече́ние ближа́йшей неде́ли.

ДОННА: Спаси́бо большо́е. До свида́ния.

ТАТЬЯНА: До свида́ния. Жела́ю вам уда́чи.

A job interview.

Donna Lewis, a recent graduate from an American university with a major in international relations and a minor in Russian, has scheduled a job interview at a Western company in Moscow. She enters the office building and is greeted by a receptionist.

RECEPTIONIST: Good morning. May I help you?

DONNA: Hello, I have an appointment with Mr. Sudakov in the personnel department.

RECEPTIONIST: And your name is?

DONNA: Donna Lewis. I spoke to Mr. Sudakov's secretary yesterday by phone. She told me to come here at ten o'clock.

RECEPTIONIST: One moment, please. (*He dials the personnel office.*) Michael Sergeevich, there's a young woman here who says she has an appointment with you . . . Okay, I'll send her up.

The receptionist hangs up the phone and turns to Donna.

RECEPTIONIST: Mr. Sudakov will see you now. Take the elevator down the hall to the third floor. His office is room number 350.

DONNA: Thank you.

Donna finds the office and knocks on the door.

MIKHAIL SUDAKOV: Come in. Hello. Miss Lewis?

DONNA: Yes. How do you do? (*shaking hands*)

MIKHAIL SUDAKOV: I'm Michael Sudakov. Pleased to meet you. Please, have a seat. So, you would like to work for our company?

DONNA: Very much so.

MIKHAIL SUDAKOV: Well, tell me a little about yourself and why you are interested in working for us.

DONNA: Well, I graduated from the University of Pittsburgh in Pennsylvania three years ago. I have a major in international relations and a minor in Russian. After graduating, I worked in marketing for a few years, but I always wanted to utilize my language skills. So I took an intensive Russian language course at the Pushkin Institute in Moscow.

MIKHAIL SUDAKOV: And when was that?

DONNA: Just this summer.

MIKHAIL SUDAKOV: So you just finished your studies?

DONNA: Yes, we had our finals last week.

MIKHAIL SUDAKOV: I see. Well, judging from your conversation, you probably passed your exams with flying colors. Your conversational Russian is excellent! That is definitely a strong asset.

DONNA: Thank you.

MIKHAIL SUDAKOV: Now, tell me, what do you know about our company and what kind of work do you think you would be able to handle?

DONNA: I know that your company markets a large number of American products. This appears to be an exciting and challenging endeavor. I would love to be involved in some aspect of marketing research and translation, with the hope of developing managerial skills.

MIKHAIL SUDAKOV: You seem to be highly motivated. There might be some opportunities right now for a junior training position in our marketing department. Again, your Russian skills will be quite valuable.

There's a knock at the door, and a woman enters the office.

MIKHAIL SUDAKOV: Ah, here's Tatyana Vorobyev, our assistant personnel manager. She has some forms for you to complete.

DONNA: Thank you.

TATYAYA: Will you come this way, please?

In Ms. Vorobyev's office.

TATYAYA: Here are two copies of our employment application form. You can keep one for your records and return one copy to this office. Frankly, I would return the form in person to make sure it gets here. Do we have your address and phone number in case we need to reach you?

DONNA: I moved since I last spoke to Mr. Sudakov. My new address is 14/21 Smolenskaya, apartment 205. The phone number there is 291-5702. By the way, do you have any idea as to when I can expect to hear from you?

TANYA: I think we'll be able to let you know something within a week or so.

DONNA: Thank you very much. Good-bye.

TANYA: Good-bye. Good luck!

B. ПРИМЕЧАНИЯ (Notes)

1. In this context собесе́дование (discussion, conversation) means "interview." The term интервью́ is primarily used when referring to a radio, television, or newspaper reporter's interview of some prominent personality.

2. Сте́пень бакала́вра (bachelor's degree) is used in reference to American and British degrees only. The approximate Russian equivalent of a B.A. is a дипло́м, normally awarded after the completion of a four-year program of study at a university or specialized institute. The full term for this degree is дипло́м об оконча́нии университе́та/институ́та (diploma upon graduation from a university/institute). Дипло́м can also be used to refer to an award or certificate issued for some achievement; e.g., дипло́м чемпиона́та ми́ра, a world championship award, or a research project undertaken to satisfy an institution's graduation requirements, as in a degree or senior thesis. Все преподава́тели счита́ли её дипло́м отли́чным. (All her instructors thought her senior thesis was excellent.)

3. The adjective дежу́рный/дежу́рная is used to describe anyone who is on duty, whether it be a civilian or a military establishment; e.g., дежу́рный администра́тор (hotel manager on duty), дежу́рный врач (physician on duty), дежу́рный офице́р (officer on duty). Used alone as a noun (see Lesson 2) дежу́рный/дежу́рная refers more specifically to a receptionist, a hotel floor attendant, or a security guard on duty. In a more obvious reference to the word's French derivation, (from *du jour*) the expression дежу́рное блю́до means "the special of the day" (*plat du jour*).

4. Обраща́ться/обрати́ться (к чему/кому) can either mean "to turn to something or someone for information or assistance" or simply "to turn to face someone." Ду́маю, что вам лу́чше обрати́ться к врачу́. (I think you had better see a doctor.) Они́ обрати́лись ко мне за по́мощью. (They turned to me for help.) Она́ обрати́лась лицо́м к ма́тери и запла́кала. (She turned to face her mother and started to cry.)

5. Remember that the verb име́ть (to have) is primarily used with abstract notions: име́ть де́ло (to have dealings with), име́ть пра́во (to have the right), име́ть значе́ние (to matter, to have significance). "To have" in the physical sense is expressed by у + a pronoun/noun in the genitive case + есть. У него́ есть о́чень хоро́шая кварти́ра. (He has a very nice apartment.)

6. Росси́йский is used to refer specifically to groups or institutions within the Russian Federation. The more general term, ру́сский, applies to any person, literary work, or group that is simply of Russian origin.

7. The term заинтересо́ванный (interested) implies a significant degree of interest and motivation to learn about or participate in some activity. To express a general interest in something, use э́то мне интере́сно or э́то меня́ интересу́ет (that's interesting to me).

8. Another term you might hear for "job application" is заявле́ние о приёме на рабо́ту.

9. The verb полага́ться is often used in the impersonal expression так полага́ется (it is the custom, this is the way it is done). Here it is used with the colloquial meaning of relying or counting on something. На конце́ртах полага́ется сдать пальто́ в гардеро́б. (It is customary to check your coat at concerts.) На э́то не сто́ит полага́ться. (You shouldn't count on it.)

C. ГРАММАТИКА И СЛОВОУПОТРЕБЛЕНИЕ (Grammar and Usage)

1. ПОВЕЛИТЕЛЬНОЕ НАКЛОНЕНИЕ (THE IMPERATIVE MOOD)

A) "YOU" IMPERATIVES

The imperative is formed by replacing the third person plural, present tense ending with the appropriate imperative ending. The imperative endings are: -и (familiar, singular) and -ите (plural, or polite, singular) for verbs whose stem ends in a consonant; -й and -йте for verbs whose stem ends in a vowel; and -ь and -ьте for verbs whose stem ends in a consonant and whose first person singular form is *not* stressed. Note that the reflexive verbs work the same way, but they retain the -ся/-сь suffix. For example, говори́ть (to speak) → говор-я́т → говори́(те), посыла́ть (to send) → посыла́-ют → посыла́й(те), отве́тить* (to answer)→ отве́т-ят → отве́ть(те), стара́ться (to try)→ стара́-ются → стара́йся/стара́йтесь.

Note that the stress of the imperative form usually falls on the same syllable as in the first person singular.

Расскажи́те немно́го о себе́.
Tell me a little about yourself.

Говори́те погро́мче, пожа́луйста. Вас плохо слы́шно.
Speak a little louder, please. I can hardly hear you.

Начни́ заполня́ть анке́ты, как то́лько прие́дешь домо́й.
Start filling out the forms as soon as you get home.

*Note the 1st person stress: я отве́чу.

Гото́вьте уро́ки во́время.
Prepare the lessons on time.

Отве́тьте на все вопро́сы сейча́с же!
Answer all of the questions right now!.

Стара́йся слу́шать бо́лее внима́тельно.
Try to listen more attentively.

Гото́вьтесь к отъе́зду. Нас уже́ ждут на вокза́ле!
Get ready to leave. They're already waiting for us at the station!

в) "LET'S"

To express "let's" commands* the imperative is formed by using дава́й (familiar, singular) or дава́йте (plural, or polite, singular) plus an imperfective infinitive.

Дава́й(те) отдыха́ть.
Let's rest.

Дава́й(те) чита́ть.
Let's read.

Alternatively, the first person plural form may be used. In this case, the future imperfective form conveys a general wish or command, while the perfective implies an immediate call to action.

Бу́дем наде́яться, что вы ско́ро найдёте рабо́ту.
Let's hope you find a job soon.

Возьмёмся за де́ло!
Let's get down to business!

А сейча́с переведём эти докуме́нты на ру́сский.
And now, let's translate these documents into Russian.

Дава́й/те and the first person plural form used together adds extra emphasis to "let's" commands.

*See Уро́к 9 for a more extensive explanation of дава́й(те) usage.

Дава́й/те уже́ зако́нчим э́тот докла́д!
Let's get this report finished!

Дава́йте уже́ бу́дем иска́ть рабо́ту!
Let's look for jobs already!

Be sure not to confuse дава́й (те) with the true imperative forms дай and да́йте which mean "Give!"

Дай мне э́ту учётную кни́гу из тре́тьего я́щика.
Give me the ledger that's in the third drawer.

Да́йте мне, пожа́луйста, два биле́та на 20 часо́в.
Please give me two tickets for 8 o'clock.

C) THIRD-PERSON IMPERATIVES

To express an imperative of the form "let him/her/them" do something, use the particle пусть, or the more colloquial пуска́й, followed by the subject and the third person perfective form of the verb in either the present or future tense.

Зна́ешь, я не хочу́ туда́ е́хать. Пусть они́ е́дут без меня́!
You know, I don't want to go there. Let them go without me!

Е́сли она́ жела́ет там рабо́тать, пусть она́ пода́ст заявле́ние о приёме на рабо́ту.
If she wants to work there, let her submit a job application.

Пуска́й они́ са́ми чита́ют письмо́!
Let them read the letters themselves!

D) THE IMPERATIVE AND ASPECT

As you will note from the preceding examples, the imperative is used to make commands or urge someone to do something. As in other tenses and moods, imperative verbs have perfective and imperfective forms.

The imperfective form is generally used:

- when referring to frequent or continuous actions, or when no immediate or specific result is expected.

Держи́те меня́ в ку́рсе после́дних собы́тий!
Keep me informed of the latest events!

Пыта́йтесь приходи́ть к нам поча́ще!
Try to come visit us more often!

Принима́й во внима́ние э́ти но́вые пра́вила.
Keep these new rules in mind.

Ве́чером занима́йтесь в библиоте́ке. Там гора́здо ти́ше.
Study in the library in the evening. It's much quieter there.

- to request that an action be performed in a certain way.

Пожа́луйста, говори́те гро́мче, вас не слы́шно.
Please speak louder. I can't hear you.

- to express polite exhortations and conventional invitations.

Заходи́те к нам, когда́ у вас бу́дет вре́мя!
Drop by when you have time!

Бери́те, пожа́луйста, ко́фе или чай!
Please have some coffee or tea!

Сади́тесь, пожа́луйста!
Please have a seat!

The perfective form, on the other hand, is generally used to request a single or immediate action, whose completion is expected.

Расскажи́те мне немно́го о себе́
Tell me a little about yourself.

Перейдём к де́лу!
Let's get down to business!

Объясни́те, пожа́луйста, почему́ вы жела́ете рабо́тать у нас!
Please explain why you want to work for us!

Отдади́те нам оди́н экземпля́р анке́ты.

Turn in one copy of the form to us.

E) NEGATIVE IMPERATIVES

Negative commands are normally given with the imperfective form of the verb.

Не чита́йте эти расска́зы. Они соверше́нно неинтере́сны.

Don't read these stories. They're entirely uninteresting.

Не покупа́йте биле́ты на конце́рт. Мы переду́мали.

Don't buy any tickets for the concert. We changed our mind.

Negative warnings or admonitions are also generally expressed using the imperfective infinitive form of verbs. These admonitions have an impersonal quality; i.e., they do not address a specific individual but are stated more as general prohibitions.

Здесь нельзя́ кури́ть!

Smoking is not permitted here!

Не тро́гать!

Don't touch!

Не ходи́ть по траве́!

Keep off the grass! (lit., Don't walk on the grass!)

The perfective aspect, on the other hand, is used with negative imperatives to warn an individual against some action that might inadvertently be performed.

Не потеря́йте эти докуме́нты. Они́ очень важны́.

Don't lose these documents. They're very important.

Не заболе́й! Ты нам о́чень ну́жен!

Don't get sick! We need you badly!

Не упади́те! На у́лицах очень ско́льзко.

Don't fall! The streets are very slippery.

Sometimes, the imperative of смотре́ть is added to negative admonitions for emphasis.

Смотри́, не купа́йся в э́том озере!
Watch out, now. Don't swim in that lake!

Смотри́те, не опозда́йте на по́езд!
Make sure you don't miss the train!

Finally, note that the verbs слы́шать (to hear) and ви́деть (to see) have no imperative forms because these are involuntary physical attributes. If you want someone to listen or to look at something, use the imperative forms of слу́шать (слу́шай/те!) and смотре́ть (смотри́/те!).

Слу́шайте, я уже́ вам сказа́л, что не пойду́ на конце́рт!
Listen, I already told you that I'm not going to the concert!

Е́сли вы не зна́ете, что зна́чит э́то сло́во, посмотри́те его́ в словаре́.
If you don't know what this word means, look it up in the dictionary.

2. УСЛОВНАЯ ЧАСТИЦА «БЫ» (THE CONDITIONAL PARTICLE БЫ)

The particle бы appears in many common constructions. It is generally placed immediately before or after the past tense form of a verb. It is used:

• to express a general wish, intention, or suggestion.

Я бы хоте́л проводи́ть иссле́дования росси́йского ры́нка.
I would like to do a study of the Russian market.

Я бы занесла́ анке́ту ли́чно, так как по́чта рабо́тает не о́чень надёжно.
I would hand-carry the form because the post office is not very reliable.

Зна́чит, вы хоте́ли бы рабо́тать в на́шей фи́рме?
So, you would like to work for our company?

Каки́е обя́занности вы смогли́ бы исполня́ть?
What duties would you be able to perform?

• to describe a hypothetical situation: the conditions and the likely result. In this case бы appears in both clauses, and the condition is introduced with е́сли бы.

Если бы я знал, что она уже приехала, я бы закончил собрание пораньше.

If I had known that she had already arrived, I would have finished the meeting earlier.

Если б* она позвонила заранее, мы могли бы назначить встречу в три часа.

If she had called earlier, we could have scheduled an appointment for three o'clock.

- to express "whatever," "whoever," "however," etc. The basic formula is: question word + бы + ни + past tense of verb.

Во что бы то ни стало, я обязательно встречусь с ними сегодня.

Whatever it takes, I'll definitely meet with them today.

Как бы то ни было, вы должны заполнить эту анкету.

No matter what, you must complete this form.

Куда бы он ни ездил, его всегда тепло встречают.

Wherever he travels, he is always greeted warmly.

Где бы я ни искал работу, мне говорили, что вакансий нет.

Wherever I looked for a job, they said there were no openings.

Кого бы я ни спрашивал об этом, никто не мог мне помочь.

Whomever I asked about this, no one could help me.

- in polite injunctions, when a direct or blunt command might not be appropriate.

У меня уже три дня голова болит. —Вам бы сходить к врачу.

I've had a headache for three days now. —Perhaps you'd better see a doctor.

Уже очень поздно. Нам бы домой поехать.

It's getting late. Perhaps we'd better head home.

*Note that after если, бы may be contracted to б.

3. НАРЕЧИЯ (ADVERBS)

Adverbs are unchanging forms that describe an action. Typically, they answer the questions how, when, why, and where.

A) GENERAL INFORMATION

Many Russian adverbs are derived from adjectives by replacing the adjective endings -ый or -ий with -o or -e. They are, therefore, identical to neuter short-form adjectives. Although there is no firm rule about which adverbial endings to use, the "soft-ending" -ий usually becomes -e, while -ый becomes -o. For example:

external	вне́шний	вне́шне	externally
sincere	и́скренний	и́скренне	sincerely
extreme	кра́йний	кра́йне	extremely
interesting	интере́сный	интере́сно	interestingly
active	акти́вный	акти́вно	actively
fluent	бе́глый	бе́гло	fluently
difficult	тру́дный	тру́дно	difficultly
personal	ли́чный	ли́чно	personally
urgent	сро́чный	сро́чно	urgently

Я и́скренне жела́ю вам успе́хов в ва́шей рабо́те.
I sincerely wish you success in your work.

Мы кра́йне обра́довались прие́зду но́вых колле́г.
We were extremely pleased about the arrival of our new colleagues.

Они́ о́чень интере́сно расска́зывали о свои́х путеше́ствиях по Сиби́ри.
Their stories about their travels in Siberia were very interesting.

Вы совсе́м бе́гло говори́те по-ру́сски.
You speak Russian quite fluently.

Я ли́чно счита́ю э́ту рабо́ту о́чень поле́зной.
I personally consider this work to be very useful.

Нам на́до бы́ло сро́чно созва́ть слу́жащих на собра́ние.
We urgently had to call the employees to a meeting.

As in English, there are special forms for adverbs of space and time.

здесь	here	пото́м	afterward
сюда́	(to) there	тогда́	then
там	there	ча́сто	often
туда́	(to) there	ре́дко	seldom
бли́зко	near	всегда́	always
далеко́	far	сейча́с	now

Remember that здесь and там answer the question Где? (Where?) and indicate location, while сюда́ and туда́ answer the question Куда́? (Where to?) and indicate direction.

Игорь рабо́тает здесь (в го́роде), а живёт в при́городе.
Igor works here (in the city), but he lives in the suburbs.

По́сле ва́шей бесе́ды с Татья́ной Воробьёвой, пожа́луйста, верни́тесь сюда́.
Please come back here after you speak with Tatyana Vorobyeva.

Тогда́ and пото́м can both be translated into English as "then," but they are used differently. Тогда́ refers to the moment at which something occurs, while пото́м specifies what happened following another event.

Снача́ла я на́чал учи́ться в Моско́вском университе́те, а пото́м я перешёл в Институ́т Пу́шкина.
I started my studies at Moscow University, and then transferred to the Pushkin Institute.

Я зако́нчил интенси́вный курс в про́шлом году́. Тогда́ я осозна́л, каки́е больши́е измене́ния происходи́ли в Росси́и.
I completed the intensive course last year. I then (at that point) realized what great changes were taking place in Russia.

C) ADVERBS OF MANNER

Many adverbs of manner are formed with the preposition по- + the dative, masculine, or singular form of the appropriate adjective. For example, по-друго́му (in a different way), по-ра́зному (in various ways), по-пре́жнему (as before).

Я бы подошёл к э́той ситуа́ции совсе́м по-друго́му.
I would have approached that situation quite differently.

Мы справля́емся с дефици́том сырья́ по-ра́зному.
We are dealing with the shortage of raw materials in various ways.

Пита́ние бы́ло восстано́влено, и сейча́с всё рабо́тает по-пре́жнему.
The power was restored and now everything is going along as before.

Note that поэ́тому (therefore) is written as one word.

Заве́дующая отде́лом пока́ ещё в командиро́вке. Поэ́тому до пя́тницы мы не мо́жем встре́титья с ней.
The department manager is still away on business. We, therefore, won't be able to meet with her before Friday.

4. ТА́КЖЕ VERSUS ТО́ЖЕ

Both та́кже and то́же mean "also," "too," or "as well," but they are used differently. То́же is used primarily when referring to old information; i.e., to someone or something that has already been mentioned. Та́кже is primarily used when referring to new information.

Вы око́нчили Моско́вский университе́т? Я то́же око́нчил э́тот университе́т.
You graduated from Moscow University? I graduated from that university, too.

Расскажи́те мне, что вам изве́стно о на́шей фи́рме, а та́кже каки́е обя́занности вы бы хоте́ли исполня́ть.
Tell me what you know about our company, and also what duties you would like to perform.

Она́ зако́нчила университе́т, а та́кже рабо́тала не́сколько лет в о́бласти ма́ркетинга.
She graduated from the university, and also (in addition) worked in marketing for a few years.

D. ИДИОМАТИКА (Idiomatic Usage)

SPEAKING IN TONGUES . . .

Russians are great talkers, so many sayings have to do with the tongue.

Язы́к мой—враг мой. (ME AND MY BIG MOUTH; LIT., MY TONGUE—MY NEMESIS)

Всё проходи́ло весьма́ хорошо́ до того́, как я нево́льно оби́дел секрета́ршу. Язы́к мой—враг мой!
> Everything was going quite well until I inadvertently offended the secretary. Me and my big mouth!

На языке́ (ON THE TIP OF THE TONGUE)

Во вре́мя интервью́ на языке́ у меня́ было ещё мно́го вопро́сов, но почему́-то мне не удало́сь их зада́ть.
> I had many other questions on the tip of my tongue during the interview, but for some reason I didn't get to ask them.

Распуска́ть/распусти́ть язы́к (TO TALK TOO MUCH; LIT., TO LET OUT ONE'S TONGUE)

Снача́ла он мне показа́лся о́чень ро́бким, а к концу́ собесе́дования он здо́рово распусти́л язы́к.
> At first he seemed very timid, but by the end of the interview he really began wagging his tongue.

Найти́ о́бщий язы́к (TO FIND A COMMON LANGUAGE)

По́сле интервью́, я по́нял, что мы с ва́ми нашли́ о́бщий язы́к.
> After the interview, I realized that you and I found a common language.

Говори́ть на ра́зных языка́х (TO SPEAK A DIFFERENT LANGUAGE)

Бы́ло совсе́м бесполе́зно разгова́ривать с ней. Мы про́сто говори́ли на ра́зных языка́х.
> It was quite useless talking with her. We just weren't speaking the same language.

Язы́к без косте́й (A LOOSE TONGUE; LIT., A TONGUE WITHOUT BONES)

По-мо́ему, бы́ло бы опа́сно назна́чить её в наш отде́л. У неё язы́к без косте́й.

I think it would be dangerous to assign her to our department. She's got a loose tongue.

Проглоти́ть язы́к (TO REFUSE TO SPEAK; LIT., TO SWALLOW ONE'S TONGUE)

Когда́ я зада́л ему́ вопро́с о его́ предыду́щей до́лжности, он как бу́дто проглоти́л язы́к.

When I asked him about his previous job, he acted as if the cat got his tongue.

E. СТРОГО ПО ДЕЛУ
(Strictly Business)

ВОЗМОЖНОСТИ ПО ТРУДОУСТРОЙСТВУ
(EMPLOYMENT OPPORTUNITIES)

The steadily increasing number of Western firms forming joint ventures, opening up branches, and trading with the Russian Federation has resulted in many new employment opportunities for Americans with a reasonably good command of Russian. There are employment opportunities with American and European international firms in Russia as well as in the United States with Russian companies, particularly banks eager to open overseas branches.

Advertisements for executive-level positions in Russian banks, for example, are placed in various domestic finance journals such as «Коммерса́нт» and English language periodicals such as *The Economist.* Typical listings include openings for top-level management positions for persons with experience in international banking, portfolio management, financial and corporate law, and personnel management. Mid-level managers and advisor positions have been offered to persons with experience in strategic planning, auditing and accounting, international economic relations, and investment project management. These ads usually stipulate that Russian fluency is desirable. Salaries are competitive with comparable positions in the United States.

The English-language newspaper *The Moscow Times,* which publishes a Job Opportunies section twice weekly, regularly advertises for copy editors (техни́ческие реда́кторы), advertisement managers (менеджеры по рекла́ме), and computer publishing specialists (специали́сты компью́терной вёрстки) whose native language is English but who also have a good command of Russian. Subscription managers (менеджеры по подпи́ске) with a humanities background and willingness to travel extensively within the Содру́жество Незави́симых Госуда́рств (Commonwealth of Independent States]) or СНГ (CIS), are regularly sought by distributors of both Russian and English-language magazines such as *The Moscow Times,* Витри́на (*Window*), *Cosmopolitan,* Капита́л *(Capital), Playboy,* and *Good Housekeeping.* Computer companies that are expanding their operations in the CIS are also in need of sales managers, product marketing managers, and education sales managers.

In addition to full-time positions, short-term internships are offered by American corporations with branches in the Russian Federation, such as Coca Cola, CNN, and AT&T. Various export-import firms, such as World Healthcare Systems, which exports medical and dental equipment to Russia, frequently post openings for short- or long-term employment at their Russian offices.

Generally, businesses in Russia place great emphasis on communicative abilities in Russian. Candidates with specialized training in commerce, finance, law, electronics, and journalism, in addition to fluency in Russian, enjoy a distinct advantage. On the other hand, recent college graduates in such fields as political science and international relations with a working knowledge of Russian have been hired in trainee positions with international companies in Moscow and St. Petersburg. Whereas it is best to do as much preliminary research about job opportunities as possible, jobs are often found by merely being at the right place at the right time. Patience and persistence are required.

It goes without saying that any experience gained in either short-term employment or internship program participation will be invaluable for further career advancement either within the Russian market or international operations.

A comprehensive list of American companies operating in the Russian Federation can be obtained from the U.S. Department of Commerce, International Trade Administration, Washington, D.C. 20230.

In contrast to job application procedures in the U.S., there is no standard resume form used by applicants for positions with Russian firms. In general, application forms, if they exist at all, vary considerably from company to company. Obtaining employment "по знако́мству" (through personal connections) is still the most prevalent practice. The personal interview is also of considerable importance. When forms require a statement about language skills, aplicants should specify the level of their fluency in Russian and whether the applicant has oral, written, and/or reading skills in various languages.

The following are correspondence excerpts from a personnel search firm to a Russian bank in Moscow that is seeking a person to fill a managerial position. The letter outlines the job qualifications, search method, and candidate selection procedures. The vocabulary that follows should help you understand the letter.

Г-н Моро́зов И.С.
Нача́льник Управле́ня
организа́ции рабо́ты персона́ла[10]
Банк Национальный Кредит
ул. Огарева; 9-2
103009 Москва; Россия

Уважа́емый И́горь Серге́еевич!
Хоте́л бы поблагодари́ть Вас за предоста́вленную возмо́жность[11] встре́титься с Вами ещё раз. В продолже́ние вчера́шнего разгово́ра направля́ю Вам наше предложе́ние[12] о заполне́нии пози́ции Управля́ющего Отделе́нием[13] в Вашем ба́нке. Оно опи́сывает ме́тод нашей рабо́ты, вре́мя, необходи́мое[14] для заверше́ния[15] прое́кта, и сто́имость[16] рабо́ты.

ДОЛЖНОСТЬ
По на́шему мне́нию,[17] кандида́т на ука́занную до́лжность до́лжен быть профессиона́лом-иностра́нецем,[18] име́ющим необходи́мый о́пыт, нако́пленный[19] в результа́те рабо́ты в ба́нковской сфе́ре ра́звитых стран.[20] Его основно́й зада́чей будет построе́ние работы Отделе́ния по за́падному образцу́[21] и установле́ние свя́зей[22] с той ча́стью клие́нтов Банка, кото́рая предста́вленна как физи́ческими, так и юриди́ческими ли́цами-иностра́нцами, и, в основно́м, представи́тельствами[23] за́падных компа́ний в России. При этом мы понима́ем, что основно́й упо́р[24] будет сде́лан им не на неме́дленное получе́ние при́были,[25] а на постепе́нное[26] перенесе́ние[27] моде́ли работы Отделе́ния на рабо́ту други́х структу́р Банка. Мы

полага́ем, что в подчине́нии[28] у Управля́ющего бу́дут находи́ться та́кже в основно́м[29] иноста́нцы, кото́рые с тече́нием вре́мени бу́дут замеща́ться[30] росси́йским персона́лом, проше́дшим необходи́мую подгото́вку внутри́ Отделе́ния. Мы уве́рены, что тако́го кандида́та мо́жно бу́дет найти́ в Москве́ или С. Петербу́рге, среди́ уже́ рабо́тающих иностра́нцев, знако́мых с росси́йской специ́фикой, либо, в кра́йнем слу́чае, среди́ тех, кто сейча́с за рубежо́м,[31] но ра́нее был и рабо́тал в Росси́и. Наш о́пыт[32] пока́зывает, что расту́щий ры́нок рабо́чей си́лы позволя́ет в не́которых слу́чаях находи́ть необходи́мых зарубе́жных[33] профессиона́лов не перенося́ по́иск за грани́цу. Это позволя́ет нам сократи́ть вре́мя по́иска[34] и уме́ньшить расхо́ды.[35]

ПРОЦЕСС ПОИСКА

Подро́бное пи́сьменное определе́ние до́лжности

По́сле встреч с клие́нтом пи́шется подро́бное определе́ние до́лжности. Это определе́ние составля́ется по четырём основны́м направле́ниям:[36]

- компа́ния клие́нта и её о́бласть де́ятельности[37]
- до́лжность, на кото́рую необходи́мо найти́ кандида́та
- ка́чества[38] идеа́льного кандида́та и его квалифика́ция
- за́работная пла́та[39] и возмо́жности продвиже́ния по слу́жбе

Вы́бор и оце́нка из мно́жества кандида́тов

Проце́сс по́иска мо́жет заключа́ть в себе́ како́й-нибудь оди́н или все три похо́да одновреме́нно, напра́вленные на удовлетворе́ние тре́бований клие́нта. Э́тими подхо́дами явля́ются:

<u>Прямо́й по́иск</u> По́иск кандида́тов в подходя́щих компа́ниях и други́х организа́циях, а та́кже определе́ние исто́чников информа́ции по возмо́жным кандида́там в ну́жной о́бласти и среди́ со́тен свя́зей, кото́рые мы испо́льзуем в виду́ отсу́тствия организо́ванных исто́чников информа́ции в Росси́и.

<u>По́иск в ба́нке да́нных</u> По́иск в ба́нке да́нных фи́рмы для определе́ния потенциа́льных кандида́тов и люде́й, кото́рые мо́гут вы́вести на кандида́тов.

<u>По́иск с по́мощью средств информа́ции</u> Рекла́ма, наце́ленная на удовлетворе́ние запро́сов ка́ждого конкре́тного прое́кта. Этот подхо́д испо́льзуется в исключи́тельных слу́чаях и то́лько по согласова́нию с клие́нтом.

СЛОВАРЬ (Vocabulary)

1. организация работы персонала	personnel department
2. предоставленная возможность	a provided opportunity
3. предложение	proposal
4. управляющий отделением	section or department chief
5. необходимое	essential
6. завершение	completion
7. стоимость	cost
8. по нашему мнению	in our opinion
9. профессионал-иностранец	a foreign professional
10. накопленный	accumulated, acquired
11. развитая страна	developed country
12. образец	model, fashion
13. установление связей	establishing ties (contacts)
14. представительство	representative
15. упор	emphasis, stress
16. прибыль	profit
17. постепенное	gradual
18. перенесение	transfer
19. в подчинении у (кого)	subordinate to
20. в основном	primarily
21. замещаться	to be replaced
22. за рубежом	abroad
23. опыт	experience
24. зарубежный	foreign
25. поиск	search
26. расходы	expenses
27. направление	direction
28. область деятельности	area of activity
29. качество	quality
30. заработная плата	wage, salary
31. продвижение по службе	advancement, promotion
32. подход	approach
33. подходящий	suitable, appropriate
34. источник	source
35. банк данных	data bank
36. средства информации	information media
37. запросы	demands, requirements
38. исключительный	exceptional
39. согласование	agreement, consent

Here are a few typical want ads in Russian. Note that age requirements are a standard practice.

Российская компьютерная компания

ищет

МЕНЕДЖЕРА ПО ОРГАНИЗАЦИИ ПРОДАЖ ВЫЧИСЛИТЕЛЬНОЙ ТЕХНИКИ

Необходимо: высшее экономическое образование.

Желательно: знание английского языка.

Опыт аналогичной деятельности не менее 2 лет.

Хорошее знание маркетинговой деятельности.

Самостоятельность в вопросах планирования.

Возраст до 45 лет.

Конкурентноспособная зарплата.

Хорошая возможность карьерного роста в

Динамично развиающейся компании.

Обращайтесь по телефону 913-2942.

Russian Computer Company

seeks a

COMPUTER SALES MANAGER

Requirements: University degree in Economics.

Knowledge of English desirable.

Minimum 2 years experience in computer sales.

Good knowledge of marketing procedures.

Self-starter in planning.

Age under 45.

Competitive salary.

Good opportunity for career growth with

a dynamically developing computer company.

Telephone: 913-2942

Российское издательство ищет # КОРРЕКТОРА Грамотность Ответственность Среднее или высшее образование Опыт работы—минимум 1 год. Возраст до 35 лет Тел. 332-01-73.	Russian Publishing House seeks # EDITOR Must be literate, responsible Secondary or Higher education Minimum 1 year work experience Age under 35 Tel. 332-01-73
Домостроительная фирма ищет # АРХИТЕКТОРОВ Необходимо: опыт работы Возраст до 35 лет Рекомендации Тел. 347-71-56	Housing Construction Company seeks # ARCHITECTS Requirements: Work experience Age under 45 References Tel. 347-71-56

УПРАЖНЕНИЯ (Exercises)

A. Впиши́те ну́жные слова́ повели́тельного наклоне́ния в про́пусках.
(Insert the required imperative words in the blanks.)

1. _____, пожа́луйста, и _____мне
   (have a seat)   (tell me)
   немно́го о себе́.

2. _____эту анке́ту, тогда́ _____ко мне в каби́нет.
   (fill out)   (come in)

3. Здесь нельзя́ _____!
   (smoking)

4. Пожа́луйста, _____погро́мче, я вас не по́нял.
   (speak)

5. Оди́н экземпля́р _____нам, пожа́луйста.
   (submit, turn in)

B. Составьте предложе́ния, преврати́в ука́занное и́мя прилага́ительное в соотве́тствующее наре́чие и переведи́те результа́т на англи́йский. (Compose sentences by converting the indicated adjectives into adverbs, and translate the result into English.)

ОБРАЗЕЦ: Она очень (интересный) рассказывала о своей семье.
Она очень интере́сно расска́зывала о свое́й семье́.
She tells a very interesting story about her family.

1. К сожале́нию, по́чта не о́чень (надёжный) рабо́тает.
2. Я ду́маю, что мне будет очень (трудный) запо́лнить анке́ту.
3. Мы зна́ем, что вы дово́льно (беглый) говори́те по-ру́сски.
4. Он (личный) занёс запо́лненную анке́ту.
5. Она сказа́ла, что они сейча́с очень (активный) и́щут (seeking) рабо́ту.

C. Переведи́те сле́дующие предложе́ния с англи́йского на ру́сский. (Translate the following sentences from English to Russian.)

1. I would like to have the opportunity to use my knowledge of Russian.
2. I finished the intensive Russian language course in March. I then realized that many foreign companies were actively engaged in the Russian market.
3. When will you let me know the results of the interview?
4. My major was international relations, but I also studied Russian.
5. Did your new assistant graduate from Moscow University? I graduated from there, too!
6. Since I last met with you, I changed my address.
7. If necessary, I'll fill out another application form.
8. What kind of duties will I be performing?
9. After our discussion I realized that we are on the same wavelength.
10. I don't think we should hire him. He's really got a loose tongue.

ПРЕДЛАГАЕМЫЕ ЗАНЯТИЯ
(Suggested Activity)

Write a brief résumé for yourself in Russian, indicating your experience and interest in some particular position.

УРОК 6

А. ДИАЛОГ

Пе́рвый день на рабо́те.

Ива́н Кусто́в был при́нят на до́лжность помо́щника ме́неджера в моско́вском филиа́ле одно́й америка́нской компа́нии. Мануэ́л Не́льсон, его нача́льник, знако́мит Ива́на с осо́бенностями его но́вой рабо́ты.

НЕЛЬСОН: **Доброе утро, Ива́н! Мне сказа́ли, что вы сего́дня прие́хали пора́ньше.**

ИВАН: **Да, движе́ние в Москве́ соверше́нно непредсказу́емо, а я не хоте́л опа́здывать.**

НЕЛЬСОН: **А как далеко́ вам прихо́дится добира́ться[1] до рабо́ты?**

ИВАН: **Вообще́-то киломе́тров де́сять[2], но в час пик я всегда́ застрева́ю в про́бках[3] на Садо́вом кольце́.[4]**

НЕЛЬСОН: **Да, я прекра́сно вас понима́ю. К сча́стью, я живу́ бли́зко от метро́ и поэ́тому добира́юсь до рабо́ты без пробле́м. Тем не ме́нее, как вы могли́ заме́тить, у нас есть автостоя́нка[5] для сотру́дников фи́рмы. Наде́юсь, что это хоть как-то вам помо́жет.**

ИВАН: **Это, действи́тельно, очень удо́бно. Сотру́дникам очень тру́дно найти́ ме́сто на у́лице, а платны́е стоя́нки, осо́бенно в це́нтре, дово́льно дороги́е.**

НЕЛЬСОН: **Хорошо́, а тепе́рь я хоте́л бы ознако́мить вас с не́которыми наибо́лее о́бщими пра́вилами вну́тренного распоря́дка на́шего о́фиса. Я та́кже покажу́ вам ваше рабо́чее ме́сто.**

Не́льсон прово́дит Ива́на в кабине́т, кото́рый занима́ет ещё одна́ сотру́дница.

НЕЛЬСОН: **Иван, познако́мьтесь, пожа́луйста, с Ната́шей Миро́новой. Она рабо́тает у нас уже́ два го́да.**

ИВАН: **Рад познако́миться.**

НАТАША: Взаимно.

НЕЛЬСОН: Тепе́рь о распоря́дке рабо́ты. Мы начина́ем рабо́тать в де́вять часо́в утра́ и зака́нчиваем в пять часо́в дня. Оди́н час отво́дится[6] на обе́денный переры́в, но в о́фисе обяза́тельно до́лжен кто-нибудь находи́ться. По́зже мы дади́м вам про́пуск[7] к замку́ центра́льного вхо́да. Вам та́кже необходи́мо запо́лнить не́сколько анке́т для нало́говой инспе́кции. Ната́ша помо́жет вам разобра́ться со все́ми э́тими форма́льностями. По́сле того́, как вы запо́лните все докуме́нты, зайди́те ко мне в кабине́т, и я расскажу́ вам о ва́ших обя́занностях.[8]

Запо́лнив все анке́ты, Ива́н вме́сте с Ната́шей идёт в кабине́т Не́льсона.

НЕЛЬСОН: Уже́ все запо́лнили? Каки́е-нибудь вопро́сы?

ИВАН: Всё в поря́дке. В да́нный моме́нт, у меня́ ещё нет никаки́х вопро́сов.

НЕЛЬСОН: Хорошо́, Ива́н. Я хоте́л бы пригласи́ть вас пообе́дать вме́сте в час дня. Ната́ша, ты смо́жешь к нам присоедини́ться?[9]

НАТАША: С удово́льствием, то́лько на́до попроси́ть Алексе́я побы́ть в о́фисе. Как пра́вило, он обе́дает в по́лдень.

Ната́ша ухо́дит.

НЕЛЬСОН: Поско́льку вы так хорошо́ владе́ете англи́йским, с ва́ми бу́дет рабо́тать оди́н из на́ших ме́неджеров, кото́рого перево́дят в Москву́ из центра́льного о́фиса компа́нии в По́ртленде. Он помо́жет вам подгото́виться к ва́шему перево́ду в Му́рманск[10] и разъясни́т, каки́е у вас бу́дут обя́занности в ка́честве ме́неджера региона́льного представи́тельства.[11]

ИВАН: Да, кста́ти, я забы́л вам сказа́ть, что у меня́ там есть ро́дственники.

НЕЛЬСОН: Вот и замеча́тельно! Вы, наве́рное, быва́ли там и пре́жде и знако́мы с го́родом?

ИВАН: Да, я быва́л там не́сколько раз. Пра́вда, э́то бы́ло давно́. Но мои́ ро́дственники де́ржат меня́ в ку́рсе всех ме́стных собы́тий.

НЕЛЬСОН: **Как вам изве́стно, мы плани́руем откры́ть на́ше торго́вое представи́тельство пря́мо на террито́рии Му́рманского по́рта.**

ИВАН: **Могу́ предста́вить, кака́я интере́сная и в то же вре́мя сло́жная рабо́та мне предстои́т.**

НЕЛЬСОН: **Не волну́йтесь. Я уве́рен, что вы с ней отли́чно спра́витесь!**

First day on the job.

Ivan Kustov has just been hired as a junior manager trainee with the Moscow office of an American company. Manuel Nelson, his supervisor, familiarizes Ivan with his new duties.

NELSON: Good morning, Ivan. I see you came a little early today.

IVAN: Yes, the traffic situation in Moscow is very unpredictable, and I didn't want to be late.

NELSON: Do you have far to drive from home?

IVAN: It's only about ten kilometers, but I always get stuck in a traffic jam on the Ring during rush hours.

NELSON: Yes, I know exactly what you mean. Fortunately, I live near the metro, so I can get here easily. As you can see, we do have a special parking area for our employees. I hope that helps.

IVAN: Yes, quite a bit, actually. It is very hard to find parking on the street, and the parking lots are very expensive, especially in the center.

NELSON: Now, I'd like go over some of the general in-house regulations. And I'll also show you where you will be working.

Nelson leads Ivan to the office he will share with another Russian employee.

NELSON: Ivan, please meet Natasha Mironova. She has been with us for two years now.

IVAN: Very pleased to meet you.

NATASHA: Likewise.

NELSON: Now, about our working hours. We start at nine and finish at five. You can take an hour for lunch, but make sure someone is in the office during your absence. We'll give you a security badge and code number to unlock the front door. You will also have to complete these various tax and social security forms. Natasha can help you with all the paperwork. After you finish filling out the forms, come into my office, and I'll go over some of your duties.

Having completed the personnel and tax forms, Ivan is accompanied by Natasha back to Nelson's office.

NELSON: Ah, all finished with the forms? Any questions?

IVAN: The forms are all done. I can't think of any other questions at the moment.

NELSON: Now then, Ivan. I would like to invite you to lunch today at one o'clock. Natasha, can you join us?

NATASHA: I'd love to. I'll ask Alex to watch our office. He usually eats at twelve.

Natasha leaves.

NELSON: Now, since you have a good command of English, I would like you to train with one of our American managers who is being transferred to Moscow from our headquarters in Portland. He will help you prepare for your relocation to Murmansk and tell you exactly what is expected of our regional office managers.

IVAN: Yes, by the way, I forgot to mention that I have several cousins who live there.

NELSON: That's wonderful! You probably know the city well then, from previous visits?

IVAN: Yes, I've been there several times. Actually, that was a long time ago. But my relatives have kept me up to date on local events.

NELSON: As you know, we're hoping to establish a trade office right at the Murmansk port area.

IVAN: I can see what an interesting and challenging job lies ahead of me.

NELSON: Don't worry. I'm sure you'll be able to handle it!

B. ПРИМЕЧАНИЯ

1. The verb добира́ться/добра́ться (to reach a destination) is usually followed by the preposition до and a noun in the genitive case. Как вы добра́лись до рабо́ты сего́дня у́тром? (Did you get to work okay this morning?)

2. Approximate units of time or distance can be expressed by placing the number after the unit. Compare: Они верну́тся с рабо́ты че́рез пятна́дцать мину́т. (They'll be back from work in fifteen minutes.) Наве́рное, они́ верну́тся мину́т че́рез пятна́дцать. (They'll probably be back from work in about fifteen minutes.) Наш офис располо́жен ро́вно в десяти́ киломе́трах от це́нтра го́рода. (Our office is exactly ten kilometers from the center of town.) Стадио́н далеко́ отсю́да? —Нет, всего́ киломе́тра два. (Is the stadium far from here? —No, it's just about two kilometers.)

3. Про́бка literally means "cork stopper," but it is commonly used to refer to a traffic jam. Ну и про́бка! Так мы никогда́ не доберёмся до рабо́ты! (What a traffic jam! We'll never get to work on time!) Почему́ тебе́ так тру́дно вы́нуть про́бку из буты́лки? —Хорошо́, тогда́ дай мне што́пор! (Why are you having such a hard time uncorking the bottle? —Well, then give me a corkscrew!) It also appears in the colloquial expression глуп как про́бка (dumb as they come): Зна́ешь, это совсе́м бесполе́зно пыта́ться объясни́ть ему́, в чём де́ло! —Зна́ю, он глуп как про́бка. (You know, it's quite useless trying to explain what's going on to him! —I know, he's as dumb as they come.)

4. The Ring, also known as the Boulevard Ring, refers to the Садо́вое кольцо́, which is a major circular traffic artery in central Moscow.

5. Автостоя́нка refers to any parking lot or area; paid parking lots are пла́тные стоя́нки.

6. Отводи́ть has several different meanings: "to lead, to take away, to deflect, to allot, to allow" or "to assign something to someone or something." Один час отво́дится на обе́денный переры́в. (One hour is allotted/allowed for a lunch break.) Он обы́чно отво́дит дете́й в шко́лу. (He usually walks the children to school.) Наш но́вый фехтова́льщик очень ло́вко отво́дит уда́ры. (Our new fencer deflects attacks very skillfully.) Я пыта́лась спроси́ть у него́, почему́ уво́лили Ко́лю, но он вся́кий раз очень ло́вко отво́дит ка́ждый неприя́тный вопро́с. (I tried to ask him why Kolya was fired, but he cleverly deflects every uncomfortable question.) Мы реши́ли отвести́ это помеще́ние для мастерско́й. (We decided to designate this area as a workshop.) Я не мог отвести́ от неё глаз. (I couldn't take my eyes off her.)

7. Here про́пуск refers to a pass, permit, or password. In other contexts, it can also indicate an omission, failure to attend, or a blank space in a written exercise. Извини́те, я не могу́ впусти́ть вас без про́пуска. (I'm sorry, I can't let you in without a pass.) Из-за мно́гих про́пусков официа́льных заседа́ний, нам пришло́сь его́ уво́лить. (We had to let him go because he missed so many official meetings.)

8. Обя́занность (obligation, duty, responsibility) should be distinguished from до́лжность, which also implies a duty but in an employment context refers to a specific position or job. Она́ вам объясни́т, каки́е у вас бу́дут обя́занности. (She will explain what your duties will be.) Ива́на то́лько что назна́чили на до́лжность помо́щника ме́неджера. (Ivan was just appointed to the position of assistant manager.)

9. Note that the verb присоедини́ться (to join, to be added) is used with к + dative case. Мо́жно к вам присоедини́ться? (May I join you?)

10. Му́рманск is located about 1,200 miles north of Moscow on the Kola Gulf of the Barents Sea. Only a small village before the First World War, the city grew rapidly after 1915 when its port and rail line to Petrograd were built after the Central Powers cut off the Russian Baltic and Black Sea supply routes. Since the port is ice-free, it was also a major supply base and port for Allied convoys during the the Second World War. Today, with a population of 500,000, Murmansk is Russia's largest northern naval base and fishing center. In addition to fish canneries, sawmills, textile factories, and breweries, the city houses a major polar research institute.

11. Представи́тельство (representation, mission) is used in such expressions as вое́нное представи́тельство (military mission), америка́нское представи́тельство при ООН (the American Mission to the UN), and представи́тельство на́шей фи́рмы в Москве́ (our company's office in Moscow).

С. ГРАММА́ТИКА И СЛОВОУПОТРЕБЛЕ́НИЕ

1. ВИ́ДЫ ГЛАГО́ЛОВ В БУ́ДУЩЕМ ВРЕ́МЕНИ (ASPECT IN THE FUTURE TENSE)

Remember that the key difference between the imperfective and perfective aspects of verbs is that perfective verbs express a completed action with emphasis on the result of that action, whereas imperfective verbs describe an activity that was, is, or will take place, but not necessarily be completed.

The imperfective future tense is used to express or describe an action that will be taking place repeatedly or for an indefinite period of time. Emphasis is on the manner in which the action is performed, but not on the result or eventual completion of the action.

The imperfective future is formed using the future tense of быть plus the imperfective infinitive of the main verb.

Вот кабинéт, где мы бýдем рабóтать.
Here's the office where we'll be working.

Вам бýдет помогáть одúн из нáших мéнеджеров.
One of our managers will be helping you.

B) THE PERFECTIVE FUTURE

Perfective verbs in the future tense are used to express the intended completion of a single action and the result of that action. Since perfective verbs have no present tense, the future tense is formed by simply conjugating the infinitive.

Я сейчáс покажý вам вáше рабóчее мéсто.
I'll show you your workstation now.

Онá помóжет вам разобрáться с этими формáльностями.
She will help you deal with these (one-time) formalities.

Как тóлько вы запóлните анкéты, зайдúте ко мне в кабинéт.
As soon as you fill out the forms, come into my office.

Although you will recall that the imperfective aspect is generally used after adverbs such as часто (often), всегда (always), редко (seldom), and иногда (sometimes), in the future tense, the perfective aspect can also be used with these adverbs to express a potential action. Compare:

Я знáю, что онú всегдá вам помóгут.
I know that they will always help you.
(whenever you need help they will give it you—perfective)

Я знáю, что онú бýдут вам помогáть кáждый день.
I know that they will help you every day.
(help will be given repeatedly—imperfective)

2. НЕОПРЕДЕЛЁННЫЕ НАРЕЧИЯ И МЕСТОИМЕНИЯ (INDEFINITE ADVERBS AND PRONOUNS)

A) ADVERBS

Question words of time, place, and manner, such as где, куда́, как, and когда́, can be combined with the suffix -то or -нибудь to form indefinite adverbs, such as где-то/где-нибудь (somewhere/anywhere), куда-то/куда-нибудь (to somewhere/to anywhere), когда́-то/когда́-нибудь (sometime/any time). As a general rule, the -нибудь forms are used in questions, with the future tense, after imperatives, and in conditional and subjunctive constructions, while the -то forms are used primarily in past- and present-tense statements unless a repeated action is involved.

The suffix -то is used when the speaker is referring to a particular but unidentified place, time, or manner. It is generally translated into English as the prefix "some-".

Я наде́юсь, что это руково́дство хоть как-то вам помо́жет.
I hope that this manual will help you somehow.

Час наза́д они куда́-то ушли́.
They went somewhere an hour ago.

Я где-то оста́вил запо́лненные докуме́нты.
I left the completed documents somewhere.

Ка́жется, я когда́-то ви́дел этот фильм.
It seems to me that I saw that film some time ago.

The suffix -нибудь is used when the speaker has no particular place, time, or manner in mind. It often translates into English as the prefix "any-".

Вы бы хоте́ли куда́-нибудь пое́хать в воскресе́нье?
Would you like to go anywhere on Sunday?

Вы когда́-нибудь бы́ли в Му́рманске?
Were you ever (at any time) in Murmansk?

Ваш брат где-нибудь сейча́с рабо́тает?
Is your brother working anywhere now?

Шесто́й уро́к

Я наде́юсь, что вы как-нибудь спра́витесь с э́той но́вой до́лжностью.
I hope that you will somehow cope with this new position.

B) PRONOUNS AND ADJECTIVES

Like indefinite adverbs, indefinite pronouns and adjectives can be formed by adding the suffix -то, -нибудь, or -либо to the pronouns кто, что, or како́й. -Либо forms imply an even greater degree of indefiniteness than -нибудь.

Он яви́лся в конто́ру без каки́х-либо докуме́нтов.
He reported to the office without any documents at all.

Кто-то позвони́л сего́дня у́тром, но я не по́мню, как его́ зову́т.
Someone called this morning, but I can't remember his name.

В о́фисе обяза́тельно до́лжен кто-нибудь находи́ться.
Someone must be in the office.

Он что-то сказа́л, но я его́ не рассль́шал.
He said something, but I didn't hear him.

Она́ спра́шивала что-нибудь об опла́чиваемом о́тпуске?
Did she ask anything about a paid vacation?

Мы получи́ли от него́ како́е-то письмо́, но я его́ ещё не чита́л.
We got some kind of letter from him, but I haven't read it yet.

У вас есть каки́е-нибудь вопро́сы?
Do you have any questions?

D. ИДИОМАТИКА

ON THE JOB.

Following are some work-related expressions that may come in handy.

Рабо́та не пы́льная (AN EASY JOB)

У него́ о́чень не пы́льная рабо́та.
He's got a pretty cushy job.

Удержа́ться на рабо́те (TO HOLD DOWN A JOB)

Я не понима́ю, почему́ он никогда́ не мог удержа́ться на рабо́те.
I don't understand why he was never able to hold down a job.

Заши́ться с рабо́той (TO BE OVERWHELMED WITH WORK; LIT., TO BE SEWN UP WITH WORK)

Де́ло в том, что я по́лностью заши́лся с рабо́той и поэ́тому у меня́ совсе́м нет свобо́дного вре́мени!
As a matter of fact, I'm snowed under with work, so I don't have any free time at all!

Рабо́та не гре́ет (WORK IS NOT SATISFYING.; LIT., WORK IS NOT PROVIDING ANY WARMTH.)

С тех пор как кома́ндует но́вое нача́льство, рабо́та меня́ не гре́ет.
Ever since I got a new boss, I don't find my work rewarding.

Горе́ть на рабо́те (TO LIVE FOR ONE'S WORK; LIT., TO BE BURNING UP ON THE JOB)

Ка́жется, что она́ гори́т на рабо́те.
It seems she's married to her job.

Ле́вая рабо́та (A JOB OFF-THE-BOOKS, MOONLIGHTING; LIT., WORK ON THE LEFT)

Мне сказа́ли, что по выходны́м ваш сотру́дник занима́ется ле́вой рабо́той в по́льзу на́ших конкуре́нтов.
I was told that your associate is moonlighting for our competitors on weekends.

Хло́потная рабо́та (A DEMANDING JOB INVOLVING A LOT OF RUNNING AROUND)

Хотя́ зарпла́та прили́чная, така́я хло́потная рабо́та меня́ не интересу́ет.
Although the pay is pretty good, I'm not interested in a job that involves so much scurrying about.

Допоздна́ заси́живаться на рабо́те (TO WORK LONG HOURS)

У неё интере́сная рабо́та, но зачасту́ю ей прихо́дится заси́живаться допоздна́.
She has an interesting job, but she often has to work late.

E. СТРОГО ПО ДЕЛУ

ПОВЕДЕНИЕ НА РАБОТЕ (ON-THE-JOB CONDUCT)

The relationship between employees and their supervisors in Russian companies is not too different than in America—it is generally informal. Of course, the personality of managers can affect any workplace atmosphere.

The form of address between employees and their superiors is usually on the polite level (вы) where persons address each other by their first name and patronymic (e.g., Михаи́л Петро́вич). Coworkers at any level often opt for and switch to the familiar form of address (ты) once they get to know one another. As a foreigner, it is best to wait until someone suggests switching to ты: Говори́те со мной на ты. (Use ты with me.). If you feel comfortable doing so yourself, you may ask: Мо́жно с Ва́ми на ты? (May I use ты with you?) The very formal equivalent of Mr. (господи́н) or Mrs. (госпожа́) is still primarily reserved for addressing foreigners. Foreigners who visit Russian institutions should start their communication with господин/госпожа until such time as the host or hostess suggests a less formal mode.

The dress code in large corporations and government institutions is generally traditional; i.e., suits and ties for men, and dresses and suits for women. Foreign visitors to such institutions should dress accordingly, lest the Russian host misinterpret informal attire as disrespectful.

Women in the Workplace

Despite the decades of extolling equality (ра́венство) between men and women under the Soviet system and Western influences during the post-Soviet period, Russia remains a male-dominated society. Although women occupy top-level positions in the biological sciences and the arts, they are sparsely represented in key positions in the business world, largely because networking is male-dominated. The few social groups and organizations that are attempting to battle male chauvinism are generally unpopular and limited in activity.

The culturally ingrained male chauvinist attitude extends toward foreign businesswomen as well. However, as more Russian businessmen become "westernized," women in the business world, particularly from the West, are becoming more tolerated, if not accepted as equals. Women in business, whether native or foreign, have been more successful when they display a conservative, neat appearance and serious behavior. A certain aloofness is also helpful in winning respect. Nevertheless, foreign businesswomen should accept certain established cultural traits on the part of Russian men, such as hand kissing, door opening, and the presentation of flowers, which for the most part constitute signs of respect.

УПРАЖНЕНИЯ

A. Поста́вьте глаго́лы из ско́бок в ну́жную фо́рму. (Place the verbs in parentheses in the appropriate form.)

1. За́втра мы_____(работать) весь день в но́вом о́фисе.
2. Че́рез пять мину́т я_____(показывать/показать) вам ва́ше рабо́чее ме́сто.
3. _____(заходить/зайти) ко мне в кабине́т, когда́ _____(заполнять/заполнить) анке́ту.
4. Я зна́ю, что на сле́дующей неде́ле он ка́ждый день_____(опаздывать/опоздать) на рабо́ту.
5. Когда́ вы мне _____(помогать/помочь) с этими форма́льностями?
6. За́втра я_____(спрашивать/спросить) господи́на Не́льсона о но́вой до́лжности.

B. Впишите по смыслу частицу -то или -нибудь. (Insert the particle -то or -нибудь according to context.)

1. У вас есть какие_____вопросы?
2. Вы когда_____были в Мурманске?
3. Два часа назад они куда_____пошли.
4. Я знаю, что я где_____в вашем офисе оставил мои документы.
5. Я уверен, что вы как_____справитесь с этой проблемой.
6. Кто_____был в офисе, когда мы обедали, но я не знаю, как его зовут.
7. Надо вам что_____принести завтра?

C. Переведите следующие предложения на русский язык. (Translate the following sentences into Russian.)

1. Do you have a long way to drive to work?
2. I hope that she will be able to help you somehow.
3. I'll be working late every day next week.
4. Someone has to stay in the office during lunch hour.
5. Tomorrow I'll show you your new office.
6. You'll have to fill out several tax forms.
7. Don't worry, I know she will always give you a hand (help).
8. She said something about the new job, but I didn't hear her.
9. Can you join us for lunch?
10. My relatives keep me informed of events there.

УРОК 7

А. ДИАЛОГ

В продово́льственном магази́не.

Ша́нти, америка́нская аспира́нтка, изуча́ющая ру́сский язы́к и литерату́ру, то́лько что прие́хала в Москву́. Дми́трий, её ста́рый знако́мый, пригласи́л Ша́нти прогуля́ться по це́нтру Москвы́. Во вре́мя прогу́лки они реша́ют зайти́ в большо́й продово́льственный магази́н за́падного образца́ на Но́вом Арба́те[1]. Захо́дят в магази́н Дми́трий берёт теле́жку для проду́ктов.

ШАНТИ: **Ого́! Так мно́го люде́й! Но о́череди совсе́м не таки́е больши́е, как я себе́ предста́вила.**

ДМИТРИЙ: **Да, э́то оди́н из са́мых больши́х продово́льственных магази́нов[2] за́падного образца́ в Москве́. Мно́гие иностра́нцы, живу́щие в столи́це, хо́дят сюда́. Ита́к, что бы ты хоте́ла купи́ть?**

ШАНТИ: **Так, вот у меня́ спи́сок, пре́жде всего́ соль и са́хар.**

ДМИТРИЙ: **Са́хар, вот в том отде́ле.**

ШАНТИ: **Замеча́тельно. Тепе́рь каки́х-нибудь овоще́й и фру́ктов. Да, и ещё сы́ра.**

ДМИТРИЙ: **За овоща́ми и фру́ктами, коне́чно, лу́чше сходи́ть на ры́нок[3].**

ШАНТИ: **Почему́?**

ДМИТРИЙ: **Фру́кты и о́вощи там о́чень све́жие, да и це́ны пони́же. Приходя́ на ры́нок, лю́ди обы́чно закупа́ются на неде́лю вперёд.**

ШАНТИ: **Хорошо́, э́то пото́м. А как насчёт моло́чных проду́ктов?**

ДМИТРИЙ: **Вот моло́чный отде́л—пря́мо пе́ред на́ми.**

Подхо́дят к витри́не.

ДМИТРИЙ: Здесь не́сколько сорто́в молока́, но я всегда́ предпочита́ю вот э́то в паке́тах. Оно́ мо́жет храни́ться не́сколько ме́сяцев. Что тебе́ бо́льше нра́вится?

ШАНТИ: А э́то молоко́ о́чень жи́рное?

Дмитрий смеётся.

ШАНТИ: Почему́ ты смеёшься?

ДМИТРИЙ: Сра́зу ви́дно, что ты иностра́нка. Ру́сские обы́чно э́тим не интересу́ются.

ШАНТИ: Ди́ма, ты же зна́ешь, что я на дие́те.

ДМИТРИЙ: Да-да, коне́чно. Сейча́с спро́сим у прода́вщицы. Прости́те, де́вушка, како́й жи́рности[4] э́то молоко́ в па́чках?

ПРОДАВЩИ́ЦА: Всего́ четы́ре проце́нта.

ШАНТИ: Четы́ре проце́нта? Э́то же о́чень мно́го! А есть ли у вас снято́е молоко́?

ПРОДАВЩИ́ЦА: Нет, э́то всё, что у нас есть.

ШАНТИ: Ну да ла́дно, наде́юсь, что для одного́ ра́за сойдёт.

ДМИТРИЙ: По пра́вде говоря́, я бо́льше люблю́ сли́вки[5]. В них бо́льше жи́ра, чем в молоке́, и они́ прекра́сно подхо́дят к ча́ю и́ли ко́фе. Кста́ти, здесь есть таки́е проду́кты, как кефи́р,[6] ря́женка и́ли топлёное молоко́, о кото́рых в Аме́рике и не слы́шали. Вот, наприме́р, творо́г, кото́рый мы обы́чно еди́м со смета́ной.

ШАНТИ: Звучи́т о́чень зама́нчиво, но дава́й попро́буем всего́ понемно́жку. Как ты ду́маешь, с чего́ мы начнём?

ДМИТРИЙ: С творога́.

ШАНТИ: Преле́стно. Ещё хоте́лось бы како́го-нибудь сы́ра.

ДМИТРИЙ: Здесь не́сколько сорто́в. Вот «Росси́йский», а вот э́то «бры́нза» —ки́слый ове́чий сыр, кото́рый едя́т на Кавка́зе.

ШАНТИ: Ну и ла́дно, вы́берем что́-нибудь по своему́ вку́су.

Подхо́дит о́чередь Шанти.

ШАНТИ: Взвесьте, пожалуйста, грамм триста голландского сыра, и ещё дайте два пакета молока, бутылку ряженки, пачку творога, и банку[7] сметаны.

ПРОДАВЩИЦА: Вам сыр нарезать?

ШАНТИ: Спасибо, не надо.

Шанти кладёт продукты в авоську[8] и отходит. Продавщица кричит ей вдогонку.

ПРОДАВЩИЦА: Девушка, девушка, подождите!

ШАНТИ: Да-да, я что-то забыла?

ПРОДАВЩИЦА: Естественно, вы забыли заплатить.

ШАНТИ: Но я ещё не всё купила.

ДМИТРИЙ: Видишь ли, здесь ты должна платить в каждом отделе, а не при выходе из магазина.

ШАНТИ: Извините, я не знала. Вот, пожалуйста ...

ПРОДАВЩИЦА: Ничего, вот сдача и чек.

Шанти и Дмитрий берут покупки и отходят от прилавка.

ШАНТИ: Мне так стыдно! Я и не подозревала, что нужно платить за всё отдельно.[9]

ДМИТРИЙ: Не надо, успокойся. Ты же не знала. Таково большинство наших магазинов, хотя есть и магазины самообслуживания. Мы их называем "универсамы," точь-в-точь[10] американские супермаркеты. Есть у нас и магазины, работающие круглосуточно.

ШАНТИ: Вот это замечательно, теперь буду ходить только туда.

ДМИТРИЙ: О чём ты говоришь! Хорошо, что нам ещё нужно?

ШАНТИ: Свежий хлеб, курица ... по моему, всё.

At a supermarket.

Shanti, an American graduate student studying Russian, has just arrived in Moscow for a summer language course. Her old friend Dmitry has invited Shanti for a stroll around downtown Moscow where they do some shopping at a large western-style food store on the Arbat. They go into the store, and Dmitry goes for a shopping cart.

SHANTI: Wow! What a crowd! But the lines are not as long as I expected.

DMITRY: This is one of Moscow's largest western-style food stores. Many foreigners who live here do their shopping here. Okay, so what do you need to get?

SHANTI: Let's see. I have a list here. First of all, some salt and sugar.

DMITRY: The sugar's this way.

SHANTI: Great. And now some fruits and vegatables. Oh, yes, and some cheese.

DMITRY: We'd be better off going to the farmer's market for the fruits and vegetables.

SHANTI: Why?

DMITRY: The produce is fresh and much cheaper. People usually go there on the weekend and stock up for a whole week.

SHANTI: Okay, we'll do that later. What about the dairy stuff?

DMITRY: The dairy section is right in front of us.

They walk up to the showcase.

DMITRY: They have several brands here. I'd advise you to get this packaged milk. It keeps for several months without spoiling. What kind do you want?

SHANTI: Is that milk high in fat content?

Dmitry laughs.

SHANTI: Why are you laughing?

DMITRY: You can tell right away that you're a foreigner. Russians usually don't care about that.

SHANTI: Dima, you know I'm on a diet.

DMITRY: Yes, of course. Let's ask the saleswoman. Excuse me, Miss, what is the fat content of the packaged milk?

SALESWOMAN: Only four percent.

SHANTI: Four percent? That's so high. Do you have any skim milk?

SALESWOMAN: No, this is all we have.

SHANTI: Well, I guess it'll be all right this one time.

DMITRY: Frankly, I prefer cream. It's much richer than milk and goes great with tea or coffee. You know, I'll bet there are a lot of the dairy products here, like *kefir* and fermented, baked milk that you've never even heard of in America. Here, take *tvorog*, for example, which we often eat with sour cream.

SHANTI: That all sounds very enticing, but let's try them a little at a time. What do you think I should start with?

DMITRY: With the *tvorog*.

SHANTI: Okay. I'd also like to get some cheese.

DMITRY: There are a few kinds here: there's domestic "Russian" or "brynza," a sharp sheep's milk cheese that's quite popular in the Caucasus.

SHANTI: Well then, pick out something you like.

It's Shanti's turn to be served.

SHANTI: Please give me about three hundred grams of Holland cheese, two cartons of milk, a bottle of baked milk, a box of cottage cheese, and a jar of sour cream.

CLERK: Do you want the cheese sliced?

SHANTI: No thank you.

Shanti puts the products in her shopping bag and walks away. The clerk calls after her.

CLERK: Miss! Miss! Come back!

SHANTI: Yes? Did I forget something?

CLERK: Yes! You forgot to pay.

SHANTI: But I'm not done shopping.

DMITRY: Here you have to pay separately at each section of the store. There is no single check-out counter.

SHANTI: Oh, I'm sorry. I didn't know. Here you are . . .

CLERK: No problem. Here's your change and your receipt.

Shanti and Dmitry take their groceries and move off to another part of the store.

SHANTI: I'm so embarrassed! I had no idea you have to pay separately for everything.

DMITRY: Don't be embarrassed. You didn't know. That's our typical system, although there are some self-service stores. We call them универсамы, and they're just like American supermarkets. We also have stores that are open twenty-four hours a day.

SHANTI: Maybe I should stick to those from now on.

DMITRY: Don't be silly! So, what else do we need?

SHANTI: Fresh bread, chicken . . . I guess that's it.

В. ПРИМЕЧАНИЯ

1. The Irish Arbat supermarket is located near the intersection of Но́вый Арба́т (the Arbat pedestrian mall) and Садо́вое кольцо́ (the Boulevard Ring) in Moscow. This very busy and popular shopping area is easily reached by either of two subway lines with nearby stations, the Арба́тская ста́нция of the Ки́ровская-Фру́нзенская ли́ния and the Филёвская ли́ния.

2. Ирла́ндский Дом (Irish House), the supermarket referred to here. Its business hours are from 10:00 A.M. to 11:00 P.M. daily. Other prominent western-style food stores in Moscow include Супермаркет Садо́вого Кольца́ (Garden Ring Supermarket), located at Бульва́р Садового Кольца 1; "Foodland," in the Sadko Arcade of the Expocenter, at Красногварде́йский проспе́кт 12 (open 7 days); and

the Julius Meinl Supermarket, on Ле́нинский проспе́кт 146 (open daily from 10:00 A.M. to 8:00 P.M.). There is a Kalinka Stockman food supermarket in Moscow (Заце́пский вал 4/8) and one in St. Petersburg (Финля́ндкий проспект 1).

3. In most Russian cities, there are both open and enclosed farmer's markets where produce, meats, and poultry are sold by private vendors. Both domestically grown produce and imported fruits and vegetables are now available at these markets. Whether or not you intend to buy something, the markets are always bustling with activity and deserve a visit. The major farmers' markets in Moscow are the Черёмушкинский (Ломоно́совский проспект 1), Центра́льный (Цветно́й бульва́р 15), Ри́жский (Проспект ми́ра 94-6), Дорогоми́ловский (Можа́йский вал 10), Яросла́вский (Проспект мира 122), and the Дани́ловский (улица Мы́тная 74). In St. Petersburg the Кузне́чный (Кузнечный переулок 3) and the Некра́совский markets are the most popular. These are ruble-only markets, and as in most Russian farmers' markets, bargaining with vendors is expected.

4. Note the use of the genitive case in questions about type, quantity, and size. Како́й жи́рности этот сыр? (What's the fat content of this cheese?) Како́го цве́та ваша маши́на? (What's the color of your car?) Како́го ро́ста ваш брат? (How tall is your brother?)

5. Сли́вки is a cream that is usually taken off the upper portion of non-homogenized milk for use with coffee, tea, and fruit. Milk containing less than 4% fat is not readily available in Russian stores, but some stores catering to the Western community do offer skim milk (снято́е or обезжи́ренное молоко́).

6. Russians are very fond of dairy products. Кефи́р is a cultured, fermented milk product similar to unflavored yogurt, but generally thin enough to drink. It is a common part of the breakfast meal. Ря́женка is baked whole milk, additionally fermented with sour cream. Простоква́ша is a rather thick sour milk, somewhat similar to buttermilk. Топлённое молоко is whole, baked milk similar in consistency to condensed milk. It is used either warmed or chilled with the skin that formed during baking left in place. Творо́г, somewhat similar to dry cottage cheese, is often eaten as a sweet dish, topped with sour cream and sugar. It constitutes the basic ingredient of such traditional Russian dishes as па́сха (a pyramid-shaped cake eaten at Easter) and сы́рники (cheese pancakes).

7. Ба́нка is a general term referring to a container for foods, usually a tin (ба́нка горо́ха, a can of peas) or a jar (банка варе́нья, a jar of jam).

8. When shopping, particularly at food stores, it's a good idea to bring some kind of shopping bag (су́мка для поку́пок), or the ubiquitous Russian string bag (аво́ська), as bags are generally not provided by the stores.

9. The system of purchase and payment in most Russian retail stores, particularly state-owned food stores, involves the following procedure: the customer notes the price of the desired item as displayed in a showcase. The customer then goes to a centrally located cashier, pays for the noted price, obtains a receipt, and returns to the counter where the receipt is exchanged for the desired item. In recent years, there has been an increasing tendency in many larger food stores to allow the purchase of items directly at the individual counter (прилáвок).

10. Note that the adverb точь-в-точь (just like, exactly) is followed by nouns in the nominative case. Онá точь-в-точь отéц. (She looks exactly like her father.)

C. ГРАММАТИКА И СЛОВОУПОТРЕБЛЕНИЕ

1. УПОТРЕБЛЕНИЕ ПРЕДЛОГА «НА» С ВИНИТЕЛЬНЫМ ПАДЕЖОМ (THE PREPOSITION НА WITH THE ACCUSATIVE CASE)

The prepositions в and на are used with the accusative case to denote movement *toward* some object or place (кудá?). Unfortunately, there are no hard and fast rules for determining which preposition goes with which noun, but there are considerably fewer nouns introduced by на. The most common include:

вокзáл	station	рьінок	market
завóд	plant (factory)	курóрт	resort
конферéнция	conference	óпера	opera
концéрт	concert	съезд	congress
лéкция	lecture	ýлица	street
плóщадь	square	урóк	lesson
пóчта	post office	факультéт	academic department
рабóта	work	óстров	island
собрáние	meeting	вьіставка	exhibit
свáдьба	wedding	вéчер	evening party

Русские обьічно хóдят на рьінок раз в недéлю за фрýктами и овощáми.
Russians usually go the market once a week to buy fruits and vegetables.

Они пошли́ на по́чту за ма́рками.
They went to the post office for stamps.

Сего́дня ве́чером мы идём на интере́сный концерт.
We're going to an interesting concert this evening.

На plus the accusative case is also used:

   • to indicate the time period of a future event or action.

Они обы́чно закупа́ют проду́кты на всю неде́лю.
They usually stock up on groceries for an entire week.

Они пое́дут в Москву́ на три ме́сяца.
They're going to Moscow for three months.

   • to indicate the purpose of an intended action, suggestion, or invitation.

Она прие́хала в Росси́ю на ле́тние ку́рсы.
She came to Russia for (to take) summer courses.

В Аме́рике часто быва́ют ски́дки на продово́льственные това́ры.
Discounts on food products are frequently offered in America.

Она пригласи́ла нас на чай.
She invited us for tea.

У них переры́в на обе́д с ча́са до двух.
Their lunch break is from one to two (lit., their break for lunch is from one to two).

   • in comparisons of age.

Ва́ша сестра́ моло́же меня́ на два го́да.
Your sister is two years younger than I am.

Я ста́рше вас на пять лет.
I'm five years older than you.

   • after the verbs жа́ловаться (to complain), наде́яться (to hope, rely on), and in the expressions обраща́ть внима́ние (to pay attention), оказывать давление (to exert pressure), производить впечатление (to make an impression).

Они всегда жалуются на качество продуктов.
They're always complaining about the quality of the produce.

Вы, конечно, знаете, что мы очень надеемся на вас.
You, of course, know that we are relying on you very much.

Я прошу вас обращать внимание на инструкции в руководстве.
Please pay attention to the instructions in the manual.

Начальник почему-то всегда оказывает давление на нового сотрудника.
For some reason the boss is always putting pressure on the new worker.

Новый рынок производит на меня неплохое впечатление.
The new market makes a pretty good impression on me.

2. УПОТРЕБЛЕНИЕ ПРИЛАГАТЕЛЬНЫХ В ПОЛНОЙ И КРАТКОЙ ФОРМАХ (USE OF LONG- AND SHORT-FORM ADJECTIVES)

Most Russian adjectives have a long (attributive) and short (predicative) form. Most short-form adjectives are derived from their long form by dropping the ending from the masculine singular form or the final vowel from the feminine, neuter, and plural forms. For example: богатый → богат; богатая → богата; богатое → богато; богатые → богаты.

The long form normally precedes the noun it modifies, while the short, predicative, form normally follows the noun and is connected to it by a verb.

The short-form is generally used to describe a temporary or relative quality, while the long-from refers to an absolute or permanent quality.

В этом магазине замечательный ассортимент продуктов.
This store has a remarkable assortment of foods.

Вчерашний обед был замечателен.
Yesterday's dinner was remarkable.

Она очень увéренная молодáя жéнщина.
  She is a very confident young woman.

Она увéрена, что он никогдá не слы́шал о кефи́ре.
  She is convinced that he has never heard of kefir.

Все приглашённые гóсти приéхали вóвремя.
  All of the invited guests arrived on time.

Мóжешь считáть, что ты ужé приглашён на чай.
  You can consider yourself (to be) invited to tea.

Моя́ женá очень занятáя жéнщина.
  My wife is a very busy woman.

Онá не мóжет сейчáс говори́ть с вáми. Онá занятá.
  She can't talk to you right now. She's busy.

  The short form must be used:

  • when the adjective is followed by a qualifying noun or phrase.

Она очень спосóбна к математике.
  She's very good at math.

Они больны́ гри́ппом.
  They're sick with the flu.

Все студéнты готóвы к экзáменам.
  All the students are ready for the exams.

  • when the subject is followed by a qualifying word or phrase.

Все цéны в этих магази́нах вполнé достýпны.
  All the prices in these stores are quite affordable.

Ассортимéнт фрýктов на ры́нке очень богáт.
  The variety of fruits at the market is very rich.

  • when the subject is это, всё, or что.

Всё было совсем ясно.
Everything was quite clear.

Безусловно, это вам будет очень легко.
Without a doubt, that'll be very easy for you.

D. ИДИОМАТИКА

MONEY, MONEY, MONEY!

Idioms concerning money, or the lack of it, are universal, and Russian is certainly no exception.

У меня купило притупило. (I DON'T HAVE ANY MONEY LEFT; LIT., MY PURSE IS BARE.)

Я очень хотел купить этот торт, но у меня купило притупило.
I really wanted to buy that cake, but I'm out of cash.

Ровным счётом. (PRECISELY; LIT., BY A FLAT COUNT)

К сожалению, у меня осталось ровным счётом три тысячи рублей.
Unfortunately, I just have precisely three thousand rubles left.

И дёшево и сердито (CHEAP AND GOOD)

Пойдём на рынок. Там продукты можно купить и дёшево и сердито!
Let's go to the market. The produce there is cheap and good!

Не при деньгах (TO BE SHORT OF CASH)

Я бы очень хотел пообедать в ресторане, но я не при деньгах.
I wish I could go out to dinner, but I'm short of cash.

Сорить деньгами (TO SQUANDER MONEY CARELESSLY)

Не удивительно, что она не при деньгах. Она всегда сорит деньгами!
It's no wonder she's broke. She is always spending money like water!

Бешеные деньги (CRAZY PRICES)

У них отличная ку́хня, но я никагда́ не бу́ду плати́ть таки́е бе́шеные
де́ньги.

The food is great there, but I refuse to pay those crazy prices.

Ни за каки́е де́ньги (NOT FOR ANY PRICE)

Учи́тывая ка́чество това́ров там, я ни за каки́е де́ньги их не куплю́!
Considering the quality of the merchandise there, I wouldn't buy that
stuff at any price!

Е. СТРОГО ПО ДЕЛУ

РАСПРЕДЕЛЕНИЕ И СБЫТ ПРОДУКЦИИ
(COMMODITY MARKETING AND DISTRIBUTION)

In contrast to the well-developed wholesale and retail distribution systems
in the United States and most western industrialized countries, commodity distribution in Russia is still comparatively primitive and often
quite erratic. Western firms interested in marketing their goods in Russia must be prepared to deal with a variety of distribution methods that
often involve the training and support of their Russian distributor
(распредели́тели) partners.

Efficient and rapid transport of goods (транспортиро́вка това́ров) is
still somewhat hampered by an insufficiently developed system of major
roadways (сеть магистра́льных доро́г), which are not always open to
year-round trucking. Nevertheless, as the process of privatization and
free marketing continues, a concomitant rise in the number of truckers
who either enter into contracts with specific companies or operate independently in the wholesale distribution of goods (о́птовое распределе́ние
това́ров) has slowly begun to resemble Western methods. Some Western firms have established their own distribution systems.

РОЗНИЧНОЕ РАСПРЕДЕЛЕНИЕ (RETAIL DISTRIBUTION)

The principal outlets for retail distribution include the long-established
network of large government-owned food stores (гастроно́мы), joint venture (совме́стное предприя́тие) stores, the various open markets
(ры́нки), kiosks (кио́ски), and the ubiquitous street counters and flea
markets (толку́чки). Many Western food and nonfood products are now

being sold through all of these outlets, including such products as Mars bars, Whiskas pet foods, Uncle Ben's sauces, Coca-Cola, European chocolates, wines and liquors, Kodak film, and cigarettes. Foreign visitors and tourists should be cautious when purchasing some of these products at the smaller kiosks because of possible adulteration, particularly of imported beverages. Kiosks in the central districts of Moscow and St. Petersburg also offer imported clothing (импортная одéжда), computer accessories (компьютерные принадлéжности), compact discs (компáкт-дúски), and a wide variety of electronic equipment (тéхника).

Major western consumer goods companies such as Master Foods, Procter and Gamble, and Coca-Cola are successfully marketing their products outside the major Russian cities. Another, perhaps less conventional channel of retail distribution are the shuttle tradesmen (челноки) who go abroad to sell inexpensive Russian-made goods and return with foreign consumer goods in high demand. This method of retailing is having the effect of opening Russia's market to foreign competition, while at the same time bringing in much needed capital.

Updated information on marketing possibilities and procedures can be obtained from the Business Information Service for the Newly Independent States (BISNIS), Room 7413, U. S. Department of Commerce, International Trade Administration, Washington, D.C. 20230. Regular BISNIS reports can be accessed on the internet at http:// www.itaip.doc.gov/bulletin/bulletin/html. The e-mail address for additional information is bisnis@usita.gov.

УПРАЖНЕНИЯ

A. Заполните прóпуски, выбирáя подходящую фóрму прилагáтельных укáзанных в скóбках, и переведúте полýченные предложéния на английский язык.

1. В этом магазúне очень _____ (богатый/богат/богаты) ассортимéнт продýктов.

2. _____ (Приглашённый/Приглашён/Приглашёны) на чай стýдент очень хорошó говорúт по-русски.

3. Я вполнé _____ (уверен/уверенный/уверено), что нóвый магазúн рабóтает крýглые сýтки.

4. Свéжие óвощи и фрýкты продаются по очень _____ (доступным/доступные/доступен) цéнам.

5. Я ду́маю, что но́вый ры́нок уже́ _____ (закры́тый/закры́та/закры́т).

6. Широко́ _____ (распространены́/распространённые/распространён) в Аме́рике распрода́жи по́льзуются большо́й популя́рностью.

B. Переведи́те сле́дующие предложе́ния на ру́сский язы́к. Обраща́йте внима́ние на испо́льзование пра́вильны предло́гов и падеже́й.

1. We seldom have discounts on food products.
2. They went to the market for fruits and vegetables.
3. We invited them to dinner last week.
4. They told me that their lunch break is from one to two.
5. My sister is going to Russia for (to take) summer courses.
6. When we go to the market we usually stock up for several weeks.
7. Cream goes great with tea and coffee.
8. Is there anything here on sale (reduced prices)?
9. There's an exchange booth around the corner.
10. What's the fat content of packaged milk (milk in the packages)?

ПРЕДЛАГАЕМЫЕ ЗАНЯТИЯ

On your next trip to the supermarket, write out a shopping list in Russian, indicating the type and amount of product to be purchased.

УРОК 8

А. ДИАЛОГ

Экскурсия по Санкт-Петербургу.

В течение своего кратковременного визита в Москву, американский бизнесмен Джим Поррино и его жена Нэнси решили посетить Санкт-Петербург до возвращения в Соединённые Штаты. На вокзале их встречает Марья Истюхина, профессиональный гид из туристического агентства Тройка.

МАРЬЯ: Добро пожаловать в Санкт-Петербург! Как прошла поездка?

ДЖИМ: Спасибо, хорошо. Ночью,[1] правда, совсем ничего не было видно.

НЭНСИ: И мне тоже не спалось. Наверное, я переволновалась.

МАРЬЯ: Ничего, сегодня ночью выспитесь.[2] А сейчас нам предстоит многое увидеть, мы запланировали великолепную экскурсию. Кстати, а можно я буду с вами на ты?

ДЖИМ: Конечно.

МАРЬЯ: За те три дня, которые у нас есть, мы как раз успеем осмотреть основные достопримечательности. С чего бы вы хотели начать?

ДЖИМ: Я думаю, нам лучше довериться тебе.

НЭНСИ: Конечно, очень хочется побывать в Эрмитаже.[3] Многие его сравнивают с Лувром в Париже.

МАРЬЯ: В Эрмитаже больше коллекция классики, в особенности Леонардо да Винчи, такое вы увидите только здесь.

НЭНСИ: Что же, тогда начнём с Эрмитажа?

МАРЬЯ: Давайте пойдём туда завтра утром, для того чтобы провести там, по крайней мере, несколько часов до обеда. А пока, давайте начнём нашу пешую эксурсию по Невскому в сторону Адмиралтейства.[4]

Выхо́дят на Не́вский[5] проспе́кт.[6]

НЭНСИ: **Нам куда́?**

МАРЬЯ: **Пойдём к Дворцо́вой пло́щади,[7] это напра́во. Мы уви́дим по пути́ бы́вший дворе́ц Стро́ганова, Каза́нский собо́р,[8] Гости́ный двор[9] и Дом кни́ги, бы́вшее зда́ние компа́нии Зи́нгера по произво́дству швейных маши́нок.**

НЭНСИ: **Стро́ганов, очень похо́же на беф-стро́ганов.**

МАРЬЯ: **И впра́вду. По́вар гра́фа Стро́ганова пе́рвым доба́вил смета́ны к горчи́чному соусу и назва́л но́вое блю́до беф-стро́ганов. Как вам, наве́рное, изве́стно, гра́фу очень понра́вилось.**

НЭНСИ: **Как интере́сно!**

На Не́вском проспе́кте.

ДЖИМ: **В большинстве́ своём, архитекту́ра очень похо́жа на за́падно-европе́йскую.**

МАРЬЯ: **Пётр Вели́кий, основа́вший этот го́род в 1703 году́, и его́ пото́мки[10] пригласи́ли италья́нских, францу́зских и неме́цких архите́кторов для прое́ктов основны́х зда́ний го́рода, в том числе́, собо́ров и церкве́й. Хотя́ вот там спра́ва, е́сли смотре́ть вдоль кана́ла Грибое́дова, вы уви́дите своеобра́зное архитекту́рное исключе́ние.**

НЭНСИ: **Ого́, очень похо́же на Собо́р Васи́лия Блаже́нного на Кра́сной пло́щади в Москве́!**

МАРЬЯ: **Ты права́, это собо́р Спа́са на Крови́. Постро́ен как подо́бие Собо́ра Васи́лия Блаже́нного в 1882 году́ на ме́сте уби́йства царя́ Алекса́ндра II.**

Прихо́дят на Дворцо́вую пло́щадь.

МАРЬЯ: **Впечатля́ет, не пра́вда ли?**

НЭНСИ: **Замеча́тельно, и пло́щадь така́я огро́мная! А что это за коло́нна в це́нтре?**

МАРЬЯ: Это Алекса́ндровская коло́нна. Она была́ постро́ена в 1819 году́ в честь побе́ды над Наполео́ном.[11] Её высота́ 47.5 ме́тров.[12] А там сле́ва располо́жен Зи́мний дворе́ц, кото́рый был постро́ен по прое́кту италья́нского архите́ктора Растре́лли.

ДЖИМ: Так хо́чется уви́деть экспона́ты внутри́!

На сле́дующий день Джим и Нэнси возвраща́ются к Эрмита́жу. Ма́рья ждёт их у вхо́да.

МАРЬЯ: Каки́е произведе́ния иску́сства вам осо́бенно нра́вятся?

НЭНСИ: Я люблю́ импрессиони́стов, здесь есть их карти́ны?

МАРЬЯ: Разуме́ется, мы уви́дим шеде́вры Пикассо, Матисса, Писсаро, Моне и Гогена.

ДЖИМ: А я бы ещё хотел уви́деть собра́ние произведе́ний Да Ви́нчи.

МАРЬЯ: Туда́ мы то́же пройдём. Это отде́льный зал, где вы́ставлены то́лько его произведе́ния.

НЭНСИ: Собра́ние в Эрмита́же отража́ет исключи́тельно за́падно-европе́йское иску́сство?

МАРЬЯ: Нет, почему́ же? Здесь есть замеча́тельные образцы́ гре́ческих мастеро́в, перси́дской и кита́йской жи́вописи и скульпту́ры.[13]

ДЖИМ: А как насчёт ру́сской живопи́си?

МАРЬЯ: Произведе́ния ру́сских мастеро́в, гла́вным образом, вы́ставлены в Госуда́рственном Русском Музее. Это бы́вший дворе́ц Вели́кого Кня́зя Миха́ила, бра́та Алекса́ндра I и Никола́я I. Если жела́ете, мы можем пойти́ туда́ за́втра.

НЭНСИ: Да, прекра́сно!

ДЖИМ: Дава́йте начнём!

Посмотре́в не́сколько за́лов, где вы́ставлены произведе́ния мастеро́в испа́нских и флама́ндских школ 16-го и 17-го веко́в, все трое вхо́дят в за́лы импрессиони́стов.

ДЖИМ: Смотри́, Нэнси, нет ли у твое́й ма́мы ко́пии вот э́той карти́ны?

НЭНСИ: Ну, что ты, не узна́л? Это «Де́вушка с ве́ером» Ренуа́ра!

МАРЬЯ: А в сосе́днем за́ле, уви́дите не́которые шедре́вры други́х францу́зских мастеро́в, в том числе́ «Бульва́р Монма́ртр в Пари́же» Писсарро́, «Дере́вня на берегу́ Се́ны» Сисле́я, «Же́нщина, держа́щая плод» Гоге́на.

НЭНСИ: Это чуде́сно!

ДЖИМ: А как насчёт карти́н Да Ви́нчи?

МАРЬЯ: Мы сейча́с туда́. Они́ вы́ставлены ря́дом с за́лом, где нахо́дятся произведе́ния Рафаэ́ля и Тициа́на.

ДЖИМ: Прекра́сно!

Спустя́ не́сколько часо́в, все тро́е выхо́дят из музе́я.

МАРЬЯ: Как вам понра́вился Эрмита́ж?

НЭНСИ: Несомне́нно, здесь потряса́ющая колле́кция произведе́ний иску́сства!

ДЖИМ: Да, и помеще́ния то́же внуши́тельные. Мо́жно себе́ предста́вить, как жила́ ца́рская семья́!

Огля́дываясь вокру́г, Джим и Нэнси ви́дят интере́сные на вид зда́ния, располо́женные на островке́ Невы́.

НЭНСИ: А что это за зда́ние с высо́ким шпи́лем?

МАРЬЯ: Это Петропа́вловский собо́р. Он был постро́ен в 1732 году́ по прое́кту Трези́ни. Собо́р нахо́дится на террито́рии Петропа́вловской кре́пости, зало́женной в 1703-ом году́. Кре́пость дала́ нача́ло го́роду, и должна́ была́ защища́ть Петербу́рг от вторже́ний с мо́ря.[14]

ДЖИМ: А сего́дня мы успе́ем туда́ попа́сть?

МАРЬЯ: Ду́маю, что да. Но сперва́ дава́йте пообе́даем.

A tour of St. Petersburg.

During a brief stay in Moscow, American businessman Jim Porrino and his wife, Nancy, have arranged to be met in St. Petersburg by a professional guide for a tour of the city prior to returning to the United States. Marya Istyukhina, a tour guide from the Troika Tours Agency, is waiting for them at the Moscow Station in St. Petersburg.

MARYA: Welcome to St. Petersburg! How was the trip?

JIM: Fine, thanks. We didn't see much, though, since we traveled at night.

NANCY: And I didn't sleep too well. I guess I was too excited.

MARYA: Well, you'll sleep fine tonight. And now we have plenty to see. We intend to give you a royal tour of the sights. Incidentally, may I call you ты?

JIM: Of course.

MARYA: I think we can just about manage to see the city's main attractions in the three days that you're going to be here. What would you like to start with?

JIM: I think we'd best rely on you.

NANCY: Of course, we would very much like to visit the Hermitage. I hear that it rivals the Louvre in Paris.

MARYA: The Hermitage has a rather large collection of classical masterpieces, particularly of Leonardo da Vinci, that can be seen only there.

NANCY: So, do we start at the Hermitage?

MARYA: Let's go tomorrow morning so we can spend at least several hours there before lunch. For now, I thought we could start our walking tour by going down Nevskiy to the Admiralty.

They leave the hotel and go to Nevsky Prospekt.

NANCY: Which way do we go now?

MARYA: Let's go toward Palace Square, to the right. On the way, we'll be passing the former Stroganoff palace, the Kazan Cathedral, the Gostiny Dvor department store, and the House of Books, the former site of the Singer Sewing Machine Company.

NANCY: Stroganoff—that name reminds me of beef Stroganoff.

MARYA: You're right. Count Stroganoff's French cook was the first to add some sour cream to a basic mustard sauce and called this new dish beef Stroganoff. As you probably know, the count was quite pleased.

NANCY: How interesting!

Along Nevsky Prospekt.

JIM: Most of the buildings remind me of Western European architecture.

MARYA: Peter the Great, who founded the city in 1703, and his immediate successors engaged Italian, French, and German architects to design the city's principal buildings, including cathedrals and churches. However, if you look to the right, near the end of the Griboyedov Canal, you will see a distinctive architectural exception.

NANCY: Oh yes, that looks very much like St. Basil's Cathedral in Red Square in Moscow!

MARYA: You're right, the cathedral is called Savior on the Blood. It's modeled after the St. Basil Cathedral and was built in 1882 on the spot where Czar Alexander II was assasinated.

They enter Palace Square.

MARYA: Impressive, isn't it?

NANCY: It's magnificent and so expansive! What is that tall column in the center?

MARYA: That's the Alexander Column. It was built in 1819 to commemorate Russia's victory over Napoleon. It's 47.5 meters high. And there to your left is the Winter Palace, which was designed by the Italian architect Rastrelli.

JIM: I can't wait to see the exhibits there.

The next day, Jim and Nancy return to the Hermitage, where Marya is waiting for them at the entrance.

MARYA: Is there any particular type of art that appeals to you?

NANCY: I like the Impressionist paintings. Are there any examples of that period here?

MARYA: Of course. We can see some fine examples of Picasso and Matisse, Pissarro, Monet, and Gauguin.

JIM: I'd like to see the da Vinci collections.

MARYA: We can go there, too. In fact, there is a special room containing only his works.

NANCY: Is the Hermitage's collections limited to Western European art?

MARYA: No, not at all. You can also see some fine examples of classical Greek, Persian, and Chinese paintings and sculpture.

JIM: And what about Russian paintings?

MARYA: The works of Russian masters are primarily exhibited at the Russian State Museum, formerly the palace of Grand Duke Michael, brother of Alexander I and Nicholas I. If you like, we can go there tomorrow.

NANCY: Oh yes, that would be great!

JIM: Well, let's get started!

After viewing several halls of Spanish and Flemish paintings of the sixteenth and seventeenth century, the three go to the rooms with Impressionist paintings.

JIM: Look, Nancy, doesn't your mother have a copy of that painting?

NANCY: Of course, don't you recognize it? It's Renoir's *Girl With a Fan*.

MARYA: And in the next room, you'll find some works by other French masters, including Pissarro's *Boulevard Montmartre in Paris,* Sisley's *Village on the Bank of the Seine,* and Gauguin's *Young Woman Holding a Fruit.*

NANCY: This is wonderful!

JIM: Now, what about the da Vinci paintings?

MARYA: Yes, we'll go there next. They're right next to the room with paintings by Rafael and Titian.

JIM: Great!

Several hours later, the three leave the museum.

MARYA: Well, how did you like the Hermitage?

NANCY: It certainly has a fantastic collection of masterpieces.

JIM: And what about the rooms themselves? You really get a good feeling of how the royal family lived.

As Nancy and Jim look around them they catch sight of some interesting buildings situated on a small island in the Neva River.

NANCY: What is that building with the tall spire?

MARYA: That's the Peter and Paul Cathedral. It was built in 1732 and designed by the Italian architect Trezzini. The cathedral stands in the center of the Peter and Paul fortress, which was erected in 1703 to protect St. Petersburg against invasions from the sea.

JIM: Will we have time to go there today?

MARYA: I think so. But first, let's have lunch.

B. ПРИМЕЧАНИЯ

1. The fastest express trains between Moscow and St. Petersburg leave around midnight and reach the other city around eight or nine in the morning.

2. Выспаться (lit., to sleep oneself out) means to get the amount of sleep one needs to feel rested. Из-за твоего храпéния прóшлой нóчью я не выспался. (Thanks to your snoring, I couldn't get a good night's sleep.)

3. The principal collections of the Hermitage Museum are housed in the Winter Palace (Зимний дворец), which is the largest of the five buildings that comprise the museum. The smaller adjoining buildings were built under Catherine the Great in 1771 to accommodate her growing collection of artworks.

4. The admiralty building (Адмиралтейство), at the north end of Nevskiy Prospekt, was built in 1704, primarily as a dockyard. Ships were built there until 1844. In 1928 a golden cupola and spire were added to the building. It currently houses naval offices.

5. Nevskiy Prospekt (Невский проспект) is named after the Neva (Нева) river on whose delta St. Petersburg is situated. The river divides into several canals that run through the city and lead to the Volga River. The principal section of Nevskiy Prospekt extends from the Admiralty (Адмиралтейство) to the Square of the Uprising (площадь Восстания). The other half of Nevskiy Prospekt extends

from the Square of the Uprising to the Alexander Nevsky monastery (Алекса́ндро-Не́вская ла́вра).

6. Remember that in Russian only the descriptive word of geographical sites, organizations, and institutions is capitalized: Кра́сная пло́щадь (Red Square), Не́вский проспе́кт (Nevsky Prospect), Зи́мний дворе́ц (the Winter Palace). However, there are some exceptions, among them certain institutions and international organizations: Сове́т Безопа́сности ООН (UN Security Council), Сове́т Мини́стров (Council of Ministers), Соединённые Шта́ты Аме́рики (United States of America).

7. Palace Square (Дворцо́вая пло́щадь) is adjacent to the Admiralty and is the site of the Winter Palace, the Hermitage, the Alexander column, and the former General Staff Building (зда́ние Гла́вного шта́ба).

8. The Kazan Cathedral (Каза́нский собор) on Nevskiy Prospekt was built in 1801. During the Soviet period it was converted to the Museum of Atheism and Religion.

9. Гости́ный двор (Merchants' Arcade) was built in the eighteenth century as an open trade center and bazaar. It was severely damaged during World War II, then restored in the 1950s. It presently functions as a department store.

10. St. Petersburg's most active period of new construction in the baroque, neoclassical, and classical Roman style took place under Catherine the Great (1762–1796), followed by Alexander I (1801–1825), Nicholas I (1825–1855), Alexander II (1855–1881), and Alexander III (1881–1894).

11. The triumphal arch (триумфа́льная а́рка) in the center of the General Staff Building, designed by C. I. Rossi in the same year, was also built to commemorate Napoleon's defeat in Russia.

12. One meter equals approximately three feet, so the column's height is about 143 feet. The column is crowned by a figurine of an angel whose face ostensibly resembles that of Alexander I, who is standing on a snake with a Napoleon-like face.

13. Other collections in the Hermitage include many bronze, silver, porcelain, and metal artefacts from ancient Egypt, Turkey, Greece, and Rome.

14. In addition to its protective function, the Peter and Paul Fortress was also used to incarcerate political opponents of the czars, very much like the Tower of London. The cathedral is the burial place of all the czars beginning with Peter the Great (except Peter II) and now includes the remains of Nicholas II.

C. ГРАММАТИКА И СЛОВОУПОТРЕБЛЕНИЕ

1. РАЗМЕРЫ И РАССТОЯНИЯ (DIMENSIONS AND DISTANCE)

In Russian, dimensions are expressed with the preposition в + a number in the accusative case. The unit and type of dimension (height, length, width) should be in the instrumental case.

Алекса́ндровская коло́нна в со́рок семь ме́тров высото́й.
The Alexander Column is forty-seven meters high.

Гла́вная у́лица приме́рно в три́дцать ме́тров ширино́й.
The main street is about thirty meters wide.

In journalistic or colloquial usage the preposition is often omitted.

В черте́ Петербу́рга Нева́ образу́ет дугу́ длино́й 13 киломе́тров.
The Neva forms a 13-kilometer long arch within the city limits of St. Petersburg.

В э́том ме́сте, мне ка́жется, что река́ шириной о́коло 500 ме́тров.
I think the river is about 500 meters wide at this point.

Note that the word for height (высота́) is used only for inanimate objects. To denote the height of person, use рост.

Его́ брат в 180 сатиме́тров ро́стом.
His brother is 180 centimeters tall.

In questions, the type of dimension is in the genitive case.

Како́й высоты́ это зда́ние?
How tall is this building?

Како́го ро́ста ваш брат?
How tall is your brother?

Како́й ширины́ река́ в э́том ме́сте?
How wide is the river at this point?

To denote the distance from one object to another the preposition в + the prepositional case is used.

Петродворе́ц располо́жен в двадцати́ девяти́* киломе́трах от Санкт-Петербу́рга.
   Peterhof is twenty-nine kilometers from St. Petersburg.

Па́вловск лежи́т в двадцати́ пяти́ киломе́трах к ю́гу от Санкт-Петербу́рга и в трёх киломе́трах от Пу́шкина.
   Pavlovsk lies twenty-five kilometers south of St. Petersburg and three kilometers from Pushkin.

2. ГЛАГОЛЫ ЗВАТЬ/ПОЗВАТЬ, НАЗЫВАТЬ(СЯ)/НАЗВАТЬ (СЯ) (THE VERBS ЗВАТЬ/ПОЗВАТЬ AND НАЗЫВАТЬ(СЯ)/НАЗВАТЬ(СЯ)

As you already know, the verb звать (to call) is used to indicate a person's name.

Его зову́т Пётр.
   His name is Peter. (lit., They call him Peter.)

The verbs звать/позва́ть and называ́ть/назва́ть also refer to calling out to or addressing someone. As in the above example, the object of the verb is in the accusative case.

Кто назва́л/позва́л† меня́?
   Who called me?

Твой па́па зовёт тебя́.
   Your father is calling you.

When the verb называть/назвать is used to describe a noun by attributing some quality to it, the noun is in the accusative case, but the quality is in the instrumental case.

Нельзя́ назва́ть это зда́ние но́вым.
   You could hardly call that building new.

*See Appendix for declension of numbers.
†Although either verb can be used to mean "to call," назва́ть is more frequently used to mean "to call someone by their name."

Я бы не назвал его гением, но он всё-таки справится с заданием!
I wouldn't exactly call him a genius, but he'll get the job done!

Давайте будем называть вещи своими именами!
Let's call a spade a spade! (lit., Let's call things by their own names!)

When calling by phone, the verb звонить/позвонить is used. A person called should be in the dative case, while a place would be in the accusative case, introduced by the preposition в or на.

Кому вы сейчас звоните?
Who are you calling now?

Вам надо позвонить в бюро путешествий, чтобы подтвердить вашу бронь.
You've got to call the travel bureau to confirm your reservations.

Я несколько раз звонил на почту, но никто не ответил.
I called the post office several times, but no one answered.

Ты позвонила в туристское агентство, чтобы узнать, когда начинается эксурсия?
Did you call the tourist agency to find out when the tour begins?

The reflexive form называться is used in naming objects.

Эта площадь называется площадь Декабристов.
This square is called Decembrist Square.

When referring to an object's former name, the name should be in the instrumental case.

Раньше она называлась Сенатской площадью.
It was previously called Senate Square.

The verb называться is also used idiomatically to mean "as they say" or "that is to say."

Состояние новых домов не было очень хорошим. Они были, что называется, недоделаны.
The condition of the new buildings was not very good. They were, what one would say, unfinished.

D. ИДИОМАТИКА

THE ART OF PATIENCE.

Various degrees of patience and impatience are derived from the verb терпеть.

Терпе́ние и труд всё перетру́т. (PATIENCE AND EFFORT OVERCOME ALL OBSTACLES.)

Зна́ешь, я про́сто не могу́ реши́ть эту сло́жную математи́ческую зада́чу! — Ничего́, терпе́ние и труд всё перетру́т.

You know, I simply can't solve this complex math problem! —That's okay. Just be patient and persistent, and you'll do it.

Набра́ться терпе́ния (TO HAVE PATIENCE)

Прошло́ уже́ две неде́ли, а ещё не получи́л ответ на моё письмо́! —Набери́тесь терпе́ния, мой друг. Вы ещё его́ полу́чите.

Two weeks have gone by, and I still haven't received an answer to my letter —Have patience, my friend. You'll get an answer.

The following expressions all mean "to lose one's patience," with an increasing degree of severity.

Потеря́ть терпе́ние (TO LOSE ONE'S PATIENCE/TEMPER)

Я уже́ три часа́ жду эксурсово́да. Потеря́л терпе́ние. Пойду́ в музей без него́!

I've been waiting three hours for our guide. I've lost my patience. I'm going to the museum without him!

Вы́вести из терпе́ния (TO TRY SOMEONE'S PATIENCE)

Како́й он дура́к. Я бо́льше не буду спо́рить с ним. Он вы́вел меня́ из терпе́ния!

What a fool he is! I'm not arguing with him any longer. He's really trying my patience!

Терпе́ть не могу́! (I CAN'T STAND IT ANYMORE!)

Они веду́т себя́ бессо́вестно. Терпе́ть не могу́!

Their behavior is unconscionable. I can't stand it anymore!

Терпе́ние ло́пнуло! (MY PATIENCE HAS RUN OUT!)

Это уже сли́шком, терпе́ние у меня́ ло́пнуло!
Now, that's really too much! My patience has run out!

Вся́кому терпению есть преде́л. (THERE'S A LIMIT TO ONE'S PATIENCE.)

Вся́кому терпе́нию есть преде́л. Это уже́ тре́тий раз, как они́ отложи́ли экску́рсию!
There's a limit to one's patience. This is the third time they've postponed the tour!

The following expressions convey impatient anticipation.

Ждать с нетерпе́нием (TO AWAIT WITH IMPATIENCE)

Оста́лось то́лько де́сять мину́т до нача́ла экску́рсии. —Да, зна́ю. Жду с больши́м нетерпе́нием!
Just ten minutes and the tour will begin. —Yes, I know. I just can't wait!

Невтерпёж (TO BE IMPATIENT)

Ско́ро у нас бу́дут кани́кулы. Мне невтерпёж пое́хать в Москву́!
Our vacation is coming up soon. I can't wait to go to Moscow!

Е. СТРОГО ПО ДЕЛУ

ПОЕЗДКИ ПО РОССИИ (TRAVEL IN RUSSIA)

Although travel to and within Russia for foreigners has become much easier to arrange in recent years, certain rules and procedures, particularly as they apply to business travel, should be kept in mind. In order to obtain a business visa, the applicant must be sponsored by some recognized governmental or commercial Russian organization (but not by a single individual). Such organizations should be contacted at least one month prior to your desired arrival, as you must present a copy of the host's invitation together with your visa application. The turnaround time for a visa is about two weeks.

Most foreign passengers fly into and depart from Moscow's Sheremetyevo-2 airport (or the Pulkovo-2 airport in St. Petersburg). For other destinations within Russia reservations are generally required 72 hours in advance and should be made from the United States or a reliable travel agent in Russia. Aeroflot no longer offers domestic service as these routes were turned over to various regional airline companies, many of which have not been very dependable. An exception is the Transaero company (Moscow headquarters) which enjoys a good safety record.

Many find that train travel between cities that are relatively close is much more convenient and relaxing than air travel. The night train between Moscow and St. Petersburg leaves one city at midnight and arrives in the other city at about eight in the morning. Of the two classes of cars available (мя́гкий ваго́н, "soft car," and жёсткий ваго́н, "hard car"), most foreigners prefer the first-class, "soft" compartment, which has two berths instead of the usual four. A first-class sleeper is also called междунаро́дный спа́льный ваго́н, "international sleeper car," and a second-class sleeper with four berths is мягкий спа́льный ваго́н, "soft sleeper." You can purchase a whole compartment, when available, if you do not wish to share it. In any case, the least desirable cars are the third-class, open "bunk" cars (жёсткие плацка́ртные ваго́ны) and the ваго́ны-сиде́ния, "sitting cars," unless the trip is a very short one.

Arrivals to and departures from Russia by train, bus, or car (via Helsinki, Prague, or Warsaw, for example), usually involve fairly lengthy and thorough customs inspections.

Car rental agencies in Moscow and at large city airports include Avis, Hertz, and Budget Rent-a-Car. However, unless you can readily read Russian signs and are fairly familiar with Moscow and St. Petersburg streets, driving can be a trying experience. You may want to consider renting a car with a driver.

Vehicular traffic in Moscow and St. Petersburg has increased tremendously in the past few years, and the streets are not easy to navigate. Street and traffic signs are not always readily visible, and traffic violations are easily committed. Traffic officers (гаи́шники) are known to be particularly keen on tracking foreign drivers. If a driver is stopped for a minor violation, the fine is usually paid on the spot. More serious violations involving injuries or drunken driving can result in heavy fines and incarceration.

The alternative for intracity travel is taxis, of which there are plenty, or the excellent subway (метро) systems in Moscow and St. Petersburg. It is a good idea to establish the taxi fare before boarding the vehicle, and it's best not to enter a taxi that already has another passenger.

Visitors who have an adequate command of Russian can independently engage guides to the principal sites of historical and cultural interest.

Some native guides advertise themselves in the city's central locations, for example, Red Square (Красная площадь) in Moscow or Palace Square (Дворцовая площадь) in St. Petersburg. Fees for their services should be established prior to any agreement (Ско́лько вы берёте за эксу́рсию? What do you charge for a sightseeing tour?).

Guided in-house tours in various foreign languages, including English, are also offered at many principal museuems and points of interest, such as the Hermitage Museum in St. Petersburg, the Catherine Palace (Екатеринский дворец) in Pushkin, the Kremlin palaces and cathedrals (Кремлёвские дворцы и соборы) in Moscow, the Pushkin and Tretyakov museums in Moscow, the medieval catacombs of the Pechersk Monastery (катакомбы Печерской лавры) outside of Kiev, and others.

УПРАЖНЕНИЯ

A. Соста́вьте вопро́сы, на кото́рые отвеча́ли бы сле́дующие предложе́ния. Укажи́те на како́й слог па́дает ударе́ние. (Compose questions that would answer the following sentences. Indicate the stress marks.)

1. Александровская колонна в сорок семь метров высотой.
2. Мой отец ростом примерно в 180 сентиметров.
3. В этом месте Нева шириной в триста метров.
4. Эта улица длиной примерно в три километра.
5. Мой сын ростом в 170 см, а дочь в 165 см.

B. В пропусках вставьте подходящие глаголы в нужной форме.

1. Она мне_____вчера вечером.
       (called)
2. Я думаю, что твой отец тебя_____.
                                (is calling)
3. Как раньше_____эта площадь?
          (was called)
4. Мне кажется, что они_____их дочь Татьяной.
                         (named)
5. Я забыл, как_____эти старые здания.
          (are called)

C. Переведите следующие предложения на русский язык.

1. Is Palace square very from here? —No, it's only a one kilometer. We can walk (go by foot) there.
2. The Catherine Palace in Pushkin is located about 25 kilometers from the center of St. Petersburg.
3. Ask him how much he charges for a tour of the Hermitage.
4. This was formerly called Senate Square.
5. I just can't wait for her any longer. My patience has run out!
6. You can certainly call that a very impressive building!
7. How long is the Neva River?
8. These buildings were designed by the Italian architect Rastrelli.
9. I just can't wait to see the exhibits at the Hermitage.
10. The museum has a very large collection of Impressionist masterpieces.

УРОК 9

A. ДИАЛОГ

Совме́стное предприя́тие.

Америка́нский бизнесме́н, заинтересо́ванный в возмо́жности созда́ния совме́стного предприя́тия с находя́щейся в Екатеринбу́рге[1] ру́сской фи́рмой по произво́дству стройматериа́лов, про́сит организова́ть ему́ посеще́ние заво́да э́той фи́рмы.

БРАУН: **Я был бы о́чень призна́телен, е́сли бы вы организова́ли мне посеще́ние одного́ из ва́ших заво́дов-изготови́телей.**

СМИРНОВ: **Е́сли вам бу́дет удо́бно, я бу́ду рад показа́ть вам оди́н из на́ших крупне́йших заво́дов сего́дня же.**

БРАУН: **Э́то бы́ло бы прекра́сно. Смо́жем ли мы пое́хать туда́ по́сле обе́да, ска́жем, в два часа́?**

СМИРНОВ: **Обы́чно у нас обе́дают в два часа́.[2] Дава́йте лу́чше пообе́даем вме́сте здесь в гости́нице, а пото́м отсю́да пое́дем пря́мо на заво́д.**

БРАУН: **Хорошо́, дава́йте!**

СМИРНОВ: **Зна́чит, договори́лись. Я вас бу́ду ждать в рестора́не в два часа́.**

На заво́де.

МОРОЗОВА: **Очень ра́да приве́тствовать вас на на́шем заво́де, господи́н[3] Бра́ун.**

БРАУН: **Спаси́бо. Я рад э́той возмо́жности. Заво́д произво́дит на меня́ неплохо́е впечатле́ние. Строи́тельные материа́лы из пенопла́ста по́льзуются у вас больши́м спро́сом?**

МОРОЗОВА: **Да, в связи́ с ускоря́ющимися те́мпами домостро́ения у нас, спрос на на́шу проду́кцию[4] превыша́ет предложе́ние. Как сле́дствие, заво́д рабо́тает с по́лной нагру́зкой.[5] Причём мы получа́ем мно́го зака́зов как от оте́чественных[6] клие́нтов, так и от зарубе́жных[7] зака́зчиков.[8]**

БРАУН: Вы выпуска́ете большо́й ассортиме́нт строи́тельных материа́лов?

СМИРНОВ: Да, в про́шлом году́ мы как раз на́чали произво́дство пеноблоков, подходя́щих к строи́тельству и малоэта́жных жилы́х домо́в, и комме́рческих зда́ний. Тем не ме́нее, на́ша ба́за,[9] к сожале́нию, недоста́точна для постоя́нной разрабо́тки но́вой продукции. Кро́ме этого́ мы хоте́ли бы увели́чить годово́й объём выпуска́емой проду́кции, разнообра́зить её ассортиме́нт и улу́чшить ка́чество на́шей проду́кции, что́бы она была́ на у́ровне мировы́х станда́ртов.

БРАУН: Вот в э́том мы могли́ бы вам помо́чь.

МОРОЗОВА: Спаси́бо, и действи́тельно, дополни́тельные капита́ловложе́ния и укрупне́ние ба́зы явля́ются на́шими первоочередны́ми зада́чами.

БРАУН: А как насчёт контро́ля за ка́чеством, господи́н Смирно́в?

СМИРНОВ: Для этого у нас есть отде́л по контро́лю за ка́чеством. Коне́чно, при усло́виях совме́стного предприя́тия, оконча́-тельная приёмка осуществля́лась бы та́кже и ва́шими инже-не́рами.

БРАУН: У вас есть на заво́де усло́вия для обуче́ния специали́стов?

МОРОЗОВА: У нас есть не́сколько ку́рсов для обуче́ния инже-не́ров- специали́стов, в том числе́ и вече́рний факульте́т.

БРАУН: Мне бы хоте́лось посмотре́ть програ́мму стажиро́вки,[10] если это возмо́жно. Вполне́ вероя́тно, что мы отпра́вим к вам не́скольких специали́стов из на́шего прое́ктного и произ-во́дственного соста́ва для их уча́стия в програ́мме обуче́ния.

СМИРНОВ: Да, это бы́ло бы очень поле́зно.

БРАУН: А как у вас обстоя́т дела́[11] с благосостоя́нием рабо́чих и медици́нским обслу́живанием на заво́де?

МОРОЗОВА: Мы наде́емся, что при усло́виях совме́стного предприя́тия[12] мы смо́жем вы́делить бо́льше средств[13] на э́ти це́ли. Разуме́ется, на заво́де име́ется кабине́т медобслу́живания, кото́рый рабо́тает круглосу́точно, на слу́чаи травм или оказа́ния пе́рвой по́мощи.

БРАУН: Ско́лько рабо́чих за́нято на ва́шем заво́де?

МОРОЗОВА: В настоя́щее вре́мя приме́рно две́сти рабо́чих.

БРАУН: Все они́ чле́ны профсою́за?

МОРОЗОВА: Все, кро́ме нача́льников не́которых цехо́в.

БРАУН: Кста́ти, если у нас ещё оста́лось вре́мя, я бы хоте́л осмотре́ть пре́ссовые це́хи и, мо́жет быть, поговори́ть с произво́дственным ма́стером о технологи́ческой[14] ли́нии и но́рмах техни́ческой безопа́сности.

МОРОЗОВА: Зна́ете, мне не хвата́ет вре́мени. Че́рез полчаса́ мне на́до бу́дет пое́хать в аэропо́рт. Приезжа́ет мой муж из Берли́на.

БРАУН: Ваш муж? Я не знал, что вы за́мужем. А я-то хоте́л пригласи́ть вас на обе́д сего́дня ве́чером.

МОРОЗОВА: Ничего́. Мо́жно пообе́дать вме́сте втроём в друго́й раз. Зна́чит, так: дава́йте встре́тимся ещё раз за́втра утром. Тогда́ мы смо́жем заня́ться обсужде́нием этих вопро́сов, и в том числе́ не́которых дета́лей по созда́нию совме́стного предприя́тия.

БРАУН: Окей. И ещё мне хоте́лось бы обсуди́ть не́сколько вопро́сов по ма́ркетингу проду́кции и составле́нию прайс-листов.[15]

МОРОЗОВА: Эти вопро́сы мы, безусло́вно, поста́вим на пове́стку дня. Дава́йте встре́тимся в гости́нице в де́вять часо́в утра́, если это вам бу́дет удо́бно.

БРАУН: Да, это меня́ вполне́ устра́ивает.[16]

A joint venture.

An American business executive who is considering a joint venture agreement with a Russian building materials company in Ekaterinburg would like to see the company's factory.

BROWN: I would very much appreciate your arranging a visit to one of your manufacturing plants.

SMIRNOV: I will be happy to show you one of our larger plants today, if that is convenient.

BROWN: That would be wonderful. Would it be possible to go there after lunch, say about two P.M.?

SMIRNOV: Actually, we usually have lunch at two. Why don't we have lunch together here at the hotel and then go directly to the plant?

BROWN: Great.

SMIRNOV: Agreed, then. I'll see you in the restaurant at two o'clock.

At the plant.

MOROZOVA: I'm very pleased to welcome you to our plant, Mr. Brown.

BROWN: Thank you. Your facilities are quite impressive. Is there a great demand for plastic foam construction materials in your country?

MOROZOVA: Yes, there is. You see, because of the accelerating rate of housing construction here, the demand for these products is exceeding supply, so we're operating at full capacity. Moreover, we're getting orders from both domestic and foreign clients.

BROWN: Do you produce a wide range of materials?

SMIRNOV: Yes. Just last year we started producing foam blocks that are quite suitable for low-rise dwellings and commercial buildings. Nevertheless, our production facilities are not quite adequate for ongoing new product development. Besides, we would like to increase our annual output, diversify our products, and bring them up to international standards.

BROWN: That's precisely where we might be able to help you.

MOROZOVA: Thank you. Additional capital investment and plant expansion are our first priority items.

BROWN: What about quality control, Mr. Smirnov?

SMIRNOV: That's taken care of by our quality control department, but of course in a joint venture operation final inspection would also be carried out by your engineering staff.

BROWN: Do you have any training facilities at your plant?

MOROZOVA: We have several departments for engineer training, including an evening school at the plant.

BROWN: I would like to learn more about the training program, if possible. We will probably want to bring some of our own design and production staff to work with you in training.

SMIRNOV: Oh, that would be very useful.

BROWN: What about worker welfare and plant medical facilities?

MOROZOVA: We hope to be able to allocate more funds for that purpose in a joint venture. Of course, we do have a plant medical station that operates around the clock to deal with injuries and emergencies.

BROWN: How many workers are employed at your plant?

MOROZOVA: At present, approximately two hundred.

BROWN: Are they all union members?

MOROZOVA: All except a few shop supervisors.

BROWN: By the way, if we still have some time I'd like to take a look at the moulding shops and perhaps talk to some foremen about your production line and safety standards.

MOROZOVA: I'm afraid I don't have the time to arrange that now. I have to leave for the airport in half an hour. My husband is arriving from Berlin.

BROWN: Your husband? I didn't know you were married! And I was going to invite you to dinner this evening.

MOROZOVA: That's okay. We can have dinner together another time, all three of us. So, let's meet again tomorrow morning. We can then take up these questions as well as some of the details about the joint venture agreement.

BROWN: Okay. I'd also like to discuss product marketing and price lists.

MOROZOVA: We'll certainly include those points on the agenda. Let's meet at the hotel at nine in the morning, if that's convenient for you.

BROWN: Nine o'clock is fine.

B. ПРИМЕЧАНИЯ

1. Ekaterinburg (Екатеринбу́рг), located 1,667 kilometers (1,000 miles) east of Moscow with a population of approximately 1.5 million, is the major industrial city of the Свердло́вская о́бласть (Sverdlovsk Region). Its principal manufactured products include electronic equipment, chemicals, building materials, plastics, pharmaceuticals, and machine tools. Among its various cultural and historic sites is what is left of the House of Ipatyev (Дом Ипа́тьева), where Czar Nicholas II and his family were murdered in July, 1918. The U.S. Department of Commerce maintains an American Business Center in the city (Луначáрская у́лица, 80, тел. 3432-55-56-89) to provide information and assistance to interested American businessmen.

2. Russian meals usually follow the European pattern. За́втрак (breakfast) is usually eaten between 6 A.M. and 9 A.M., обе́д (lunch) is normally the biggest meal and is eaten between 1 p.m. and 3 P.M. У́жин (dinner) is light and is eaten between 7 P.M. and 9 P.M.

3. It is now quite common for Russians to use the pre-revolutionary titles господи́н (Mr.) and госпожá (Mrs.) in formal situations. These terms were applied almost exclusively to western foreigners during the Soviet period. Note that there is no contemporary Russian equivalent for Ms. The term for "Ladies and Gentlemen" is Да́мы и господá. In less formal settings (at work, school, social occasions) Russians address each other by the first and patronymic names, if they are not very close friends.

4. Проду́кция can mean "production, product(s), or output." Note that the word проду́кция itself is used in the singular form but can stand for plural objects, particularly when preceded by adjectives: гото́вая проду́кция (finished products), товáрная проду́кция (marketable products). The plural проду́кты generally refers to food products, produce.

5. По́лная нагру́зка also means "full work load." У него́ о́чень большáя нагру́зка. (He has a very heavy workload.)

6. Оте́чественный refers to the fatherland (from the word оте́ц) and is commonly translated as "domestic" or "home" when referring to manufactured goods and services.

7. Зарубе́жный (lit. beyond the frontier) can be translated as "foreign" or "abroad," e.g., зарубе́жные страны (countries abroad).

8. Закáзчик (customer, client), is derived from the verb закáзывать/заказáть (to order); i.e., one who places an order.

9. As in English, the Russian word бáза (base) has a wide range of usages. In business situations, it can mean a material and technical base (материáльно-техни́ческая бáза), a financial base (финáнсовая

база), a source of raw materials (сырьева́я ба́за), or a container depot (конте́йнерная ба́за). As applied to computers, ба́за да́нных means a database program. It can also refer to a military location, such as вое́нно-морска́я ба́за (naval base).

10. Стажиро́вка can refer to practical training, a probationary period, or a temporary position. Неда́вние выпускники́ Екатеринбу́ргской бизнес-шко́лы пришли́ в на́ше совме́тное предприя́тие на стажиро́вку. (Recent graduates of the Ekaterinburg Business School have joined our joint venture company as interns.) По́сле того́, как она́ прошла́ трёхмеся́чную стажиро́вку у нас, она́ реши́ла иска́ть другу́ю рабо́ту. (After undergoing a three-month period of on-the-job training with us, she decided to look for other work.)

11. The word де́ло can have a variety of meanings, including "business; affair; endeavor; deal"; e.g., суде́бное де́ло (lawsuit), ли́чное де́ло (personal affair), нечи́стое де́ло (monkey business), го́рное де́ло (mining), до́хлое де́ло (bad business), пусто́е де́ло (a vain endeavor, a waste of time). It is also used in the common expression Как у вас дела́? (How are things?).

12. Совме́стное предприя́тие (often abbreviated as СП) is a joint venture, normally involving a Russian and a foreign company. A joint stock company, on the other hand, is акционе́рное о́бщество, a society or company that issues stocks.

13. The plural word сре́дства (means) can be used in the monetary sense as in жить по сре́дствам (to live within your means) or in the sense of physical facilities as in the сре́дства ма́ссовой информа́ции or СМИ (mass media; lit. means of mass information). The singular form сре́дство can also indicate a remedy for some condition, such as сре́дство от ка́шля (cough medicine).

14. Технологи́ческая ли́ния is a production line. The noun техноло́гия, which here refers to a manufacturing process, is also the general term for "technology." На́ша долгосро́чная зада́ча-расшире́ние ассортиме́нта проду́кции за счёт поку́пки но́вых технологи́ческих ли́ний. (Our long-term task is to expand the diversity of our products by acquiring new technology.)

15. An increasing number of English words are becoming part of the Russian business vocabulary. For example: ма́ркетинг, прайс-лист, ноу-ха́у, би́знес, бизнесме́н, бро́кер, ме́неджер, etc.

16. Устра́ивать/устро́ить can mean "to organize, to arrange, to settle." Вы устро́или свои́ дела́? (Have you settled your affairs?) It can also mean "to suit (someone)." Вас устра́ивают но́вые усло́вия контра́кта? (Do the new contract provisions suit you?)

C. ГРАММАТИКА И СЛОВОУПОТРЕБЛЕНИЕ

1. СОСЛАГАТЕЛЬНОЕ НАКЛОНЕНИЕ (THE SUBJUNCTIVE MOOD)

While the indicative mood is used for statements of fact or realistic situations, the subjunctive mood is used to describe situations that are hypothetical or contrary to fact. It is formed with the particle бы and the past tense of the verb.

Они́ бы подписа́ли контра́кт, но заво́д ещё не был постро́ен.
They would have signed the contract, but the plant wasn't built yet.

Мы бы пое́хали в Ло́ндон, но у нас не́ было де́нег.
We would have traveled to London, but we didn't have any money.

The subjunctive mood is also used to express a desire or wish.

Я бы хоте́л посмотре́ть програ́мму обуче́ния.
I would like to see the training program.
I would have liked to have seen the training program.

Мы бы с удово́льствием пошли́ в кино́.
We would very much like to go to the movies.
We would have gone to the movies with pleasure.

Note that in the examples above, the Russian sentence can refer to the past, present, or future. Since the subjunctive mood in Russian is not associated with tense, the context of the statement reveals the intended meaning.

The conjunction чтобы may be used instead of бы when requesting that an action be performed (or not performed) by someone else. Чтобы is commonly used following the verbs хоте́ть (to want), проси́ть* (to request), наста́ивать (to insist), and тре́бовать (to require).

*The verb проси́ть/попроси́ть can also be used with the infinitive to request that some action be performed by another person.

Я прошу́ вас отвезти́ его́ в аэропо́рт.
Please take him to the airport (lit., I ask you to take him to the airport).

Я хочу, чтобы они пришли в гостиницу в девять часов.
I want them to come to the hotel at nine o' clock.

Они не хотят, чтобы мы обсуждали этот вопрос сегодня.
They don't want us to discuss this question today.

Мы их попросили, чтобы они поставили эти вопросы на повестку дня.
We asked them to put these questions on the agenda.

Она настаивала на том, чтобы мы посетили новый завод в пригороде.
She insisted that we visit the new plant in the suburbs.

Начальник всегда требует, чтобы служащие приходили на работу вовремя.
The boss always demands that the employees come to work on time.

2. УСЛОВНЫЕ КОНСТРУКЦИИ—ЕСЛИ
(CONDITIONAL "IF" CLAUSES)

"If" clauses are used to describe the conditions required for an action to occur. In Russian they are introduced by если. If the conditions and the related consequence depict a realistic situation that is likely to occur, an indicative mood should be used in both the "if" and the main clause.

Если он завтра придёт в гостиницу, мы сможем обсудить проект контракта.
If he comes to the hotel tomorrow, we'll be able to discuss the draft contract (he will probably come).

Если они уже обсудили этот вопрос, они, наверное, договорились встретиться ещё раз в субботу.
If they already discussed this problem, they have probably agreed to meet again on Saturday (they probably have discussed the problem).

Если господина Брауна уже отвезли в гостиницу, я позвоню ему сегодня вечером.
If they already drove Mr. Brown to the hotel, I'll phone him this evening (Mr. Brown was probably driven to the hotel).

However, when the conditions and related consequences are unlikely to occur, the subjunctive form should be used in both the "if" and main clause. The tense must be derived from the context.

Бы́ло бы поле́зно, е́сли бы они́ смогли́ встре́титься с на́ми.
It would have been useful if they had been able to meet with us (but they didn't meet with us).

Е́сли бы он пришёл в гости́ницу, мы могли́ бы обсуди́ть прое́кт контра́кта.
If he had come to the hotel, we could have discussed the draft contract (but he didn't come).
If he were to come to the hotel, we could discuss the draft contract (but he probably won't come).

3. ЛИ VERSUS ЕСЛИ

Ли, meaning "whether or not," is sometimes confused with е́сли because they can both be translated in English as "if." It is therefore important to remember that whenever "whether or not" *could* be used in English, ли *must* be used in Russian.

Мы не зна́ем, захотя́т ли наши клие́нты подписа́ть но́вый контра́кт.
We don't know if (whether or not) our customers will want to sign the new contract.

Вы не зна́ете, на́чали ли уже́ произво́дство но́вой моде́ли?
Do you know if (whether or not) they have already started producing the new model?

Е́сли is used in all other cases.

Е́сли вы не хоти́те пойти́ туда́, я пойду́ оди́н.
If you don't want to go there, I'll go alone.

Е́сли я получу́ прое́кт сего́дня ве́чером, я вам позвоню́.
If I get the draft copy this evening, I'll give you a call.

Note that the position of ли can be changed for emphasis. It is always placed immediately following the emphasized element. Compare:

Я не зна́ю, господи́на Бра́уна отвезли́ ли в гости́ницу.

I don't know if they drove Mr. Brown to the hotel (they may have driven someone else to the hotel).

Я не зна́ю, не в гости́ницу ли отвезли́ господи́на Бра́уна.

I don't know if they drove Mr. Brown to the hotel (they may have driven him somewhere else).

Вы не зна́ете, не нача́ли ли произво́дство но́вой моде́ли?

Do you know if (whether or not) that's a new model they've started producing?

4. ЯВЛЯ́ТЬСЯ/ЯВИ́ТЬСЯ (TO APPEAR, TO BE)

The verb явля́ться in the imperfective aspect essentially means "to be" and is primarily used to define a subject in more formal or official speech and in periodical texts. Of the two or more nouns linked by the verb явля́ться, the subject defined is in the nominative case and the definition ascribed to it is the instrumental case.

Расшире́ние ассортиме́нта проду́кции явля́ется на́шей гла́вной зада́чей.

An expansion of our product line is our principal task.

Контра́кт явля́ется основно́й фо́рмой юриди́ческих соглаше́ний.

The contract is the basic form of legal agreements.

Господи́н Бра́ун явля́ется президе́нтом большо́й фи́рмы.

Mr. Brown is the president of a large company.

Note that явля́ться is almost exclusively used in the third person, as first person usage would reflect a certain pomposity.

The perfective forms of явля́ться are яви́ться and появи́ться. Яви́ться means "to appear," "to report," or "to arrive" somewhere in an official capacity, where movement from one place to another is involved. It answers the question Куда́? (Where to?). Появи́ться means "to appear" or "to show up" in a place, and answers the question Где? (Where?).

Куда́ мне на́до яви́ться за про́пуском?

Where do I have to report for a pass?

Завтра мне надо будет явиться в суд.
 I have to appear at court tomorrow.

Я попросил его явиться сюда за новым назначением.
 I asked him to report here for his new assignment.

Я не знаю, когда или где появятся нужные нам материалы.
 I don't know where or when the materials we need will show up.

Вчера в местной газете, появилась интересная статья о новом совместном предприятии.
 An interesting article about a new joint venture appeared in yesterday's local paper.

D. ИДИОМАТИКА

AGREED!

There are several ways to express agreement in Russian. In formal situations, you may use:

Договорились! (AGREED!)
Давайте встретимся на заводе в пять часов. —Договорились!
 Let's meet at the plant at five o' clock. —Agreed!

Я согласен/согласна.* (I AGREE.)
Я считаю, что нам необходимо начать производство новой модели как можно скорее. Вы согласны? —Я согласен/согласна.
 I think it is essential for us to start production of the new model as soon as possible. Do you agree? —I agree.

In more informal contexts, you can use:

Давайте! (LET's!)
Давайте поедем сейчас на завод. —Давайте!
 Let's go to the plant now. —Okay!

*This expression can also be used to express agreement with an opinion or viewpoint.

Окей!* (OKAY!)

Ребя́та! Пое́хали на тусо́вку! —Оке́й, пое́хали!
　　Hey, guys, let's take off for the concert!—All right, let's go!

Certain expressions are appropriate in any situation:

Хорошо́! (GOOD!)

Наконе́ц, они́ подписа́ли контра́кт! —Хорошо́! Тепе́рь мо́жно нача́ть
произво́дство.
　　They finally signed the contract! —Good! Now we can start
　　production.

Вы не хоти́те поу́жинать в це́нтре сего́дня ве́чером? —Хорошо́! Дава́йте
встре́тимся у вхо́да в метро́.
　　Would you like to have dinner downtown this evening? —Sure! Let's
　　meet at the subway entrance.

Отли́чно! (EXCELLENT!)

Ма́ма, я пра́вильно отве́тила на все вопро́сы! —Отли́чно! Я о́чень
горжу́сь тобо́й!
　　Mom, I answered all the questions correctly! —Excellent! I am very
　　proud of you!

Вас пригласи́ли уча́ствовать в перегово́рах. Вы пойдёте? —Отли́чно!
Коне́чно пойду́!
　　You have been invited to participate in the negotiations. Will you go?
　　—Excellent! Of course, I will!

Finally, to express somewhat reluctant or matter-of-fact agreement, use

Ла́дно! (ALL RIGHT!)

Мы сейча́с идём в парк, ты идёшь с на́ми? —Ла́дно, иду́.
　　We're going to the park now, are you coming with us? —Okay, I'm
　　coming.

When preceded by ну, reluctance is emphasized.

---

*This English expression is now commonly used to express agreement or approval. It is much
less formal and is heard most often among young people.

Почему́ ты не хо́чешь пойти́ с на́ми на вечери́нку? Бу́дет ве́село! —Ну, ла́дно, пойду́, но за́втра мне на́до ра́но встава́ть!-

Why don't you want to go with us to the party with us? You'll have a good time! —Well, all right, I'll go, but I've got to get up early tomorrow!

E. СТРОГО ПО ДЕЛУ

ВОЗМОЖНОСТИ ДЛЯ КАПИТАЛОВЛОЖЕНИЙ (INVESTMENT OPPORTUNITIES)

In response to the growing number of commercial opportunities in the countries of the former Soviet Union, the U.S. Department of Commerce, in concert with the U.S. Agency for International Development, operates a number of American Business Centers (ABCs) that are designed to encourage U.S. companies to explore trade and investment opportunities and to assist them in conducting business more effectively. ABCs are now located in a large number of Russian cities, including Moscow, St. Petersburg, Yekaterinburg, and Novosibirsk.

In any contemplated business venture, the American businessman is encouraged to engage, first of all, a reliable and experienced Russian consultant (о́пытный консульта́нт) who knows English, as well as a Russian-speaking American adviser, since interpreters (перево́дчики) may not always be sufficiently competent to convey the required business terminology. There are a large number of consulting firms in the major Russian cities that employ bilingual consultants. A good place to start are such long-standing, reputable firms as Deloite & Touche with offices in Moscow and St. Petersburg, or the American Business Centers in Russia, whose addresses can be obtained from the U.S. Department of Commerce Business Information Service, Room H-7413, Washington, D.C. 20230.

One of the safest and most successful types of investment has been the purchase of franchises (френча́йзы). Some of the better known American franchises currently operating in Russia are McDonald's, Alpha-Graphics, Micro-Edge, Baskin-Robbins, and Computerland. Franchises are seen as a powerful stimulus to the process of privatization (приватиза́ция) by offering Russian businessmen an opportunity to acquire their own shops without the fear of losing their savings in a constantly changing economy, particularly if the franchises are associated with established Western companies.

As the process of privatization (приватизáция) continues to develop in the former Soviet Union, so too do opportunities for foreign investment (инострáнное капиталовложéние) in various sectors of the Russian economy. Although the laws and regulations governing the conduct of commerce (торгóвое прáво) are still in flux, the potential of return on investments would seem to outweigh the risks inherent in any susbstantial financial undertaking (финáнсовое начинáние).

Informational sources for American businessmen interested in investment opportunities include the Business Information Service of the Newly Independent States (U.S. Department of Commerce, Room H-7413, Washington, D.C. 20230; tel. 202-482-4655), the Export-Import Bank (811 Vermont Avenue, NW, Washington, D.C. 20230; tel. 202-565-3210), the International Trade Commission (500 E St., SW, Washington, D.C. 20436; tel. 202-205-2000), and the Overseas Private Investment Corporation (1100 New York Avenue, NW, Washington, D.C. 20527; tel. 202-336-8799). The latter organization (OPIC) is a self-financed U.S. agency that provides American businessmen with direct loans (прямы́е зáймы) or loan guarantees (гарáнтии зáймов), as well as insurance against a broad range of political risks (страхóвка капиталовложéний от политúческих рúсков), expropriation (экспроприáция), and currency inconvertibility (неконвертúруемость валю́ты). For a nominal fee, OPIC also offers investment consultation.

The principal vehicles for foreign investment in Russia are the joint stock companies (акционéрные óбщества), which are actually shareholder societies; limited liability companies (обществá огранúченой отвéтсвенности); and partnerships (товáрищества). All of these must be registered with the Ministry of Finance (Министéрство финáнсов) and are subject to various taxes such as a profit tax (налóги на прúбыли), local or regional taxes (мéстные/райóнные налóги), value-added tax or VAT (налóг на добáвленную стóимость), property tax (налóг на недвúжимость), sales tax (налóг с оборóта), and an advertising tax (налóг на рекламúрование). Western investors/partners in the aforementioned enterprises are also subject to a transfer tax (налóг на дéнежные перевóды загранúцу) on any dividends (дивидéнды) transferred to the investor's foreign residence. Companies that are wholly foreign-owned (фúрмы, пóлностью принадлежáщие инострáнцам) are also usually registered as joint stock companies and are increasingly becoming a popular method of direct investment because the registration procedure for such firms is less complicated.

Other avenues open to foreign investors include the purchase of securities (це́нные бума́ги) on Russian exchanges (би́ржи), partial or whole acquisition of a small or medium-sized privatized enterprise (части́чное или по́лное приобрете́ние приватизи́рованного предприя́тия), purchase of shares (а́кции) in Western investment funds such as the Russia Value Fund with principal investments in the oil and gas industry (San Antonio Capital, 15750 IH 10, West, San Antonio, TX 78249), the Russian Partners Fund, fully insured by OPIC, which provides equity (маржа́) in large privatized enterprises (Paine Webber Russia Partners Fund, 1285 Avenue of the Americas, 14th flr., New York, NY 10019), and the Lehman Brothers Russian Fund, engaged in large industrial investments (Lehman Brothers Russia Fund, 3 World Financial Center, 16th flr., New York, NY 10285) among others. An additional good source for information about the Russian emerging securities market is the *Russian Investor* newsletter (Global Investor Publishing, 50 Follen St, Suite 216, Cambridge, MA 02138; tel. 617-864-4999, email 75107.2343@compuserve.com).

УПРАЖНЕНИЯ

A. 1) Переведи́те сле́дующие усло́вные предложе́ния изъяви́тельного наклоне́ния на англи́йский язы́к; 2) По́льзуясь сослага́тельным наклоне́нием, замени́те получа́емые действи́тельные констру́кции гипотети́ческими; 3) Переведи́те получа́емые предложе́ния сослага́тельного наклонения. ((1)Translate the following conditional indicative sentences into English. (2) Then convert these real situations into hypothetical ones by placing them into the subjunctive mood. (3) Translate the new subjunctive sentences.)

Example: Е́сли перево́дчики приду́т на заво́д во́ время, мы смо́жем нача́ть перегово́ры до обе́да.

(1) [translation] If the interpreters arrive at the plant in time, we can begin the negotiations before lunch.

(2) [conversion] Е́сли бы перево́дчики пришли́ на заво́д во́время, мы смогли́ бы нача́ть перегово́ры до обе́да.

(3) [translation] If the interpreters were to arrive at the plant in time, we would be able to begin the negotiations before lunch.*

---

*Note that this sentence could be translated as: "If the interpreters had arrived on time we could have begun the negotiations before lunch" because there is no tense associated with the subjunctive mood.

1. Если вы начнёте произво́дство но́вой моде́ли к ма́рту, мы смо́жем к вам отпра́вить на́ших специали́стов в этом ме́сяце.
2. Если мы подпи́шем но́вый контра́кт, они откро́ют но́вый заво́д в этом году́.
3. Если они́ смо́гут созда́ть совме́стное предприя́тие, они́ увели́чат годово́й объём выпуска́емой проду́кции.
4. Если вы смо́жете встре́титься со мной сего́дня ве́чером, я покажу́ вам програ́мму обуче́ния.
5. Если они́ улу́чшат ка́чество проду́кции, у них бу́дет бо́льше зака́зчиков.

B. В сле́дующих предложе́ниях впиши́те глаго́л в ну́жной фо́рме.

1. Если мы _____ра́но у́тром, мы смо́жем пое́хать на
   _____have breakfast_____
   заво́д пря́мо из гости́ницы.
2. Если бы они_____бо́льше средств на но́вый прое́кт,
   _____had allocated_____
   мы_____ произво́дство но́вой моде́ли в про́шлом
   _____could have begun_____
   году́.
3. _____на заво́де. Там есть хоро́шая столо́вая (cafeteria).
   __Let's have lunch__
4. _____этот вопро́с сего́дня. Мне на́до отдохну́ть.
   __Let's not discuss__
5. _____обсуди́ть пове́стку дня на за́втра.
   __I would like__

C. Переведи́те сле́дующие предложе́ния на ру́сский язы́к. Обраща́йте внима́ние на подходя́щие фо́рмы в усло́вных предложе́ниях.

1. I don't know if they have signed the contract.
2. If it's convenient for you, we can discuss the contract this evening.
3. We would like to increase our annual production and diversify our product line.
4. We have already agreed to meet tomorrow at the hotel.
5. I asked him if the plant is operating at full capacity.

УРОК 10

А. ДИАЛОГ

Но́вости по телеви́зору.

Поу́жинав у себя́ до́ма, Оле́г и На́дя Каса́ткины собира́ются смотре́ть телеви́зор со свои́м го́стем, Ро́бертом.

РОБЕРТ: **Всё бы́ло о́чень вку́сно, На́дя. Спаси́бо огро́мное!**

НАДЯ: **Пожа́луйста. Очень ра́да, что тебе́ понра́вилось. Пра́вда, должна́ сказа́ть, что, в основно́м, гото́вила моя́ ба́бушка.**

РОБЕРТ: **Пра́вда? Она замеча́тельно гото́вит! А где она́ сейча́с?**

НАДЯ: **Пое́хала к сестре́ в Переде́лкино.¹ Вернётся за́втра или послеза́втра. Уже́ почти́ во́семь часо́в! Мо́жет посмо́трим но́вости?**

ОЛЕГ: **Зна́ешь, На́дя, дава́й лу́чше посмо́трим но́вости по тре́тьему кана́лу² в де́вять.**

РОБЕРТ: **А чем вам не нра́вятся но́вости в во́семь?**

ОЛЕГ: **Мне ка́жется, что они́ предподно́сят далеко́ не объекти́вную тракто́вку³ фа́ктов. И вообще́ эта ста́нция представля́ет лишь официа́льные взгля́ды прави́тельства.**

НАДЯ: **Да хва́тит⁴ уже́, Оле́г! Ты про́сто не согла́сен с ны́нешним полити́ческим ку́рсом прави́тельства.⁵ Я наоборо́т счита́ю, что они́ даю́т че́стное освеще́ние⁶ собы́тий.**

ОЛЕГ: **Хорошо́. Дава́й сде́лаем так. Посмо́трим о́бе переда́чи и пусть Ро́берт пото́м разреши́т наш спор. Ты согла́сен, Роберт?**

РОБЕРТ: **Да-да, коне́чно. Мне и самому́ бу́дет интере́сно улови́ть каку́ю-либо тенденцио́зность. А эти но́вости в де́вять передаю́тся по ча́стному кана́лу?**

НАДЯ: **Да, по ча́стному. У нас уже́ появи́лось не́сколько ча́стных телекомпа́ний.**

РОБЕРТ: **И они́, есте́ственно, пока́зывают мно́го рекла́мы?**

ОЛЕГ: Ну, естéственно. Зачастýю, прáвда, вся реклáма[7] прохóдит в сáмом начáле или концé передáчи. (Олег смóтрит на часы́.) Порá, нóвости ужé начались. (включáет телевúзор)

ДИКТОР: . . . Вчерá на заседáнии Государственной Дýмы бы́ло при́нято постановлéние о крити́ческой оцéнке дéятельности прави́тельства по исполнéнию федерáльного бюджéта в пéрвом квартáле гóда. Постановлéние об этом бы́ло при́нято пóсле отчёта пéрвого вице-премьéра прави́тельства. Вы́ступая[8] в Госдýме, вице-премьéр призвáл депутáтов поддержáть плáны прави́тельства по кардинáльному повышéнию тéмпов собирáемости налóгов. Характеризýя ны́нешнюю экономи́ческую ситуáцию, он назвáл ее «непростóй, но и не безнадёжной.» По егó словáм, дохóды от налóгов за предыдýщие три квартáла оказáлись значи́тельно ни́же заплани́рованных и объясни́л это тем, что «на фóне снижáющихся тéмпов инфля́ции, продолжáлся спад произвóдства . . .»

Вскоре после окончания программы новостей Олег переключает телевизор на третий канал.

ОЛЕГ: Давайте тепéрь послýшаем другýю тóчку зрéния.

ДИКТОР: Репортáж составил наш корреспондент из Влади-востóка, Андрей Глушин. Сейчас нóвости о кри́зисе бюд-жéта. На послéднем заседáнии Дума оцени́ла[9] бюджéтную поли́тику прави́тельства как неудовлетвори́тельную и 325[10] голосáми при́няла постановлéние рéзко осуждáющее неспосóбность прави́тельства дорабóтать окончáтельную вéрсию бюджéта на пéрвый квартáл нóвого гóда. В постановлéнии отмечáется пóлная неприéмлемость заплани́-рованного дефици́та в 24 триллиóна рублéй. Государственная Дума потрéбовала объяснéний у отвéтственных лиц . . .[11]

ОЛЕГ: Тепéрь ви́дите рáзницу?

РОБЕРТ: Ви́дишь ли, Олег...

НАДЯ: Ну что, Олéг, мне ещё не поня́тно, на что ты жáлуешь-ся. Ди́ктор пéрвого канáла прóсто сообщáет о попы́тке прави́тельства найти́ объяснéние трýдному положéнию.

ОЛЕГ: Чего тут объяснять? Ясно, что первая программа пытается оправдывать совершенно недопустимое положение!

НАДЯ: Недопустимое?! Что ты подразумеваешь под недопустимым? Перестань преувеличивать! Уже начинаешь выступать, как какой-то политик!

ОЛЕГ: Называй меня, как хочешь! Меня интересует правда, а не оправдывание!

РОБЕРТ: (перебивает разговор) Смотрите, показывают очень смешную рекламу!

ОЛЕГ: Рекламу? Да, да. По этому каналу показывают очень забавные рекламы.

НАДЯ: Ну, по крайней мере, с этим мы согласны!

TV news.

Oleg and Nadya Kasatkin have just finished dinner at their apartment and are about to watch TV with their guest, Robert.

ROBERT: That was delicious, Nadya, thank you very much!

NADYA: You're welcome. I'm glad you enjoyed it. Actually my grandmother did most of the cooking.

ROBERT: Really? She's a great cook! Where is she?

NADYA: She went to see her sister in Peredelkino. She'll probably be back in a day or two. Oh, look, it's almost eight. Do you want to watch the news?

OLEG: You know, Nadya, I prefer to watch the news program on Channel 3 at nine.

ROBERT: What don't you like about the eight o'clock news?

OLEG: I think their reporting is far from objective. That station just gives the official government point of view.

NADYA: Oh, come on, Oleg! You just don't agree with some of the government's policies. I think the reporting is reasonably fair.

OLEG: Okay. Let's do this. We'll watch both programs and let Robert settle our argument. Do you agree, Robert?

ROBERT: Yes, of course. I'll be very interested to see if I can detect any bias. And the news at nine are a privately owned station?

NADYA: Yes. Actually, there are a number of nongovernment stations operating now.

ROBERT: And they, naturally, show a lot of commercials?

OLEG: Well, what else? But in most cases, all the commercials are shown at once, usually at the beginning of a newscast. (*Oleg looks at his watch.*) Oh, the news has already started! (*He turns on the TV.*)

ANNOUNCER: . . . The Russian State Duma adopted a resolution yesterday criticizing the government's handling of the federal budget for the first quarter of the year. The resolution was adopted following a report presented by a government minister that called upon the Duma to support the government's plan to accelerate tax collection. The minister characterized the current economic situation as "difficult but not hopeless." The minister went on to say that tax receipts for the first three months of the year were considerably less than anticipated and attributed this shortfall to "the continuing drop in productivity against the backdrop of lower inflation rates . . ."

Soon after the news program is over, Oleg switches to Channel 3.

OLEG: Now let's listen to a different viewpoint.

ANNOUNCER: . . . that report was prepared by our correspondent in Vladivostok, Andrey Glushin. And now news about the budget crisis. In its last session, the federal Duma labeled the government's budget policies as "unsatisfactory" and adopted a resolution supported by 325 deputies which strongly criticized the government's inability to manage the federal budget during the first quarter of the year. The resolution termed the twenty-four trillion ruble deficit "completely unacceptable" and demanded an explanation on the part of the executive branch . . .

OLEG: Now do you see the difference?

ROBERT: Well, Oleg . . .

NADYA: Oleg, I still don't see what you're complaining about. The newscaster on Channel 1 was merely reporting the government's efforts to explain a difficult situation.

OLEG: What's there to explain? The first program was obviously trying to make excuses for a completely intolerable situation!

NADYA: Intolerable? What do you mean by intolerable? Stop exaggerating! You're beginning to sound just like some politician!

OLEG: Call me what you want! I'm interested in the truth, not excuses!

ROBERT: (*interrupting the conversation*) Look! This commercial is pretty funny!

OLEG: Commercial? Oh yeah, they've got very amusing commercials on this station.

NADYA: Well, at least we can agree on that!

B. ПРИМЕЧАНИЯ

1. Переде́лкино is a small village located twelve miles southwest of Moscow. It is best known as the former residence and burial site of Бори́с Пастерна́к, author of «До́ктор Жива́го». You can ride to Переде́лкино on an electric suburban train (электри́чка) from the Kiev railroad station (Ки́евский вокза́л) in Moscow. The Pasternak House is open to the public Thursdays to Sundays from 10 A.M. to 4 P.M. Pasternak's grave (моги́ла Пастерна́ка) is one mile south of the house.

2. There are five network TV stations serving Moscow, as well as several pay cable channels. St. Petersburg has two local channels. Commercial TV stations include the НТВ (Незави́симое телеви́дение, Independent Television), and ТВ-6 Москва́.

3. Тракто́вка фа́ктов literally means "treatment of facts."

4. Хва́тит! literally means "Enough!, That'll do!" Хва́тит мне спо́рить с тобо́й! (I've had enough of arguing with you!) С меня́ хва́тит! (I've had enough!)

5. Оста́нкино ТВ station is the government-owned facility that broadcasts on Channel 1, called "Росси́я".

6. Освеще́ние собы́тий (lit. illumination of events) is used here in the figurative sense to mean news coverage. По-мо́ему, освеще́ние собы́тий по э́тому кана́лу о́чень объекти́вно. (I think the news coverage on this channel is very objective.) Пе́рвый кана́л заслужи́л

международное призна́ние за своё освеще́ние собы́тий по по́воду переселе́ния бе́женцев. (Channel 1 earned international acclaim for their coverage of the refugee resettlement.)

7. Note that рекла́ма can refer to a television, print, or radio ad. Вся рекла́ма прохо́дит в самом нача́ле переда́чи. (All the commercials are shown at the beginning of the program.) Вы ви́дели вот э́ту заба́вную рекла́му о стира́льном порошке́? (Did you see that funny ad for soap powder?)

8. Выступа́я is an adverbial participle that means "while addressing," or "in addressing." The verb выступа́ть can also mean "to appear" or "to present one's views" on the air, in print, or before some group. Сего́дня ве́чером президе́нт выступа́ет по телеви́зору. (The president will be appearing on TV tonight.) Э́тот писа́тель ча́сто выступа́ет в на́шей газе́те. (This writer often appears in our newspaper.)

9. Оцени́ть is a commonly used verb meaning "to estimate, to judge, to evaluate." Они оцени́ли наше иму́щество в сто ты́сяч до́лларов. (They appraised our property at one hundred thousand dollars.) Мы оцени́ли его выступле́ние как соверше́нно бесполе́зное. (We judged his address to be completely useless.)

10. Note the use of the instrumental case to mean "by a vote of 325". The numeral written out would be тремя́ста́ми двадцатью́ пятью́. Законопрое́кт был при́нят четырьмя́ста́ми голоса́ми за и двумя́ста́ми про́тив. (The bill was adopted after a vote of four hundred for and two hundred against it.)

11. Отве́тственные ли́ца literally means "person responsible"; i.e., officials responsible for policymaking.

C. ГРАММАТИКА И СЛОВОУПОТРЕБЛЕНИЕ

1. ДЕЙСТВИТЕЛЬНЫЕ И СТРАДАТЕЛЬНЫЕ ПРИЧАСТИЯ (ACTIVE AND PASSIVE VOICE PARTICIPLES)

Russian participles retain the characteristics of both an adjective and a verb (and are therefore often called "verbal adjectives"). Like verbs, they reflect tense and voice, and, like adjectives, they agree with the nouns they modify in case, number, and gender.

a) Действи́тельные прича́стия настоя́щего вре́мени (PRESENT ACTIVE PARTICIPLES)

Present active participles are formed only from imperfective verbs by replacing the final -т of the third person plural form of the verb with -щий, -щая, -щее, or -щие. For example: получа́ть→получа́ют→ получа́ющий/ая/ее/ие (receiving). This form frequently corresponds to the -ing form in English and is used to describe an action occurring simultaneously with the action of the main verb.

Ста́нции, не получа́ющие подде́ржку от прави́тельства, нахо́дятся в финансовой зави́симости от зри́тельской аудито́рии. поже́ртвований от зри́телей.
Stations not receiving government support depend on viewer contributions.

Делега́ты, обсужда́ющие этот вопро́с, наве́рное, бу́дут встреча́ться ещё раз на сле́дующей неде́ле.
The delegates discussing this question will probably meet again next week.

Remember that participles can be replaced with кото́рый clauses, which are used much more frequently in conversation.

Ста́нции, кото́рые не получа́ют подде́ржку от прави́тельства, нахо́дятся в финансовой зави́симости от зри́тельской аудито́рии.
Stations that do not receive government support depend on viewer contributions.

Делега́ты, кото́рые обсужда́ют этот вопро́с, бу́дут встреча́ться ещё раз на сле́дующей неде́ле.
The delegates who are discussing this question will probably meet again next week.

Frequently, as in the above case, the preferred English translation is rendered by "who," "which," and "that" clauses rather than the corresponding English -ing form of the verb. Also note that, whereas in the English the participle normally follows the modified noun, Russian participles can be placed either before or after the nouns they modify.

Не получа́ющие подде́ржку от прави́тельства ста́нции нахо́дятся в
фина́нсовой зави́симости от зри́тельской аудито́рии.
Stations not receiving governmental support depend on viewer
contributions.

In the above example there is considerable distance between the
participle получа́ющие and the noun it modifies: ста́нции. This is a
typical participle construction in formal and printed literature. The
modified nouns can easily be identified and related to their verbal
adjective by noting the agreement in case, number, gender, and, of
course, logic.

Програ́ммы, представля́ющие лишь официа́льные взгля́ды, не
по́льзуются большо́й популя́рностью.
Представля́ющие лишь официа́льные взгля́ды програ́ммы не
по́льзуются большо́й популя́рностью.
The programs presenting official views only are not very popular.

Once again, the preceding sentences with partciples could also be rendered with a кото́рый clause.

Програ́ммы, кото́рые представля́ют лишь официа́льные взгля́ды, не
по́льзуются большо́й популя́рностью.
Programs that present only official news are not very popular.

У нас име́ется не́сколько незави́симо рабо́тающих телеста́нций.
We have several independently operating TV stations.

У нас име́ется не́сколько телеста́нций, кото́рые рабо́тают незави́симо.
We have several TV stations that operate independently.

Иду́щие в по́льзу телестанци́й нало́ги собира́ются прави́тельством.
Taxes used to support TV stations are collected by the government.

Прави́тельство собира́ет нало́ги, иду́щие в по́льзу телеста́нций.
The government collects taxes that go to support TV stations.

Прави́тельство собира́ет нало́ги, кото́рые иду́т в по́льзу телеста́нций.
The government collects taxes that go to support TV stations.

b) Действи́тельные прича́стия проше́дшего вре́мени (PAST TENSE
  ACTIVE PARTICIPLES)

Past active participles are formed by replacing the past tense ending
of an imperfective or perfective verb with -вший, -вшая, -вшее, -вшие
(in the appropriate case endings). For example: посмотре́ть → посмотре́л
→ посмотре́вший (having watched/watched) or смотре́ть → смотре́л →
смотре́вший (were watching). This form is used to denote an action that
occurred prior to the action of the main verb.

Зри́тели, посмотре́вшие вчера́шнюю переда́чу по тре́тьему кана́лу,
бы́ли очень разочаро́ваны выступле́нием нового веду́щего.
  The viewers who watched yesterday's broadcast on Channel 3 were
  very disappointed by the new anchorperson's presentation. (perfective)

Зри́тели, смотре́вшие но́вости по второ́му кана́лу, реши́ли перек-
лючи́ться на друго́й кана́л.
  The viewers, having seen the news on Channel 2, decided to switch to
  another channel. (imperfective)

Verbs in the past tense that do not end in -л in the third person singular,
masculine form take the participial suffix -ший, e.g., помога́ть → помо́г
→ помо́гший (having helped/had helped); принести́ → принёс →
принёсший (brought/had brought).

Помо́гшие мне перевести́ эту статью́ колле́ги прекра́сно владе́ют
ру́сским языко́м.
  The colleagues who helped me translate this article have an excellent
  command of Russian.

Принёсший мне сего́дня у́тром русские газе́ты студе́нт за́втра ве́чером
уезжа́ет в Москву́.
  The student who brought me the Russian newspapers this morning is
  leaving for Moscow tomorrow evening.

Past tense participles can also be replaced with кото́рый clauses.

Ста́нции, кото́рые получа́ли подде́ржку от прави́тельства, не пла́тят
нало́ги.
  Stations that were receiving governmental support do not pay taxes.

Студе́нт, кото́рый сего́дня у́тром принёс мне ру́сские газе́ты, за́втра ве́чером уезжа́ет в Москву́.

The student, who brought me the Russian newspapers this morning, is leaving for Moscow tomorrow evening.

c) Действи́тельные прича́стия, образо́ванные от возвра́тных глаго́лов (ACTIVE VOICE PARTICIPLES FORMED FROM REFLEXIVE VERBS)

Remember that active participles formed from reflexive verbs retain the -ся suffix regardless of whether the suffix is preceded by a vowel or consonant.

Скла́дывающаяся у нас систе́ма приватиза́ции влечёт за собо́й мно́го затрудне́ний.

Our developing system of privatization entails many difficulties.

Мы говори́ли с дру́гом, затрудня́вшимся отвеча́ть на эти вопро́сы.

We were speaking with a friend who was having difficulty in answering these questions.

2. СТРАДАТЕЛЬНЫЕ ПРИЧАСТИЯ НАСТОЯЩЕГО ВРЕМЕНИ (PASSIVE PRESENT PARTICIPLES)

In most cases, passive present tense participles are formed by adding the appropriate adjectival ending (-ый, -ая, -ое, -ие,) to the first person plural form of imperfective verbs. Remember that only verbs that normally take a direct object can be used in the passive voice, and the direct object then becomes the subject of the passive verb. For example, плани́ровать → плани́руем → плани́руемый (being planned).

Програ́ммы, плани́руемые но́вой ста́нцией, представля́ют значи́тельный интере́с.

The programs being planned by the new station are of considerable interest.

Мно́гие из иностра́нных изде́лий, реклами́руемых по ру́сскому телеви́дению, мне весьма́ знако́мы.

I am quite familiar with many of the foreign products being advertised on Russian TV.

Although you should be able to recognize and form present tense passive participles, they are used primarily in formal, scientific, and technical correspondence, and in literature. More commonly, and particularly in colloquial usage, the passive voice is rendered by a reflexive verb or simply by the third person plural form of the verb when no agent of action is specified.

Нало́ги собира́ются прави́тельством.
Taxes are collected by the government.

По суббо́там, по пе́рвому кана́лу, часто передаю́т очень интере́сные програ́ммы о после́дних зарубе́жных фи́льмах.
On Saturdays, Channel 1 often broadcasts very interesting programs about the latest foreign films.

Здесь говоря́т по-русски.
Russian is spoken here.

3. СТРАДАТЕЛЬНЫЕ ПРИЧАСТИЯ ПРОШЕДШЕГО ВРЕМЕНИ (PAST PASSIVE PARTICIPLES)

Remember that long-form participles are used as adjectives, whereas short-form participles can only be used when some form of the verb "to be" comes between the noun and the relevant participle.

Пи́сьма, напи́санные мои́м бра́том, лежа́т на столе́.
The letters written by my brother are lying on the table. (long form)

Эти пи́сьма бы́ли напи́саны мои́м бра́том.
These letters were written by my brother. (short form)

A) LONG-FORM PARTICIPLES

The long-form (attributive) past passive participles decline like adjectives and are formed from perfective transitive verbs (those that take a direct object) by replacing the infinitive ending -ть with -нн- (for most verbs ending in -ать/-ять), -енн- (for most verbs ending in -ить),* or -т- (for a limited number of Conjugation I verbs) and adding the appropri-

---

*Consonant mutations often occur in verbs endng in -ить: приготóвить (to prepare) → приготóвленный (prepared) предстáвить (to represent, present) → предстáвленный (represented, presented) купи́ть (to buy) → ку́пленный (bought, purchased) постáвить (to place, put) → постáвленный (placed, put).

ate adjectival ending.* Like the present passive forms, the past passive participles are primarily used in formal correspondence and literature. Here are some examples:

to write	написа́ть	напи́санный/ая/ое/ые	written
to support	поддержа́ть	подде́ржанный	supported
to transmit	переда́ть	пере́данный	transmitted
to receive	получи́ть	полу́ченный	received
to include, to switch on	включи́ть	включённый	included, switched on
to begin	нача́ть	на́чатый	begun

Пи́сьма, напи́санные ва́шим бра́том, наконе́ц пришли́ сего́дня утром.
The letters written by your brother finally arrived this morning.

Куда́ вы положи́ли полу́ченные на́ми вчера́ докуме́нты?
Where did you put the documents we received yesterday?

Вопро́сы, поста́вленные на сего́дняшнюю пове́стку дня, нам показа́лись очень актуа́льными.
We felt that the questions placed on today's agenda are very urgent.

Програ́ммы, пере́данные новой ста́нцией, фина́нсировались ча́стными поже́ртвователями.
The programs broadcast by the new station were financed by private contributors.

Все изде́лия, включённые в эту рекла́му, произво́дятся за грани́цей.
All the items included into this ad are produced abroad.

B) SHORT-FORM PASSIVE PARTICIPLES

Short-form passive participles are formed from their long-form counterparts by dropping the adjectival endings and adding nothing for the masculine form, -a for feminine, -o for neuter, or -ы for plural. Only one -н- is retained from past passive participles formed with -нн-.

Письмо́ бы́ло напи́сано твои́м бра́том.
The letter was written by your brother.

*There are a few verbs whose past passive participles do not conform to these rules: найти (to find) → на́йденный (found), уви́деть (to see) → уви́денный (seen), укра́сть (to steal) → укра́денный (stolen), and съесть (to eat up) → съе́денный (eaten up).

Телеви́зор был включён ро́вно в во́семь часо́в.
　The TV was turned on at exactly eight o' clock.

Прое́кт зако́на был поддёржан большинство́м делега́тов.
　The draft bill was supported by a majority of the delegates.

Вопро́с был поста́влен на пове́стку дня, но не был обсуждён.
　The question was placed on the agenda, but it wasn't discussed.

Вы не зна́ете, кем бы́ли ку́плены но́вые компью́теры?
　Do you know who bought the new computers?

Мне сказа́ли, что вчера́ апте́ка была́ закры́та весь день на учёт.
　I was told that the pharmacy was closed all day yesterday to take
　inventory.

D. ИДИОМАТИКА

FACT OR FICTION?

Here are some useful expressions about hearsay and news.

Вот ещё но́вости! (THAT'S NEWS TO ME!)

Ты слы́шал, что заве́дующий вы́шел в отста́вку? —Вот ещё
но́вости!
　Did you hear that the manager resigned? —Well, how do you
　like that!

Худы́е ве́сти не лежа́т на ме́сте. (BAD NEWS TRAVELS FAST.)

Я то́лько что узна́л, что фи́рма уво́лит двухсо́т слу́жащих! — Да, зна́ю.
Худы́е ве́сти не лежа́т на ме́сте.
　I just found out that the company is going to fire 200 employees!
　— Yes, I know. Bad news travels fast.

Слу́хами земля́ по́лнится (TO HEAR SOMETHING THROUGH THE
GRAVEVINE; LIT., THE WORLD GETS FILLED WITH GOSSIP)

This expression is used to avoid naming a source of information.

Откýда ты знáешь, что я прúнял нóвую дóлжность? —Слýхами земля́ пóлнится.

How did you know I was taking a new job? —I heard it through the grapevine.

По слýхам (THROUGH HEARSAY)

По слýхам, президéнт сегóдня вéчером не выступáет по телевúдению.
Rumor has it that the president's not going to appear on TV tonight.

Откры́ть Амéрику! (SO, WHAT ELSE IS NEW!; LIT., TO DISCOVER AMERICA)

Знаешь, снóва повы́сят цéну на хлеб! —Ну, Амéрику откры́л!
You know, they're going to raise the price of bread again! — So, what else is new?

E. СТРОГО ПО ДЕЛУ

РЕКЛАМА ПО ТЕЛЕВИДЕНИЮ (ADVERTISING ON TELEVISION)

Revenue from advertising has become a vital source of income for both government and privately owned stations. In a striking departure from former practice, the principal, state-owned TV station, Остáнкино, Channel 1, for example, established its own in-house advertising agency (сóбственное агéнтство по реклáме) which sells airtime at rates ranging from $3,000 to $25,000 per minute. This station operates around the clock and reaches a potential viewing audience (зрúтели) of 200 million across the entire territory of the former Soviet Union. The other state-owned TV stations charge somewhat less, but they also have a shorter broadcast day. Russian TV and Radio (Россúйское телевúдение и рáдио), on Channel 2 and St. Petersburg, Channel 5, operate about 18 hours daily with potential viewing and listening audiences of 140 and 90 million, respectively.

The Channel 2 station was created as a spin-off from Остáнкино and is operated as a joint stock company (акционéрное óбщество) with 51 percent of the shares owned by the state. The news programs on this channel (Вéсти) are considered to be more impartial (беспристрáстный) than the «Врéмя» news programs on Channel 1.

The largest and fastest growing privately owned station is Moscow-based TV-6, which was begun as a joint venture with the Turner Broadcasting System in 1993. TV-6 operates 20 hours daily and has a potential audience of 60 million viewers in 60 cities. Its advertising rates range from $1,000 to $5,000 per minute. The other rapidly developing privately owned stations are Independent TV (НТВ—Незави́симое телеви́дение), which reaches a potential audience of 100 million in European Russia, but broadcasts for only 8 hours daily, and TV Channel 2X2, (Телекана́л 2X2) which is owned by nineteen individual investors (ча́стные инве́сторы) and often includes English-language programming from CBS and Russian-dubbed news from the BBC. It operates 15 hours daily, has a potential viewing audience of 25 million in the Moscow region, and charges $800 to $1,000 per minute for advertising air time.

Most frequently advertised items include banking and investment services, followed by travel and real estate opportunities, electronic appliances, and the usual broad range of consumer products, both foreign and domestic. Airtime for ads can be arranged directly with the stations or with the help of a rapdily growing number of both Western and Russian agencies that offer a full range of services for advertising in the media, including TV and radio. Some of the more prominent agencies in Moscow are Ко́смос-ТВ, Arrange Media Service, and Светорекла́ма TV. These and other agencies can also provide market research (изуче́ние ры́нка).

УПРАЖНЕНИЯ

A. В сле́дующих предложе́ниях замени́те прида́точные предложе́ния действи́тельными прича́стями настоя́щего вре́мени. (Replace the subordinate clauses with present active participles in the following sentences.)

ОБРАЗЕЦ: Лю́ди, кото́рые де́лают поже́ртвования на ста́нции, ре́дко смо́трят комме́рческие переда́чи.
Лю́ди, де́лающие поже́ртвования на ста́нции, ре́дко смо́трят комме́рческие переда́чи.

1. Нало́ги, кото́рые иду́т в по́льзу телеста́нций, собира́ются прави́тельством.
2. Програ́ммы, кото́рые представля́ют официа́льные взгля́ды прави́тельства, не опла́чиваются рекла́мами.

3. Ста́нции, кото́рые рабо́тают незави́симо, не получа́ют подде́ржку от прави́тельства.

4. Зри́тели, кото́рые лю́бят спорт, всегда смо́трят футбо́льные ма́тчи по телви́зору по воскресе́ньям.

5. Студе́нты, кото́рые затрудня́ются отвеча́ть на эти вопро́сы, должны́ занима́ться поча́ще.

B. В да́нных предложе́ниях замени́те прида́точные предложе́ния действи́тельными прича́стиями проше́дшего вре́мени. (Replace the subordinate clauses with active past tense participles. Be careful about using the corresponding imperfective or perfective form of the participle).

1. Зри́тели, кото́рые о́чень внима́тельно следи́ли за новостя́ми, легко́ мо́гли суди́ть об объекти́вности освеще́ния собы́тий.

2. Мои́ друзья́, кото́рые вчера́ купи́ли но́вые ла́мпы, сказа́ли мне, что их реклами́руют по телеви́дению.

3. Сосе́д, кото́рый согласи́лся с жено́й, то́же счита́ет, что репорта́ж по второ́му кана́лу весьма́ беспристра́стен.

4. Зри́тели, кото́рые посмотре́ли втору́ю програ́мму, жа́ловались на коли́чество рекла́м.

C. Замени́те прида́точные предложе́ния страда́тельными прича́стиями настоя́щего вре́мени. (Replace the subordinate clauses with present passive participles.)

1. Проду́кты, кото́рые реклами́руют по телеви́зору, по́льзуются большо́й популя́рностью.

2. Проце́сс приватиза́ции, кото́рый плани́рует прави́тельство, наве́рное, бу́дет продолжа́ться в тече́ние мно́гих лет.

3. По-мо́ему, ка́чество това́ров, кото́рые предлага́ют зарубе́жные фи́рмы, о́чень хоро́шее.

4. Поже́ртвования, кото́рые получа́ют станции, иду́т на нало́ги.

D. Переведи́те сле́дующие предложе́ния с английского языка́ на ру́сский, по́льзуясь прича́стиями в подходя́щих места́х. (Translate the following sentences from English to Russian using participles wherever appropriate.)

1. The programs being paid for by commercials are very popular.

2. The taxes received by the government go to support several TV stations.

3. Some commercial stations that are being supported by the government also receive listener contributions.
4. We usually watch the news on Channel 3 at 10 P.M. because the reporting is not biased.
5. There are several independently operating stations in our city.
6. Most of the commercials on Channel 2 are shown at the beginning of the program.
7. The stations that receive financial support from viewers usually do not show commercials.
8. The computers purchased by our university are very popular.
9. When we arrived home, the TV was already turned on.
10. The letters written by your uncle were received (by us) yesterday.

ПРЕДЛАГАЕМЫЕ ЗАНЯТИЯ

Find the TV listings in a fairly current Russian newspaper and compare the type of programming on the various channels. Select the programs you find interesting. Compare the offerings to U.S. programs. Alternatively, consult your local cable TV listings, and try to find a Russian news program. Compare the coverage, in both style and content, to U.S. news programs.

УРОК 11

А. ДИАЛОГ

Откры́тие ба́нковского счёта.[1]

Америка́нский бизнесме́н Ма́ртин Ча́вез, кото́рый намерева́ется откры́ть в Москве́ представи́тельство свое́й американской компа́нии, и сопровожда́ющий его́ ру́сский колле́га Арка́дий Фи́рсов захо́дят в отделе́ние ба́нка "Росси́йский Креди́т"[2] с це́лью откры́ть счёт. Они́ направля́ются в кабине́т ба́нковской слу́жащей Ве́ры Каза́нской.

КАЗА́НСКАЯ: Ну, с, чем могу́ быть поле́зна?

ЧА́ВЕЗ: Я сейча́с открыва́ю представи́тельство на́шей фи́рмы, и поэ́тому нам необходи́мо завести́[3] корпорати́вный счёт в ба́нке.

КАЗА́НСКАЯ: Наш банк с удово́льствием возьмёт на себя́ э́ту зада́чу. Вы уже́ прошли́ через все форма́льности, свя́занные с регистра́цией о́фиса?

ЧА́ВЕЗ: (повора́чиваясь к Фи́рсову) Спаси́бо Арка́дию, почти́ все форма́льности уже́ позади́, не так ли, Арка́дий?

ФИ́РСОВ: То́чно. Не да́лее[4] чем сего́дня утром, мы получи́ли после́дний докуме́нт, подтвержда́ющий ликви́дность и платёжеспосо́бность компа́нии. Вот заве́ренная ру́сская ко́пия.

КАЗА́НСКАЯ: (просма́тривает докуме́нт) Что ж, всё в ажу́ре.[5] Вы, наве́рное, уже́ зна́ете, каки́е услу́ги предоставля́ет наш банк. Како́й счёт вы хоте́ли бы откры́ть?

ЧА́ВЕЗ: Пре́жде всего́ мне пона́добится ли́чный теку́щий[6] счёт, поско́льку я бу́ду здесь находи́ться по кра́йней ме́ре год.

КАЗА́НСКАЯ: Мы мо́жем Вам предложи́ть как сро́чный, так и бессро́чный счёт.

ЧА́ВЕЗ: И вы предлага́ете проце́нты[7] по вкла́дам?

КАЗА́НСКАЯ: Коне́чно, но Вы должны́ понима́ть, что проце́нты по сро́чному вкла́ду не́сколько вы́ше, чем по бессро́чному. Но при этом Вы обязу́етесь не снима́ть[8] де́ньги с этого счёта в тече́ние огово́ренного сро́ка. Чем до́льше срок, тем[9] вы́ше проце́нт вы́плат.

ЧА́ВЕЗ: Так-так. Ну для себя́ самого́ я откро́ю, поло́жим, бессро́чный счёт. А что каса́ется на́шего корпорати́вного счёта, мо́жем ли мы откры́ть как рублёвый, так и до́лларовый счета́?

КАЗА́НСКАЯ: Почему́ бы[10] и нет? Кста́ти, а не хоте́ли бы Вы име́ть корпорати́вную ка́рту в на́шем ба́нке? Нали́чие этой ка́рты упроща́ет[11] проце́сс вы́плат и эконо́мит Ва́ше вре́мя.

ЧА́ВЕЗ: Неплоха́я иде́я. Да, и ещё мне хоте́лось бы получи́ть аккредити́в от Ва́шего ба́нка.

КАЗА́НСКАЯ: Это одна́ из на́ших станда́ртных услу́г. Сра́зу же по́сле откры́тия счёта с нача́льным вкла́дом мы смо́жем заня́ться его составле́нием.[12]

ЧА́ВЕЗ: Могу́ ли я откры́ть счёт пря́мо сейчас?

КАЗА́НСКИЙ: Вам сле́дует обрати́ться[13] в тре́тье окно́. То́лько потре́буется па́спорт.[14] Пото́м зайди́те опя́ть ко мне, и мы вплотну́ю займёмся аккредити́вом.

ЧА́ВЕЗ: Спаси́бо. (Ча́вез и Фи́рсов направля́ются к две́ри.)

КАЗА́НСКАЯ: Совсе́м забы́ла спроси́ть Вас! Вы бу́дете получа́ть зарпла́ту от Ва́шего ба́нка в Шта́тах или от ме́стного ба́нка?

ЧА́ВЕЗ: Из Шта́тов.

КАЗА́НСКАЯ: В тако́м слу́чае, так как у нас име́ются корреспонде́нтские соглаше́ния с большинство́м из америка́нских ба́нков, если Вы жела́ете, мы могли́ бы переводи́ть Ва́шу зарпла́ту непосре́дственно на ваш счёт у нас.

ЧА́ВЕЗ: Спаси́бо. Я поду́маю об этом.

ФИ́РСОВ: (гля́дя на свои́ часы́) Ма́ртин, зна́ете, че́рез два́дцать мину́т у меня́ назна́чена встре́ча в офисе. Дава́йте встре́тимся там же, когда́ Вы освободи́тесь здесь, ла́дно?

ЧА́ВЕЗ: Хорошо́. Пока́.

Откры́в счёт в «Росси́йском Креди́те» Ча́вез сно́ва захо́дит в кабине́т Каза́нской.

КАЗАНСКАЯ: Всё в поря́дке?

ЧАВЕЗ: Да, тепе́рь мо́жно заня́ться де́лом!

КАЗАНСКАЯ: Дава́йте . . . Ита́к, како́го ро́да аккредити́в Вам ну́жен?

ЧАВЕЗ: Че́стно говоря́, я не о́чень уве́рен . . .

КАЗАНСКАЯ: Вы выступа́ете как зака́зчик и́ли как поста́вщик?

ЧАВЕЗ: Как зака́зчик.

КАЗАНСКАЯ: В тако́м слу́чае, наилу́чшим реше́нием бу́дет отзывно́й[15] аккредити́в, поско́льку э́то даёт Вам свобо́ду прекрати́ть вы́платы ещё до нача́ла поста́вки.

ЧАВЕЗ: А креди́т бу́дет предоста́влен в СКВ?[16]

КАЗАНСКАЯ: Есте́ственно. Запо́лните, пожа́луйста, вот э́ту фо́рму. Е́сли Вам зара́нее изве́стен банк поставщика́, э́то значи́тельно уско́рит де́ло.

ЧАВЕЗ: Сего́дня ве́чером Арка́дий мне обо всём расска́жет.

КАЗАНСКАЯ: Хорошо́. Что—нибудь ещё?

ЧАВЕЗ: Нет, пока́ всё, спаси́бо.

КАЗАНСКАЯ: Вот моя́ визи́тка.[17] Е́сли бу́дут вопро́сы, звони́те.

ЧАВЕЗ: Спаси́бо ещё раз за Ва́шу по́мощь!

КАЗАНСКАЯ: Что Вы, не сто́ит.[18]

Opening a bank account.

American businessman Martin Chavez, who is opening a Moscow office of his stateside company, is accompanied by a Russian colleague, Arkady Firsov, to a branch of the Russian Credit Bank to open a corporate account. They proceed to the office of bank officer Vera Kazanskaya.

KAZANSKAYA: So, how can I be of service?

CHAVEZ: I'm here to open an office for our company, and I would like to open a corporate account.

KAZANSKAYA: Our bank would be happy to arrange that for you. Have you already taken care of all the formalities regarding registering your office?

CHAVEZ: (turning to Firsov) Thanks to Arkady, I think almost all the formalities are behind us. Right, Arkady?

FIRSOV: Yes. Just this morning we received the last document certifying the liquidity and payment capabilities of the company. Here's a certified Russian translation.

KAZANSKAYA: (looking over the document) Very good. Everything seems to be in order, then. Well, as you may know, our bank provides a full range of services. What type of account would you like to open?

CHAVEZ: First of all, I'll need a personal checking account since I'll probably be here for at least a year.

KAZANSKAYA: We offer both time-deposit and non-fixed term accounts.

CHAVEZ: Do those accounts yield interest?

KAZANSKAYA: Certainly, but time-deposit accounts have a higher interest rate than non-fixed term accounts. However, you cannot withdraw any funds for a fixed period of time. The longer the period, the higher the interest.

CHAVEZ: I see. Well, for my own personal use, I think a non-fixed term account will do. Now, as to our corporate account, can we open both dollar and ruble accounts?

KAZANSKAYA: By all means. Incidentally, would you like a corporate card issued by our bank? It would simplify transactions and save you time.

CHAVEZ: Not a bad idea. Oh, yes, I'd also like to get a letter of credit issued by your bank.

KAZANSKAYA: That's one of our standard services. As soon as you open an account with an initial deposit, we can process it for you.

CHAVEZ: Can I open the account right now?

KAZANSKAYA: You can take care of that at Window 3. You'll just need your passport. Afterward, come back to see me, and we'll deal with the letter of credit.

CHAVEZ: Thank you. (Chavez and Firsov start for the door.)

KAZANSKAYA: Oh, yes, I completely forgot to ask you. Will you be receiving your salary directly from the States or through a local bank?

CHAVEZ: From the States.

KAZANSKAYA: In that case, since we maintain correspondent relations with most major banks in the States, if you wish, we can arrange to have your salary checks deposited directly into your account here.

CHAVEZ: Thank you. I'll think about it.

FIRSOV: (looking at his watch) Martin, I've got an appointment at the office in twenty minutes. Why don't you meet me there when you get through here, okay?

CHAVEZ: Fine. I'll see you later.

Having opened an account, Chavez returns to Kazanskaya's office.

KAZANSKAYA: Everything in order?

CHAVEZ: Yes, I think we're in business now!

KAZANSKAYA: Now, what type of letter of credit do you need?

CHAVEZ: Frankly, I'm not really sure . . .

KAZANSKAYA: Will you be using the letter as the buyer or seller?

CHAVEZ: As the buyer.

KAZANSKAYA: In that case, the best solution would be a revocable letter that gives you the freedom to withdraw the credit at any time prior to delivery.

CHAVEZ: And the credit will be in freely convertible currency?

KAZANSKAYA. Of course. Just fill out this form. If you already know the seller's bank, that will speed up the process considerably.

CHAVEZ: Arkady will give me all the information this evening.

KAZANSKAYA: Good. Is there anything else I can help you with?

CHAVEZ: No, that's all for now. Thank you.

KAZANSKAYA: Here's my business card. If you have any questions, call me.

CHAVEZ: Thanks again for your help.

KAZANSKAYA: Not at all.

B. ПРИМЕЧАНИЯ

1. The noun счёт has the irregular plural счета. Be sure not to confuse it with the older plural form счёты, which is now used almost exclusively in reference to an abacus. Счёт has a variety of meanings, in addition to "account." Дайте мне счёт, пожалуйста. (May I have the check, please.) Какой был счёт? (What was the score?) Не беспокойтесь, это всё будет за мой счёт. (Don't worry, this will all be at my expense.) В конечном счёте, они решили не обменивать свои доллары. (In the final analysis, they decided not to exchange their dollars.) Они у нас на хорошем счету. (We regard them in good standing.)

2. Note that the title of a book, newspaper, or institution in quotation marks is not declined if preceded by the noun that defines it. Compare: Они были в банке «Российский Кредит». (They were at the Российский Кредит bank.) Они открыли счёт в «Российском Кредите». (They opened an account at the Российский Кредит.) Мы часто читаем газету «Комсомольская Правда». (We often read the newspaper Комсомольская Правда.) Мы часто читаем «Комсомольскую Правду». (We often read Комсомольская Правда.)

3. Завести here means "to acquire" but the verb заводить/завести has a number of other meanings as well. Он сел в машину и быстро завёл мотор. (He got into the car and quickly started the motor.) Она действительно, умеет завести* его. (She really knows how to attract his attention.)

4. Не далее как (as recently as) is commonly used when discussing business in Russian. Не далее, как вчера, он открыл у нас счёт, а сегодня он решил закрыть его. (It was only yesterday that he opened an account with us, and today he decided to close it.) Не далее, чем сегодня, он наводил справки об открытии счёта. (Just this morning he was asking about opening an account.)

5. В ажуре (from the French *à jour*) is a more formal way of saying "up to date." Все счета в ажуре. (All the accounts are up to date.) This expression is also used colloquially to express that everything is in order: Всё у нас в полном ажуре. Сейчас, нам осталось только подождать приезда гостей. (Everything here is all set. Now we can just wait for the guests to arrive.)

*This meaning implies emotional and/or sexual arousal.

6. Теку́щий счёт is a demand deposit or current account. This term can also refer to a checking account, where available. Сберега́тельный счёт is a savings account.

7. Note that the term "interest" as applied to a bank account or investment is normally rendered by the plural проце́нты, which literally means "percent."

8. "To withdraw money from an account" can be rendered by either снима́ть/снять or брать/взять (де́ньги) со счёта.

9. Чем . . . тем is a "the more . . . the more" comparative construction. Both чем and тем are followed by the short form of the comparative adjective.* Чем скоре́е вы откро́ете счёт, тем ле́гче нам бу́дет вы́дать вам аккредити́в. (The sooner you open an account, the easier it will be for us to issue a letter of credit.) Ско́лько де́нег я до́лжен положи́ть на э́тот счёт? —Чем бо́льше, тем лу́чше! (How much money do I have to put into this account? —The more the better!)

10. Here the particle бы adds a polite affirmation to something taken for granted: Почему́ бы и нет. (But of course there would be no problem.) A response of "Почему́ нет?" (Why not?) might be interpreted as condescending. In general, when in doubt, it is better to err on the side of politeness and use бы in all responses or requests.

11. The verb упроща́ть/упрости́ть (to simplify) also has a pejorative meaning. Вы совсе́м упроща́ете о́чень сло́жный вопро́с. (You're completely oversimplifying a very complex problem.)

12. Заня́ться составле́нием is a somewhat formal business expression that means "to draw documents." Мы сейча́с занима́емся составле́нием необходи́мого вам безотзы́вного аккредити́ва. (We are now in the process of drawing up the straight L/C you require.)

13. Remember that обраща́ться/обрати́ться is followed by в/на plus the accusative case to indicate a place (куда́), к plus the dative case to indicate a person (кому́), and за plus the instrumental case to express the object sought. Они́ обрати́лись к нам за по́мощью. (They turned to us for help.) Я ему́ посове́товал обрати́ться в тре́тье окно́ за информа́цией об откры́тии счёта. (I advised him to go to Window 3 for information about opening an account.)

14. A passport is also required for cashing traveler's checks or exchanging money at a bank. Passports are not required for changing dollars to rubles at exchange booths (обме́н валю́ты) in retail stores or hotels.

15. Отзывно́й аккредити́в is a revocable L/C usually issued by a purchaser's bank to the seller's bank. Безотзы́вный аккредитив is a straight or irrevocable L/C.

*See Lesson 12 for discussion of comparative forms of adjectives.

16. СКВ stands for свобóдно конверти́руемая валю́та (freely convertible currency).

17. Визи́тка derives from визи́тная ка́рточка.

18. Не сто́ит is a shortened form of "не сто́ит благода́рности" (lit., no thanks are necessary).

C. ГРАММАТИКА И СЛОВОУПОТРЕБЛЕНИЕ

1. ПРЕДЛОГИ, ВЫРАЖАЮЩИЕ ПРОСТРАНСТВЕННЫЕ ОТНОШЕНИЯ (PREPOSITIONS DENOTING SPATIAL RELATIONSHIPS)

A) DIRECTION VERSUS LOCATION

Russian differentiates between location (stationary) and direction (movement). The prepositions у, в, and на are used to indicate location. To express temporary location, generally in relation to people, use у + the genitive case.

Они стоя́т в о́череди у второ́го окна́.
They're standing in line at Window 2.

Она́ бу́дет вас ждать у вы́хода из ба́нка.
She'll be waiting for you at the bank exit.

To indicate where something is permanently located or where some regular activity takes place, use на or в* + the prepositional case.

Вы мо́жете предъяви́ть де́нежный перево́д к опла́те во второ́м окне́.†
You can redeem a money order at the second window.

Де́нежные перево́ды получа́ют на по́чте.
Money orders are obtained at the post office.

---

*See Appendix for a list of nouns that require на or в.
†Either на or в can be used with окно to render different meanings.

Вдруг он появи́лся в окне́.
He suddenly appeared at the window.

На окне́ стоя́л большо́й цвето́чный горшо́к.
There was a big flowerpot on the windowsill.

Ско́лько у вас есть на ва́шем счету́?*

How much do you have in your account?

> When used with the Accusative Case, на and в express movement toward a location (always inanimate).

Вам на́до обрати́ться в тре́тье окно́.

You'll have to go to Window 3.

Они́ вста́ли в о́чередь.

They got in line.

Они́ то́лько что пошли́ на по́чту.

They just left for the post office.

Ско́лько рубле́й вы жела́ете положи́ть на сро́чный счёт?

How many rubles do you want to put into the time-deposit account?

> The preposition к is always followed by the dative case and generally indicates movement toward someone or something.

Они́ пое́хали к мое́й сестре́ в дере́вню.

They went to see my sister in the country.

Обменя́в свои́ до́ллары на рубли́, я сно́ва подошёл к тре́тьему окну́.†

After having exchanged my dollars for rubles, I went back to Window 3.

Она́ подошла́ ко мне и спроси́ла, где нахо́дится пункт обме́на валю́ты.

She came up to me and asked where the exchange booth was.

Скажи́те, пожа́луйста, э́то о́чередь к пе́рвому окну́?

Tell me, please, is this line for (lit., toward) Window 1?

в) OTHER USES OF THE PREPOSITION на

> The preposition на followed by the Accusative Case has a number of meanings that denote exchange, allocation, expenditure, and purpose. These are frequently translated as "for" in English.

---

*Note the special prepositional ending in this construction. The "normal" prepositional ending appears in such expressions as в коне́чном счёте (in the last analysis).

†The expression к тре́тьему окну́ places greater emphasis on movement *toward* the third window, whereas в тре́тье окно emphasizes the destination of movement.

Я хочу́ обменя́ть сто до́лларов на рубли́.

I want to exchange a hundred dollars for rubles.

У нас о́чень большо́й спрос на иностра́нные маши́ны.

There is a big demand for foreign cars in our country.

Вам вы́писали реце́пт на но́вое лека́рство?

Were you given a prescription for the new medicine?

Мы тепе́рь получа́ем мно́го зака́зов на эле́ктроприбо́ры.

We are now getting a lot of orders for electric appliances.

На бессро́чный счёт я положу́ оста́вшуюся су́мму, на ежедне́вные расхо́ды.

I'll put the rest of the money into the non-fixed term account for everyday expenses.

2. ПОДЧИНИТЕЛЬНЫЕ СОЮЗЫ (SUBORDINATING CONJUNCTIONS)

A good command of connective words and phrases will help your Russian speech flow more smoothly. The Russian language has many subordinating conjunctions, used to introduce or connect clauses. Following are the most common:

потому что	because
из-за того, что	for the reason that
поско́льку	as long as
пока́	while, until
несмотря́ на то, что	in spite of the fact
впро́чем	however
одна́ко	although, however
с тех пор, как	since the time that
по́сле того́, как	after
как то́лько	as soon as
пре́жде чем	before
чтобы	in order to, for

The expressions ввиду́ того что (in view of the fact that), всле́дствие того что (as a consequence of the fact that), в связи с тем что (in connection with the fact that) are frequently used in more formal and official communication.

Он откры́л сро́чный счёт, потому́ что* он хоте́л име́ть бо́лее высо́кие проце́нты по своему́ вкла́ду.

    He opened a time-deposit account because he wanted to earn greater interest.

Из-за того́ что они́ не отплати́ли подохо́дные нало́ги, у них бы́ли неприя́тности.

    Because they didn't pay their income tax, they had problems.

Поско́льку вы уже́ обменя́ли ва́ши до́ллары, мо́жно бо́льше не заходи́ть в банк.

    Since you have already exchanged your dollars, there's no need to drop by the bank.

Пока́ вы оформля́ете докуме́нты, я схожу́ в кио́ск за газе́той.

    While you're processing the documents, I'll run over to the kiosk for a newspaper.

Дава́йте подождём в кафе́, пока́† банк не откро́ется.

    Let's wait in the cafe until the bank opens.

Несмотря́ на то, что он забы́л взять с собо́й па́спорт, мы откры́ли ему́ ба́нковский счёт.

    In spite of the fact that he forgot to bring his passport with him, we opened a bank account for him.

Мы получи́ли ва́ше письмо́ насчёт откры́тия сро́чного счёта. Впро́чем, мы не мо́жем зако́нчить оформле́ние вкла́да из-за отсу́тствия необходи́мых нам да́нных.

    We received your letter concerning the opening of a time-deposit account. However, we are unable to complete the necessary paperwork due to a lack of required information.

Он о́чень у́мный студе́нт, одна́ко он ча́сто отсу́тствует на заня́тиях.

    He's a very smart student, but he frequently misses classes.

Что она́ де́лала с тех пор, как око́нчила университе́т?

    What has she been doing since she graduated from the unversity?

---

*Note that it is not considered good style to begin a sentence with потому что.
†Note that пока́ не (until) is followed by a perfective verb.

Он вернулся в свой офис после того, как открыл новый счёт в банке.
He returned to his office after he opened a new account at the bank.

Она осознала, что она забыла свой паспорт, как только вошла в банк.
She realized she forgot her passport as soon as she walked into
the bank.

Вы должны заполнить эту форму, прежде чем обменять деньги.
You've got to fill out this form before you can exchange money.

Note that чтобы is used with the infinitive when the subject of both
clauses is the same.

Чтобы открыть вам счёт, мне необходимо увидеть ваш паспорт.
I have to see your passport in order to open an account for you.

Otherwise, it is used with the past tense:

Я передал ему мой паспорт, чтобы он мог открыть мне счёт.
I gave him my passport so that he could open an account for me.

D. ИДИОМАТИКА

ALL WORK AND NO PLAY . . .

Here are a few words and expressions concerned with finance and business relations, some of which are frequently used in jest.

Артист (A CROOK)

Осторожно, когда занимаешься делом с ним. Он настоящийй артист!
Watch out when you do business with him. He's a real con artist!

Деляга (A HUSTLER)

Этот деляга своего не упустит
That hustler is always looking out for number one.

Риск—благоро́дное де́ло. (Nothing ventured, nothing gained.; lit., Risk is a noble venture.)

Я бы вложи́л куш в это но́вое предприя́тие, но ведь это большо́й риск! —Ну, вот. Риск —благоро́дное дело!
I would invest a tidy sum into that new enterprise, but it's very risky! —Well, then. Nothing ventured, nothing gained!

Де́ло в шля́пе. (It's in the bag.)

Де́ло в шля́пе. Я получи́л повыше́ние зарпла́ты.
It's in the bag! I got my raise.

Дела́ иду́т, конто́ра пи́шет. (Business as usual.)

Как дела́? —Дела́ иду́т, конто́ра пи́шет. Рубль даду́т, а два запи́шут.
How are things? —Business as usual. They give you one ruble and charge you two.

And if you think a situation is ominous you can say:

Де́ло па́хнет кероси́ном (This means trouble.; lit., The matter smells of kerosene.)

Конто́ра уже́ три дня подря́д не рабо́тает. Де́ло па́хнет кероси́ном.
The office has been closed for three days in a row. This means trouble.

Де́ло таба́к (All is lost.; lit., a tobacco situation)

А что, господа́, де́ло таба́к? Управле́ние объявля́ет банкро́тство!
Well, gentlemen, we're up the creek, eh? The board is declaring bankruptcy!

On the other hand, after a good day's work, one can say:

Ко́нчил де́ло, гуля́й сме́ло. (Work is done, now take off!)

А что, уже́ шесть часо́в. Ко́нчил де́ло, гуля́й сме́ло!
Well, it's already six. Work is done, time for fun!

Е. СТРОГО ПО ДЕЛУ

БАНКОВСКИЕ УСЛУГИ (BANKING SERVICES)

The proliferation of Russian banks following privatization has occurred primarily among commercial banks (коммéрческие бáнки), which cater mainly to large, institutional clients. The state savings bank of the Russian Federation (Сберегáтельный банк Росси́йской Федерáции), which is generally ranked first among all Russian banks, is still the principal provider of commercial savings accounts (сберегáтельные счетá для делово́го предприя́тия) and checking accounts (текýщие счетá). However, many Russian banks are now diversifying and are beginning to turn more attention to individual depositors (чáстные вклáдчики) to whom lower interests (бóлее ни́зкие процéнты) can be offered.

The top-ranked Russian banks are licensed to conduct the full range of banking transactions (бáнковские операции) in foreign currencies (инострáнная валю́та), within the Russian Federation as well as abroad (за рубежóм). They also are entitled to open accounts with any foreign correspondent bank (банк-корреспондéнт). A few of the most reliable banks with the largest assets (акти́вы) include the aforementioned Сбербанк РФ, the state-run Foreign Trade Bank (Внешторгбанк РФ), the Russian Credit Bank (Росси́йский креди́тный банк), Inkombank (Инкомбанк), the Capitol Bank (Столи́чный банк), and МОСТ банк, all of which have branches in most large Russian cities.

All major banks issue and offer cash advances (дéнежный авáнс) against major Western credit cards (креди́тные кáрточки) and accept and sell American Express, VISA, and Thomas Cook traveler's checks (доро́жные чéки). Many have ATMs (кáссовые автомáты) in center city locations, shopping centers, and international hotels (e.g., in Moscow along Тверскáя ýлица, Нóвый Арбáт, and the ГУМ department store). Some banks also offer their clients safe deposit boxes (сейф для хранéния цéнностей). Many American expatriates working and living in Russia nevertheless make primary use of local offices of American Express, for example, to obtain cash as they need it, and therefore do not open personal accounts at Russian banks.

Although most major credit cards are generally accepted by Russian banks and commercial establishments, their use by Russian citizens is illegal. The use of "plastic" by Russians is generally limited to debit cards (дéбитовые кáрточки). A number of Russian banks have obtained licenses to issue these cards with one of the regular credit card logos, such as Visa or MasterCard. The requirements for these "credit" cards usually include a certain set minimum in an established account, a security deposit (депо́зит в ка́честе поручи́тельства), an annual fee (ежего́дный внос), cash withdrawal charges (пла́та за сня́тия со счёта), and purchase charges (пла́та за поку́пки).

Updated information on retail banking in Russia can be obtained from the U.S. Department of Commerce BISNIS bulletin (tel. 202-482-4655). Additional information on the ratings of Russian banks is available from the World Wide Internet Network at http://www.emn.ru/rating/method.html.

УПРАЖНЕНИЯ

A. Запо́лните про́пуски, по́льзуясь ну́жными предло́гами (на, в, у, к, по) и слова́ми в ну́жной фо́рме. Укажи́те, на како́й слог па́дает ударе́ние. (Fill in the blanks using the required prepositions на, в, у, к, по and words in their correct form. Indicate stress marks.)

1. Какую сумму вы желаете положить_____?
   (into your account)

2. Эта очередь _____?
   (for Window 3)

3. Вы можете получать денежные переводы _____.
   (at Window 4)

4. Когда вы освободитесь, ждите меня_____.
   (at the subway exit)

5. Я хотел бы обменять _____.
   (one hundred dollars for rubles)

6. После того, как вы откроете счёт, зайдите опять_____,
   (my office [to me])
   и мы займёмся аккредитивом.

7. _____они открыли бессрочный счёт?
   (At which bank)

8. Я сове́тую вам обратиться _____ об
   (Mr. Smirnov for information)
   открытии нового счёта.

9. Они стоят в очереди_____.
   (at Window 2)

10. Какие проценты можно получать_____?
    (on deposits in your bank)

B. Переведи́те вышеприведённые предложе́ния на англи́йский язы́к. (Translate the sentences in A into English.)

C. Переведи́те сле́дующие предложе́ния с англи́йского языка на ру́сский.

1. I would like to get a straight L/C (letter of credit) from your bank.
2. We can have your salary deposited directly into your account at our bank.
3. The interest paid on a time-deposit account is much greater than on demand-deposit accounts.
4. Do you have both ruble and foreign currency accounts?
5. The issuance of letters of credit is one of our standard services.
6. The longer the time-deposit period, the more interest (is paid).
7. Since I'm going to be here for two years, I'll need a personal account.
8. In order to open an account I'll have to see your passport.
9. In spite of the fact that he doesn't have an account in our bank, we issued a letter of credit upon the recommendation (по рекомменда́ции) of Mrs. Kazanskaya.
10. Well, everything seems in be in order. Now we can get down to business!

УРОК 12

A. ДИАЛОГ

Посеще́ние кинофестива́ля.

В суббо́ту ве́чером по́сле фи́льма две четы́[1] у́жинают в сосе́днем рестора́не и обсужда́ют то́лько что уви́денный фильм.

ТАНЯ: Ну, и как вам понра́вился э́тот фильм?

САРА: Сюже́т был о́чень волну́ющий и драмати́чный, а в пла́не игры́ актёров, э́то был оди́н из лу́чших фи́льмов, кото́рый я когда́-либо ви́дела. Гла́вный геро́й, пра́вда, немно́жечко переи́грывал, а в остально́м . . .

ЛУИС: Немно́жечко переи́грывал?! Я бы сказа́л, что э́то исполне́ние бы́ло чуть ли не смехотво́рным, осо́бенно во вре́мя сце́ны с пикнико́м.

ИГОРЬ: Да, мо́жет быть, э́то бы́ло слегка́ глупова́то,[2] но смешны́ми э́тих актёров я бы не назва́л.

ТАНЯ: Но вы упуска́ете и́з виду, что фильм заду́мывался как мета́фора. Его́ нельзя́ воспринима́ть напряму́ю, и уж тем бо́лее сце́ну на пикнике́.

САРА: Да, всё ещё и происходи́ло-то во сне . . .

ЛУИС: Глу́пый сон како́й-то!

САРА: Ну ла́дно, ла́дно, ты вы́сказал своё мне́ние. И тем не ме́нее съёмки[3] бы́ли великоле́пными.

ТАНЯ: Да, э́тот режиссёр всегда́ рабо́тает с одни́м и тем же опера́тором. У них небыва́лая сла́женность, не пра́вда ли?

ИГОРЬ: Позво́лю себе́ в э́том усомни́ться. Мне ка́жется, что с таки́ми актёрами режиссёр мог рассчи́тывать на лу́чшее исполне́ние.

ТАНЯ: Но ведь э́то осо́бый стиль игры́! Мне ли́чно понра́вилось.

САРА: И мне то́же. Вам не меша́ло то, что фильм шёл на францу́зском?

ИГОРЬ: Да в о́бщем-то, нет . . . Но если б бы́ло побо́льше разгово́ра, тогда́ без субти́тров бы́ло бы значи́тельно сложне́е всё поня́ть. А то, по большо́му счёту мне бы́ло нева́жно, что фильм был на францу́зском!

ТАНЯ: Ну, Игорь, тебе́ же всегда́ хвата́ло[4] на́ших дома́шних разгово́ров—мне ка́жется ты мог бы наслади́ться относи́тельным молча́нием. Шу́тки в сто́рону, мы уже́ привы́кли к фи́льмам на други́х языка́х.

ИГОРЬ: Это ве́рно. На́ших фи́льмов ста́ло несравне́нно ме́ньше за после́дние го́ды, так что нас завали́ли[5] зарубе́жными.

ТАНЯ: Так и есть, но большинство́ из них дубли́ровано.

ЛУИС: Зна́чит, наве́рное, би́знес по озву́чиванию[6] фи́льмов до́лжен процвета́ть!

ИГОРЬ: Пря́мо в то́чку! Вы, наве́рное, подме́тили, ско́лько ва́ших фи́льмов пока́зывают по на́шему телеви́дению в дубли́-рованном вариа́нте?

САРА: Не да́лее чем вчера́, мы посмотре́ли «Унесённые ве́тром». Нам бы́ло, действи́тельно, заба́вно слы́шать, как Кларк Гейбл говори́л на чи́стом ру́сском языке́!

ТАНЯ: Да, «Унесённые ве́тром»—оди́н из мои́х са́мых люби́мых фи́льмов . . .

ИГОРЬ: Ну, а мне таки́е фи́льмы что-то так себе́.[7]

САРА: Да уж, зна́ю что в твоём вку́се, небо́сь[8] детекти́вы и нау́чная фанта́стика.

ЛУИС: Что тут говори́ть—ка́ждому своё. Да, а как давно́ у вас начали́сь э́ти междунаро́дные кинофестива́ли?

ИГОРЬ: Поря́дочно.[9] Это уже́ ста́ло моско́вской тради́цией. Как вы мо́жете себе́ предста́вить, до перестро́йки все фи́льмы подверга́лись[10] стро́гой цензу́ре. Сейча́с э́то, сла́ва, бо́гу отошло́ . . .

САРА: Наве́рное, э́то па́лка о двух конца́х?[11]

ТАНЯ: В како́м смы́сле?

СА́РА: Ну как же, вели́кое мно́жество соверше́нно безвку́сных фи́льмов с избы́тком се́кса или наси́лия абсолю́тно не де́лают честь стране́, где они́ бы́ли сня́ты.

И́ГОРЬ: Наве́рное да, но, с друго́й стороны́, у вся́кого должно́ быть пра́во вы́бора. Не так ли?

СА́РА: Да, вы пра́вы.

И́ГОРЬ: Это предме́т да́внего спо́ра, каки́е фи́льмы ввози́ть и пока́зывать. Но в све́те вышеупомя́нутой цензу́ры немудрено́, что мно́гих привлека́ет всё но́вое и тем бо́лее заграни́чное.

ТА́НЯ: Но и это то́же постепе́нно прохо́дит.

СА́РА: А вот и официа́нт . . . И́горь, Та́ня, разреши́те нам . . . вы бы́ли так добры́!

И́ГОРЬ: Ни в ко́ем слу́чае![12] Вы на́ши го́сти, и, зна́чит, мы угоща́ем.

Attending a film festival.

Saturday evening, after a film, two couples have dinner at a nearby restaurant and share their opinions.

TANYA: So, how did you like the film?

SARAH: The story was rather powerful and dramatic, and as for the acting, this was one of the best films I've ever seen. Although maybe the main character was somewhat overplayed, but as for the rest . . .

LUIS: Somewhat overplayed? I would say the acting bordered on the ridiculous, especially during the scene at the picnic.

IGOR: Yes, maybe it was a little silly perhaps, but I wouldn't say that the acting was ridiculous.

TANYA: But you're losing sight of the fact that the entire film was a metaphor. It wasn't supposed to be taken so literally, especially the picnic scene.

SARAH: And it was a dream anyway . . .

LUIS: A silly dream, I would say!

SARAH: Okay, okay, you're entitled to your opinion. But I still think the cinematography was spectacular!

TANYA: Yes, this director always works with the same cinematographer. They make a great team, don't they?

IGOR: I'm not so sure about that. I think the director could have elicited better performances from his cast.

TANYA: But that's a particular style of acting! I liked it.

SARAH: Me, too. Did anyone have trouble with the film being in French?

IGOR: Generally, no . . . Well, if there had been more dialogue it might have been somewhat more difficult to understand everything without the subtitles. So I suppose it really didn't make any difference that the film was in French!

TANYA: Well, Igor, you often complain about too much dialogue at home— I thought you'd enjoy the relative silence. Seriously, though, we're pretty used to seeing foreign films.

IGOR: Yes, there have been far fewer domestic films in recent years, so we've been swamped with foreign films.

TANYA: Yes, but most are dubbed.

LUIS: So I guess the film dubbing business is doing pretty well!

IGOR: Absolutely! You've probably noticed a lot of your films dubbed into Russian on TV.

SARAH: As a matter of fact, just yesterday we saw *Gone with the Wind*. I got such a kick out of hearing Clark Gable speak perfect Russian!

TANYA: Oh, *Gone with the Wind* is one of my favorite films . . .

IGOR: Well, that kind of film is not exactly my cup of tea.

SARAH: Yes, I know what you like—suspense and science fiction, most likely.

LUIS: Well, to each his own. Incidentally, how long have you had these international film festivals?

IGOR: Oh, for quite some time. It's become a real Moscow tradition. As you can imagine, before perestroika all films were subject to a strict censorship process. Thank God that's over . . .

SARAH: I guess that's a double-edged sword.

TANYA: What do you mean?

SARAH: Well, I think there are an awful lot of tasteless films with excessive violence and sex that don't do much credit to the country where they're made.

IGOR: I suppose so, but, on the other hand, everyone should have the right to choose. Don't you agree?

SARAH: Yes, you're right.

IGOR: There has always been a lot of controversy about what kind of films should be imported. But given our relatively recent restrictive policies, it's no wonder that many here were fascinated with anything foreign and new.

TANYA: But that, too, is gradually changing.

SARAH: Oh, here comes the waiter . . . Igor, Tanya, please let us get this . . . You've been so kind.

IGOR: Absolutely not! You are our guests, and this is our treat.

B. ПРИМЕЧАНИЯ

1. The word чета́ (couple) can also be used in the construction: не чета́ + dative case, meaning "to be no match for something." Ты посмотре́л бы, каки́е у них фи́льмы пока́зывают—не чета́ на́шим документа́льным фи́льмам. (You should have seen the films they're showing there—no match for our documentaries.)

2. The diminutive suffix -оват(ый)/-еват(ый) used with adjectives (or -овато/-евато used with adverbs) denotes a certain incompleteness and usually means "somewhat" or "rather." Этот фильм глупова́тый. (This film is rather silly.) Это кварти́ра дорогова́та. (This is a rather expensive apartment.) Она́ хитрова́то отве́тила на мой вопро́с. (She answered my question rather cunningly.)

3. Here съёмка refers to shooting a picture, but it can also mean "removal," "surveying," or "plotting." По́сле съёмки ста́рого обору́дования, на заво́де ничего́ не оста́лось. (There was nothing left in the plant after the removal of the old equipment.) Во вре́мя войны́ мы занима́лись возду́шной съёмкой промы́шленных це́нтров. (During the war we did aerial surveys of industrial centers.)

4. Хвата́ть/хвати́ть (to catch) can be used in an impersonal construction with the genitive case to mean "to suffice, to have enough." Фотоплёнки нам хва́тит на ме́сяц. (We have enough film for a month.) Мне уже́ хвати́ло таки́х разгово́ров! (I've had enough of these conversations!) Хва́тит тебе жа́ловаться! (Enough of your complaining!)

5. Note that завали́ть (to overload, to cram, to swamp) is followed by the instrumental case. Реда́кцию завали́ли рабо́той. (The editors were snowed under with work.) Прила́вок зава́лен коро́бками. (The counter is piled high with boxes.) Завали́ть is also used in the sense of failing at some activity. К сожале́нию, он завали́л экза́мен. (Unfortunately, he failed the exam.)

6. Озву́чивание literally means "adding sound" to something.

7. Что-то так себе́ (lit., something that's so-so) is a polite way of saying that something is not to your liking. You could also say: Таки́е фи́льмы не по мне. (Those are not my kind of films.); or Таки́е фи́льмы не в моём вку́се. (Such films are not to my taste.).

8. Небо́сь is a colloquial expression meaning "most likely," "I suppose," "I dare say." Вы, небо́сь, мно́го иностра́нных фи́льмов ви́дели. (I suppose you've seen many foreign films.) Ну, а курсово́й экза́мен? Небо́сь, сдал? (And your final exam? I take it you passed?)

9. Поря́дочно here means "a fair amount." It can also mean "fairly well," "decently." Вчера́ мы поря́дочно уста́ли. (Yesterday we were pretty tired.) Он поря́дочно поёт. (He sings pretty decently.) На вечери́нке мы поря́дочно вы́пили. (We had a fair amount to drink at the party.)

10. Подверга́ться/подве́ргнуться followed by the dative case means "to be subjected to, to undergo" and is used in passive constructions. Все иностра́нные журна́лы подверга́лись цензу́ре. (All foreign magazines were subject to censorship.) The nonreflexive form подверга́ть/подве́ргнуть, however, takes an object. Рецензе́нты подве́ргли но́вую кни́гу ре́зкой кри́тике. (The reviewers sharply criticized the new book.) Все сотру́дники профе́ссора подве́ргли его́ вы́воды сомне́нию. (All of the professor's associates called his conclusions into question.)

11. Па́лка о двух конца́х literally means "a stick with two ends."

12. The word слу́чай appears in many useful expressions involving the word "case." For example, во вся́ком слу́чае (in any case), в проти́вном слу́чае (otherwise), в тако́м слу́чае (in that case), в кра́йнем слу́чае (as a last resort), на вся́кий слу́чай (just in case), на кра́йний слу́чай (in case of emergency). Во вся́ком слу́чае, вы мо́жете откры́ть и рублёвый, и валю́тный счета́. (In any case, you can open both a ruble and hard currency account.) Е́сли у вас уже́ име́ются биле́ты на спекта́кль, вы мо́жете войти́ в зал. В проти́вном слу́чае, вам придётся купи́ть биле́ты в ка́ссе. (If you already have tickets for the show, you can go into the theater. Otherwise, you'll have to buy tickets at the box office.) В тако́м слу́чае, мне на́до снача́ла обменя́ть до́ллары на рубли́. (In that case, I'll first have to change dollars for rubles.) В кра́йнем слу́чае, вы, коне́чно, мо́жете отклони́ть их приглаше́ние. (If worse comes to worst, you can of course decline their invitation.) Пого́да у нас о́чень

непредсказу́емая. На вся́кий слу́чай возьми́ с собо́й зо́нтик. (Our weather is very unpredictable. Take an umbrella with you just in case.) На кра́йний слу́чай, позвони́те мне, вот по этому но́меру. (In case of an emergency, call me at this number.)

С. ГРАММАТИКА И СЛОВОУПОТРЕБЛЕНИЕ

1. УМЕНЬШИТЕЛЬНЫЕ И УВЕЛИЧИТЕЛЬНЫЕ СУЩЕСТВИТЕЛЬНЫЕ (DIMINUTIVE AND AUGMENTATIVE NOUNS)

Diminutive and augmentative nouns are primarily used in colloquial speech. As the names imply, diminutive nouns denote smallness—до́мик (a little house)—but they are also used to convey affection—па́почка (dear daddy), disparagement—сыно́к профе́ссора (teacher's pet), or scorn—анекдо́тик (silly little joke). On the other hand, augmentative nouns are used to denote largeness—бороди́ща (a massive beard), as well as nuances both negative—дурачи́на (an immense fool), and positive—голоси́ще (a mighty voice).

Feminine noun diminutives normally take the suffixes -ка, -ичка, and -ица. For example, неде́лька (week), води́чка (nice little water), страни́чка* (little page), мину́точка (a little minute), про́сьбица (a little request).

Ну и неде́лька!
What a week!

Вы ви́дели на́шу страни́чку на интерне́те?
Did you see our home page on the Internet?

Подожди́те мину́точку!
Wait just a second!

У меня́ к тебе́ про́сьбица.
I have a little favor to ask of you.

Masculine diminutive suffixes are -ец, -ик, -чик, -ок, -ёк. For example, бра́тец (little brother; old chap), до́мик (little house), денёк (an affec-

---

*Титуа́льная страни́чка is a home page on the World Wide Web.

tionate reference to a particular day), го́дик (an affectionate reference to a particular year), автомоби́льчик (little car), карма́нчик* (little pocket).

Ну, бра́тец, не хо́чешь за́втра на да́чу?
Well, old chap, how about going to the dacha tomorrow?

Ви́дишь вот этот до́мик в конце́ у́лицы? Там же живёт моя́ мать.
Do you see that little house at the end of the street? That's where my mother lives.

Ну и го́дик! Нам действи́тельно повезло́!
That sure was some year! We really lucked out!

Masculine augmentative suffixes include -ина, -ище, and -ища. For example, доми́на (a huge house), уми́ще (a great mind), ручи́ща (a mighty hand). Some augmentatives carry negative connotations associated with political events such as the Ежо́вщина, a reign of terror during the Stalin years when the NKVD[†] was headed by Никола́й Ежо́в.

В тридца́тых года́х, почти́ все его́ ро́дственники поги́бли во вре́мя Ежо́вщины.
In the thirties almost all his relatives perished during the Yezhov reign of terror.

A number of diminutive and augmentative forms have a different meaning altogether from the regular form.

AUGMENTATIVE/ DIMINUTIVE	MEANING	ORIGIN
голо́вка по́ршня	piston head	голова́—head
доро́жка	path	доро́га—road
кры́шка	lid, cap	кры́ша—roof
значо́к	badge, lapel pin	знак—sign
волосо́к	filament	во́лос—hair
площа́дка	athletic court, launch pad	пло́щадь—square
зре́лище	spectacle, show	зре́ние—sight, vision
кла́дбище	cemetery	класть—to place
чудо́вище	monster	чу́до—miracle, wonder

*Do not confuse this with карма́нник or карма́нщик (a pickpocket).
†NKVD = Наро́дный комиссариат вну́тренних дел—People's Commissariat for Internal Affairs.

Смотри! Ничего не получится. Ты забыл снять крышку с линзы!
Look here! You won't get anything. You forgot to take the cap off the lens!

Наши хозяева подарили нам вот эти прекрасные значки на память.
Our hosts gave us these great pins as a memento.

За этим жилым домом находится большая теннисная площадка.
There's a big tennis court behind this apartment house.

Московский цирк — действительно потрясающее зрелище.
The Moscow circus is truly a spectacular show.

Вчера ночью мне снилось, что в нашем бассейне появилось ужасное морское чудовище .
Last night I dreamed that a horrible sea monster appeared in our pool.

2. СРАВНИТЕЛЬНАЯ СТЕПЕНЬ ПРИЛАГАТЕЛЬНЫХ (THE COMPARATIVE DEGREE OF ADJECTIVES)

In English comparatives can be formed by using "more/less" or by adding the suffix -er to the adjective. Likewise in Russian, you can use the words более (more) or менее (less) plus a long form adjective, or you can use the suffix -ee, e.g., интересный → интереснее. Более/менее is used when the adjective precedes the noun, while the -ee suffix is used when the adjective follows the noun (i.e., when it follows "to be," which is omitted in the present tense). Compare:

Это более популярный фильм.
This is a more popular film.

Этот фильм популярнее.
This film is more popular.

Я так устал. Кажется, что сегодня вечером мне бы понравился менее сложный фильм.
I'm so tired. I think I would have enjoyed seeing a less complex film tonight.

Как вам понра́вилась кинематогра́фия? —Она́ мне понра́вилась, а Игорь счита́л её ме́нее впечатля́ющей.

How did you like the cinematograpy? —I liked it, but Igor was less impressed.

Мы в восто́рге от возмо́жности встре́титься с Та́ней! —А она́ ещё бо́лее в восто́рге от встре́чи с ва́ми!

We're very excited about meeting Tanya! —She's even more excited about meeting you!

Note that бо́лее and ме́нее, as well as the -ee ending, do not change. The long adjectives, however, decline as usual. In colloquial usage, the -ee ending is often rendered as -ей.

Како́й краси́вый теа́тр! —Большо́й теа́тр ещё краси́вей!

What a beautiful theatre! —The Bolshoi is even more beautiful!

You are probably already familiar with many of the irregular comparative forms of adjectives.* Here are some of the most frequently used irregular forms:

	ADJECTIVE	COMPARATIVE	
big	большо́й	бо́льше	bigger
small	ма́ленький	ме́ньше	smaller
bad	плохо́й	ху́же	worse
good	хоро́ший	лу́чше	better
old	ста́рый	ста́рше	older (for people)
		старе́е	older (for things)
young	молодо́й	моло́же	younger
early	ра́нний	ра́ньше	earlier
late	по́здний	по́зже	later

When directly comparing two things, чем means "than."

Но́вые фи́льмы бо́лее интере́сные, чем ста́рые.

The new films are more interesting than the old ones.

Пе́рвые кинофестива́ли бы́ли бо́лее уда́чными, чем после́дние.

The first film festivals were more successful than the latest ones.

*See Appendix for more extensive list of irregular comparative forms.

The -ee form is always used when comparing whole phrases or infinitives.

В этом году́ у нас бы́ло ме́ньше таки́х фи́льмов, чем в предыду́щие го́ды.
This year we've had fewer of these films than in previous years.

Мно́гие счита́ют, что чита́ть ле́гче, чем разгова́ривать.
Many believe it's easier to read than to speak.

Чем can be replaced by the genitive case with the -ee comparative form
if declinable nouns are compared.

Иностра́нные фи́льмы интере́снее оте́чественных.
Foreign films are more interesting than domestic ones.

Гора́здо (much) is used for added emphasis.

Она́ зараба́тывает гора́здо бо́льше меня́.
She earns much more than I do.

Note that гора́здо can be followed by either the long or short comparative adjective.

Он счита́ет, что детекти́вы гора́здо драмати́чнее, чем рома́ны про
любо́вь.
Он счита́ет, что детекти́вы гора́здо бо́лее драмати́чны, чем рома́ны про
любо́вь.
He thinks that mysteries are much more dramatic than love stories.

To compare quantities, such as age, use the prepositon на.

Я ста́рше бра́та на три го́да.
I'm three years older than my brother.

На ско́лько его́ сестра́ моло́же ва́шей? —Она́ на де́сять лет моло́же.
How much younger is his sister than yours? —She's ten years younger.

Шумовы́е эффе́кты в пересня́том фи́льме бы́ли гора́здо лу́чше.
—Пра́вильно, но по́длинный фильм ста́рее* на три́дцать лет!
The remake had better special effects. —Yes, but the original is thirty
years older!

*Note that the comparative ста́рее is used with inanimate objects.

3. ПРЕВОСХОДНАЯ СТЕПЕНЬ ПРИЛАГАТЕЛЬНЫХ (THE SUPERLATIVE DEGREE OF ADJECTIVES)

The superlative degree of adjectives is used when comparing three or more items. It is usually formed with са́мый plus the long-form adjective, e.g., са́мый интере́сный фильм (the most interesting film). Both са́мый and the adjective are declined and agree with the modified noun in case, number, and gender.

«Унесённые ве́тром»—мой са́мый люби́мый иностра́нный фильм.
Gone With the Wind is my favorite foreign film.

«Война́ и Мир»—оди́н из са́мых захва́тывающих рома́нов, кото́рый я когда́-либо чита́л.
War and Peace is one of the most compelling novels I have ever read.

Они живу́т в са́мом большо́м до́ме на на́шей у́лице.
They live in the biggest house on our street.

В про́шлом году́ я провёл три ме́сяца в одно́м из са́мых краси́вых италья́нских городо́в.
Last year I spent three months in one of the most beautiful Italian cities.

Russian also has a suffix similar to the English -est, but these simple superlative adjectives are used to indicate a high degree of quality or an absolute comparison without reference to other items. These adjectives are formed by adding -ейший (or -айший if the stem ends in -г, -к, -х) to the stem of the adjective; e.g., но́вый → нове́йший (newest, latest), интере́сный → интере́снейший (most interesting, very interesting). When adding -айший, -г, -к, and -х change to -ж, -ч, -ш, respectively.

На э́той вы́ставке пока́зывают нове́йшие достиже́ния компью́терной технологии.
The latest achievements of computer technology are being shown at this exhibit.

Интере́снейшие иностра́нные фи́льмы пока́зывают во второ́м за́ле.
The most interesting foreign films are being shown in the second hall.

Достое́вский—велича́йший ру́сский писа́тель.
Dostoevsky is the greatest Russian writer.

Вы не зна́ете, где здесь ближа́йшая остано́вка авто́буса?
Do you happen to know where the nearest bus stop is around here?

Some short-form comparative adjectives can also function as superlatives: лу́чший (best, better), ху́дший (worst, worse), ста́рший (oldest, elder), мла́дший* (youngest, younger). Compare:

Это не лу́чший вариа́нт.
That's not the best option.

Нельзя́ ли найти́ лу́чший слова́рь?
Can't you find a better dictionary?

Мой мла́дший сын у́чится на тре́тьем ку́рсе в университе́те.
My youngest son is in his third year at the university.

Я вчера́ встре́тился с его́ мла́дшим сы́ном.
I met his younger/youngest son yesterday.

В ху́дшем слу́чае, я туда́ пойду́ оди́н.
In the worst case, I'll go there alone.

The superlative forms наибо́лее (the most) and наиме́нее (the least) are used primarily in formal writing, literature, and journalism, and do not decline. You should only learn to recognize them.

Делега́ты при́няли реше́ние по наибо́лее актуа́льным вопро́сам.
The delegates adopted a resolution on the most pressing problems.

Иссле́дователям пришло́сь прибе́гнуть к наиме́нее то́чному ме́тоду ана́лиза.
The investigators had to resort to the least accurate method of analysis.

The following superlatives, also characteristic of journalistic style, decline like regular adjectives: наибо́льший (the greatest), наивы́сший (the highest), наиме́ньший (the smallest), and наилу́чший (the very best).

*Ста́рший and мла́дший are used only with animate nouns.

Наибо́льшее коли́чество законопрое́ктов каса́ется экономи́ческих рефо́рм.

    The greatest number of legislative bills is concerned with economic reforms.

Арти́сты всегда́ стремя́тся к наивы́сшей сте́пени соверше́нства.

    Artists always strive for the highest degree of perfection.

Но́вые предпринима́тели и́щут инвести́ции с наиме́ньшим ри́ском.

    The new entrepeneurs are looking for investments with the smallest risk.

Все рецензе́нты бы́ли согла́сны с тем, что за после́дние два́дцать лет это бы́ло наилу́чшее представле́ние «Ча́йки» Че́хова.

    All the critics agreed that this was the best performance of Chekhov's *The Seagull* in the last twenty years.

    The superlative наилу́чший is also often used in closing salutations and expressions of good wishes.

(Жела́ю Вам) всего́ наилу́чшего!

    (I wish you) all the very best!

(Посыла́ю Вам) наилу́чшие пожела́ния.

    (Sending you) very best wishes.

D. ИДИОМАТИКА

AT THE MOVIES.

Russians love to discuss and argue. Here are some expressions you're likely to hear or use yourself.

О вку́сах не спо́рят. (IT'S NO USE ARGUING ABOUT TASTE.)

Я по́нял, что фильм тебе́ совсе́м не понра́вился, но что тут говори́ть—о вку́сах не спо́рят.

    I gathered that you didn't like the film at all, but what can you say—it's no use arguing about tastes.

На вкус и цвет това́рища нет. (TO EACH HIS/HER OWN; LIT., THERE'S NO COMPANION TO SHARE YOUR TASTE AND COLOR PREFERENCES.)

Я не бу́ду спо́рить с ва́ми насчёт этого фи́льма—на вкус и цвет това́рища нет.

I'm not going to argue with you about that film—to each his own.

Берёт за́ душу. (IT GOES RIGHT TO THE HEART.)

Я чуть бы́ло не запла́кал по оконча́нию фи́льма. —Зна́ю, эта исто́рия действи́тельно берёт за́ душу.

I almost started to cry at the end of the film. —That story really goes right to the heart.

Си́льный (IMPRESSIVE, POWERFUL)

Мы все бы́ли глубоко́ тро́нуты игро́й актёров. —Да, это действи́тельно си́льный фильм.

We were all deeply touched by the actors' performances. —Yes, it was really a very moving film.

Боеви́к (A BOX-OFFICE HIT)

Ты уже́ ви́дел после́дний фильм Михалко́ва? —А как же, этот фильм ведь супербоеви́к!

Did you see Mikhalkov's last film? —How could I not see it, it was a box-office sensation!

Е. СТРОГО ПО ДЕЛУ

ИСТОРИЯ ФИЛЬМОВ И КИНЕМАТОГРАФИЯ
(FILM HISTORY AND FILM INDUSTRY)

As an official medium of the government, films during the Soviet period generally adhered to the views and policies of those in power at the time. The earlier films were therefore produced as the art form of the Revolution. Although the so-called golden era of Soviet film production (кинематогра́фия) witnessed such well-known films as Eisenstein's «Броненосец Потёмкин» *(The Battleship Potemkin)*, 1926; «Октя́брь» *(October)*, 1927; «Алекса́ндр Не́вский» *(Alexander Nevsky)*, 1938; «Ива́н

Грозный» *(Ivan the Terrible)*, 1941–1946; Pudovkin's «Мать» *(Mother)*, 1926; and «Конец Санкт-Петербурга» *(End of St. Petersburg)*, most of these films, particularly of the earlier period, were more popular abroad than in Russia.

During World War II and the next two decades, the dominant theme of Soviet films was the war. Those films included «Летя́т журавли́» *(The Cranes Are Flying)*, 1957, and «Балла́да о солда́те» *(The Ballad of a Soldier)*, 1959, both of which also enjoyed considerable popularity in the West. The postwar period also saw the release of a few films based on classics of Russian literature such as Chekhov's «Да́ма с соба́чкой» *(Lady with the Lapdog)*, 1960, Turgenev's «Дворя́нское гнездо́» *(A Nest of the Gentry)*, 1969, and Tolstoy's «Война́ и мир» *(War and Peace)*, 1967. By the 1970s, as restrictions on film topics were somewhat lessened, Soviet films became much less constrained by the tenets of "Socialist Realism" and increasingly dealt with contemporary themes as reflected by «Андре́й Рублёв» and the science-fiction film «Соля́рис», *(Solaris)* directed by Andrei Tarkovsky, who died in exile in Paris but was later rehabilitated as an artist.

The post-perestroika films have addressed political and social issues head-on. «Покая́ние» *(Repentance)* depicts life under Stalin, «Легко́ ли быть молоды́м?» *(Is It Easy to Be Young?)*, a Latvian film directed by Juris Podnieks, offers social criticism. «Останови́лся по́езд» *(A Train Has Stopped)* is a study of local corruption, and «Ма́ленькая Ве́ра» *(Little Vera)* constituted a strong indictment of Soviet family life. More recent films include those directed by Nikita Mikhalkov, most notably, «Утомлённые со́лнцем» *(Burnt by the Sun)*, which won both a Cannes Film Festival prize and an Academy Award for the best foreign film in 1995, and a film directed by Sergei Bodrov, «Кавка́зский пле́нник» *(Prisoner of the Caucasus)*, which won a Cannes Film Festival Audience Prize in 1996.

Although movie attendance in Russia had been at record heights during the 1970s and 1980s, that number dropped precipitously during the 1990s. With much less leisure time available, Russians increasingly turned to television and videos for entertainment. Concomitantly, Russian film production has been significantly reduced, partly due to economic restraints placed on an industry formerly fully subsidized by the state, and partially due to the flood of foreign imports.

In the process of adapting to a market economy (ры́ночная эконо́мика), many professionals in the film industry have formed production companies that offer video and film services, including the preparation of advertising clips (рекла́мные киноматериа́лы) and promotional films (рекла́мные фи́льмы), for both domestic and foreign companies. These companies also provide camera crews (киносъёмочные кома́нды), interpreters (перево́дчики), and vehicle and equipment rentals (автомаши́ны и аппара́ты на прока́т). Two such companies are located in St. Petersburg: Novokom, and Maksim Golant. A Moscow-based company is the Babylon Company.

УПРАЖНЕНИЯ

A. Запо́лните про́пуски, испо́льзуя сравни́тельную или превосхо́дную сте́пень ну́жных прилага́тельных. (Fill in the blanks with either the comparative or superlative forms of the required adjectives.)

1. Мне ка́жется, что пе́рвый фильм_____, чем второ́й.
   (was more interesting)

2. _____из иностра́нных фи́льмов пока́зывали на про́шлой
   (The best)
   неде́ле.

3. Игра́ гла́вного геро́я была́ _____исполне́ния
   (was much worse than)
   други́х актёров.

4. По-мо́ему, после́дние и́мпортные фи́льмы бы́ли
   _____из тех, кото́рые я когда́-то ви́дел.
   (most exciting)

5. Я люблю́ _____приключе́нческие фи́льмы.
   (more dramatic)

6. Вообщем-то, большинство́ из фи́льмов, кото́рые пока́зывают по
   на́шему телеви́дению, _____.
   (are much less interesting)

7. Мне ка́жется, что режиссёр до́лжен был рассчи́тывать на _____
   (better)
   исполне́ние роле́й.

8. Сце́на с пикнико́м была́_____сце́ной фи́льма.
   (the most ridiculous)

9. А ты счита́ешь, что твои́ люби́мые детекти́вы_____
   (less ridiculous than)
   фи́льмы, кото́рые пока́зывают на фестива́ле?

10. Ты что, хо́чешь сказа́ть, что твой вкус_____?
    (better than mine)

B. Переведи́те сле́дующие предложе́ния с англи́йского языка́ на
ру́сский. Укажи́те куда́ па́дает ударе́ние.

1. Do you think it is easier to translate from Russian to English than
   to translate from English to Russian?
2. The very latest films are more complex than the old ones.
3. It is much colder in Moscow in the winter than in Washington.
4. The new foreign films are more interesting than our domestic
   films.
5. They lived in one of the most beautiful houses in the city.
6. I don't know what the weather will be like. But just in case, take an
   umbrella.
7. In case of an emergency, call me at the office. I'll be there until
   eleven.
8. Their home page on the internet is more interesting than ours.
9. He grew (отпусти́л) such an immense beard that I hardly
   recognized him.
10. What a week that was! We were really swamped with work!

C. Переведи́те сле́дующие предложе́ния на ру́сский язы́к, по́льзуясь
подходя́щими прилага́тельными в просто́й фо́рме превосхо́дной
сте́пени. (Translate the following sentences into Russian, using the
simple superlative form of the appropriate adjectives.)

1. Can you tell me where the nearest subway station is?
2. Which is the best Russian-English dictionary?
3. His youngest son played (испо́лнил) the role of the hero.
4. In your opinion, who is greatest Russian writer of the nineteenth
   century?
5. I wish you the very best!
6. In the worst case, I'll have to spend the weekend (выходны́е)
   alone.
7. The film is concerned with the latest achievements of technology.
8. The best solution to this problem is a double-edged sword.
9. These films were subjected to the most severe censorship.
10. This is one of our oldest traditions.

ПРЕДЛАГАЕМЫЕ ЗАНЯТИЯ

Rent one of the classic older Russian films such as Eisenstein's *The Battleship Potemkin* or *Alexander Nevsky* as well as more modern films such as *Little Vera, Repentance,* and the award-winning *Burnt by the Sun.* Compare the stylistic, social, and political changes reflected in them. Try to follow along as much as possible without reading the English subtitles.

УРОК 13

A. ДИАЛОГ

Компью́терная вы́ставка в Ирку́тске.[1]

Ива́н Кулико́в и Фёдор Посто́вский, программи́сты Русско-Азиатского Ба́нка в Ирку́тске, пришли́ на вы́ставку компью́терной те́хники Комтек.

ИВА́Н: **Смотри́, Фёдор, вот стенд фи́рмы Эппл, погля́дим?**

ФЁДОР: **Да, дава́й, я хочу́ посмотре́ть на их нови́нки.**

ПРЕДСТАВИТЕЛЬ ЭППЛ: **Здра́вствуйте, чем могу́ быть поле́зна?**

ИВА́Н: **Я бы хоте́л ознако́миться с после́дними моде́лями ваших компью́теров.**

ПРЕДСТАВИТЕЛЬ: **Вас интересу́ет лэпто́п[2] или стациона́рная моде́ль?**

ИВА́Н: **Меня́ интересу́ет стациона́рная моде́ль с большо́й операти́вной па́мятью.**

ПРЕДСТАВИТЕЛЬ: **Тогда́ вас заинтересу́ет вот эта моде́ль, одна из наибо́лее мо́щных из всех предста́вленных здесь. Мне ка́жется, что вы найдёте операти́вную па́мять и вмести́мость винче́стера[3] внуши́тельными.**

ФЁДОР: **А какова́ та́ктовая частота́ проце́ссора?**

ПРЕДСТАВИТЕЛЬ: **Са́мая высо́кая частота́ на рынке! Есть ещё и други́е превосхо́дные характери́стики этой моде́ли, как наприме́р, два скоростны́х после́довательных по́рта, высокоскоростна́я видеока́рта, шесть расшири́тельных гнезд. Ёмкость кэша са́мая больша́я, кото́рая име́ется в прода́же.**

ИВА́Н: **Да, дово́льно впечатля́ющие характери́стики. А каково́ разреше́ние мо́нитора?**

ПРЕДСТАВИТЕЛЬ: **Разреше́ние этой моде́ли 1280 x 1024.**

Представи́тель включа́ет компью́тер.

ФЁДОР: (присвистывает) **Ничего́ себе́!**

ИВАН: **А звук како́в?**

ПРЕДСТАВИТЕЛЬ: Эта моде́ль име́ет сте́рео звукопереда́чу и звукоза́пись[4]. Вот э́тот монито́р име́ет встро́енные сте́рео дина́мики и микрофо́н. Кста́ти, посмотри́те, пожа́луйста, прекра́сное ка́чество цветно́го изображе́ния. Да́нный мо́нитор облада́ет пло́ским экра́ном с минима́льным отсве́чиванием.

ИВАН: Да, ви́дно. Вы зна́ете, большинство́ обору́дования, с кото́рым нам прихо́дится ста́лкиваться[5] совмести́мо со станда́ртом Ай-Би-Эм.* Возмо́жно ли подключе́ние э́той моде́ли к компью́терной се́ти ти́па Ай-Би-Эм?

ПРЕДСТАВИТЕЛЬ: Да, коне́чно. Она́ име́ет отли́чное преинсталл-и́рованное програ́ммное обеспе́чение, позволя́ющее рабо́тать с програ́ммами напи́санными для **DOS** и **Windows**.[6]

ФЁДОР: **Скажи́те, а мо́жно ли перевести́ програ́ммы, напи́санные для Макинто́ш, в фо́рмат Windows?**

ПРЕДСТАВИТЕЛЬ: Нет пробле́м. Мы предлага́ем не́сколько паке́тов програ́мм для подо́бных це́лей. Я сове́тую вам посети́ть отде́л на́шей экспози́ции, посвящённый про-гра́ммному обеспе́чению, кото́рый нахо́дится в павильо́не 4 на второ́м этаже́. Но́мер сте́нда, по-мо́ему, 503. Там же, я ду́маю, вы найдёте то, что вас интересу́ет.

ИВАН: **Хорошо́. И после́дний вопро́с. Как насчёт обслу́живания и техни́ческой подде́ржки?**

ПРЕДСТАВИТЕЛЬ: Мы предлага́ем по́лную гара́нтию, послегаранти́йное обслу́живание и техни́ческую подде́ржду.

ФЁДОР: **Како́в гаранти́йный срок?**

ПРЕДСТАВИТЕЛЬ: **Как обы́чно—два го́да.**

ИВАН: **Ну, спаси́бо вам за всю информа́цию.**

ПРЕДСТАВИТЕЛЬ: **Не́ за что. Почему́ бы вам не взять вот э́ти катало́ги и прейскура́нт? Вот моя́ визи́тная ка́рточка. Если у вас ещё возни́кнут вопро́сы, или вы захоти́те помести́ть зака́з**

*An IBM compatible computer is also referred to as ИБМ-совмести́мый компью́тер.

у нас, пожа́луйста, позвони́те мне и́ли обраща́йтесь в наш гла́вный о́фис в Москве́.

ФЁДОР: Спаси́бо.

ПРЕДСТАВИТЕЛЬ: Да, кста́ти, мо́жет быть вы хоти́те подписа́ться[7] на наш катало́г? Мы бы тогда́ посыла́ли вам са́мую све́жую информа́цию.

ФЁДОР: Почему́ бы и нет? Вот моя́ визи́тка . . . Ита́к, Иван, что у нас тепе́рь по пла́ну?

ИВАН: Мне хоте́лось бы посмотре́ть на ска́неры Хьюлетт-Пакка́рд.

ФЁДОР: (гля́дя на часы́) Иван, по́сле э́того пойдём что-нибудь перекуси́ть, хорошо́?

ИВАН: Хоро́шая иде́я.

ФЁДОР: Замеча́тельно! Я ужа́сно проголода́лся[8]! Ты не по́мнишь, когда́ э́та вы́ставка закрыва́ется?

ИВАН: Ду́маю, что вы́ставка рабо́тает с девяти́ утра́ до шести́ ве́чера.

ФЁДОР: Зна́чит, у нас ещё уйма́[9] вре́мени . . .

At a computer show in Irkutsk.

Ivan Kulikov and Fedor Postovsky, programmers at the Russo-Asiatic Bank in Irkutsk, arrive at the Comtek computer show.

IVAN: Oh, look, Fedor. There's the Apple booth. Do you want to take a look?

FEDOR: Let's go. I want to see their new stuff.

REPRESENTATIVE: Hello. May I help you?

IVAN: I'd like to see your latest computer line.

REPRESENTATIVE: Are you interested in a laptop or desktop model?

IVAN: A desktop model with a large memory capacity.

REPRESENTATIVE: Then you'll want to see this one, one of our most powerful desk top models shown here. I think you'll find the RAM and hard-disk capacity impressive.

FEDOR: And what's the speed of the processor?

REPRESENTATIVE: It's the fastest on the market! It also has some very nice features like two high-speed serial ports, an accelerated graphics card, six PCI expansion slots, and it has the largest cache capacity available.

IVAN: That's pretty impressive. What about the monitor's resolution?

REPRESENTATIVE: This model has a resolution of 1280 by 1024.

The sales representative turns on the computer.

FEDOR: (whistles) Oh, how nice!

IVAN: And the sound?

REPRESENTATIVE: This model has stereo sound, both in and out. The display unit you see has integrated hi-fi stereo speakers and a microphone. Incidentally, just take a look at the superb color graphics. The display has a vertically flat, low curvature screen, and notice that there's hardly any glare.

IVAN: Yes, I see that. You know, much of our equipment where we work is IBM-compatible. Can we connect this machine to an IBM-type network?

REPRESENTATIVE: Certainly. It comes bundled with excellent, factory-installed software that enables you to run all Windows and DOS programs.

FEDOR: Tell me, what about transferring Macintosh programs to Window formats?

REPRESENTATIVE: No problem. We have several software packages that will do that for you. I'd suggest that you visit our software display on the second floor of Hall Number 4, Booth Number 503. I think you'll find what you need there.

IVAN: Great! One last question. What about servicing and technical support?

REPRESENTATIVE: We offer full warranty and post-warranty servicing and support.

FEDOR: What's the warranty period?

REPRESENTATIVE: The usual two years.

IVAN: Well, thanks for all the information.

REPRESENTATIVE: Not at all. Why don't you take some brochures and our price list? Here's my business card. Don't hesitate to call me or write our main office in Moscow if you have any questions or if you'd like to place an order.

FEDOR: Thanks.

REPRESENTATIVE: By the way, would you like to be on our mailing list so we can send you updated information?

FEDOR: Sure, why not? Here's my business card . . . So, Ivan, what's next?

IVAN: I'd like to take a look at the Hewlett-Packard scanners.

FEDOR: (looking at his watch) Ivan, how about getting a bite to eat after this?

IVAN: Good idea.

FEDOR: Great! I'm starving! Do you remember when the exhibit closes?

IVAN: I think the exhibit hours were 9 A.M. to 6 P.M.

FEDOR: So, we still have plenty of time . . .

B. ПРИМЕЧАНИЯ

1. Иркутск is located approximately 5,000 kilometers (3,000 miles) southeast of Moscow at the confluence of the Angara and Irkut Rivers, which lead into nearby Lake Baikal (озеро Байкал), the world's deepest fresh water lake (maximum depth 5,714 feet). The city has a population of approximately 700,000 and is the main industrial, cultural, scientific, and commercial center of eastern Siberia. With its international airport and a principal stop on the Trans-Siberian Railway, Irkutsk serves as the gateway to Mongolia, China, and the Far East. In addition to a major hydroelectric plant, the city houses numerous gold and diamond processing, machine-tool, construction material, and food processing plants. The Geography Institute of the Russian Academy of Sciences Siberian Branch (Институт географии Сибирского отделения Российской Академии Наук) is also located here.

2. A "laptop" computer is also known as дорожный компьютер, портативный компьютер, or ноутбук.

3. The literal translation жёсткий диск (hard disk) is also used.

4. Звукозапись is any kind of audio recording. The verb записывать/записать refers to both audio or video recordings. Мы записали весь концерт на плёнку. (We recorded the entire concert on tape.)

Они записа́ли на́ше исполне́ние пье́сы на видеока́меру. (They recorded our performance of the play on a camcorder.) Remember that запи́сывать/записа́ть has the primary meaning of "to take notes" or "to write something down." Вы записа́ли техни́ческие характери́стики э́той моде́ли? (Did you write down the specs of this model?)

5. Ста́лкиваться/столкну́ться here has the colloquial meaning of "to encounter." The verb's primary meaning is "to collide with" or "to run into something" (literally or figuratively). В э́том вопро́се на́ши интере́сы столкну́лись. (Our interests clashed on this point.) Вчера́ я случа́йно столкну́лся со свои́м бы́вшим ученико́м. (Yesterday I happened to bump into a former pupil of mine.) На у́лице бы́ло всего́ две маши́ны, и они́ столкну́лись! (There were just two cars traveling on the street, and they collided!

6. It has become common practice in Russian technical literature to leave certain terms like Windows and DOS in English.

7. Подписа́ться literally means "to subscribe to" or "to sign up to receive something." Мы уже́ подписа́лись на журна́л «Коммерса́нт». (We have already subscribed to the journal *Kommersant*.) Подписа́ться followed by the preposition под and a noun in the instrumental case means "to subscribe to an idea or suggestion." По́сле того́, как мы разъясни́ли цель прое́кта, они незамедли́тельно подписа́лись под на́шим предложе́нием. (After we clarified the purpose of our project, they promptly agreed to our proposal.)

8. Other common expressions of hunger include: Я го́лоден/голодна́ как зверь. (I'm hungry as a beast.) Я го́лоден/голодна́ как волк! (I'm hungry as a wolf!), and Умира́ю от го́лода! (I'm dying of hunger!).

9. The popular colloquial expression у́йма (heaps, tons, lots) is used only in the singular and must be followed by the genitive case. Для того́, чтобы получи́ть ну́жную мне информа́цию, мне пришло́сь пережи́ть у́йму тру́дностей. (I had to go through hell and high water to get the information I needed.) У меня́ для вас у́йма новосте́й. (I have tons of news for you.) У него́ уйма де́нег. (He has tons of money.) У меня́ у́йма дел. (I've got a bunch of things to do.)

C. ГРАММАТИКА И СЛОВОУПОТРЕБЛЕНИЕ

1. ПРИЛАГАТЕЛЬНЫЕ «КАКОВ» И «КАКОЙ» (THE ADJECTIVES КАКОВ AND КАКОЙ)

The adjectives како́в/какова́/каково́/каковы́ (what) and тако́в/такова́/таково́/таковы́ (such) are used with the verb "to be," whereas како́й/

какáя/какóе/какúе (which) and такóй/такáя/такóе/такúе (such) are used as part of a noun phrase that can be used with any verb. Compare:

Каковá тáктовая частотá процéссора?
What is the speed of the processor?

Какýю тáктовую частотý испóльзуют на этой модéли?
Which processor speed is used with this model?

Каковы́ звуковы́е характери́стики этого компью́тера?
What are the sound specs of this computer?

Какúе звуковы́е характери́стики вас интересýют?
Which sound specs are you interested in?

Какóв гаранти́йный срок у вáших компью́теров?
What is the warranty period for your computers?

Какúе гаранти́йные срóки предлагáет вáша фи́рма?
What warranty periods does your company offer?

The какóв-type adjectives are also used to express strong feelings about something or someone.

А погóда-то каковá!
What weather we're having!

Какóв is frequently used in combination with такóв in such expressions as "каковá мать, таковá и дочь" (like mother, like daughter). Такóв can also be used to express similarity, as in "just like," "such is."

Таковó нáше положéние.
Such is our situation.

Все эти компью́теры таковы́.
All of these computers are like that.

Таковá ценá, котóрую мы должны́ плати́ть.
That's the price we'll have to pay.

And таков appears in the colloquial expression:

И был таков.
And that was the last we heard of him.

2. ГЛАГОЛЫ, УПРАВЛЯЮЩИЕ ТВОРИТЕЛЬНЫМ ПАДЕЖОМ (VERBS GOVERNING THE INSTRUMENTAL CASE)

Although there are no hard and fast rules for determining which verbs govern the instrumental case, many verbs fall into the category that is concerned with control, use, and attitude.* Some of the most common include:

обладáть	to possess, to be possessed of
интересовáться	to be interesed in
пóльзоваться/воспóльзоватся	to use, to make use of
управлять	to govern, to control
гордиться	to be proud of
владéть	to own, have a command of, to know how to use
располагáть	to have at one's disposal, to have available
завéдовать	to manage, to be in charge of
любовáться	to admire
пренебрегáть/пренебрéчь	to disregard, to neglect, to scorn
увлекáться/увлéчься	to develop a fascination for, to become enamored with

Все нóвые лэптóпы обладáют шáровым указáтелем, дисковóдом для неперезапи́сываемых компáктных звукоди́сков.
All of the new laptops are equipped with a trackball and CD-ROM drive.

Мы всегдá интересовáлись компью́терной технолóгией.
We were always interested in computer technology.

С пóмощью дáнного прогрáммного обеспéчения, мóжно пóльзоваться и рýсским и англи́йским шри́фтами.
Both Russian and English fonts can be used with this software.

*In general, when learning new verbs try to associate them with the corresponding interrogative pronoun (to possess—обладать чем; to fear—бояться чего/кого; to facilitate—способствовать чему, etc.)

Представи́тель воспо́льзовался слу́чаем, чтобы ознако́мить нас с
нове́йшими моде́лями при́нтеров.

The representative took the opportunity to acquaint us with the newest
models of printers.

Коне́чно, мы о́чень горди́мся на́шими тала́нтливыми студе́нтами.

Of course we are very proud of our talented students.

Мы располага́ем больши́м вы́бором ра́зных моде́лей
компью́теров.

We have available a large selection of various computer
models.

Он увлека́лся компью́терами да́же до того́, как он на́чал говори́ть!

He's been fascinated with computers since before he could talk!

Nouns derived from these verbs also govern the instrumental case:
владе́ние (possession), Заве́дующий (manager), увлече́ние (fascination, enthusiasm), пренебреже́ние (neglect, disregard, scorn).

Заве́дующий магази́ном уже́ пое́хал домо́й.

The store manager has already gone home.

Я совсе́м не разделя́ю его́ увлече́ние телеви́дением.

I do not at all share his fascination with television.

Его́ обвини́ли в пренебреже́нии свои́м обя́занностям.

He was accused of dereliction of duty.

D. ИДИОМАТИКА

DO YOU REMEMBER . . . ?

The word па́мять (memory) is an important factor in computer technology, but it also appears in a number of Russian idiomatic expressions. Here are a few of them:

Дари́ть/получи́ть на па́мять (TO GIVE/RECEIVE AS A MEMENTO)

Она́ подари́ла мне на па́мять собра́ние её стихо́в.
She gave me a collection of her poems as a memento.

Дай бог па́мяти! (IF I COULD ONLY REMEMBER!; LIT., GOD GIVE ME MEMORY!)

А, вот идёт наш но́вый сотру́дник . . . Э, как же его́ зову́т, дай бог па́мяти . . .
Oh, here comes our new associate . . . Ah, what's his name now, if I only could remember . . .

Бежа́ть без па́мяти (TO RUN LIKE CRAZY; LIT., TO RUN WITHOUT THINKING)

Серге́й схвати́л паке́т и без па́мяти побежа́л на по́чту.
Sergey grabbed the package and ran to the post office like a bat out of hell.

Люби́ть/влюби́ться без па́мяти (TO BE MADLY IN LOVE)

Соверше́нно я́сно, что он без па́мяти лю́бит дочь на́шего нача́льника.
It's perfectly obvious that he's madly in love with our boss's daughter.

Дыря́вая па́мять (A MEMORY LIKE A SIEVE)

Как э́то мо́жет быть, что он уже́ забы́л мою́ фами́лию?—В э́том ма́ло удиви́тельного—у него́ дыря́вая па́мять.
How is it possible that he already forgot my name?—Don't be surprised—he's got a memory like a sieve.

Вы́лететь из па́мяти (TO SLIP ONE'S MIND)

Почему́ вы мне зара́нее не сказа́ли, что у них нет компью́тера?—Я не зна́ю, это про́сто вы́летело у меня из па́мяти.
Why didn't you tell me sooner that they don't have a computer?—I don't know, it just slipped my mind.

Если па́мять не изменя́ет (IF MEMORY SERVES)

Если мне не изменя́ет па́мять, это то же са́мое програ́ммное обеспе́чение, кото́рое мы испо́льзовали в про́шлом году́.
If my memory serves me correctly, this is the same software we used last year.

Вре́заться в па́мять (TO BE ETCHED INTO ONE'S MEMORY)

То, что произошло́ там, си́льно вре́залось в мою́ па́мять.
What occurred there has stuck vividly in my mind.

E. СТРОГО ПО ДЕЛУ

КОМПЬЮТЕРЫ (COMPUTERS)

The computer and software business in Russia has been expanding rapidly along with the telecommunications industry. IBM-compatible computers still account for the largest portion of the market, although Apple computer sales increased significantly in the mid-nineties and the company expanded its distributorship to Belarus, Georgia, Armenia, Lithuania, and Latvia. The major American computer and software companies with offices in the principal Russian cities now include IBM, Intel, Digital, SUN Microsystems, Apple, Hewlett-Packard, Packard-Bell, and Microsoft. There are many computer sales and service companies in the principal Russian cities. Warranties (гара́нтии) do not always apply when purchasing equipment, so it is advisable to inquire about service support (се́рвисная подде́ржка) and post-warranty maintenance (послегаранти́йное обслу́живание). A number of western firms offer full system installation (по́лная систе́мная устано́вка). In addition to extensive advertising in selected business-oriented journals such as «Коммерса́нт», «Де́ньги», and «Деловы́е лю́ди», all brands of computers and peripherals are regulary promoted at frequent international computer exhibits in many Russian cities. Updated information about the status of computer technology developments can also be obtained from the Computer Business Russia newsletter (email: farish@glas.apc.org or from its Internet address: http://koi.www.online.ru/emain/ecomp/cbr).

The following diagram will help you become familiar with some basic Russian computer terminology. Of the many Russian fonts (шрифт) and keyboard layouts (раскладка клавиатуры) available on the market, most English-speaking users find the phonetic-equivalent layout the most convenient.

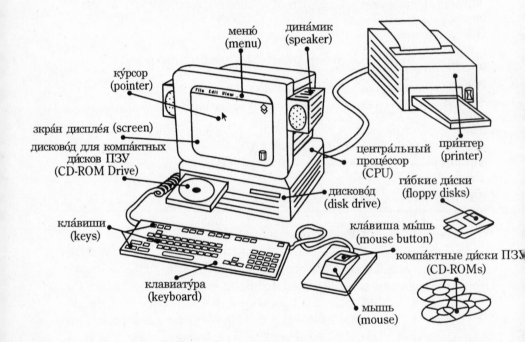

меню́
(menu)

дина́мик
(speaker)

ку́рсор
(pointer)

зкра́н дисппле́я (screen)

дисково́д для компа́ктных
ди́сков ПЗУ
(CD-ROM Drive)

центра́льный
проце́ссор
(CPU)

при́нтер
(printer)

ги́бкие ди́ски
(floppy disks)

дисково́д
(disk drive)

кла́виши
(keys)

кла́виша мы́шь
(mouse button)

компа́ктные ди́ски ПЗУ
(CD-ROMs)

клавиату́ра
(keyboard)

мышь
(mouse)

The following are additional computer terms you might find useful.

ба́за да́нных	data base
вход в систе́му	login
дисково́д для ги́бких ди́сков	floppy disk drive
диск с удво́енной пло́тностью	double-density disk
загружа́ть да́нные/файл	to load data/file
ЗУ (запомина́ющее устро́йство)	memory
ЗУ с произво́льным поря́дком
выборки	RAM

Интеловский	Intel-based
лазерный диск	laser disk
локальная сеть	LAN (local area network)
многоабонентский	multi-user
модем	modem
настольные издательские средства	desktop publishing
обработка текстов	word processing
объединительная плата	mother board
оптическое распознавание символов	OCR (optical character recognition)
пакетные задания	batched jobs
пароль	password
повторять начальную загрузку	to reboot
ПЗУ (постоянное запоминающее устройство)	ROM
пространство на диске	disk space
резервное устройство	backup
сохранять	to save
управляемый в режиме меню	menu-driven
полный отказ системы	system crash
сжатие данных	data crunching
справочное руководство для пользователей	user's manual
образ	icon
идентификатор пользователя	user ID

УПРАЖНЕНИЯ

A. В следующих предложениях впишите подходящее местоимение или прилагательное в нужной форме. (Insert the required form of the appropriate pronoun or adjective in the following sentences.)

1. _____ (какой/каков) гарантийный срок у этого принтера?
2. _____ (какие/каковы) модели вас интересуют?
3. _____ (каково/какое/ разрешение этого монитора?
4. _____ (таков/такой) компьютер, который мы хотели купить
5. _____ (какие/каковы) технические характеристики этой модели?
6. Все новые модели компьютеров _____ (такие/таковы/каковы/какие)

7. _____(такие/какие/каковы) новые модели у вас в продаже?

8. _____(таков/каков/какой) их финансовое положение?

9. Выставка будет_____(открытый/открыт) до девяти вечера.

10. Я _____(голодн(ый)(ая)/голод(ен)(на)) как волк.

B. Заполните пропуски, используя нужную форму подходящего глагола, прилагательного, существительного. (Fill in the blanks by using the required form of the appropriate verb, adjective, or noun.)

1. Мы_____новейшими моделями компьютеров.
   (are interested in)

2. Все эти мониторы имеют_____.
   (a flat screen)

3. _____можно пользоваться на этих компьютерах?
   (Which fonts)

4. Вот эта модель _____.
   (is very popular [enjoys popularity])

5. Вы не знаете, где сейчас _____?
   (the store manager)

6. К сожалению, они пренебрегли _____пользования
   (the rules)

_____.
   (these computers)

7. Они прекрасно владеют _____текстовой обработки (word
   (the new system)
processing).

8. Мы_____большим выбором новейших моделей.
   (have available)

9. _____ лэптопы с большой оперативной памятью.
   (We are interested in)

10. Мы бы хотели_____ с _____ваших сканеров.
   (become acquainted)   (latest models)

C. Переведите следующие предложения с английского языка на русский. Укажите, куда падает ударение. (Translate the following sentences into Russian. Indicate stress marks.)

1. I asked the store manager about servicing and technical support.
2. They were interested in computers with a large memory.
3. The representative took the opportunity to demonstrate IBM-compatible computers.
4. The software section of our exhibit is on the second floor.

5. What is the processor speed of these models?
6. What kind of fonts do you use in these computers?
7. Can you give me some information about the specs of this scanner?
8. You can switch the fonts or language by a single click of the hot key.
9. Would you like to get on our mailing list for receiving catalogs?
10. We have heaps of time left. Why don't we go back to the exhibit to see the rest of the stands?

УРОК 14

А. ДИАЛОГ

В антикварном магазине.

Перед возвращением в США Йоко и её муж Дэнис, заядлые коллекционеры антиквариата, думают о том, что они могут себе позволить приобрести что-нибудь из русских предметов старины.[1] С ними их русский друг Борис.

БОРИС: У вас есть на примете[2] какие-то определённые предметы антиквариата, которые вы хотели бы купить?

ЙОКО: Вообще-то нет. Единственное, о чём я слышала, так это об иконах.

БОРИС: Да? Это не лучший вариант. Во-первых, подлинные иконы считаются культурным достоянием государства и по закону не могут быть вывезены из страны. Конечно, есть очень много поддельных икон, которые спекулянты сбывают[3] ничего не подозревающим туристам. Я уверен, что это не то, что вы хотите.

ЙОКО: Вот как. Тогда что бы вы посоветовали?

БОРИС: Вообще-то, зайдя в антикварный магазин, вы увидите много вещей, которые могут вас заинтересовать: скажем, латунные самовары, серебряные столовые наборы, фарфор, музыкальные шкатулки . . .[4]

ДЭНИС: А где нам лучше искать такие вещи?

БОРИС: Так как мы уже на Арбате, давайте начнём вот здесь. Как раз есть несколько интересных магазинов подальше по этой улице. А если у нас будет время, можно посмотреть и другие места. У вас паспорта с собой?

ЙОКО: Да, у меня паспорт с собой. А он мне может понадобиться?

БОРИС: Обязательно. Продавец попросит его у вас, заполняя декларацию на вывоз подлинных предметов антиквариата.

Вам ну́жно бу́дет предоста́вить её на тамо́жне при вы́езде из страны́.

В антиква́рном магази́не «Рарите́т».

ЙОКО: **Посмотри́ на э́тот краси́вый фарфо́ровый серви́з! Что ты ду́маешь? Он тебе́ нра́вится?**

ДЭНИС: **Да, ничего́ себе́. И рису́нок мне нра́вится. Но мне ка́жется, что он для нас сли́шком до́рог.**

ЙОКО: (обраща́ясь к продавщи́це) **Извини́те, вы мо́жете мне сказа́ть, когда́ и где э́тот серви́з сде́лан?**

ПРОДАВЩИЦА: **Да, коне́чно. Э́тот серви́з, изгото́вленный в Гже́ли,[5] дати́руется середи́ной восемна́дцатого ве́ка. По́лный набо́р рассчи́тан на шесть персо́н и состои́т из блю́дец, ча́шек, са́харницы и ма́ленького ча́йника.**

ЙОКО: **Вы принима́ете до́ллары?**

ПРОДАВЩИЦА: **К сожале́нию, нет. Но пря́мо за ва́ми пункт обме́на валю́ты. Вы мо́жете купи́ть сто́лько[6] рубле́й, ско́лько вам пона́добится для поку́пки.**

ДЭНИС: **Ну, мы всё-таки должны́ снача́ла поду́мать.**

В магази́не «Ико́ны».

ЙОКО: **Мне о́чень нра́вятся э́ти лату́нные самова́ры. Я ду́маю, что мы мо́жем купи́ть самова́р.**

ДЭНИС: **Вот э́тот о́чень своеобра́зный. Посмотри́те, у него́ на боку́ каки́е-то гравиро́ванные меда́ли. Бори́с, вы мо́жете прочита́ть, что там напи́сано?**

БОРИС: **Да, я разбира́ю слова́. Самова́р был сде́лан компа́нией Алекса́ндра Ду́бова в 1910 году́ в Ту́ле.[7]**

ЙОКО: **Дава́й ку́пим его́! Я уже́ давно́ хоте́ла приобрести́ настоя́щий самова́р.**

БОРИС: **Я рад, что вы нашли́ то, что хоте́ли. Кста́ти, мо́жет быть вы хоте́ли бы ещё купи́ть ма́ленький подходя́щий к нему́ зава́рочный ча́йник,[8] кото́рый ста́вят на самова́р?**

ЙОКО: Это то, что нужно!

At an antique shop.

Before returning to the States, Yoko and her husband, Dennis, who are avid antique collectors, decide to see what they might be able to afford in the way of a Russian antique. They are accompanied by their friend, Boris.

BORIS: Do you have any idea what kind of antiques you would like to buy?

YOKO: Not really. The only antiques I have heard about are icons.

BORIS: Really? Well, I wouldn't recommend that. First of all, genuine icons are considered state art and cannot be legally exported. Of course, there are a lot of fake icons that are often hawked to unsuspecting tourists. But I'm sure you wouldn't want one of those.

YOKO: Well, then what would you suggest?

BORIS: Well, there are number of interesting items that might suggest themselves once you see them in an antique shop: brass samovars, a silverware service, porcelain, music boxes . . .

DENNIS: Where do you suggest we start looking?

BORIS: Since we're already on Arbat, we can start right here. There are a couple of interesting shops just down the street. If we have time we can also take a look at some other places. Do you have your passports?

YOKO: Yes, I do. Will I need it?

BORIS: Definitely. The clerk will need it to fill out the required form for genuine antiques. You'll have to present the form to customs when you leave.

At the Raritet antique store.

YOKO: Oh, look at that beautiful porcelain tea set! What do you think? Do you like it?

DENNIS: Yeah, it's pretty nice. And I like that design. But I wonder if it's too expensive for us.

YOKO: (*addressing the saleswoman*) Excuse me, can you tell me where and when this tea set was made?

SALESWOMAN: Yes, of course. The set dates to the mid-eighteenth century, and was made in Gzhel. The entire set is a service for six and consists of saucers, cups, a sugar bowl, and a small teapot.

YOKO: Do you accept dollars?

SALESWOMAN: No, sorry. But we have a foreign exchange booth right behind you. You can change the amount you need to rubles and then make your purchase.

DENNIS: Well, let's think about this for a while.

At the Ikoni store.

YOKO: These brass samovars are really nice. I think we might get one.

DENNIS: This one looks quite impressive. See, it's got medals engraved on the side. Can you read what's written on them, Boris?

BORIS: Yes, I can just make it out. The samovar was made in 1910 by the Aleksandr Dubov company in the city of Tula.

YOKO: Yes, let's buy it. I've always wanted a genuine samovar.

BORIS: I'm glad you found what you want. You might want to get a matching teapot that goes on top of the samovar.

YOKO: Oh, yes!

B. ПРИМЕЧАНИЯ

1. Рýсские предмéты старины́ literally means "Russian objects of ancient times."

2. Примéта means "sign," "token," "omen," but it is also used in the expression быть на примéте (to have in mind). Когдá зéркало упáло нá пол и рассколóлось на мéлкие куски́, мать сказáла: «Плохáя примéта.» (When the mirror fell on the floor and split into small pieces, mother said: "It's a bad omen.") А у тебя́ есть ктó-нибудь на примéте? (Do you have anyone in mind?)

3. Сбывáть/сбыть (to sell) also has the colloquial meaning of "to dump something off on someone." Наконéц, я сбыл с рук эти бесполéзные шмóтки. (I finally got these useless old clothes off my hands.) The noun сбыт (sales) usually refers to large-scale marketing. Сбыт влечёт за собóй не тóлько продáжу товáров, но тáкже и изучéние

рынка, спроса и интересов покупателей. (Sales not only entails the selling of merchandise, but also a study of the market and consumer demand and interests.)

4. Шкатулки are among the best known Russian handicrafts. These intricately hand-painted, lacquered boxes were first produced in 1796 in the village of Fedoskino, outside of Moscow. Later the nearby village of Palekh became the center for that craft, and it remains so today.

5. Owing to the rich clay deposits in that region, the village of Гжель, near Moscow, became a center for the manufacture of porcelain wares in the early eighteenth century. The Russian word фарфор (porcelain) originates from Turkish *(farfur)*.

6. Столько + a noun in the genitive case + сколько means "as much . . . as . . .": На Арбате иногда бывают столько туристов, сколько москвичей. (Sometimes there are as many tourists on Arbat as there are Muscovites.)

7. The first samovar factory in Tula was opened in 1778 by the arms manufacturer Ф.И. Лисицын. Founded in the twelfth century, Tula currently has a population of approximately 600,000. Its principal industries include metal-working, machine tools, knitwear, sugar-refining, and bakery products. Leo Tolstoy's estate «Ясная Поляна,» where he lived for sixty years and wrote «Война и Мир» and «Анна Каренина», is 14 kilometers (about 8 miles) to the south of the city.

8. Заварочный чайник (brewing teapot) is used to make a concentrated solution of tea that is diluted with the water drawn from the spigot of the samovar.

C. ГРАММАТИКА И СЛОВОУПОТРЕБЛЕНИЕ

1. УПТРЕБЛЕНИЕ СЛОВА «ЧТО» (THE USE OF ЧТО)

Что is most commonly used to ask questions or to introduce a subordinate clause.

Что они сейчас делают?
What are they doing now?

Я думаю, что они купят самовар.
I think that they'll buy a samovar.

Что can also introduce a clause that describes a substantivized adjective, or the pronouns всё and то.

Гла́вное, что вам на́до сде́лать — это получи́ть па́спорт.
The main thing that you have to do is get a passport.

Еди́нственное, о чём я слы́шала, так это об ико́нах.
The only thing that I've heard about are icons.

Пе́рвое, чем на́до занима́ться, так это подгото́вкой к экза́мену.
The first thing you have to get busy with is to prepare for the exam.

Мы купи́ли всё, что мне на́до бы́ло приобрести́.
We bought everything that I needed to get.

Я уже́ тебе́ рассказа́л всё, что я зна́ю об этих предме́тах.
I already told you everything that I know about these objects.

Я рад, что вы нашли́ то, что хоте́ли.
I'm glad that you found what you wanted.

Это то, что мне ну́жно.
That's just what I need.

Всё начало́сь с того́, что я столкну́лся со свои́м бы́вшим колле́гой.
It all began with my running into my former colleague.

Что is also used as a particle in certain emphatic expressions.

Ты что, не ви́дел, что там случи́лось?
What's with you, didn't you see what happened there?

А я что, не жела́ю прийти́ на ве́чер?
And what about me, don't you think I want to come to the party?

Ты что, с ума́ сошёл?
Have you gone nuts, or what?

2. ДЕЕПРИЧАСТИЯ (VERBAL ADVERBS)

Verbal adverbs, also known as gerunds, are indeclinable forms that are often translated into English with the -ing form of a verb. They are used to describe an action taking place at the same time as or prior to the action of the main verb. Be careful not to confuse them with present participles (also translated with the -ing form), which act as adjectives and must agree with the nouns they modify. Compare:

Тури́сты, заполня́ющие деклара́цию на вы́воз предме́тов антиквариа́та, гото́вятся к вы́езду из страны́. (participle)
The tourists filling out the declaration form for exporting antiques are getting ready to leave the country.

Заполня́я деклара́цию на тамо́жне, тури́сты ча́сто проверя́ют, ско́лько у них оста́лось иностра́нной валю́ты. (gerund)
While filling out their declaration forms, the tourists often check to see how much foreign currency they have left.

In most cases gerund phrases can be replaced by a phrase beginning with когда́ (when).

Когда́ тури́сты заполня́ют деклара́ции, они́ ча́сто проверя́ют, ско́лько у них оста́лось иностра́нной валю́ты.
When tourists fill out their declaration forms, they often check to see how much foreign currency they have left.

A) FORMATION OF IMPERFECTIVE GERUNDS

Imperfective gerunds are formed by adding -я (-а after ж, ч, ш, щ) to the present tense stem of the verb. The stem of the verb is normally found by dropping the last two letters of the third person plural form; e.g., чита́ют → чита- → чита́я (reading), слы́шат → слыш- → слы́ша (hearing.) Reflexive verbs retain the -ся/-сь ending; e.g., обраща́ются → обраща- → обраща́ясь (turning to, addressing). Note that, with few exceptions, the stress in gerunds is the same as in the first person singular form of the verb.*

---

*Exceptions include the verbs гляде́ть (to watch), лежа́ть (to lie down), сиде́ть (to sit), and стоя́ть (to stand): я гляжу́/гля́дя (I am looking at/while looking at); я лежу́/лёжа (I am lying down/while lying down); я сижу́/си́дя (I am sitting/while sitting); я стою́/сто́я (I am standing/while standing).

Чита́я брошю́ру об антиквариа́те, я заме́тил, что продавщи́ца
закрыва́ла магази́н
> While reading the booklet on antiques, I noticed that the saleswoman
> was closing the store.

Получа́я де́ньги у окна́ обме́на валю́ты, я поду́мала, что я бу́ду де́лать с
ли́шними деньга́ми?
> While getting money at the exchange window, I wondered what I
> would do with the leftover rubles?

Обраща́яъ к продавцу́, я попроси́ла его́ показа́ть мне янта́рное
ожере́лье.
> Turning to the salesman, I asked him to show me an amber
> necklace.

Some common verbs, such as хоте́ть (to want) and пить (to drink), do
not have an imperfective gerund. In that case, the gerund form of a syn-
onym can be used instead. For example, you can substitute жела́ть (to
wish) for хоте́ть, or выпива́ть for пить.

Жела́я купи́ть самова́р, я зашёл в антиква́рный магази́н.
> Wanting to purchase a samovar, I dropped into an antique shop.

Выпива́я в ба́ре ча́шку ко́фе, я завёл разгово́р с сиде́вшей ря́дом со мной
де́вушкой.
> While drinking a cup of coffee at the bar, I started up a conversation
> with the young woman sitting next to me.

Other verbs with no imperfective gerunds and synonyms from which
they can be formed include:

VERB WITH NO IMPERFECTIVE GERUND	SYNONYM	GERUND
есть (to eat)	съеда́ть	съеда́я (eating)
ехать (to travel)	проезжа́ть	проезжа́я (traveling)
ждать (to wait)	ожида́ть	ожида́я (waiting)
жечь (to burn)	сжига́ть	сжига́я (burning)

B. FORMATION OF PERFECTIVE GERUNDS

Gerunds from perfective verbs ending in -ть are generally formed by replacing the final -л of the past tense masculine form with the suffix -в; e.g., прочита́ть→прочита́в (having read), завари́ть→завари́в (having brewed). The reflexive perfective gerunds have the ending -вшись; e.g., верну́ться→верну́вшись(having returned).

Gerunds derived from perfective verbs ending in -ти and -сть are generally formed by replacing the last two letters of the third person plural form with -я; e.g., приобрести́→приобрету́т→приобретя́ (having acquired), вы́везти→вы́везут→вы́везя́ (having exported), принести́→принесу́т→принеся́ (having brought).

C. PRINCIPAL USAGES OF RUSSIAN GERUNDS

Gerunds are much more common in written than in spoken language, and they should be learned only insofar as they need to be recognized.

Imperfective gerunds denote an action that is simultaneous to the action of the verb in the main clause.

Обраща́ясь к продавцу́, я заме́тил ещё оди́н интере́сный с ви́ду самова́р.
As I turned to the clerk, I noticed yet another interesting looking samovar.

Рабо́тая с компью́тером, я ча́сто слу́шаю му́зыку по ра́дио.
I often listen to music on the radio while working on the computer.

Сто́я у пу́нкта обме́на валю́ты, он вдруг почему́-то рассмея́лся.
While standing near the currency exchange window, he burst into laughter for some reason.

Note that a negated imperfective gerund can be rendered in English as "without ... -ing."

Не обраща́я внима́ния на предупрежде́ния друзе́й, она всё-таки купи́ла у спекуля́нта подде́льную ико́ну.
Without paying attention to the warnings of friends, she bought a fake icon from a huckster.

Perfective gerunds describe an action that was completed prior to the action of the main verb.

Заплати́в за ча́йник и самова́р, мы отпра́вились в друго́й магази́н.
Having paid for the teapot and samovar, we set off for another store.

Пройдя́ тамо́женный досмо́тр, пассажи́ры подгото́вились к поса́дке.
After passing through customs, the passengers got ready to board the plane.

Зара́нее запо́лнив деклара́цию, я о́чень бы́стро прошёл досмо́тр.
By completing the declaration beforehand, I went through customs very quickly.

A few additional rules about gerund constructions should be kept in mind: The subject of the gerund and the subject of the main clause are always the same. Gerunds are, therefore, not normally used with an impersonal phrase, unless the impersonal is used in the infinitive.

Заполня́я деклара́цию, мо́жно по́льзоваться карандашо́м.
When filling out the declaration, you can use a pencil.

Remember that the verb in the main clause can be in any tense or aspect as long as the two actions are simultaneous, in the case of imperfective gerunds, or sequential, in the case of perfective gerunds.

Получи́в деклара́цию на вы́воз антиква́рных веще́й, я её сра́зу запо́лнил.
After receiving the declaration form for exporting antiques, I filled it out immediately.

Зайдя́ в магази́н, вы уви́дите мно́го прекра́сных веще́й, кото́рые мо́гут вас заинтересова́ть.
After dropping into the store, you'll see a lot of beautiful things that might interest you.

Возвраща́ясь с рабо́ты, я обы́чно захожу́ на ры́нок за овоща́ми.
While returning from work, I usually drop by the market for vegetables.

Возвраща́ясь с рабо́ты, я ча́сто заходи́л на ры́нок за овоща́ми.
When returning from work, I often used to drop by the market for vegetables.

D. ИДИОМАТИКА

OLDER AND WISER.

По старинке (IN THE OLD-FASHIONED WAY)

Она ещё считает по старинке, на счётах.
  She still counts the old-fashioned way, on the abacus.

Тряхнуть стариной (TO GO BACK TO FORMER ACTIVITIES)

Когда он вышел в тираж, ему приходилось изредка тряхнуть стариной.
  When he retired, every once in a while he had to go back to the old
  trade.

И на старуху бывает проруха. (EVEN AN EXPERIENCED PERSON CAN
BLUNDER.)

Мне трудно поверить, что он допустил такую ошибку! —Ну, что же, и на
старуху бывает проруха.
  I can't believe he made such a mistake! —Well, after all, anyone can
  make a mistake.

Старость не радость. (OLD AGE IS NO JOY.)

Ну, что такое, Вася, ты два раза подряд промазал! —Да, знаю. Старость
не радость.
  What's with you, Vasya, you missed twice in a row! —Yeah, I know. I'm
  not what I used to be.

Стреляный воробей (AN OLD HAND; LIT., A SHOT BIRD)

Не беспокойтесь, он стреляный воробей. Его не обманешь!
  Don't worry, he's a wise old bird. You can't fool him!

Старый друг лучше новых двух. (AN OLD FRIEND IS BETTER THAN TWO
NEW ONES.)

Не беспокойся, там у тебя будут новые друзья. —Может быть, но всё же
старый друг лучше новых двух.
  Don't worry, you'll make new friends over there. —Maybe. Still, an old
  friend is better than two new ones.

E. СТРОГО ПО ДЕЛУ

ПРЕДМЕТЫ ВВОЗА И ВЫВОЗА (IMPORTS AND EXPORTS)

Although Western Europe remains Russia's largest trading partner (accounting for approximately 40 percent of exports and 41 percent of imports), the United States' trade with the NIS (Newly Independent States) has been steadily increasing along with the pace of privatization. The largest import items (предме́ты вво́за) from the United States into Russia include poultry (дома́шняя пти́ца), pork (свини́на), dairy machinery (маши́ны для моло́чной промы́шленности), machinery parts (запча́сти к маши́нам), tobacco products (таба́чные изде́лия), electrical equipment (электри́ческое обору́дование), and aircraft (самолёты). Among the principal items exported (предме́ты вы́воза) from Russia to the United States are aluminum (алюми́ний), iron (желе́зо), steel (сталь), precious stones and metals (драгоце́нные ка́мни, благоро́дные мета́ллы), inorganic chemicals (неоргани́ческие химика́ты), and nickel (ни́кель). The United States typically has a very small trade deficit with Russia, and the volume is well over \$3 billion annually. Among the U.S. export items to Russia that represent considerable prospects for growth are consumer-oriented food products (пищевы́е проду́кты широ́кого употребле́ния), particularly consumer-ready products (полуфабрика́ты и гото́вые проду́кты).

Despite the continually improving prospects for exporting goods to the Russia and the NIS, the frequently changing regulations regarding customs duties (по́шлины) and tariff rates (тари́фные ста́вки) imposed on a variety of goods have presented considerable difficulties for American exporters. Efforts are being made on the intergovermental level to improve those conditions. In any event, anyone contemplating the export of goods to Russia and the NIS should become thoroughly familiar with the documentaton required for shipping merchandise (перево́зка това́ров) in order to avoid costly delays in cargo clearance and delivery (тамо́женная очи́стка и поста́вка това́ров). The beginning exporter should locate a reliable forwarding agent (экспеди́тор) who specializes in shipping goods to Russia. Detailed information about freight forwarders and customs brokers can be obtained from The National Customs Brokers and Forwarders Association of America, Inc. (tel. 212-432-0050; fax 212-432-5709). The principal documents involved in exporting goods to Russia include a commercial invoice (счёт-фактура), a marine bill of lading (морско́й коносаме́нт) and/or air waybill (авианакладна́я), a certificate of origin (сертифика́т происхожде́ния това́ра), an export packing list (упако́вочный лист на вы́воз), and a number of pre-shipment inspection certificates such as a certificate of safety (сертифика́т о безопа́сности това́ра) and a health certificate (сертифика́т о санита́рно-гигиени́ческом контро́ле).

Updated information on export-import regulations can be obtained from the U.S. Department of Commerce, International Trade Administration Business Information Service (tel. 202-482-4655; email bisnis@usita.gov).

УПРАЖНЕНИЯ

A. Замени́те сле́дующие сло́жные предложе́ния предложе́ниями с соотве́тствующими дееприча́стными оборо́тами. (Change the following compound sentences into corresponding gerund phrases.)

ОБРАЗЕЦ: Когда́ я верну́лся с рабо́ты, я пригото́вил обе́д.
Верну́вшись с рабо́ты, я пригото́вил обе́д.

1. По́сле того́, как мы запо́лнили деклара́цию, мы вошли́ в рестора́н.
2. Когда́ я за́втракаю, я обы́чно чита́ю у́треннюю газе́ту.
3. Так как она́ не зна́ет ру́сского языка́, она́ не поняла́, о чём мы говори́ли.
4. Когда́ я возвраща́лся с рабо́ты, я обы́чно заходи́л в кни́жный магази́н.
5. По́сле того́, как вы пройдёте тамо́женный досмо́тр, вы смо́жете подгото́виться к поса́дке.
6. Пока́ мы стоя́ли в о́череди, мы завели́ интере́сный разгово́р.
7. Когда́ он вы́пил две ча́шки ко́фе, он сказа́л, что ему́ пора́ идти́ домо́й.
8. По́сле того́ как мы поменя́ли на́ши до́ллары на рубли́, мы купи́ли не́сколько предме́тов старины́.
9. Когда́ я зашёл в магази́н, я уви́дел мно́го интере́сных веще́й.
10. Когда́ я посмотре́л на ча́йный серви́з, я сра́зу реши́л купи́ть его́.

B. Впишите подходящее причастие в нужной форме. (Insert the
    appropriate gerund in the proper form.)

    1. _____декларацию, можно отвечать на вопросы на
       (When completing)
       английском языке.
    2. Мы шли по улицам_____ на время.
                              (without paying attention)
    3. _____три письма, я начал заниматься уроками.
       (After having written)
    4. _____того, что она сказала, я ещё раз спросил
       (Without understanding)
       её, сколько стоит самовар.
    5. _____домой, я поставил самовар.
          (After returning)
    6. _____за столом, мы решили сыграть в карты.
          (While sitting)
    7. _____десять километров, он вдруг сообщил, что
       (After having driven)
       мы попали не туда.
    8. _____новые документы, мы начали переводить
       (After having brought)
       текст с русского на английский.
    9. _____журнал, он передал его моему брату.
          (After reading)
    10. _____из школы, они обычно заходили в
        (When returning)
        библиотеку.

C. Переведите следующие предложения с английского языка на
    русский.

    1. While going through customs, my friends asked if I filled out a
       declaration form.
    2. I told her that I bought everything that I needed.
    3. The first thing you have to do is complete the declaration form.
    4. I'm glad you found what you wanted.
    5. What's with you, didn't you see the bus near the station?
    6. When filling out the declaration form, many tourists don't know
       how to answer some of the questions.
    7. While turning to the clerk, I asked her how much the tea
       service costs.

8. Having acquired a real samovar, she decided to buy a matching antique teapot.
9. Having paid for the samovar, we set off for another store.
10. Having dropped into the antique store, I saw a lot of interesting things.

УРОК 15

А. ДИАЛОГ

Посещéние чáстной фéрмы.

Торгóвые представи́тели америкáнской фирмы по произвóдству сельскохозя́йственного оборýдования Мáрвин Трýман и Андрея Блýмфилд бы́ли приглашены́ в Ростóвскую[1] óбласть на фéрму Ивáна Куликóва, котóрый привéтствует их в управлéнии своéй фéрмы.

ИВАН: Добрó пожáловать в Ростóв-на-Донý[2]. Наскóлько я понимáю, вы ужé имéли достáточно дéла с сельско-хозя́йственным оборýдованием в этом региóне?

МАРВИН: Да, нáша фи́рма продалá нéкоторое коли́чество комбáйнов украи́нскому прави́тельству и совсéм недáвно нéсколько комбáйнов отдéльным колхóзам[3] в Росси́йской Федерáции. А вы знакóмы с нáшим оборýдованием?

ИВАН: Ну ещё бы, я вы́слушал немáло хорóшего о вáших маши́нах!

АНДРЕЯ: Каки́е вáши основны́е культýры?

ИВАН: Ну так, у нас примéрно[4] сóрок пять гектáров[5] отдано под ози́мую пшени́цу, и ещё óколо пятнáдцати под подсóлнечник. И, наконéц, в прóшлом годý мы нáчали высевáть гибри́д кукурýзы.

МАРВИН: И какóв[6] был урожáй?

ИВАН: Очень дáже неплохóй. Мы собрáли óколо ты́сячи тонн пшени́цы, пятидесяти́ тонн кукурýзы и примéрно двáдцать пять тонн семя́н подсóлнечника.

АНДРЕЯ: Кто явля́ется вáшими основны́ми покупáтелями?

ИВАН: Мы продаём нáшу продýкцию прави́тельству, а тáкже скóлько-то поставля́ем на чáстные ры́нки в окрéстных городáх.

МАРВИН: Наскóлько я понимáю, вáша фéрма процветáет.

ИВАН: И да, и нет.

АНДРЕЯ: Что вы имеете в виду?

ИВАН: Видите ли, мне легко найти покупателей, но предлагаемые ими цены зачастую слишком низки, чтобы получить хоть какую-то прибыль.

АНДРЕЯ: Вот уж эта проблема нам знакомая. Итак, какое же оборудование вам нужно?

ИВАН: Мы уже имеем четыре трактора, три грузовика, и два комбайна, но мы определённо могли бы дополнительно использовать современное оборудование, чтобы увеличить производительность. Пойдёмте на поле, я покажу вам, что у нас имеется и что бы мы хотели приобрести.

На поле.

МАРВИН: Ваша ферма производит на меня неплохое впечатление. Вы, кстати, владеете землёй полностью?

ИВАН: Не совсем. Когда два года назад мы с женой решили обзавестись семейной фермой, то район выделил нам шестьдесят гектаров земли на двадцать лет с последующим выкупом.

МАРВИН: Понятно . . . а кто это вон на том тракторе?

ИВАН: Это моя жена Тамара. У неё золотые руки.[7]

Иван машет Тамаре рукой и представляет её американцам.

МАРВИН: Насколько я вижу, вы достаточно занятая[8] женщина на этой ферме.

ТАМАРА: Да уж, всегда есть чем заняться. К тому же нам никто особо не помогает.

АНДРЕЯ: А возможна ли помощь со стороны семьи?

ТАМАРА: Боюсь, наши дети потеряли интерес к сельской жизни. Они уехали в город на поиски[9] других видов работы.

МАРВИН: Как я вас понимаю—у нас происходит то же самое.

ТАМАРА: А сейчас прости́те меня́, я уви́жу вас приме́рно че́рез час у нас до́ма, ла́дно?

ИВАН: Ла́дно. А тепе́рь дава́йте пройдём сюда́ ...

По́сле обхо́да фе́рмы все тро́е возвраща́ются к до́му Ива́на с це́лью немно́го передохну́ть и перекуси́ть. Там их приве́тствует Тама́ра.

ТАМАРА: Ну, как вам нра́вится на́ша «планта́ция»?

АНДРЕЯ: (хихи́кает) Ага́, «планта́ция», а где у вас хлопча́тник!

ТАМАРА: (усмеха́ется) Да, хло́пка у нас нет, а вот хлопо́т[10] нема́ло!

АНДРЕЯ: Я вас поняла́. Нет, серьёзно, фе́рма у вас о́чень впечатля́ющая.

МАРВИН: И хоро́ший подбо́р культу́р.

ИВАН: Спаси́бо. Всё же, как вы ви́дите, мы вполне́ могли́ бы испо́льзовать но́вый убо́рочный комба́йн и молоти́лку.[11]

МАРВИН: Я хоте́л бы показа́ть вам ко́е-каки́е проспе́кты, кото́рые я принёс с собо́й, опи́сывающие обору́дование, вы́пускаемое на́шей фи́рмой. Мне ка́жется, вас с Тама́рой э́то мо́жет заинтересова́ть.

ТАМАРА: Спаси́бо. Есть ли у вас представи́тельство в на́шем регио́не?

АНДРЕЯ: Пока́ что у нас о́фисы то́лько в Москве́ и Ки́еве. Но мы плани́руем откры́ть ме́стный о́фис в Росто́ве в ближа́йшем бу́дущем.

ИВАН: Очень хорошо́. Само́ собо́й,[12] нам ну́жно бу́дет навести́ спра́вки о возмо́жности креди́та у на́ших ба́нков, е́сли я всё же решу́ что́-нибудь купи́ть.

МАРВИН: Разуме́ется, я вас понима́ю. Но вы, наве́рное, зна́ете, что мы мо́жем устро́ить для вас за́ймы на поку́пку обору́дования у на́ших со́бственных ба́нков под[13] сравни́тельно небольши́е проце́нты?

ИВАН: Хорошо́. Мо́жет, у нас что́-нибудь и полу́чится. Тама́ра, ты как ду́маешь?

ТАМАРА: Да уж, тот тра́ктор, на кото́ром я рабо́тала, уже́ старова́т,[14] и вся́кая почи́нка влета́ет в копе́ечку.

МАРВИН: **Обрати́тесь к нам, если у вас бу́дут вопро́сы, и мы мо́жем вам помо́чь.**

A visit to a privatized farm.

Marvin Truman and Andrea Bloomfield, sales representatives of an American agricultural machinery manufacturer, have been invited to the Rostov Oblast private farm of Ivan Kulikov, who greets them at his farm office.

IVAN: Welcome to Rostov. So, I understand you have been doing quite a bit of business in agricultural equipment in this area.

MARVIN: Yes, our company has sold a number of harvesters to the Ukrainian government and a few to some collective farms in the Russian Federation. Are you familiar with our equipment?

IVAN: Oh yes. I've only heard good things about your machines.

ANDREA: What are your principal crops?

IVAN: Well, we have about forty-five hectares given to winter wheat, and about fifteen for sunflower seed. And last year, we started to plant hybrid corn.

MARVIN: And how have your harvests been?

IVAN: Not too bad. We produced about one thousand tons of wheat, fifty tons of corn, and twenty-five tons of sunflower seed.

ANDREA: Who are your principal customers?

IVAN: We market our products to the government and deliver produce to various privately owned farmer's markets in nearby cities.

MARVIN: I gather business has been pretty good, then?

IVAN: Yes and no.

ANDREA: What do you mean?

IVAN: Well, yes, I don't have any problems finding customers, but the prices they offer are often too low for me to make a reasonable profit.

ANDREA: That sounds like a familiar problem. What about your equipment needs?

IVAN: Well, we have four tractors, three trucks, and two combines, but we could definitely use some additional modern equipment that would increase productivity. Let's go onto the fields so I can show you what we have and what I would like to have.

In the field.

MARVIN: Your farm is quite impressive. By the way, do you own the land outright?

IVAN: Not quite. When my wife and I decided to set up a farmstead two years ago, the regional government allotted us an area of sixty hectares for a period of twenty years with the option to buy.

MARVIN: I see . . . Who's that on the tractor?

IVAN: That's my wife, Tamara. She's a real handy person.

Ivan waves Tamara over and introduces her to the Americans.

MARVIN: I understand you're quite a busy woman around here.

TAMARA: Yes, there's always plenty to do. And we don't have too much help.

ANDREA: Is there any family help possible?

TAMARA: I'm afraid our children have lost interest in farm life. They've gone to the city to find different kinds of work.

MARVIN: I understand. We are experiencing that trend, too.

TAMARA: Now, if you'll excuse me, I'll see you later at the house in about an hour, okay?

IVAN: Fine. Okay. Now, if you'll follow me . . .

After a tour of the farm, the three return to Ivan's home for refreshment, where Tamara greets them.

TAMARA: So, how do you like our "plantation"?

ANDREA: (*giggles*) Yeah, "plantation." But where are the cotton plants?

TAMARA: (*grins*) Cotton we don't have, but worries we do.

ANDREA: I get it. But, seriously, your farm is very impressive.

MARVIN: And a very nice variety of crops.

IVAN: Thanks. Still, as you can see, we certainly can use a more modern harvester, and thresher.

MARVIN: I'd like to give you some brochures I brought which describe some of the equipment our company manufactures. I think you and Tamara will find the material interesting.

TAMARA: Thank you. Do you have a sales office in this area?

ANDREA: So far, our only offices are in Moscow and Kiev. But we plan to open a local office in Rostov in the near future.

IVAN: That's good. Of course, we'll have to check with our banks about financing if I decide to buy anything.

MARVIN: Yes, I understand. You may know, however, that we can arrange special loans for equipment purchases through our own banks, and at reasonable interest rates.

IVAN: Good. We may be able to do business, then. What do you think, Tamara?

TAMARA: Well, that tractor I've been driving is getting pretty old, and the repairs are becoming very costly.

MARVIN: Let us know if you have any questions or if we can be of any service.

В. ПРИМЕЧАНИЯ

1. Ростóвская óбласть (the Rostov territory), located in the southwest region of the Russian Federation, is a major grain-producing area. Its economic importance to Russia became even greater following the dissolution of the Soviet Union and the formation of an independent Ukraine, formerly the "bread basket" of the Soviet Union.

2. There are two Rostovs in the Russian Federation. The smaller city, Ростóв, with a population of approximately 40,000, is located about 100 miles northeast of Moscow on the shores of Lake Nero. Ростóв-на-Донý is a major industrial city with a population of approximately one million, located 676 miles southeast of Moscow on the Don River, near its entrance into the Sea of Azov (Азóвское мóре). Among its many enterprises is the Rostov Agricultural Machinery Company

(ПО* «Ростсельмаш», which is Russia's largest producer of agricultural equipment and which, incidentally, sponsors one of the Premier League (Вы́сшая Ли́га) soccer teams. The city is also a major port and rail hub, as well as an important cultural and scientific center. Sixteen foreign countries, including the United States, are represented by consular offices here.

3. Колхо́з (коллекти́вное хозя́йство) refers to a collective farm, as opposed to the fully state-owned совхо́з. Collective farms comprise the majority of Russian farms and account for approximately 90 percent of the country's grain production. The remaining 10 percent is produced by fully privatized farms (ча́стные фе́рмы).

4. Remember that приме́рно and приблизи́тельно, which both mean "approximately," are followed by the accusative case, whereas о́коло (around) requires the genitive case. В Росси́и ещё есть приблизи́тельно три́дцать ты́сяч бы́вших совхо́зов и колхо́зов. (There are still approximately thirty thousand former state and collective farms.) В Росто́вской о́бласти име́ется о́коло четы́рнадцати ты́сяч ча́стных ферм. (There are about fourteen thousand private farms in the Rostov Oblast.)

5. Property size in Russia is measured in terms of the гекта́р (hectare), which is equal to 10,000 sq. meters or approximately 2.5 acres.

6. Remember that како́в is used following the verb "to be," stated or understood (Како́в ваш урожа́й?—What was your harvest?), while како́й functions as an adjective that precedes the noun (Како́й урожа́й?—What kind or which harvest?). See Lesson 13.

7. Literally: She has golden hands.

8. Note the difference between занято́й (busy) and за́нятый (engaged, occupied). Я ви́жу, что вы о́чень занято́й челове́к. (I see that you're a very busy person.) Все слу́жащие, за́нятые э́тим де́лом, наве́рное, заси́живаются за рабо́той. (All the employees occupied with this case are probably keeping long hours.) Я сейча́с о́чень за́нят, у меня́ нет вре́мени трепа́ть языко́м! (I'm very busy right now; I don't have time to chat!)

9. По́иск (search) is most frequently used in the plural form (в по́исках, на по́иски). Note that the accusative case form по́иски is used after determinate verbs of motion. Они́ бе́гают по го́роду в по́исках но́вой кварти́ры. (They're running around the city in search of a new apartment.) Они́ уе́хали заграни́цу на по́иски но́вой рабо́ты. (They've gone overseas in search of new work.)

10. The pun here is based on the different meanings of the near-homophone pair хлопо́т (troubles) and хло́пок (cotton plant). Note also

*ПО «Ростсельмаш» (Произво́дственное объедине́ние «Росто́вская сельскохозя́йственная маши́на»—Rostov Agricultural Machinery Production Association)

хлопча́тник or хло́пок is a cotton plant. Хлопча́тка or, more formally, хлопча́тобума́жная ткань, is cotton fabric or cotton fiber. Хло́поты (always in the plural) means "cares, chores, worries."

11. Молоти́лка (a threshing machine) also appears in a few colloquial expressions that describe a chatterbox or someone who eats too fast. Этот чуда́к когда́-нибудь замолчи́т, молоти́лка несча́стный? (That idiot's a hopeless chatterbox, will he ever shut up?) Я то́лько что на́чал второ́е, а ты уже́ всё проглоти́л. Ну ты и молоти́лка! (I'm just beginning my second course and you've already wolfed everything down. What a thresher you are!) The verb молоти́ть/смолоти́ть can also be used to signify a fast eater. Мне не ве́рится, что ты уже́ всю по́рцию успе́л смолоти́ть! (I can't believe that you've already managed to gulp down the whole portion!).

12. The full expression is само́ собо́й разуме́ется (it goes without saying).

13. Note the use of the accusative case after под to indicate dedicating something for a specific purpose, in support of an object, or to the accompaniment of something. Мы отда́ли пять гекта́ров под ози́мную пшени́цу. (We allocated five hectars to winter wheat.) Старика́ подде́рживали по́д руки. (They were supporting the old man by the arms.) Докла́дчик сел под бу́рные аплодисме́нты. (The speaker sat down to tumultuous applause.) Они́ поста́вили нас под угро́зу. (They placed us under threat.) Они́ лю́бят обе́дать под му́зыку. (They love to dine to music.)

14. Старова́т(ый) (somewhat old) is a good example of the use of the diminutive suffix -оват(ый)/-еват(тый), meaning "somewhat," with adjectives. Дорогова́тая кварти́ра (a rather expensive apartment) По-мо́ему, этот суп кислова́т. (I think this soup is somewhat sour.)

C. ГРАММАТИКА И СЛОВОУПОТРЕБЛЕНИЕ

1. НЕОПРЕДЕЛЁННЫЕ ЧИСЛИТЕЛЬНЫЕ (INDEFINITE NUMERALS)

A number of quantitative adverbs such as доста́точно (enough, sufficient), ма́ло (a few), не́сколько (several), ско́лько (how many), сто́лько (so many), and мно́го (many, much) can function as indefinite numerals, i.e., they can refer to some quantity without a specific numerical value. When used alone, these forms govern the genitive case.

У нас доста́точно семя́н для оби́льного урожа́я.
    We have sufficient seed for an abundant harvest.

Я не знал, что у вас сто́лько подсо́лнечника.
    I didn't know that you have so much sunflower seed.

У нас оста́лось ещё мно́го вре́мени.
    We still have a lot of time left.

    When preceded by a preposition, the indefinite numerals не́сколько, ско́лько, and сто́лько decline like plural adjectives and agree in case with the nouns they modify.

Мы говори́ли о не́скольких но́вых моде́лях тра́кторов.
    We were talking about several new tractor models.

Тру́дно пове́рить, что мы встреча́лись со сто́лькими но́выми студе́нтами.
    It's difficult to believe that we met with so many new students.

    Note, however, that indefinite numerals generally do not decline when modifying animate nouns in the accusative or genitive case.

Я зна́ю мно́го ру́сских писа́телей.
    I know many Russian writers.

Я встре́тил не́сколько американских фе́рмеров.
    I met several American farmers.

    But...

Мы говори́м о мно́гих фермерах.
    We are talking about many farmers.

Они́ говори́ли о не́скольких журнали́стах, кото́рые неда́вно прие́хали из Росси́и.
    They were talking about a few journalists who recently arrived from Russia.

    Сто́лько and ско́лько are frequently used in the same clause to render "as much as..."

Мы посади́ли сто́лько семя́н, ско́лько у нас бы́ло.
We planted as much seed as we had.

Although не́сколько and не́который may both be translated into English as "several" or "a few," remember that не́который always refers to a previously specified group.

Хотя́ у нас есть не́сколько тра́кторов, не́которые из них нужда́ются в капита́льном ремо́нте.
Although we have several tractors, some of them require major repair.

У нас бы́ло не́сколько отли́чных студе́нтов. Не́которые из них тепе́рь в аспиранту́ре.
We had several excellent students. Some of them are now in graduate school.

Be sure not to confuse мно́го (a lot) and мно́гое/мно́гие (many). Мно́го governs the genitive case but does not decline itself. Мно́гое, on the other hand, declines as an adjective.

На собра́нии бы́ло мно́го фе́рмеров.
There were many farmers at the meeting.

В э́том регио́не, мно́гие фе́рмеры продаю́т свою́ проду́кцию то́лько прави́тельству.
Many farmers in this region sell their produce to the government only.

Во мно́гих слу́чаях, фе́рмеры реши́ли высева́ть гибри́дную кукуру́зу.
In many cases, the farmers decided to grow hybrid corn.

Во мно́гих отноше́ниях, э́то был наш са́мый лу́чший урожа́й.
In many respects this was our very best harvest.

When they follow the verb, не́сколько, мно́го, ма́ло, ско́лько, and сто́лько require the singular, neuter form of the verb in the past and future tense. Otherwise, the verb is plural. Мно́го and ма́ло almost invariably take the singular, neuter form of the verb.

На собра́нии бы́ло не́сколько фе́рмеров из Росто́вской о́бласти.
There were several farmers from the Rostov Oblast at the meeting.

Не́сколько фе́рмеров опозда́ли на собра́ние.
Several farmers were late for the meeting.

За́втра на заня́тиях, наве́рное, бу́дет ма́ло студе́нтов.
There will probably be just a few students at classes tomorrow.

Мно́го фе́рмеров отказа́лось от но́вого предложе́ния.
Many farmers rejected the new proposal.

Мно́го is sometimes used with a plural form of the verb to emphasize a particular activity.

К сожале́нию, мно́го студе́нтов провали́лось на выпускно́м экза́мене.
Unfortunately, many students failed the final examination.

The adverb ма́ло or the adjective ма́лый/мал (a few, little) appear in a number of frequently used expressions concerned with size, quantity, or mood. The adjectival form generally refers to size or quality, whereas the adverbial form is commonly used to denote mood.

мне малы́	too small
до́брый ма́лый	a good guy
ма́ло того́, что . . .	it was not enough that . . .
ма́ло ли что	what of it, what if
го́ря ма́ло	couldn't care less
ма́ло сказа́ть	it would be an understatement to say

Эти боти́нки мне малы́.
These shoes are too small for me.

Вы с ним знако́мы?—Я с ним с де́тства знако́м. Он до́брый ма́лый!
Do you know him?—I've known him since childhood. He's a good guy!

Ма́ло того́, что она сама́ прие́хала, она́ привезла́ всю семью́!
It wasn't enough that she came herself, but she had to bring the whole family!

Ма́ло ли что вы вы́сеяли сто́лько пшени́цы. Отку́да нам взять молоти́лки?
So what if you sowed so much wheat? Where are we going to get the threshers?

Урожа́й у них ску́ден, не хвата́ет семя́н, предлага́емые им це́ны низки́—но ему́ и го́ря ма́ло.

They have a poor harvest, a shortage of seed, the prices offered them are low—but he could care less.

Урожа́й у нас в про́шлом году́, ма́ло сказа́ть, был ску́дным—он был катастрофи́ческим!

It would be an understatement to say that our harvest last year was bad—it was catastrophic!

2. МЕЖДОМЕТИЯ (INTERJECTIONS)

Interjections add flavor to any language. Russian interjections can be categorized in two broad groups. The first group expresses various feelings and moods such as wonderment, surprise, fear, grief, etc.:

Ах!	Ah!	Ай!	Ow!
Ба!	Bah!	Ба́тюшки!	Good gracious!
О!	Oh!	Ох!	Oh me!
Эх!	Eh!	Увы́!	Alas!
Ура́!	Hurrah!	Фу!	Ugh!
Тьфу!	Bah! phooey!	У́жас!	Horrible!

Ай! Этот куст ко́лется.
Ow! This bush is prickly!

Ба́тюшки! И кто же это всё сюда́ принёс?
Dear me! Who brought all of that stuff here?

О! Тогда́ бы́ло совсе́м друго́е вре́мя!
Oh! That was a different time entirely!

Хоро́ший ли был урожа́й?—Увы́, совсе́м наоборо́т!
Did you have a good harvest?—Alas, quite to the contrary!

У́жас! Ничего́ с ним не поде́лаешь!
It's just horrible. You can't do anything with him!

The second group expresses various inducements to start or stop some action:

Брось!	Quit it!; Cut it out!	Брысь!	Shoo! [to a cat]
Прочь!	Begone!	Вон!	Get out!
Тсс!	Shsh!	Цыц!	Hush!
Шабáш!	Enough!		

Пошлú все прочь!
Get out of here, all of you!

Вон! Полюбýйся, что натворúла твоя́ лóшадь!
Get out of here! Just look at what your horse did!

Тсс! Тúше, не разбудúте дéдушку!
Shsh! Quiet, don't wake up grandpa!

Шабáш! Надоéло всё до невозмóжности.
Enough of that! I've had all I can take!

In addition, several onomatopoeic expressions simply imitate a human, animal, or object sound.

хи-хи-хи!	hee-hee-hee!	ха-ха-ха!	ha-ha-ha!
хрю-хрю!	oink-oink!	мяу-мяу	meow-meow
динь-динь-динь	ding-ding-ding	тик-так	tick-tock
бух-бух	rumble-rumble	буль-буль	gurgle-gurgle

Хи-хи-хи!—ну и шýтник вы, бáтенька.
Ha-ha-ha! Now, aren't you the little joker!

Бóдрое «хрю-хрю» доносúлось из-за сарáя, это свúньи доедáли ботвý.
A buoyant "oink-oink" was heard from the barn where the pigs were finishing up the carrot tops.

Бы́ло совсéм тúхо, тóлько хóдики издавáли вéчное «тик-так.»
Everything was rather quiet with the exception of the eternal tick-tock of the grandfather clock.

Бух-бух!—прогремéло в сторонé дерéвни. Начинáлась грозá.

A rumble-rumble sound was heard from the village. A storm was beginning.

Several sounds in the last group can be turned into verbs: мяýкать (to meow), бýлькать (to gurgle), хихúкать (to titter), курлы́кать (to coo like a crane), хохотáть (to laugh loudly).

Я не понимáю, почемý онú всё врéмя хихúкают.

I don't understand why they're tittering all the time.

Я слы́шу, как кóшка мяýкает, но её я не вúжу.

I hear a cat meowing, but I don't see it.

D. ИДИОМАТИКА

EXPRESSIONS WITH КАША.

Next to хлеб (bread), various forms of кáша (kasha, cooked cereal) have long represented a staple of the Russian diet. Consequently, quite a few idioms and expressions are associated with this food.

Сам кáшу заварúл, сам и расхлёбывай. (YOU MADE THIS MESS, NOW YOU GET OUT OF IT.; LIT., YOU BREWED THE KASHA, SO YOU UNTANGLE IT.)

Слýшай, я не смогý тебé помóчь, сам кáшу заварúл, сам и расхлёбывай.

Listen, I can't help you. You made this mess, and now you get out of it.

Мáло кáши ел. (HE'S/SHE'S STILL WET BEHIND THE EARS.; LIT., HE'S/SHE'S EATEN TOO LITTLE KASHA.)

Мой племя́ник, навéрное, не спрáвится с этой задáчей. —Ну, вúдно он ещё мáло кáши ел.

My nephew will probably be able handle this task. —Well, he's apparently still wet behind the ears.

Ка́ша во рту́ (TO MUMBLE; LIT., TO HAVE KASHA IN THE MOUTH.)

Ничего́ не пойму́, о чём ты говори́шь! У тебя́ как бу́дто ка́ша во рту́.
I can't understand a thing you're saying! You're mumbling!

Ка́ши не сва́ришь … (YOU WON'T GET ANYWHERE WITH . . . ; LIT., YOU
CAN'T EVEN MAKE KASHA . . .)

Он соверше́нно ненадёжный челове́к.—Да, с таки́м ка́ши не сва́ришь.
He's completely unreliable.—Yeah, you won't get anywhere with
his kind.

Ка́ша в голове́. (HIS/HER HEAD'S FULL OF MUSH.)

У него́ в голове́ всё перепу́талось—сплошна́я ка́ша.
He's all confused—his brain is all mush.

Ка́ши ма́слом не испо́ртишь. (YOU CAN'T HAVE TOO MUCH OF A GOOD
THING.; LIT., YOU CAN'T SPOIL KASHA WITH BUTTER.)

Слу́шай, у меня́ уже́ есть де́сять буты́лок хоро́шего вина́.—А что? Ка́ши
ма́слом не испо́ртишь.
Listen, I already have ten bottles of good wine.—So what? You can't
have too much of good thing.

Размолоти́ть в ка́шу (TO BEAT TO A PULP)

Проти́вник размолоти́л их в ка́шу.
The enemy beat them to a pulp.

Е. СТРОГО ПО ДЕЛУ

ПОЛОЖЕ́НИЕ И ПЕРСПЕКТИ́ВЫ СЕЛЬСКОГО ХОЗЯ́ЙСТВА
(STATUS AND PROSPECTS OF AGRICULTURAL DEVELOPMENT)

Although the landmass of the Russian Federation is approximately twice
that of the United States, due to generally unfavorable soil and climatic
conditions only 8 percent of the Federation's territory is considered
arable (па́хотная земля́) as compared with 20 percent in the United

States. The bulk of this land lies in the southeastern region, particularly the Krasnodar and the Rostov regions, but even these areas are frequently subject to drought (за́суха) and wind erosion (выве́тривание). Nevertheless, agricultural experts believe that the potential for grain yields (урожа́й зерновы́х культу́р) could be raised to the level of production in southern Scandinavia.

Russia's principal farm products in descending order of output include: grains (зерновы́е культу́ры), wheat (пшени́ца), barley (ячме́нь), potatoes (карто́фель), sugar beets (саха́рная свёкла), and meats (мя́со). Only sunflower seed is produced in sufficiently large quantities for export. Consequently, the country's principal agricultural imports include wheat, soybeans (со́евые бобы́), meal (мука́), fruits (фру́кты), vegetables (о́вощи), dairy products (моло́чные проду́кты), and meat. The Rostov region exports large quantities of grains to other parts of the Federation and other countries of the former Soviet Union.

Since the passage of legislation providing for the private ownership of land, the number of privately owned farms has been steadily increasing, albeit with some failures. There are approximately fourteen thousand private farms in the Rostov Oblast, accounting for approximately 7 percent of the region's cultivated land (па́хотные зе́мли о́бласти) and approximately 10 percent of the region's total agricultural output (о́бщий объём агропромы́шленного ко́мплекса). Surprisingly, in spite of considerable financial hardships and weather problems (тяжёлые фина́нсово-экономи́ческие и пого́дные усло́вия), the number of privately owned farms continues to grow. A number of private farmers in the Rostov Oblast have formed farm associations (ассоциа́ции крестья́нских хозя́йств) that provide long-term credits (долгосро́чные креди́ты) for the purchase of seed and machinery. A loan trust fund in support of this program was established with the help of the U.S. Department of Agriculture, which has been donating some of the proceeds from the sales of American soybeans to provide low-interest loans (за́ймы под небольши́е проце́нты). Although Rostov-on-the-Don is the location of a large agricultural machinery plant (Ростсельма́ш), a number of Western firms, including the John Deere Company, have been active in promoting the sales of farm machinery in the Russian Federation and the Ukrainian Republic. Some of the imported equipment has been sold outright to private farmers, but the bulk of the sales has been to government-owned collective and state farms (колхо́зы и совхо́зы) in the Russian Federation and the Ukraine.

Updated information about agricultural machinery marketing opportunities can be obtained from the Business Information Service for the Newly Independent States (BISNIS), U.S. Department of Commerce, International Trade Administration, Washington, D.C., 20230. In addition, a Russian nongovernmental organization, the Foundation for Agrarian Development and Research, organizes international electronic conferences on privatization and agrarian reform in Russia. The director of the foundation, Alexander Makeev, can be reached by e-mail: makeev@fadr. msu.ru. The American contact for these conferences is Bob Hart (e-mail: bhart@undp.org). The U.S. Department of Agriculture also provides information on Russian grain production, sales, and marketing opportunities. The Department has a Web page on the Internet (http://www. econ.ag.gov).

УПРАЖНЕНИЯ

A. Запо́лните про́пуски, по́льзуясь подходя́щими слова́ми в ну́жной фо́рме. (Fill in the blanks with the appropriate words in the required form.)

1. На вчера́шней ле́кции бы́ло _____.
   (many Russian students)

2. Мы встре́тили _____из Росто́вской о́бласти.
   (several farmers)

3. _____из ру́сских фе́рмеров на́чали выра́щивать ги́бридную
   (Some)
   кукуру́зу.

4. Я не знал, что у вас _____приватизи́рованных ферм.
   (so many)

5. Сейча́с у нас _____семя́н, что́бы получи́ть неплохо́й
   (enough)
   урожа́й.

6. _____ неда́вно_____из Владивосто́ка.
   (Several students)   (arrived)

7. Они́ наконе́ц-то договори́лись _____
   но́вого контра́кта.   (on several important articles [статья])

8. По прие́зде в Росто́в нас_____не́сколько слу́жащих из
   (were met)
   кру́пного совхо́за «Фе́никс».

9. Мы говори́ли _____, представля́юших
   (about many problems)
   взаи́мный интере́с.

10. На по́ле _____не́сколько _____
    (were standing)   (old combines)
    оте́чественного произво́дства.

B. Зако́нчите предложе́ния, вста́вив в ну́жной фо́рме подходя́щие по смы́слу слова́ из числа́ ука́занных в ско́бках. (Complete the sentences by inserting the required form of the appropriate words shown in parentheses.)

   (ско́лько, сто́лько, не́сколько, не́которые,
   мно́го, мно́гие, доста́точно, наско́лько)

   1. Мы вы́сеяли_____семя́н, _____у нас бы́ло.
   2. На про́шлой неде́ле, мы встреча́лись с
      _____интере́сными представи́телями америка́нских
      фирм.
   3. Мы обсужда́ли_____актуа́льные вопро́сы,
      кото́рые нам необходи́мо реши́ть.
   4. Ва́ши указа́ния бы́ли _____чёткими.
   5. На ры́нке бы́ло _____тури́стов из Англии.
   6. _____не согла́сны с предлага́емым им сове́том.
   7. _____у вас есть семя́н на весе́нний посе́в?
   8. _____я понима́ю, вы уже́ плани́руете расши́рить фе́рму.
   9. На́шего фе́рмера привлека́ет не_____пе́рспектива
      бога́тства, _____потре́бность быть свобо́дным,
      распоряжа́ться земле́й и всем, что на ней вы́ращено.
   10. У них уже́ есть _____комба́йнов, но _____ из
       них нужда́ются в капита́льном ремо́нте.

C. Переведи́те сле́дущие предложе́ния на ру́сский язы́к. Укажи́те куда́ па́дает ударе́ние.

   1. When we arrived at the farm we were met by Ivan and his wife.
   2. Our company sold several threshers to the Ukrainian goverment.
   3. We harvested about two thousand tons of wheat.
   4. Our children went to the city in search of new work.
   5. We allocated approximately fifteen hectares to winter wheat.
   6. The instructions he gave us were rather clear.
   7. We have been doing quite a bit of business in agricultural equipment.

8. Some of the combines are in need of major repairs.
9. We met several American farmers at the meeting last night.
10. Here are some brochures describing some of the equipment our company manufactures.

УРОК 16

А. ДИАЛОГ

На футбо́льном ма́тче.

Серге́й и Ви́ктор с опозда́нием прие́хали на футбо́льный матч ме́жду кома́ндами «Спарта́к» и «Локомоти́в».[1] Они́ приса́живаются ря́дом со свои́м дру́гом Влади́миром на трибу́не стадио́на «Лужники́».[2] Идёт второ́й тайм. Все тро́е боле́ют[3] за Спарта́к.

ВЛАДИМИР: Где вы пропада́ли?[4]

СЕРГЕЙ: Застря́ли в прокля́том движе́нии . . . Ну, како́й счёт?

ВЛАДИМИР: 3:2, в по́льзу «Локомоти́ва». На́до бы́ло ещё смотре́ть пе́рвый тайм. Игра́ была́ дово́льно груба́.

ВИКТОР: Кого́-нибудь удали́ли?[5]

ВЛАДИМИР: Ники́форова, к сожале́нию.

СЕРГЕЙ: Вот неуда́ча! Он наш лу́чший защи́тник![6]

ВЛАДИМИР: Зна́ю. Этот матч уже́ бу́дет тру́дно у них вы́играть.

Свисто́к на по́ле. Полузащи́тник Локомоти́ва Косола́пов получа́ет замеча́ние за гру́бую игру́.

СЕРГЕЙ: Ну, что э́то тако́е?! То́лько замеча́ние? Сле́довало бы дать ка́рточку![7]

Судья́ передаёт мяч игроку́ кома́нды Спарта́к, кото́рый вбра́сывает мяч в игру́ из-за боково́й ли́нии.

ВЛАДИМИР: Ла́дно, сейча́с мяч у нас. Дава́йте, ребя́та!

Спартако́вец Алиничев, дли́нным наве́сным па́сом, передаёт мяч игроку́ свое́й кома́нды Ти́хонову, кото́рый принима́ет мяч, обво́дит трёх игроко́в и продолжа́ет вести́ мяч к воро́там сопе́рника.

ВИКТОР: **Ви́дели этот пас? Како́й ло́вкий манёвр!**

ВЛАДИМИР: **Вот э́то сы́гранность! Сейча́с мы пробьёмся!**[8]

Боле́льщики Спартака́ всё бо́льше и бо́льше возбужда́ются по ме́ре[9] **продвиже́ния мяча́ к воро́там Локомоти́ва.**

ВИКТОР: **Смотри́, Ти́хонов переда́л мяч Кани́щеву! Кани́щев ведёт да́льше. Дава́й, дава́й! А сейча́с мяч обра́тно Ти́хонову!**

Ти́хонов гото́вится к уда́ру по воро́там, но ему́ даёт подно́жку защи́тник из кома́нды Локомоти́ва и отбира́ет[10] **у него́ мяч.**

СЕРГЕЙ: **Ви́дели? Да почему́ же судья́ не назна́чил штрафно́й?**

Боле́льщики Спартака́ свистя́т, крича́т «судью́ на мы́ло»! Сейча́с Локомоти́в владе́ет мячо́м и перехо́дит в контрата́ку.

ВИКТОР: **Локомоти́в приближа́ется к воро́там! Дава́й, Серёжа, вы́ручай!**[11]

Напада́ющий из кома́нды Локомоти́ва бьёт по воро́там, но врата́рь Овчи́нников руко́й ло́вит мяч. Боле́льщики одобри́тельно покри́кивают. Овчи́нников вы́бивает мяч обра́тно в игру́.

ВЛАДИМИР: **Молоде́ц врата́рь!**

СЕРГЕЙ: **Еле-еле спасли́сь.**[12]

ВИКТОР: **Ла́дно, сейча́с идёт на́ша контрата́ка.**

Спарта́ковец Але́ничев бы́стро пасу́ет мяч Ке́чинову, кото́рый ведёт мяч да́льше на полови́ну Локомоти́ва.

СЕРГЕЙ: **Вот э́то игра́. То́лько не теря́йте мяч!**

Спарта́ковские напада́ющие веду́т мяч к воро́там проти́вника, но игро́к из кома́нды Локомоти́ва па́дает на зе́млю, и судья́ даёт свисто́к.

ВИКТОР: **Невероя́тно! Он объя́вил наруше́ние! За что́ назна́чен штрафно́й?**

СЕРГЕЙ: Ты что, не ви́дел? За уда́р сопе́рника ного́й.

Судья́ даёт мяч кома́нде Локомоти́ва, и спарта́ковцы выстра́ивают оборони́тельную сте́нку для защи́ты воро́т.

СЕРГЕЙ: Кто бу́дет бить?

ВЛАДИМИР: Чугайнов, ка́жется. Их основно́й бомбарди́р!

СЕРГЕЙ: Не могу́ на это смотре́ть. Скажи́ мне, что случи́тся!

Чугайнов бьёт по мячу́, но его отбива́ет спарта́ковец—защи́тник Мамедов, кото́рый сра́зу же де́лает дли́нную переда́чу к воро́там Локомоти́ва.

ВИКТОР: Нам сего́дня везёт! Мяч сно́ва у нас!

Спарта́ковец Канищев обво́дит па́ру защи́тников Локомоти́ва и, выполня́я уда́р с лёта, передаёт мяч това́рищу по кома́нде Хлестову. Хлестов принима́ет его в прыжке́ и голово́й направля́ет мяч к воро́там Локомоти́ва. Боле́льщики в ожида́нии встаю́т, выкри́кивают своё одобре́ние, крича́т ура́.

СЕРГЕЙ: А в этот раз, мо́жет быть, нам уда́стся!

По́сланный голово́й мяч отска́кивает от шта́нги, и его остана́вливает Канищев, кото́рый гото́вится к уда́ру по воро́там.

ВЛАДИМИР: Бееееееей !!!

Врата́рь Локомоти́ва занима́ет своё ме́сто в воро́тах. Канищев, обводя́ игрока́ сре́дней ли́нии, пу́шечным уда́ром[13] забива́ет мяч в да́льний у́гол воро́т.

ВИКТОР, СЕРГЕЙ, ВЛАДИМИР: Гоооооол!!!!

СЕРГЕЙ: Сравня́ли счёт! Подождём дополни́тельного вре́мени![14]

Звучи́т свисто́к, обознача́я коне́ц второ́й полови́ны игры́.

At a soccer match.

Sergey and Viktor arrive late for a soccer match between Spartak and Lokomotiv. They join their friend Vladimir in the stands at the Luzhniki Stadium.
The game is in the second half. All three are Spartak fans.

VLADIMIR: What happened to you guys?

SERGEY: We got stuck in the damned traffic . . . So, what's the score?

VLADIMIR: Lokomotiv is leading 3 to 2. You should have seen the first half.
    The play's been pretty rough.

VIKTOR: Anybody ejected?

VLADIMIR: Unfortunately, Nikiforov.

SERGEY: Oh, no! He's our best back!

VLADIMIR: I know. It's going to be tough to win this one.

There's a whistle on the field. The referee cautions Lokomotiv's midfielder,
Kosolapov, for rough play.

SERGEY: Hey, what's that! Just a caution? He should have given him a yel-
    low card!

The referee gives the ball to a Spartak player who tosses the ball back into
play from the sidelines.

VLADIMIR: Okay, we've got the ball now. Come on, go!

Spartak player Alinichev makes a lob pass to teammate Tikhonov, who drib-
bles past three opponents and heads downfield.

VIKTOR: Did you see that pass? What a beautiful move!

VLADIMIR: That's teamwork for you. Now we'll make it!

The Spartak fans get more excited as the ball is brought closer to the Lokomotiv goal.

VIKTOR: Look, Tikhonov's passed the ball to Kanishchev. He's got it. Go, go! Now it's back to Tikhonov.

Tikhonov gets set to kick toward the net, but he is tripped by a Lokomotiv back who takes control of the ball.

SERGEY: Did you see that? Why didn't the ref call that foul and declare a penalty kick?

Spartak fans whistle and shout, "Send the ref to the showers!" Lokomotiv now goes on the offensive.

SERGEY: Lokomotiv is getting close! Come on, goalie, don't let them make it!

A Lokomotiv forward attempts a goal, but the ball is caught by Ovchinnikov, the Spartak goalie. The Spartak fans roar approval. Ovchinnikov kicks the ball back into play.

VLADIMIR: Way to go, Goalie!

SERGEY: He just barely made that save!

VIKTOR: Okay, now comes our counterattack!

Spartak's Alenichev quickly passes the ball to Kechinov, who brings the ball to the Lokomotiv half of the field.

SERGEY: That's the way to play. Just don't lose the ball!

The Spartak forwards bring the ball to the oppoent's goal, but a Lokomotiv player falls down and the referee blows the whistle.

VIKTOR: Unbelievable! He called a foul! What was the penalty for?

SERGEY: Didn't you see? He kicked an opponent.

The referee hands the ball to the Lokomotiv team, and the Spartak players line up to defend their goal.

SERGEY: Who's gonna kick?

VLADIMIR: It looks like Chugaynov. Their top kicker!

SERGEY: I can't watch. Tell me what happens!

Chugaynov kicks the ball, but it's deflected by Spartak back Mamedov, who immediately makes a long pass toward the Lokomotiv goal.

VIKTOR: Luck is with us today! We've got the ball again!

Spartak player Kanishchev manuevers around several Lokomotiv defenders, and kicking the ball in midair, passes it to teammate Khlestov. Khlestov leaps into the air and heads the ball toward the Lokomotiv goal. Spartak fans rise in expectation of a goal, cheer and shout hurrah.

SERGEY: I think we might make it this time!

Khlestov's ball bounces off the goal post, but is retrieved by Kanishchev who is now poised to kick the ball into the Lokomotiv goal.

SERGEY: Kick the baaalllll!

The Lokomotiv goalie gets set to stop an attempted goal. Kanishchev avoids a defending Lokomotiv player and slam-kicks the ball into the far corner of the net.

VIKTOR, SERGEY, VLADIMIR: Gooooooal!!!!!

SERGEY: It's tied! We go into overtime!

A whistle blows, marking the end of the second half.

В. ПРИМЕЧАНИЯ

1. Спартак and Локомотив are two of the twenty teams in the "major" league of Russian soccer. The four categories are высшая ("highest" or premier), followed by the first, second, and third leagues.

2. Лужники, formerly Ле́нинский стадио́н (Lenin Stadium), is located in the Воробьевы горы (Sparrow Hills) region of Moscow, adja-

cent to the Moscow River (Ленинские горы and Спортивная subway stations on the Кировско-Фрунзенская line). The other two major Moscow stadiums are the Олимпийский стадион (Olympic Stadium), which was built for the 1980 Olympic Games, located on Олимпийский проспект 16, and the Динамо stadium on Ленинградский проспект 36 (Динамо metro station on the Горьковско-Замоскворецкая line). The soccer season runs from the spring to fall, and the games are usually played on Saturday afternoon. Soccer remains the most popular spectator sport in Russia, followed by ice hockey (хоккей с шайбой) and basketball (баскетбол).

3. Болеть за (plus a noun in the accusative case) here means "to root for a team" or "to be an avid fan." The noun for a sports fan is болельщик. In other contexts, болеть за (plus a noun in the accusative case) or о (plus a noun in the prepositional case) can mean "to agonize over, to grieve for." Мы, действительно, болеем душой за этих бедных сирот. (We really feel for these poor orphans.) У меня болит душа о жертвах бедствия. (My heart aches for the disaster victims.)

4. Где вы пропадали? or Куда вы пропали? (Where did you disappear to?). The verb пропасть (to disappear, to be missing) is used in several common colloquial expressions: Теперь мы пропали! (Now we're done for!) Пиши пропало! (You can write it off as lost!) Пропади пропадом! У меня снова пропал зонтик! (Damn it all! I've lost my umbrella again!)

5. Удалить (to remove) can be used in several ways. У него удалили зуб. (He had a tooth extracted.) Почему Владимира не было на заводе сегодня? —Я забыл тебе сказать, что его удалили с работы. (Why wasn't Vladimir at the plant today? —I forgot to tell you that he was laid off.)

6. Substitutions are not allowed for players removed for the infraction of rules in a soccer match. Защитник (lit., defender) is a back. The Russian names for the 11 positions and their number in a soccer team are: вратарь (goalkeeper, 1), защитник (fullback, 4), полузащитник (halfback, 3), нападающий (forward or striker, 3).

7. In soccer a referee can issue a penalty card (дать карточку) to a player for a variety of reasons. A yellow card constitutes a serious warning, and a red card means expulsion from the game.

8. Пробиться (to break through, to force one's way to some objective). Наконец, им удалось пробиться сквозь густую толпу. (They finally succeeded in forcing their way through the thick crowd.)

9. По мере (+ genitive case) means "in proportion to." It is frequently translated as "as much as." Мы вам поможем по мере сил. (We'll help you as much as possible.)

10. Отбира́ть/отобра́ть (+ accusative case) followed by у (+ genitive case) means "to take something away from someone." До сих пор не понима́ю, почему́ у него́ отобра́ли все пи́сьменные принадле́жности. (To this day, I don't understand why they took away all of his writing materials.)

11. Выруча́ть means "to rescue, to help," but it can also mean "to make a profit." Мы попа́ли в больши́е затрудне́ния, а друзья́ нас вы́ручили. (We got into considerable difficulty, but our friends came to our rescue.) Он вы́ручил дово́льно мно́го де́нег от прода́жи биле́тов. (He made quite a bit of money from the sale of the tickets.)

12. Еле-еле is an emphatic variant of еле (hardly, scarcely).

13. Пу́шечный уда́р literally means a cannon shot.

14. A soccer match is played through two 45-minute periods (та́ймы). In championship games it goes into overtime (дополни́тельное вре́мя) in the event of a tie score (счёт ра́вный/ниче́йный).

С. ГРАММАТИКА И СЛОВОУПОТРЕБЛЕНИЕ

1. ОТГЛАГОЛЬНЫЕ ПРИСТАВКИ (VERBAL PREFIXES)

You are already familiar with various prefixes that can be attached to verbs to impart different meanings. For example, бро́сить (to throw) → вбро́сить (to throw into). The most common prefixes and some of their meanings are listed below, along with the most frequently associated prepositions for verbs of motion.

PREFIX	MEANING
в(о)-	in, into
вз* (о)-воз/вос	figurative or literal upward movement or feeling
вы-	movement out of
до-	movement as far as, up to, completion of an action
за-	movement behind, or over a long distance; to fasten, to secure, to seal, literally and figuratively
из(о)-ис	selection or extraction
на-	movement or action on to

*When the prefix combines with stems that begin with unvoiced consonants (к, п, с, т ф, х, ц, ч, ш, щ) the prefixes вз-, из-, раз- change to вс-, ис-, рас- respectively

o-/об-/обо	to circumvent, pass
от(о)-	movement away from, to repel, to return, detachment, reversal of action
пере-	movement across, transfer, to redo some action
под(о)-	movement under or up to
при-	approach, arrival, attach
про-	through, past
раз(о)-рас	separate, distribute, disperse, action reversal
с(о)-	removal, descent
у-	removal

The following examples illustrate how various prefixes change the meaning of the verb броса́ть/бро́сить (to throw):

Он вбро́сил мяч в игру́ из-за боково́й ли́нии.
He threw the ball back into play from the sideline.

Он вы́бросил мяч с по́ля.
He threw the ball out of the field.

Он добро́сил мяч до среди́ны по́ля.
He threw the ball as far as (up to) the middle of the field.

Он забро́сил го́лову наза́д.
He tossed his head back.

Она набро́сила шаль на пле́чи.
She tossed a shawl over her shoulders.

Мы сра́зу отбро́сили его́ но́вую тео́рию.
We immediately cast aside his new theory.

Он перебро́сил мяч че́рез площа́дку.
He threw the ball across the court.

Она подбро́сила моне́ты под стол.
She tossed the coins under the table.

Они́ разбро́сали свои́ де́ньги на ве́тер.
They squandered their money. (lit., They threw their money to the wind.)

Она вдруг сбросила с себя одеяло, и подбежала к окну.
She suddenly threw off the blanket and ran toward the window.

A number of Russian verbs exist only in a single prefixed form. Such prefixes cannot be replaced to change the verb's meaning. Here are some of the more common ones:

удалять/удалить	to remove
отвечать/ответить	to answer
восторгаться	to be delighted
доставать/достать	to fetch
затевать/затеять	to undertake, organize
исчезать/исчезнуть	to disappear

2. ИНФИНИТИВ (THE INFINITIVE)

In Russian, the infinitive has a wide variety of uses, depending on the aspect.

A. THE IMPERFECTIVE INFINITIVE

The imperfective infinitive is used:

 • after verbs denoting a beginning, continuing, or concluding action.

Диктор только что начал передавать последние новости.
The announcer just started broadcasting the latest news.

Сейчас они начинают собирать все данные о вчерашнем матче.
They're now beginning to collect all the data on yesterday's game.

Спартаковец продолжает вести мяч к воротам соперника.
The Spartak player continues to move the ball toward the opponent's goal.

По всей вероятности, они будут продолжать учиться в этом институте.
In all probability, they'll continue to study at this institute.

Мы перестали заниматься в библиотеке, потому что там слишком шумно.
We stopped studying at the library, because it's too noisy there.

Наконе́ц, он ко́нчил расска́зывать нам о пое́здке в Евро́пу.
He finally finished telling us about his trip to Europe.

• with verbs that imply preferences, tendencies, habitual actions.

Я уже́ давно́ привы́к встава́ть ра́но.
I've been used to getting up early for a long time.

Они́ предпочита́ют смотре́ть но́вости по тре́тьему кана́лу.
They prefer watching the news on Channel 3.

• with expressions denoting inadvisability or denying necessity.

Вам не на́до покупа́ть биле́ты. Вход беспла́тный.
You don't need to buy tickets. Admission is free.

Совсе́м бесполе́зно разгова́ривать с ним. Он не в ку́рсе де́ла.
It's quite useless talking to him. He's not in the know.

Не ну́жно вызыва́ть врача́. Она́ уже́ чу́вствует себя́ полу́чше.
There's no need to call a doctor. She's feeling better already.

Не сто́ит писа́ть ему́. Он никогда́ не отвеча́ет на пи́сьма.
It doesn't pay to write to him. He never answers letters.

The imperfective infinitive can also be used to express imperatives or warnings:

Молча́ть!
Silence!

Сиде́ть сми́рно!
Sit quietly!

Не кури́ть.
No smoking.

По траве́ не ходи́ть!
Keep off the grass!

Не высо́вываться из окна́.
No leaning out of the window.

Приде́рживаться пра́вой стороны́.
Keep to the right.

The perfective infinitive is used to denote an intended, requested, or implied single action.

Судье́ сле́довало бы дать ему́ ка́рточку.
The referee should have given him a penalty card.

Им бу́дет тру́дно вы́играть э́тот матч.
It's going to be difficult for them to win this game.

Я забы́л взять с собо́й ключи́ от но́мера.
I forgot to take the room key.

Мне на́до позвони́ть домо́й сейча́с же!
I've got to call home right now!

Ему́ удало́сь обвести́ трёх игроко́в.
He succeeded in getting past three players.

Она́ попроси́ла меня́ закры́ть дверь.
She asked me to close the door.

The perfective infinitive is also used to indicate that an action cannot be performed successfully.

Нельзя́ войти́* в ко́мнату. Дверь заперта́.
It's impossible to get into the room. The door's locked.

---

*Note that нельзя́ used with the imperfective infinitive means that the action is forbidden.

Нельзя́ входи́ть в ту ко́мнату. Сдаю́т экза́мены.
You can't go into that room. They're taking exams.

Я не могу́ откры́ть окно́. Оно́ зае́ло.
I can't open the window. It's stuck.

In some cases, use of the perfective or imperfective depends only on the intention of the speaker to perform or request an immediate or continuous or action.

Я хочу́ написа́ть ей письмо́ о сего́дняшнем собра́нии.
I want to write her a letter about today's meeting.

Я хочу́ писа́ть пи́сьма, но у меня отобра́ли все пи́сьменные принадле́жности.
I want to write letters, but they took away all of my writing materials.

Я сове́тую вам чита́ть газе́ты поча́ще.
I advise you to read the newspapers more often.

Я сове́тую вам прочита́ть вот э́ту статью́.
I advise you to read this article.

D. ИДИОМАТИКА

WIN OR LOSE...

Here are some expressions concerned with winning and losing games and the way they are played.

Победи́ть одно́й ле́вой (AN EASY WIN; LIT., TO WIN WITH THE LEFT HAND ALONE)

Ну вот, такого счёта я никогда́ не ожида́л! —Да, в са́мом де́ле на́ши ребя́та победи́ли одно́й ле́вой!
Well, I never expected that kind of score! —Yes, indeed, that was an easy win for our guys!

Победи́телей не су́дят. (WINNING IS WHAT MATTERS.; LIT., VICTORS ARE NOT TO BE JUDGED.)

Зна́ешь, хотя́ мы победи́ли, на́ша кома́нда игра́ла дово́льно гру́бо. —Ну и что, победи́телей не су́дят!
> You know, although we won, our team played pretty rough. —But they won, and that's what counts!

Тяну́ть рези́ну (TO DRAG THINGS OUT)

Что же он де́лает!? Оста́лось всего́ три мину́ты до конца́ та́йма!—Ты что, не по́нял? Он наро́чно тя́нет рези́ну.
> Whatever is he doing!? There's only three minutes left in the half! —Don't you get it? He's stalling on purpose.

Разбива́ть/разби́ть в пух и в прах (TO DEFEAT UTTERLY; LIT., TO BREAK INTO WIND AND POWDER)

Так, что нам сказа́ть? Нас разби́ли в пух и в прах!
> Well, what can we say? They destroyed us!

Дать подно́жку (TO TRIP SOMEONE UP)

Ви́дел, как на́шему защи́тнику да́ли подно́жку? —Да, ви́дел. Обяза́тельно бу́дет штрафно́й.
> Did you see how our back was tripped? —Yes, I did. There'll be a penalty for sure.

Проигра́ть всуху́ю (TO BE SHUT OUT)

Како́е несча́стье! Вот ещё раз на́ши ребя́та проигра́ли всуху́ю!
> What lousy luck! Our guys were shut out again!

Кла́ссный игро́к (A FIRST-CLASS PLAYER)

Э́тот Овчи́нников—вот кла́ссный игро́к!
> That Ovchinnikov is a top-notch player!

По́лный разгро́м (A TOTALLY CRUSHING DEFEAT)

Су́дя по соверше́нному отсу́тствию сы́гранности, я бою́сь, что на́ша кома́нда поте́рпит по́лный разгро́м!
> Judging by the complete absence of teamwork, I'm afraid our team's going to be completely wiped out!

E. СТРОГО ПО ДЕЛУ

ОБЩЕСТВЕННЫЙ ЭТИКЕТ (SOCIAL ETIQUETTE)

Russians are friendly and warm people who are particularly understanding and tolerant of foreign visitors. Strict formality is not a common characteristic of Russian behavior. Your Russian conversation partner will always be in near proximity to your person, sometimes slapping you gently on the shoulder, arm, or knee to emphasize a point. This is quite normal, friendly behavior and indicates a favorable disposition toward you.

Meetings for the first time and on subsequent occasions are normally accompanied by a firm handshake and direct eye-to-eye contact. Handshaking upon departing is also expected. Gloves, if worn, should be removed before shaking hands. If you are already acquainted, it is quite customary to ask about your friend's family before beginning any other topic, business or otherwise. Whether or not you have a translator, it is important to be a good listener. Any sign of disinterest, distraction, or insincerity on your part will be quickly detected. Excessively assertive or forward behavior should be avoided, particularly in a first encounter. Let your Russian hosts and acquaintances initiate the conversation.

Despite the many problems past and present faced by Russians, they are essentially very proud of their history and culture. Therefore, any knowledge you have about Russian culture, history, and current events will be of immense value in developing feelings of mutual respect and friendship. Russians are pleased to answer questions about these topics, as long as they are not too personal, such as questions about salary, housing conditions, frustrations, etc. Leave those topics for your host to bring up. In any event, at least initially, you should refrain from criticism of the people or the country as a whole. In most cases, criticism of social and economic conditions will be offered by your host once you have gained his or her confidence.

Gift giving is well ingrained in Russian custom, primarily to demonstrate that the gift giver is thinking about the host or acquaintance. Modest gifts, such as wine or flowers (always in odd numbers), or chocolates for children are quite appropriate when a visitor is invited to a private residence. You should arrive punctually for dinner parties to show that you appreciate the amount of time and effort expended by your host.

The Russian custom of toasting with vodka is well known. The drinking of alcoholic beverages also represents, to a certain extent, a genuine desire to enjoy one's company, and to develop and maintain a feeling of closeness and openness among friends. Consequently, refusing a drink can be misinterpreted as an offense to your host. Unless contraindicated by a medical problem, the visitor should go along with a few small drinks. If pressured to continue drinking, the visitor might offer the excuse of current medication problems, the need to drive home, or even religious prohibitions.

Although Russians often joke about the many superstitions that are steeped in their culture, most of them are taken seriously. Therefore, the visitor should keep the following additional common customs and superstitions in mind to avoid embarrassing situations. Your knowledge of these superstitions and customs will earn you additional respect as well.

DO'S:

- Remove your shoes when visiting a home (particularly in the winter); house slippers (тáпочки) will be provided.
- Check your overcoat at museums, public concerts, and indoor events at the cloakroom (гардерóб).

DON'TS:

- Never shake hands over a threshold.
- Don't whistle indoors.
- Never pour wine back-handed. It is considered insulting.
- Never gesture with your thumb between your first two fingers. It is considered obscene.
- Do not put your feet up on furniture or show the soles of your feet while sitting. It is considered rude.
- Avoid "rough" language in company.
- Never light a cigarette from a candle. It is considered bad luck.

УПРАЖНЕНИЯ

A. Заполните пропуски, пользуясь подходящими глаголами и нужными предлогами. (Fill in blanks using the approriate verbs and required prepositions.)

1. Судья_____ игрокá_____ пóля.
       (ejected)   (from)
2. Дéти_____ дéрево.
       (ran behind)

3. Кома́нда Спарта́к _____ матч_____ счётом 2:1.
                      (won)   (by)

4. Одну́ мину́точку, я ещё _____письмо.
                               (finish writing)

5. Она́_____ру́ку_____спи́ну.
      (placed)   (behind)

6. Врата́рь_____мяч _____ по́ля.
       (threw)   (out of)

7. Полузащи́тник _____мяч_____игру́
              (threw in)   (into)

8. Когда́ наш напада́ющий_____ ворота́м, я кри́кнул: "Бей!"
                        (neared)

9. Они́ _____сре́дней ли́нии и останови́лись.
     (ran up to)

10. Она́_____го́лову_____поду́шку и запла́кала.
      (put)   (under)

B. Впиши́те подходя́щие предло́ги и существи́тельные в ну́жном падеже́. (Insert the appropriate prepositions and nouns in the required case.)

1. Алени́чев переда́л_____.
                   (the ball to his teammate)

2. Полузащи́тник получи́л замеча́ние_____.
                             (for rough play)

3. За что судья́ объяви́л _____?
                  (foul [violation])

4. Напада́ющие веду́т мяч_____.
                     (to the opponent's goal)

5. Боле́льщики выкри́кивали_____.
                       (their approval)

6. Врата́рь отбро́сил_____.
                  (the ball back into play)

7. Но́вые игроки́ подгото́вились_____.
                        (for a medical exam)

8. Ка́нищев ло́вко обвёл_____.
                  (two defense backs)

9. К сожале́нию, они́ пропусти́ли_____.
                       (the first half)

10. Мои́ друзья́ прие́хали_____.
                  (to the game very late)

С. Переведите следующие предложения на русский язык.

1. When our striker kicked a goal, the whole stadium jumped to their feet shouting "Goal!"
2. He threw the ball into play from the sideline.
3. After he side-stepped two players, Ovchinnikov aimed the ball toward the goal.
4. The Lokomotiv player took the ball away from our fullback.
5. Our team's going on the offensive.
6. Our neighbor was laid off last week.
7. We got stuck in traffic.
8. It's going to be tough to win this one.
9. The referee decided to cancel the match.
10. Petrov kicked the ball toward the goal, but it bounced off the goal crossbar.

ПРЕДЛАГАЕМЫЕ ЗАНЯТИЯ

Try to find a Russian soccer match on one of your local cable TV stations. See if you can follow the Russian commentary.

УРОК 17

А. ДИАЛОГ

Посеще́ние поликли́ники.

Бе́верли Пола́нски и Фрэнк Си́мпсон из Це́нтра по контро́лю заболева́емости пришли́ в райо́нную поликли́нику во Влади́мире[1] по приглаше́нию свои́х колле́г Людми́лы Гера́симовой и Петра́ Шемя́кина. Америка́нские го́сти в сопровожде́нии до́ктора Шемя́кина пришли́ в поликли́нику, где их встреча́ет до́ктор Гера́симова.

ЛЮДМИЛА: **До́брое у́тро! Вы пришли́ как раз во́время! Прости́те, что я не смогла́ встре́титься с ва́ми в гости́нице, у меня́ был э́кстренный вы́зов.**

БЕВЕРЛИ: **Я наде́юсь, что мы не доставля́ем[2] вам никаки́х неудо́бств.**

ЛЮДМИЛА: **Нет, да́же наоборо́т, я специа́льно отвела́ э́то вре́мя на встре́чу с ва́ми.**

ПЁТР: (повора́чиваясь к Бе́верли и Фрэ́нку) **Поско́льку вы о́ба эпидемио́логи, мы начнём осмо́тр с отделе́ния инфекцио́нных боле́зней.**

ФРЭНК: **Отли́чно!**

ПЁТР: **Нам ну́жно пря́мо по коридо́ру, и пото́м на ли́фте на тре́тий эта́ж.**

ФРЭНК: **В после́днем письме́ вы упомяну́ли дифтери́ю. Э́то по-пре́жнему серьёзная пробле́ма?**

ПЁТР: **Бою́сь, что да.**

БЕВЕРЛИ: **У вас не хвата́ет вакци́нного материа́ла?**

ЛЮДМИЛА: **Вообще́-то на́ших запа́сов коклю́шно-дифтери́йно-столбня́чной сы́воротки[3] вполне́ доста́точно. Загво́здка[4] в том, что из-за её про́шлой нехва́тки недоста́точное коли́чество населе́ния бы́ло вакцини́ровано.**

ПЁТР: И вот теперь, даже при наличии вакцины, многие родители не хотят, чтобы их детям делали эту прививку.[5]

БЕВЕРЛИ: А это-то почему?

ЛЮДМИЛА: Отчасти от недоверия к прививкам в целом, а отчасти из-за боязни осложнений, связанных с плохой стерилизацией оборудования. И это несмотря на то, что теперь мы имеем достаточные запасы одноразовых шприцев.

Все входят в отделение инфекционных заболеваний.

БЕВЕРЛИ: Кстати о детях, я не вижу ни одного ребёнка.

ЛЮДМИЛА: Для детей у нас отдельные поликлиники. Мы можем зайти туда попозже, если вам будет угодно.

ФРЭНК: (наблюдая, как медсестра регистрирует очередного пациента) Этот пациент пришёл сделать прививку?

ЛЮДМИЛА: (смотрит в карточку больного) Нет, у неё будут брать повторный анализ слизистой оболочки глотки. Её подвергли лечению антибиотиками, и она, по-видимому, поправилась от лёгкого случая дифтерии.

БЕВЕРЛИ: Как часто вы проверяете иммунизационные листы?

ПЁТР: Как минимум раз в год. Мы просматриваем списки всех взрослых, проживающих в данном районе, и определяем, кто нуждается в прививках.

ФРЭНК: Таким образом, участковые врачи делают большинство прививок?

ПЁТР: Да, а те, кто по разным причинам не состоит в их списках, всегда могут сделать прививку в больнице. К тому же, большие предприятия имеют свои медпункты,[6] которые оказывают различные услуги, и в том числе делают прививки.

Через два часа они завершают обход отделений сердечно-сосудистых и аллергических заболеваний.

ЛЮДМИЛА: Кажется, у нас есть время для ещё одного отделения.

БЕВЕРЛИ: (глядя на часы́) Да, у нас оста́лось о́коло 45 мину́т до сле́дующего приёма. Каки́е ещё отделе́ния мы могли́ бы посмотре́ть?

ЛЮДМИЛА: Мы не ви́дели ещё отделе́ний заболева́ний дыха́тельных путе́й, желу́дочно-кише́чных заболева́ний, ко́жных, и венери́ческих заболева́ний, а та́кже лаборато́рий диагно́стики и рентгеноскопи́и.

БЕВЕРЛИ: Вы ле́чите венери́ческие боле́зни в отделе́нии ко́жных заболева́ний?

ЛЮДМИЛА: Да, е́сли хоти́те, мы мо́жем туда́ пойти́ пря́мо сейча́с.

ФРЭНК: Отли́чно, тогда́ оста́вим все остальны́е отделе́ния на за́втра, е́сли тако́е возмо́жно.

ПЁТР: Непреме́нно. Я ли́чно об э́том позабо́чусь. Да, ведь вы ещё хоте́ли посмотре́ть де́тскую поликли́нику ...

БЕВЕРЛИ: Превосхо́дно!

На сле́дующий день колле́ги встреча́ются в кабине́те до́ктора Шемя́кина для того́, чтобы собра́ть и обсуди́ть не́которые статисти́ческие да́нные.

БЕВЕРЛИ: Наско́лько я поняла́ из разгово́ра с одни́м врачо́м в де́тской поликли́нике, мно́гих дете́й не приво́дят в кли́нику, когда́ они́ заболева́ют. Я пра́вильно её поняла́?

ПЁТР: Да, вполне́. Чтобы избежа́ть возмо́жности зараже́ния в поликли́нике, мы про́сим роди́телей вызыва́ть врача́ на́ дом. А уже́ осма́тривающий врач пото́м реша́ет, сле́дует ли госпитализи́ровать больно́го.[7]

ФРЭНК: По каки́м при́знакам вы реша́ете госпитализи́ровать ребёнка?

ЛЮДМИЛА: Наприме́р, когда́ у ребёнка анги́на,[8] а ему́ неда́вно де́лали приви́вку. В проти́вном слу́чае врач то́лько берёт ана́лизы, и больно́й ребёнок остаётся до́ма.

ФРЭНК: Эта процеду́ра отно́сится и ко взро́слым, не так ли?

ЛЮДМИЛА: Вообще́-то да. Если, наприме́р, у пацие́нта температу́ра за 38°,[9] и воспалено́ го́рло, вы́званный на́ дом врач, де́лающий осмо́тр, до́лжен ли́бо[10] приня́ть реше́ние о госпитализа́ции, ли́бо взять соотве́тствующие ана́лизы и оста́вить больно́го до́ма.

БЕВЕРЛИ: Вы де́лаете повто́рные приви́вки для взро́слых?

ЛЮДМИЛА: Ра́ньше, это было че́рез ка́ждые де́сять лет, но тепе́рь, по́льзуясь адсорби́рованными анато́ксинами, мы мо́жем проводи́ть приви́вки и ча́ще по указа́нию ме́стных эпиде-мио́логов.

A visit to a polyclinic.

Beverly Polanski and Frank Simpson, from the U.S. Centers for Disease Control, are visiting the Regional Polyclinic in Vladimir at the invitation of their colleagues, Lyudmila Gerasimova and Peter Shemyakin. The American visitors, escorted by Dr. Shemyakin, arrive at the clinic and are greeted by Dr. Gerasimova.

LYUDMILA: Good morning! I see you're right on time! Sorry I couldn't join you at the hotel. I had to take care of an emergency here.

BEVERLY: I hope we're not inconveniencing you.

LYUDMILA: No, on the contrary. I set aside this time to be with you.

PETER: (turning to Beverly and Frank) Since you're both epidemiologists, shall we start the tour with the Infectious Diseases Ward?

FRANK: Excellent!

PETER: We'll just go down the hall and take the elevator to the third floor.

FRANK: You mentioned diphtheria in your last letter. Is it still a serious problem?

PETER: I'm afraid so.

BEVERLY: Are you short on vaccine materials?

LYUDMILA: Actually, our present supplies of DPT vaccine are pretty good. The problem is that, due to past shortages, not enough people were vaccinated.

PETER: And even when we have vaccines, there is considerable resistance on the part of some parents to have their children immunized.

BEVERLY: Why is that?

LYUDMILA: Partly because of an inherent distrust of vaccines and partly because of complications resulting from nonsterilized equipment, although our stock of disposable syringes has improved significantly.

The four enter the Infectious Diseases Department.

BEVERLY: Speaking of children, I don't see any here.

LYUDMILA: We have a separate pediatric polyclinic for them. We can go there later if you like.

FRANK: (observing a nurse registering a patient) Is this patient here for a vaccination?

LYUDMILA: (looking at the patient's chart) No, she's here for a follow-up throat culture. I see she's been treated with antibiotics and has apparently recovered from a mild case of diphtheria.

BEVERLY: How often do you review your immunization records?

PETER: At least once a year. We look at all of the log books for adults maintained by the district physicians and then determine which residents require immunization.

FRANK: So the district physicians do most of the immunizing?

PETER: Yes, and the people who are not on the physician's roster can get their shots at the clinic. Of course, large work sites also have health units that can provide immunization shots as well as other basic medical services.

About two hours later, the group completes a round of visits to the cardiovascular and allergy departments.

LYUDMILA: I think we have time to visit one more ward, if you'd like.

BEVERLY: (looking at her watch) Well, we have about forty-five minutes before our next appointment. What other departments can we take a look at?

LYUDMILA: We still haven't seen the respiratory tract, gastro-intestinal, dermatology and venereal diseases sections or the diagnostic and X-ray laboratories.

BEVERLY: Your STDs are treated in the dermatology section?

LYUDMILA: Yes, if you'd like we can go there now.

FRANK: Fine. Then perhaps we can visit the remaining sections tomorrow, if that's possible.

PETER: Of course. I'll personally take care of that. I know that you also want to see the pediatric polyclinic . . .

BEVERLY: Excellent!

The next day, the four colleagues meet in Dr. Shemyakin's office to discuss and collect some statistical materials.

BEVERLY: I gathered from a conversation with a physician at the pediatric polyclinic that ill children are normally not brought to the clinic. Did I understand her correctly?

PETER: Yes. In order to avoid the risk of contagion at the clinic, we ask the parents to request a home visit. The examining pediatrician will then determine whether to hospitalize the patient.

FRANK: What are your criteria for hospitalization?

LYUDMILA: For example, if an unimmunized child has a sore throat or if an immunized child has a sore throat and a pharyngeal membrane. Otherwise, we arrange for a throat culture and the parent is advised to keep the child at home.

FRANK: That procedure applies to adults, as well, right?

LYUDMILA: Generally, yes. If, for example, a patient has a temperature higher than 38° C and a sore throat, the physician making the house call will either arrange for hospitalization or take a throat culture and let the patient stay at home.

BEVERLY: Do you give adult contacts booster shots?

LYUDMILA: The interval for booster shots was ten years, but we are now giving Td immunizations to adult contacts at shorter intervals at the direction of the local epidemiologist.

B.   ПРИМЕЧАНИЯ

1. Владимир is located 190 kilometers (114 miles) northeast of Moscow. The city was founded in 1108 as a fortress by the Kievan Prince Vladimir II and destroyed during the Mongol invasion of 1238. Subsequently, under the control of Muscovy dukes, Vladimir became the administrative, cultural, and religious center of northeastern Russia until the fourteenth century. It has become a popular tourist attraction because of its many preserved cathedrals and architectural stuctures dating back to the twelveth century. With a population of approximately 400,000, the city has over fifty industries, producing machinery, tractors, chemicals, cotton textiles, and plastics.

2. Доставля́ть (to convey, to give) is often used in contexts of causing someone inconvenience, pleasure, trouble, etc. Она́ мне предоста́вила возмо́жность ознако́миться с поликли́никой. (She gave me the opportunity to become familiar with the polyclinic.) Э́то доставля́ет мне большо́е удово́льствие. (This gives me great pleasure.) Извини́те, что мы доста́вили вам мно́го хлопо́т. (Sorry for causing you a lot of trouble.)

3. Коклю́ш (pertussis); дифтери́я (diphtheria); столбня́к (tetanus); сы́воротка (serum).

4. Загво́здка (snag, rub, obstacle) is a popular word in Russia. Я хочу́ пое́хать за грани́цу —А де́ньги? —Де́ньги! Вот в чём загво́здка! (I want to go abroad —And what about money? —Money! There's the rub!)

5. The noun приви́вка (immunization, prevention) is followed by the preposition от (from) or про́тив (against) and the name of the disease in the genitive case. Мы сде́лали всем де́тям приви́вку от о́спы. (We gave all the children an inoculation against smallpox.) Alternatively, the infinitive приви́ть (to vaccinate) can be used, in which case the disease should be in the dative case. Мы приви́ли де́тям о́спу. (We vaccinated the children against smallpox.)

6. Медпу́нкт is an abbreviation derived from медици́нский пункт (lit. medical aid station). Another term for a first-aid station is здравпу́нкт, derived from здравоохрани́тельный пункт (lit. public health station).

7. Unlike medical practice in the United States, where hospitalization is chiefly concerned with clinical intervention, Russians hospitalize infected patients primarily to isolate them from the community.

8. Анги́на in Russian refers to a throat infection or inflammation, such as tonsillitis (also тонзилли́т). Be sure not to confuse it with the

heart condition angina pectoris , which in Russian is грудна́я жа́ба or стенока́рдия.

9. The normal body temperature of 98.6° F is equivalent to 37° C. Body temperature in Russia is traditionally measured in adults by placing the thermometer under the armpit (подмы́шка).

10. The disjunctive conjunction ли́бо . . . ли́бо is essentially the equivalent of и́ли . . . и́ли (either . . . or). Вы мо́жете ли́бо записа́ться на приём к врачу́ сейча́с же, ли́бо позвони́ть нам за́втра утром. (You can either make an appointment to see the doctor now, or call us tomorrow morning.)

С. ГРАММАТИКА И СЛОВОУПОТРЕБЛЕНИЕ

1. ОТНОСИТЕЛЬНЫЕ МЕСТОИМЕНИЯ: КОТОРЫЙ И ЧТО/КТО (RELATIVE PRONOUNS: КОТО́РЫЙ VERSUS ЧТО/КТО)

In Уро́к 14 you saw how что functions as a relative pronoun; i.e., to introduce a new clause. For example: всё, что ты хо́чешь (everything you want), пе́рвое, что тебе́ на́до сде́лать (the first thing you've got to do). Кто functions in a similar way: все, кто сде́лает приви́вку (everyone who gets vaccinated). Both кто and что generally have pronoun antecedents (всё, то). In other words, they refer to previously introduced pronouns, and they do not change according to case. Кото́рый, on the other hand, is used when the antecedent is a noun, and it declines for case and gender.

Тот, кто пришёл ра́но утром, уже́ пошёл домо́й.
The one who came early in the morning has already gone home.

Же́нщина, кото́рая пришла́ ра́но утром, уже́ пошла́ домо́й.
The woman who came early in the morning has already gone home.

When their antecedent is singular, кто and что normally require the masculine, singular form of the verb.

Тот, кто пришёл сего́дня у́тром, не хоте́л сде́лать приви́вку.
The one who came this morning didn't want to get vaccinated.

Пе́рвым, кто прие́хал на приём, был до́ктор Шемя́кин.
The first one who arrived at the reception was Dr. Shemyakin.

If the antecedent is plural, the verb can be either singular or plural.

Те, кто не состоя́т/состои́т в на́ших спи́сках, мо́гут сде́лать приви́вку в больни́це.
Those who are not on our roster can be vaccinated at the hospital.

Все, кто прису́тствовал/и на сва́дьбе, переночева́ли в гости́нице.
Everyone who attended the wedding stayed at the hotel overnight.

Те из нас, кто осмотре́л больно́го, поста́вили одина́ковый диа́гноз.
Those of us who examined the patient, made the same diagnosis.

Кото́рый, on the other hand, changes case according to its function in the clause. Compare:

Те, кто получа́ют приви́вку, ре́дко испы́тывают осложне́ния.
Those who get vaccinated rarely suffer complications.

Де́ти, кото́рые получа́ют приви́вку, ре́дко испы́тывают осложне́ния.
Children who get vaccinated rarely suffer complications.

Больны́е, кото́рых мы осмотре́ли, наве́рное, бы́стро вы́здоровеют.
The patients (whom) we examined will probably recover rapidly

Кото́рая can also be used instead of кто when the antecedent is a feminine and singular pronoun.

Та, кото́рая осмотре́ла ребёнка, реши́ла сде́лать ему́ приви́вку.
She (the woman) who examined the child, decided to vaccinate him.

Кто, то can also be shortened to кто, with тот shifted to a separate clause as follows:

Кто сде́лает приви́вку, тот не зарази́тся.
Anyone who gets vaccinated will not become infected.

... Or, as in the old Communist adage:

Кто не рабо́тает, тот не ест.
    Whoever does not work does not eat.

2. ЧАСТИЦЫ (PARTICLES)

Russian particles are used primarily in colloquial speech to add certain nuances to words and phrases, or to express emotions, subjective attitudes, etc. They do not decline. Following are some of the most common particles.

PARTICLE	MEANING	USAGE
a	question	end of statement
ведь	you know, after all	positive assumption
же	emphasis	emphasizes following element
бы	it would, were it so	exclamation
вот	now this, but now	contrast
ещё	yet, still	emphasizes preceding element
ну	well now	emphasizes preceding element
тоже	also that too	skepticism
-то	emphasis	emphasizes following element
хоть	at least, for example	minimum expectation, before or after emphasized element

Жва́чку тебе́ дать, а?
    So, I should give you some gum, eh?

Ну что ж ты тут стои́шь. Помоги́ мне, а?
    Well, what are you standing there for? Help me, would you?

Ведь вы ещё хоте́ли посмотре́ть де́тскую поликли́нику.
    Surely (I know that) you also wanted to see the pediatric polyclinic.

Но ведь это всем изве́стно.
    But surely everyone knows about this.

Что́ же ты де́лаешь?
    Whatever are you doing?

Это же совсем непонятно!
  Now this is something quite incomprehensible!

Лишь бы они смогли приехать пораньше.
  If only they could come a little earlier.

Тебе понравился фильм? —Ещё бы!
  Did you like the film? —And how!

Я совсем проголодался. Перекусить бы!
  I'm starved. Oh, what I wouldn't give for a little snack!

Раньше, у нас не хватало сыворотки, а вот теперь даже при наличии вакцины, многие боятся прививок.
  Previously, we were short of serum, but now, even when we have vaccines, many are afraid of getting vaccinated.

Работать со старыми шприцами было довольно трудно, а вот эти одноразовые гораздо удобнее.
  Working with the old syringes was rather difficult, but these disposable ones are much more convenient.

Он хорошо владеет компьютером? —Ещё как!
  Is he good with computers? —I'll say he is!

Ещё врачом называется!
  And he calls himself a physician!

Ну, врач!
  Some doctor!

Тоже мне врач нашёлся!
  If he's a doctor, I don't know what a doctor is!

Вообще-то запасов сыворотки достаточно.
  Well, generally speaking, our serum stock is sufficient.

Теперь-то я понимаю, почему они не хотели сделать прививку.
  Now I understand why they didn't want to be vaccinated.

Попро́буй хоть кусо́чек. Па́льчики обли́жешь!
Try at least a small piece. It's delicious!

Взять хоть Шемя́кина; он ка́ждый день рабо́тает с утра́ до но́чи, не покладая рук.
Take Shemyakin, for example. He works every day from morning to night without pause.

D. ИДИОМАТИКА

AN APPLE A DAY . . .

Following are some health related expressions:

Быть пря́мо поме́шанным на здоро́вье (TO BE A REAL HEALTH NUT)

Зачем Ви́ктор принима́ет сто́лько витами́нов? —Ведь, ты зна́ешь он пря́мо поме́шан на здоро́вье.
Why is Viktor taking so many vitamins? —Well, you know he's a real health nut.

Бу́дь(те) здоро́в(вы)! (BE HEALTHY!; TAKE CARE!)

Ну, уви́димся, когда́ верну́сь с Да́льнего Восто́ка. —Ну, ладно. Бу́дьте здоро́вы.
We'll see you when I get back from the Far East. —Well, okay, then. Take care!

Подремонти́ровать/попра́вить здоро́вье (TO RECOVER FROM
AN ILLNESS)

Я уве́рен, что че́рез не́сколько неде́ль, она́ вполне́ подремонти́рует здоро́вье.
I'm certain that she'll recover completely in a few weeks.

If you're not feeling up to par you can say:

Мне нездоро́вится.
I'm feeling a bit under the weather.

Я чу́вствую себя́ нева́жно.
I don't feel so hot.

And always remember:

Ра́но ложи́шься, ра́но встаёшь—здоро́вья, бога́тсва и ума́ наживёшь.
Early to bed, early to rise, makes a man health, wealthy, and wise.

E. СТРОГО ПО ДЕЛУ

МЕДИЦИНСКАЯ И ФАРМАЦЕВТИЧЕСКАЯ ПРОМЫШЛЕННОСТЬ (THE MEDICAL AND PHARMACEUTICAL INDUSTRY)

The medical and pharmaceutical industry was never accorded a high level of priority during the Soviet period in comparison to most other sectors of the economy. The resultant chronic shortage of advanced medical equipment, facilities, and pharmaceutical products placed a heavy reliance on imports. This situation has been exacerbated by the restricted amounts of hard currency (валю́та) allotted for the purchase of such items abroad.

The process of privatization and conversion to a market economy, along with a realistic recognition of problems in the health-care sector, have resulted in some improvements in medical supplies and facilities. Research has been undertaken at the Cardiology Center of the Russian Academy of Sciences (Нау́чный центр кардиоло́гии при Росси́йской Акаде́мии Нау́к), for example, to develop medical imaging machines. However, considerable shortages in medical equipment and medicinals persist. Medical equipment in particularly short supply include CAT scanners (компью́терные томографи́ческие ска́неры), MRIs (аппара́т для магни́тно-резона́нсного изображе́ния), kidney dialysis machines (гемодиализа́торы), ultrasound detectors (ультразвуковы́е дете́кторы), electrocardiograms (прибо́ры для электрокардиогра́ммы), and X-ray machines (рентге́новский диагности́ческий аппара́т). Pharmaceuticals in short supply include antibiotics (антибио́тики), heart and circulatory system drugs (серде́чно-сосу́дистые лека́рственные сре́дства), insulin (инсули́н), vitamins (витами́ны), blood and plasma substitutes (кровезамени́тели и плазмозамени́тели), hormones (гормо́ны), cancer medication (лека́рства от ра́ка), anesthestics (анестези́рующие срéдства), and vaccines (вакцѝны). The limited number of Russian pharmaceutical firms that are now becoming privatized are engaged primarily in the manufacture of basic drugs (основнꙋ́е лекáрственные препарáты) because they do not have the required research and testing facilities to develop advanced drug products.

A number of Western European countries have been active in promoting their products to satisfy Russia's needs. American companies have been particularly active in promoting the sale of medical equipment in the Far East (Дáльний Востóк) of Russia because the relative proximity of that area to the West Coast makes shipments more reliable and less expensive than transportation by rail via Moscow, for example. Although most U.S. equipment and pharmaceuticals are generally more expensive than medical products offered by other countries, the American items enjoy a reputation of high quality and reliability. Most medical equipment and medicines are exempt from customs duties, although they are assessed value-added taxes (налóги на добáвленную стóимость), which can make them a profitable export. A useful contact for the sale of medical equipment to the Far East is Chernay International, Inc., in Khabarovsk (Хабáровск), which has represented 28 American companies since 1987.

Major American pharmaceutical companies that have been active in exporting medicinals include Eli Lilly & Company, the Upjohn Company, and Abbott Laboratories. Among the several shipping companies that now offer reliable service between the Far East and the United States are the American President Lines, JAS Forwarding (3225 S. 116th St., Suite 177, Seattle, WA 98168; Владивостóк, 35-4 Пýшкинская ýлица; tel. 26-93-39); FESCO Intermodel (614 Norton Building, 801 Second Ave., Seattle, WA 98104, Tel. 206-583-0860); and the Sea-Land CIS Logistics Company, Sea-Land Service, Inc. (379 Thornall St., Edison, NJ 08837; Владивосток, 7 Комсомóльская улица, Тел. 7-4232-25-93-87).

Additional updated information about marketing opportunities for medical and pharmaceutical products can be obtained from the International Trade Administration of the U.S. Department of Commerce (202-482-0550; fax: 202-482-0975), or directly from a Department of Commerce Bulletin Board on the Internet (http://www.itaiep.doc.gov/bisnis/bulletin/bulletin.html).

УПРАЖНЕНИЯ

A. Запо́лните про́пуски, испо́льзуя подходя́щие местоиме́ния. Поста́вьте ну́жные зна́ки препина́ния. (Fill in the blanks with the appropriate pronoun and insert the required punctuation.)

1. Вот врач＿＿＿＿＿＿＿ сде́лал мне приви́вку.
2. После́дний из тех＿＿＿＿＿＿ пришёл на приём, очеви́дно, где́-то заблуди́лся.
3. Те из нас＿＿＿＿＿＿ посети́ли поликли́нику, сде́лали одина́ковые вы́воды.
4. В э́той пала́те нахо́дятся де́ти＿＿＿＿＿＿＿＿ра́ньше не де́лали приви́вку.
5. Я уже́ рассказа́л тебе́ всё,＿＿＿＿＿＿я зна́ю.
6. Та ＿＿＿＿＿＿пришла́ сего́дня у́тром, перенесла́ дифтери́ю.
7. ＿＿＿＿＿＿не хо́чет сде́лать приви́вку, тот не о́чень хорошо́ осведомлён о профила́ктике.
8. Все,＿＿＿＿＿＿записа́лся, полу́чат приви́вку.
9. Отделе́ние, в＿＿＿＿＿＿лечат венери́ческие боле́зни, нахо́дится на тре́тьем этаже́.
10. Пе́рвый,＿＿＿＿＿＿пришёл на приви́вку, уже́ пошёл домо́й.

B. Переведи́те сле́дующие предложе́ния на ру́сский язы́к. Укажи́те куда́ па́дает ударе́ние.

1. Let's begin our tour with the infectious diseases ward.
2. The rub is that an insufficient number of the population was vaccinated.
3. Do you have a shortage of serum?
4. Those who are not on our roster can get vaccinated at the hospital.
5. The old syringes were rather unreliable (ненадёжный), but now these disposable ones are quite convenient,
6. What was Dr. Petrov's diagnosis? —Some doctor! He examined me and didn't explain anything!
7. If only the children had registered last week!
8. Whatever is that nurse doing?
9. Please tell me something about the pediatric polyclinic.
10. The woman who came in for a follow-up throat culture had a mild case of diphtheria.

УРОК 18

А. ДИАЛОГ

В университе́те.

В фойе́ Моско́вского госуда́рственного университе́та.[1] Два студе́нта, Андре́й и Еле́на, то́лько что сда́ли экза́мен[2] по междунаро́дному пра́ву.

ЕЛЕНА: **Ну, как прошёл экза́мен, Андре́й?**

АНДРЕЙ: **Норма́льно,[3] я получи́л четы́ре.[4] Хотя́ мог бы отве́тить и лу́чше, коне́чно. А ско́лько тебе́ поста́вили?[5]**

ЕЛЕНА: **Я получи́ла пять. Мне попа́лся[6] биле́т,[7] кото́рый я о́чень хорошо́ зна́ла. Экзаменацио́нной коми́ссии очень понра́вился мой отве́т.**

АНДРЕЙ: **Молодчи́на! Ты кого́-то ждёшь?**

ЕЛЕНА: **Да, жду моего́ дру́га из США. Он прилете́л вчера́ в Москву́. Я уже́ давно́ обеща́ла показа́ть ему́ университе́т. (К Андре́ю и Еле́не подхо́дит молодо́й челове́к.) А вот, как раз и он!**

Еле́на здоро́вается с го́стем и представля́ет его́ Андре́ю.

ПАТРИК: **Вы ведь сего́дня сдава́ли экза́мены, ве́рно? Ну, как отстреля́лись?[8]**

ЕЛЕНА: (бро́сив взгляд на Андре́я) **Мы о́ба получи́ли хоро́шие оце́нки.**

ПАТРИК: **Поздравля́ю! И тепе́рь, полага́ю, вы мо́жете немно́го рассла́биться?**

ЕЛЕНА: **Не совсе́м. Мне ещё на́до дописа́ть курсову́ю рабо́ту. А сейча́с ты не хоте́л бы сходи́ть на ле́кцию по междунаро́дным отноше́ниям? Сего́дняшняя ле́кция как раз посвящена́ ру́сско-америка́нским отноше́ниям по́сле перестро́йки.**

ПАТРИК: **Здо́рово! А вы уве́рены, что мне разреша́т прису́тствовать на заня́тиях?**

АНДРЕЙ: Нет проблéм. Аудитóрия у нас óчень большáя, рассчи́тана по крáйней мéре на пятьсóт слýшателей.[9] Никтó и не замéтит одногó ли́шнего студéнта.

ПАТРИК: Давáй. Знáчит, вы óба ýчитесь на однóм[10] факультéте?[11]

АНДРЕЙ: Нет, я учýсь на факультéте экономи́ческих отношéний, на трéтьем кýрсе,[12] но в э́том семéстре мы с Елéной слýшаем оди́н и тот же курс.

Бли́же к концý лéкции.

ПРОФЕССОР: . . . Итáк, вот э́ти три глáвных понятия, я совéтую вам при́нять во внимáние. Подýмайте о том, как их мóжно примени́ть к вáшему задáнию на слéдующую лéкцию. Кстáти, в слéдующий раз вы послýшаете доклáд профéссора Пáнина, с нáшего экономи́ческого факультéта, котóрый тóлько что вернýлся с Пари́жской конферéнции Междунарóдной ассоциáции разви́тия. Поскóльку занятия ассоциáции, во мнóгом, связаны с вáшим задáнием, я увéрен, что вы найдёте его доклáд óчень интерéсным. Всё. Спаси́бо.

ПАТРИК: Лéкция былá увлекáтельной. Óчень интерéсно было услы́шать толковáние э́тих собы́тий в инóм свéте.

ЕЛЕНА: Но ведь в Амéрике вам достýпны разнообрáзные тóчки зрéния, в том числé и та, котóрая былá вы́сказана на сегóдняшней лéкции.

ПАТРИК: Достýпны, может быть, но информáцию о текýщих собы́тиях срéдний америкáнец получáет, глáвным образом, из тележурнáлов. А репортáжи в них рéдко предлагáют разли́чные трактóвки собы́тий, причём у большинствá америкáнцев нет ни врéмени, ни желáния поискáть други́е истóчники информáции.

ЕЛЕНА: То есть ты хóчешь э́тим сказáть, что америкáнцы плóхо проинформи́рованы о текýщих собы́тиях?

ПАТРИК: До нéкоторой стéпени, я бы сказáл, да.

ЕЛЕНА: Но ведь . . .

АНДРЕЙ: (глядя на часы́) Слýшайте, уже пóздно, а я бы хотéл зайти́ в Дом кни́ги до ýжина. Пáтрик, хóчешь тудá сходи́ть?

ПАТРИК: С больши́м удово́льствием! Мне позаре́з ну́жен совреме́нный ру́сско-англи́йский юриди́ческий слова́рь бизнесме́на.

ЕЛЕНА: Ну, пойдём!

В До́ме кни́ги.

АНДРЕЙ: Насто́льные[13] кни́ги, словари́ и спра́вочники нахо́дятся на второ́м этаже́. А я бу́ду в отде́ле эконо́мики, вот здесь, спра́ва.

ЕЛЕНА: Ла́дно. Встре́тимся попо́зже … А вот насто́льные кни́ги, Па́трик.

ПАТРИК: Так, дава́й посмо́трим, что тут име́ется … Ах, у меня́ уже́ есть э́то изда́ние. А я рассчи́тывал,[14] что уже́ вы́пустили бо́лее но́вое изда́ние.

ЕЛЕНА: Дава́й спро́сим … (обраща́сь к продавщи́це) Прости́те, нет ли у вас[15] бо́лее но́вых изда́ний э́того словаря́?

ПРОДАВЩИЦА: В да́нный моме́нт это еди́нственный слова́рь тако́го ро́да, кото́рый у нас име́ется.

ЕЛЕНА: Зна́ешь, Па́трик, мо́жет быть, нам лу́чше поиска́ть словари́ в кни́жных кио́сках.[16] Иногда́ там быва́ют очень вы́годные сде́лки.[17]

ПАТРИК: Дава́й … А, вот идёт Андре́й!

———————

At the university.

In the foyer of Moscow State University. Two students, Andrey and Elena, have just taken their exams in International Law.

ELENA: Well, how was the exam, Andrey?

ANDREY: Not bad, I got a four. Of course, I could have done better. What did you get?

ELENA: A five. I drew a question on a subject that I knew very well. The examination committee liked my answers.

ANDREY: Good for you! Are you waiting for somebody?

ELENA: Yes, I'm waiting for my friend from the States. He flew into Moscow yesterday, and I promised him a long time ago that I would show him the university. (A young man comes up to Andrey and Elena.) Ah, here he is!

Elena greets her guest and introduces him to Andrey.

PATRICK: You had exams today, right? How did it go?

ELENA: (glancing at Andrey) We both did very well.

PATRICK: Congratulations! So now you can relax a little.

ELENA: Well, not exactly. I still have a paper to write. But right now I thought you might like to sit in on our International Relations class. Today's lecture is on Russian-American relations after perestroika.

PATRICK: Perfect! Are you sure it's okay for me to be there?

ANDREY: No problem. It's a very big lecture hall that seats five hundred students. No one will even notice whether there's one student more or less.

PATRICK: Great. So, are you both in the same department?

ELENA: No, I'm in the Economics Department in my third year, but we're both taking this course.

Toward the end of the lecture.

PROFESSOR: ... So I would like you to keep these three principal notions in mind. Think about how they might be applied to your reading assignment for the next class. Incidentally, next time you'll hear a report by Professor Panin of our Economics Department, who has just returned from a conference of the International Development Association in Paris. Since much of the association's activity is related to your assigned topic, I'm sure you will find his talk interesting. That's all. Thank you.

PATRICK: That was fascinating. Very interesting to see these events in a different light.

ELENA: But surely in America you have access to a variety of viewpoints, including the one we heard in today's lecture.

PATRICK: Access, perhaps, but the average person in the States gets most of his information about current events from TV news programs, and their reporting rarely offers differing interpretations of events. And besides, most Americans have neither the time nor desire to look for different sources of information.

ELENA: You mean to tell me that Americans are poorly informed about current events?

PATRICK: To a certain extent, I would say, yes.

ELENA: But surely . . .

ANDREY: (*looking at his watch*) Look, it's getting late, and I'd like to get to the bookstore before dinner. Would you like to come, Patrick?

PATRICK: Yes, I'd love to go. I desperately need a good, current Russian-English commercial law dictionary.

ELENA: Let's go then.

At the bookstore.

ANDREY: The reference section is on the second floor. And I'll be in the economics section down here on the right.

ELENA: Okay, we'll see you in a little bit . . . Here's the reference section, Patrick.

PATRICK: So, let's see what they have here . . . Oh, I already have this edition. I was hoping they published a more recent one.

ELENA: Let's ask . . . (*addressing a salesperson*) Excuse me, do you have a more recent edition of this dictionary?

SALESPERSON: I'm afraid this is the only one we have right now.

ELENA: You know, Patrick, we might have better luck if we look at some of the bookstalls on the street. Sometimes you can find some good bargains there.

PATRICK: Okay, let's try . . . Ah, here comes Andrey!

B. ПРИМЕЧАНИЯ

1. The full name of Moscow State University (abbreviated МГУ) is Моско́вский госуда́рственный университе́т и́мени Ломоно́сова. It is named after the Russian eighteenth-century poet and academic Михаи́л Ломоно́сов, who founded it in 1755. The original site of the university was in the central section of Moscow on Мохова́я у́лица, where a few departments are still located. The principal "campus," which comprises approximately sixty buildings situated around the 31-story, central "wedding cake"–style tower, is located in Sparrow Hills (Воробьёвы го́ры). The university has a full-time student population of approximately 50,000. It can be reached by subway on the Kirov-Frunze line (Ки́ровско-Фру́нзенская ли́ния); the stop is University subway station (ста́нция метро́ Университе́т).

2. Экза́мен is a formal examination. Контро́льная рабо́та is a quiz. Зачёт is a test or examination. The final examination period at the university level is экзаминацио́нная се́ссия, usually referred to as се́ссия. Сдава́ть экзамен means "to take an exam." The perfective form сдать is used to refer to passing an exam. To fail an examination is провали́ться на экза́мене (lit., to fall through). Ну, как прошёл экза́мен? —К сожале́нию, я провали́лся на нём. (Well, how did the exam go? —Unfortunately, I flunked it.)

3. Норма́льно is a very common expression. Ну, как у вас идёт рабо́та? —Норма́льно. (Well, how's your work coming along? —It's okay.)

4. The Russian grading system is based on a five-point scale (пятиба́лльная систе́ма). The highest grade is a пятёрка (пять) followed by четвёрка (четы́ре), тро́йка (три), дво́йка (два), and едини́ца, which is a failing grade. A дво́йка is also considered a failing grade, but it and the единица are almost never given.

5. The verb ста́вить/поста́вить (to place) has different usages. It can refer to assigning a grade, putting on a play, setting a task, or parking a car. Профе́ссор поста́вил мне пятёрку. (The professor gave me an A.) Студе́нты на четвёртом ку́рсе поста́вили очень заба́вную пье́су Че́хова. (The fourth-year students put on a very funny play by Chekhov.) Они́ поста́вили себе́ очень тру́дную зада́чу. (They set a very difficult task for themselves.) Спроси́те его, куда́ он поста́вил маши́ну. (Ask him where he parked the car).

6. The verb попада́ться/попа́сться means "to come across." Мне попа́лась интере́сная кни́га. (I came across an interesting book.) Это письмо́ мне попа́лось соверше́нно случа́йно. (I came across this letter quite by accident.) The verb is also used in several colloquial expressions meaning "to be caught." Они́ попа́лись с поли́чным. (They were caught red-handed.) Его́ брат попа́лся на кра́же, и тепе́рь сиди́т. (His brother was caught stealing, and now he's doing time.)

7. In Russia, university students generally take oral exams. First, they draw an экзаменацио́нный биле́т (exam card) at random. They have a certain amount of time to organize their thoughts, write a few notes, and prepare to answer the question on the card. They then discuss the subject and answer additional questions posed by the examining committee.

8. Отстреля́ться literally means "to have finished firing at shooting practice." Here it is used figuratively in reference to successfully completing all of one's exams. Я сда́л после́дний экза́мен, отстреля́лся! (I passed my last exam, and that's the end of it!)

9. Слу́шатель (lit. listener) here means "student." The plural слу́шатели means audience. Likewise, the verb слу́шать (to listen to) is also used to mean "to attend a lecture" or "to take a course." Каки́е ку́рсы вы слу́шаете в э́том уче́бном году́? (What courses are you taking this year?) "To sign up for a course" is записа́ться на курс. Ты уже́ записа́лся на курс дре́вной исто́рии? (Did you sign up for the ancient history course already?)

10. Remember that оди́н in its declined forms can mean "the same." Мы с тобо́й бу́дем жить в одно́м общежи́тии. (You and I will be living in the same dormitory.) Мы с ней одного́ во́зраста. (She and I are the same age.) Нам э́то всё одно́. (That's all the same to us.)

11. Факульте́т is a major division within a university that sometimes corresponds to a department in an American university. Ка́федра is a subdivision within a факульте́т, or could be a department in a smaller institution. It can also mean a chair or professorship. Он уже́ два́дцать лет заве́дует ка́федрой матема́тики. (He's held a mathematics professorship for twenty years now.) Она́ тепе́рь у́чится на ка́федре неоргани́ческой хи́мии. (She's now studying in the department of inorganic chemistry.) Он в аспиранту́ре на физи́ческом факульте́те. (He's a graduate student in the physics department.)

12. Курс (course) here means "year." A first-year student is a первоку́рсник. A senior student at a Russian university is normally in his/her fifth year (на пя́том ку́рсе). Все первоку́рсники живу́т у нас в одно́м общежи́тии. (All our first-year students live in the same dorm.) Студе́нты пя́того ку́рса дожны́ защища́ть дипло́мную рабо́ту. (Fifth-year/senior students must defend a graduation thesis.)

13. Насто́льная literally means "on the table" and is used in the following common expressions: насто́льный те́ннис (table tennis), насто́льное руково́дство (a handbook or manual), and насто́льная полиграфи́я (desktop publishing).

14. Рассчи́тывать (to count on; to bargain) is used only in the imperfective. Мы рассчи́тывали купи́ть дом к концу́ э́того го́да. (We were hoping to buy a house by the end of this year.) На э́то я не рассчи́тывал. (That wasn't what I expected.) The perfective form of

the verb рассчита́ть means "to compute," "to calculate," "to design." Они́ уже́ рассчита́ли, ско́лько бу́дет сто́ить но́вое обору́дование? (Have they already calculated how much the new equipment will cost?) Э́тот слова́рь рассчи́тан на преподава́телей, студе́нтов и перево́дчиков. (This dictionary is intended for teachers, students, and translators.)

15. Не́т ли у вас . . . ? is a more polite way of saying У вас есть . . . ? (Do you have . . . ?). Remember that asking questions in the negative indicates greater politeness. Вы не ска́жете, где здесь нахо́дится ближа́йшая остано́вка авто́буса? (Won't you tell me where the nearest bus stop is?) Ты не хо́чешь пойти́ в кино́ сего́дня ве́чером? (Would you not like to go to the movies this evening?)

16. Along with other types of merchandise sold on the streets in major cities, the number of bookstalls has greatly proliferated in recent years. Frequently, the selection at the stalls is better than in regular bookstores.

17. Сде́лка means "bargain," "deal," or "transaction." В конце́ концо́в, они́ заключи́ли сде́лку. (They finally concluded a deal.) Они́ наста́ивали на сде́лке за нали́чный расчёт. (They insisted on a cash transaction.) Я с ним вошёл в о́чень вы́годную сде́лку. (I struck a very good bargain with him.)

C. ГРАММАТИКА И СЛОВОУПОТРЕБЛЕНИЕ

1. ГЛАГОЛЫ, ОТНОСЯЩИЕСЯ К ОБУЧЕНИЮ
(VERBS RELATED TO TEACHING AND LEARNING)

Several Russian verbs can be translated as "to learn," "to study," or "to teach," each with a specific meaning in a particular context.

Учи́ть/вы́учить means "to learn" and takes an object in the accusative case. The perfective form вы́учить implies that the material was thoroughly learned or memorized.

Они́ сейча́с у́чат четвёртый уро́к.
They are now learning the fourth lesson.

Они́ отли́чно вы́учили пе́рвые три уро́ка.
They did an excellent job of learning the first three lessons.

Учи́ть/обуча́ть/научи́ть means "to teach." The person taught is then in the accusative case and the subject taught in the dative case. This group of verbs is generally used in reference to elementary or secondary school, or nonschool contexts. To instruct or teach at the university level is most commonly expressed by the verb преподава́ть.

Я учу́ их ру́сскому языку́.
I am teaching them Russian.*

Кто вас научи́л пло́тничному де́лу?
Who taught you carpentry?

Я хочу́, что́бы она́ обучи́ла тебя́ францу́зскому языку́.
I want her to teach you French.

Он преподаёт фи́зику в МГУ.
He teaches physics at MSU.

Учи́ть/обуча́ть/научи́ть can also be used with an infinitive to mean "to teach how" to do something.

Он у́чит моего́ сы́на игра́ть на скри́пке.
He's teaching my son how to play the violin.

Кто вас научи́л води́ть маши́ну?
Who taught you how to drive a car?

Мой дя́дя обучи́л меня́ ката́ться на лы́жах.
My uncle taught me how to ski.

The reflexive form учи́ться/научи́ться means "to learn" or "to study" some subject, which can be expressed with a noun in the dative or accusative case, or with an infinitive.

Эти студе́нты у́чатся биоло́гии.
These students are studying biology.

Где вы учи́лись неме́цкому языку́?
Where did you study German?

*It might be helpful to think about this construction as introducing someone to a subject.

Они́ у́чатся игра́ть в ша́хматы.
They're learning how to play chess.

Где вы научи́лись так хорошо́ говори́ть по-ру́сски?
Where did you learn to speak Russian so well?

Учи́ться на + the accusative case means "to study, to learn to be."

Она́ учится на программи́ста.
She's studying to be a programmer.

The imperfective form учи́ться can also mean to matriculate at some institution of learning.

Моя́ сестра́ сейча́с у́чится на филологи́ческом факульте́те Ки́евского университе́та.
My sister is now studying (enrolled) in the philology department of Kiev University.

The verbs изуча́ть/изучи́ть mean "to study in depth."

Она́ уже́ пять лет изуча́ет средневеко́вую исто́рию Ита́лии.
She has been studying Italian medieval history for five years..

The perfective form изучи́ть is primarily used to express a thorough study of a particular subject to the point of mastery.

Подро́бно изучи́в э́тот сло́жный вопро́с, он нашёл оши́бку в да́нных.
Having studied the complex problem in detail, he found an error in the data.

Занима́ться (to be engaged) is used to express the idea of doing one's homework or preparing for exams.

Она́ обы́чно занима́ется в библиоте́ке, потому́ что в общежи́тии сли́шком шу́мно.
She usually does her homework/studies in the library because it's too noisy in the dormitory.

2. ПОРЯДОК СЛОВ В ПРЕДЛОЖЕНИИ (WORD ORDER)

A) DECLARATIVE SENTENCES

In Russian, word order is quite flexible because most words are heavily inflected, so that their form, rather than their position, usually indicates their function. Nevertheless, written, and often spoken, Russian normally follows a so-called neutral pattern, which generally places new information towards the end of a declarative sentence. In the examples below, the new or suggested information is underlined. Characteristically, the subject and object can vary in position but can usually be easily identified by their case endings.

Я уже́ давно́ обеща́ла показа́ть ему́ <u>университе́т</u>.*
I promised to show him the university a long time ago.

Вот э́ти три гла́вных поня́тия я <u>сове́тую вам приня́ть во внима́ние</u>.
I suggest that you consider these three principal notions.

Информа́цию о теку́щих собы́тиях сре́дний америка́нец получа́ет, бо́льшей ча́стью, из <u>тележурна́лов</u>.
The average American gets most of her information about current events from TV news programs.

B) THE POSITION OF ADJECTIVES

Russian long adjectives normally precede the nouns they modify, similar to English word order.

Мне ещё на́до дописа́ть <u>курсову́ю</u> рабо́ту.
I still have to write my term paper.

Short-form adjectives must, and long-form adjectives may, follow a linking verb; i.e., "to be." In this position, long- and short-form adjectives are often interchangeable, although the long form often implies an inherent permanent condition, whereas the short form relates to temporary states.

Аудито́рия у нас о́чень <u>больша́я</u>.
Our auditorium is very large.

*Note that the word order is almost reversed in the English translation.

Студе́нты бы́ли о́чень <u>голо́дны</u>.
The students were very hungry.

C) THE POSITION OF ADVERBS AND ADVERBIAL PHRASES

Adverbs and adverbial phrases normally precede the verbs they modify. However, if they are introducing new information, they can follow the verb.

Мне попа́лся биле́т, кото́рый я о́чень хорошо́ зна́ла.
I drew a question that I knew very well.

Мо́жет быть, лу́чше поиска́ть словари́ в кни́жных кио́сках.
Perhaps we had better look for dictionaries at the book stalls.

Он прилете́л вчера́ в Москву́.
He arrived in Moscow yesterday.

D) THE POSITION OF PRONOUNS

Object pronouns can either precede or follow a verb.

На ле́кции я их не ви́дел.
Я не ви́дел их на ле́кции.
I didn't see them at the lecture.

Вы да́ли ему́ слова́рь?
Вы ему́ да́ли слова́рь?
Did you give him the dictionary?

E) INTERROGATIVE SENTENCES

If a sentence begins with a question word (как, когда́, куда́, где, etc.), the verb normally precedes the noun, particularly if the latter represents new information.

Как прошёл экза́мен?
How did the exam go?

Когда́ закрыва́ется кни́жный магази́н?
When does the bookstore close?

Куда́ идёт э́тот авто́бус?
Where is this bus going?

However, a pronoun must precede the verb in these types of questions.

Как он прошёл?
How did it go?

Когда́ он закрыва́ется?
When does it close?

Куда́ он идёт?
Where is it going?

If the interrogative sentence is not introduced by a question word, the word order can be the same as in a declarative sentence, and intonation determines the meaning.

Вы о́ба у́читесь на одно́м факульте́те.
You are both studying in the same department.

Вы о́ба у́читесь на одно́м факульте́те?
Are you both studying in the same department?

In general, the flexibility of word order is much greater in spoken Russian, where both intonation and the variable placement of words can shift the emphasis of meanings or express various emotions.

Мы получи́ли хоро́шие оце́нки.
We got good grades.

Оце́нки мы получи́ли <u>хоро́шие</u>!
The grades we got were good!

<u>Хоро́шие</u> оце́нки мы получи́ли!
It was good grades that we got!

The two latter "expressive" sentences do not follow the neutral order of placing new information at the end of the sentence. Again, emphasis would depend on intonation. Compare the following "neutral" and "expressive" versions:

Нам лу́чше поиска́ть словари́ в кни́жных кио́сках.
We had better look for dictionaries at the bookstalls.

Словари́, нам лу́чше поиска́ть в кни́жных кио́сках!
Now dictionaries are something we had better be looking for at the bookstalls!

D. ИДИОМАТИКА

LIVE AND LEARN.

Here are some expressions reflecting various attitudes toward learning and wisdom.

Век живи́ век учи́сь! (Live and learn!)

This expression is sometimes followed by the somewhat pessimistic и дурако́м умрёшь (but you'll die a fool).

Ско́лько живу́, никогда́ тако́го живо́тного не встреча́л!—Вот, век живи́, век учи́сь.
I've never seen an animal like that in all my life. —Well, there you are, live and learn!

Учи́ться никогда́ не по́здно. (It's never too late to learn.)

И по́сле сто́льких лет ты реши́л поступа́ть в университе́т? —Да, ведь учи́ться никогда́ не по́здно.
After so many years you've decided to apply to a university? —Well yes, after all it's never too late to learn!

Учи́ться на у́дочку* (to just get by)

Твой това́рищ по ко́мнате, наве́рное, отли́чник? —Да нет, у́чится так себе́, на у́дочку.
I suppose your roommate is a top student? —Not at all! He's just getting by, getting C's.

*Удочка is a diminutive form for удовлетвори́тельно (satisfactory or passing). An A-student is отли́чник.

Не учи́ учёного. (DON'T TEACH A SCHOLAR.; I.E., AN OLD FOX DOESN'T NEED TO BE TAUGHT TRICKS.)

Послу́шайте, по-мо́ему, это де́лается по-друго́му. —Не учи́ учёного, сыно́к.
    Listen, I think you're doing this wrong! —Don't tell an expert what to do, sonny!

Не учи́ меня́ жить! (DON'T TELL ME HOW TO LIVE!)

Ну вот, ты же совсе́м запусти́л учёбу! —Зна́ешь, ма́ма, не учи́ меня́ жить!
    Now just look at that, you've completely neglected your studies! —Look, Mom, don't tell me how to live!

Уче́нье свет, а неуче́нье тьма. (KNOWLEDGE IS LIGHT, BUT IGNORANCE IS DARKNESS.)

This saying is a light-hearted reminder about the importance of study, often expressed jokingly.

И заче́м тебе́ вся э́та нау́ка? —Ну как же: уче́нье свет, а неуче́нье тьма.
    What do you need all this studying for? —Well, now, knowledge is light but ignorance is darkness.

Вот тебе́ нау́ка! (LET THAT BE A LESSON TO YOU!)

Вчера́ я провали́лся на экза́мене, и тепе́рь меня́ мо́гут исключи́ть из институ́та. —Вот тебе́ нау́ка! Ме́ньше на́до лоботря́сничать!
    I failed my exam yesterday and now I may get expelled from the institute. —Well, let that be a lesson to you! You shouldn't have goofed off so much!

Учи́ть/научи́ть уму́-ра́зуму (TO TEACH SOMEONE SOME SENSE)

Уж они́-то нау́чат тебя́ уму́-ра́зуму, дружки́ твои́.
    Yeah, well, your buddies will knock some sense into you for sure.

Ему́/ей э́тот уро́к пошёл впрок. (THAT WAS A GOOD LESSON FOR HIM/HER.)

Су́дя по тому́, что она́ ста́ла лу́чше учи́ться по́сле разгово́ра с отцо́м, ей
э́тот уро́к пошёл впрок.

The talk with her father was apparently a good lesson for her since she
subsequently started to do better in her studies.

Е. СТРОГО ПО ДЕЛУ

ИЗДАТЕЛЬСКОЕ ДЕЛО (BOOK PUBLISHING)

Russians are avid readers. Certainly one of the positive aspects of the
early Communist years was the great emphasis placed on raising the literacy rate of the population, even if this was a self-serving goal. In any
event, the literacy rate (гра́мотность) in Russia is one of the highest in
the world, 98 percent. As part of the Soviet literacy campaign, books were
relatively inexpensive, although the quality of printing, paper, and binding was obviously of secondary importance. During the Soviet period
quality art books were frequently printed in Czechoslovakia or Italy.
Today, many glossy-type news and trade journals are still being printed
in Finland (e.g., Коммерса́нт, Деловы́е лю́ди, Ито́ги) or the Netherlands
(e.g., БизнессКласс).

Following the collapse of the USSR, the publishing monopoly held by
the State Publishing Company (Госизда́т) was ended, and the number of
non-state publishers rapidly increased from 235 before perestroika to approximately 2,000. However, the actual book output and number of titles
declined by nearly a third in comparison to the pre-perestroika period.
The genres most adversely affected were children's books (де́тские
кни́ги), textbooks (уче́бники), and scientific publications (нау́чные
произведе́ния). Russian private publishers consequently turned to areas
of greater demand and profitability such as detective fiction (детекти́вы),
erotica (эро́тика), popular medicine (наро́дная медици́на),* business
manuals, and foreign language commercial and technical dictionaries.
The largest Russian publisher of the latter is Изда́тельство «Ру́сский
язы́к» (Russian Language Publishing House) in Moscow. There are a
few firms that have formed partnerships with Western publishers, such
as John Wiley & Sons (Изда́тельство Нау́ка-Уа́йли), also located in
Moscow.

*Popular and homeopathic medicine has a long tradition in Russia. The recent, newly revived
interest in it is partially attributable to inadequate public health care and expensive private medical care.

Russian authors are presently free to conduct contract terms and copyright negotiations at home or abroad without official approval of the former All-Union Agency for Authors' Rights (Всесоюзное агéнтство по áвторским правáм), which was replaced by the Russian Agency for Intellectual Property (РАИС— Росси́йское агéнство интеллектуáльной со́бственности). The functions of РАИС are actually carried out by the Russian Authors' Society (Росси́йское áвторское о́бщество), which is directly under the patronage of the Russian Federation presidency. Although the Russian Federation has approved legislation for its adherence to the Berne Convention on copyright protection, the difficulty of enforcement has resulted in the continued pirating (пирáтсво, нарушéние áвторского прáва) of works by popular writers.

Although international book fairs are still occasionally organized in Russia, their appeal to the general public has somewhat lessened as Western literature has become readily available. Marketing possibilities for Western publishers are still being pursued and investigated through various promotional events such as those organized by the Interforum Services Limited, London (tel. 44-171-381-8914); WP International, Inc., New York (tel. 212- 702-4830); and the Expocenter, Moscow (tel. 7-095-05-66-50 and 268-1340).

УПРАЖНЕНИЯ

A. Впиши́те подходя́щий глагóл в ну́жной фóрме. (Insert the correct form of the appropriate verb.)

1. Мне придётся _____нóвый урóк к концу́ недéли.
(learn thoroughly)

2. Я _____свою́ дочь води́ть автомаши́ну.
(am teaching)

3. Каки́е ку́рсы вы бу́дете_____в слéдующем
(taking)
семéстре?

4. На какóм факультéте они́_____?
(studying)

5. Скóлько лет вы ужé_____немéцкий язы́к?
(studying)

6. Вчерá вéчером я_____ в читáльном зáле нóвой
(was studying)
библиотéки.

7. Кто_____ва́шего бра́та ру́сскому языку́?
       (is teaching)

8. Ты уже́_____на курс америка́нской исто́рии?
       (sign up)

9. Они́_____англи́йскому языку́ в петрогра́дском
       (studied)
   университе́те.

10. Он мне пообеща́л_____меня́ игра́ть в ша́хматы.
       (teach)

B. Запо́лните про́пуски, по́льзуясь подходя́щими предло́гами и существи́тельными и́ли местоиме́ниями в ну́жном падеже́. (Fill in the blanks using the appropriate prepositions, nouns, or pronouns in the required case.)

1. На́ши де́ти тепе́рь у́чатся_____.
       (English)

2. Я бою́сь, что на́ша дочь провали́лась _____.
       (examination)

3. Наш сосе́д у́чит_____ _____.
       (our uncle)   (German)

4. Наши́_____тепе́рь у́чатся _____.
       (sons)   (at Moscow University)

5. Мой сын_____, а дочь у́чится_____.
       (in graduate school)   (in her third year)

6. Я ещё не записа́лся _____.
       (for all my courses)

7. _____вы учи́ли_____?
    (Whom)   (Russian)

8. Её брат у́чится_____.
       (to be a lawyer)

9. Мне разреша́т прису́тствовать_____?
       (classes)

10. Мы ждём_____ _____.
       (our friends)   (from London)

C. Переведи́те сле́дующие предложе́ния на ру́сский язы́к. Обраща́йте внима́ние на поря́док слов в предложе́нии. (Translate the following sentences into Russian. Pay attention to the word order.)

1. I was told that you passed your exams today.

2. Our auditorium is very large.

3. We are both studying in the same department.

4. The lecture concerns Russian-American relations.

5. Perhaps we had better look for dictionaries at the book stalls.
6. How did the exam go? —The professor gave me an A.
7. Do you know when the bookstore opens? —It usually opens at 9 A.M.
8. How long have you been studying Russian?
9. Our friends took their examination last week.
10. I have to finish writing my term paper by the end of the week.

УРОК 19

А. ДИАЛОГ

Переговóры по контрáкту.

Продолжáя разговóр о возмóжности создáния совмéстного предприя́тия в Росси́и, америкáнский бизнесмéн Фил Брáун и егó адвокáт вернýлись в Екатеринбýрг для переговóров по контрáкту на постáвку нóвого оборýдования и техни́ческой пóмощи для свои́х росси́йских партнёров.

БРАУН: Я надéюсь, что Вы получи́ли моё письмó с основны́ми услóвиями предлагáемого контрáкта?

СМИРНОВ: Безуслóвно, и бóлее тогó, совéт управля́ющих нáшего завóда одóбрил большинствó пýнктов. Однáко нéкоторые детáли трéбуют доработки. Напримéр, услóвия оплáты при достáвке материáлов нуждáются[1] в уточнéнии.

БРАУН: Несомнéнно. Поэ́тому—то я и пригласи́л сюдá госпожý Бáтлер. Эллен, разреши́те взгляну́ть на чернови́к[2] контрáкта, пожáлуйста?

БАТЛЕР: Однý секýнду. Вот óба экземпля́ра: рýсский и англи́йский. У Вас есть кóпия, господи́н Смирнóв?

СМИРНОВ: Да, пря́мо прéдо мной на столé.

БАТЛЕР: Господá, давáйте начнём пря́мо с пýнктов, трéбующих уточнéния.

СМИРНОВ: Хорошó. Начнём с услóвий постáвки, срóков постáвки, и упакóвки оборýдования. Итáк, какóй спóсоб оплáты при постáвке вас бóльше устрáивает?

БРАУН: Обы́чно мы испóльзуем безотзы́вный аккредити́в на 80 процéнтов óбщей сýммы постáвки в течéние трёх недéль с подписáния контрáкта. Вам э́то подхóдит?

СМИРНОВ: Вполнé, я дýмаю нам такóе под си́лу.[3] Что касáется спóсобов отгрýзки и достáвки, нам хотéлось бы получáть оборýдование и материáлы на услóвиях с.и.ф.[4]

БРАУН: (поворачиваясь к Батлер) **Мы ведь обычно посылаем ф.а.с.,**[5] **не правда ли?**

БАТЛЕР: **Да, но я думаю, мы можем пойти навстречу господину Смирнову, ведь речь идёт о дорогом и сложном оборудовании.**

СМИРНОВ: **Я также предполагаю, что всё оборудование будет сдаваться «под ключ»?**

БАТЛЕР: **Совершенно верно. Теперь один вопрос о стоимости: наши цифры не включают импортные пошлины, поскольку мы рассчитываем, что это будет оплачено вашей стороной.**

СМИРНОВ: Хорошо, наверное, этот пункт будет включён в раздел взаимообязанностей обеих сторон.

БРАУН: **Есть ещё несколько мелких деталей в вопросе совместного арбитража в случае возникающих разногласий.**

СМИРНОВ: Да, да, это, действительно, очень важно. Мы попросим наших юристов встретиться с госпожой Батлер завтра утром, если это будет вам удобно.

БАТЛЕР: **Да, завтрашнее утро меня вполне устраивает. Мне также кажется, что мы должны включить условие «форс-мажор»**[6] **в окончательную версию контракта.**

БРАУН: **Будем надеяться, что нам не придётся применять этот пункт, но всё же, наверное, его необходимо включить в контракт.**

СМИРНОВ: **Безусловно. На завтрашней встрече нам также хотелось бы внести некоторые поправки, в особенности к статьям об установке и техническом обслуживании оборудования. Хотя я понимаю, что оборудование будет сдаваться «под ключ», мы считаем что проект контракта недостаточно отражает условия подготовки нашего местного персонала.**

БАТЛЕР: **И действительно, нам, пожалуй, придётся пересмотреть эти условия, поскольку стоимость подготовки персонала не была включена в изначальную сумму контракта.**

СМИРНОВ: **А вот с этим, возможно, будет проблема. Мы рассчитывали на то, что в эту сумму уже включены расходы на обучение персонала.**

БРАУН: Так-так. Ну что ж, мы могли́ бы части́чно оплати́ть по́шлины на ввоз при усло́вии, что ва́ша сторона́ берёт на себя́ хоть часть сто́имости переподгото́вки персона́ла. (повора́чивается к Батлер) Как Вы счита́ете?

БА́ТЛЕР: По-мо́ему, э́то сле́дует обсуди́ть. Нам ну́жно бо́лее то́чно знать, что из себя́ представля́ют тамо́женные по́шлины.

БРАУН: Как Вы смо́трите на тако́й компроми́сс, господи́н Смирно́в?

СМИРНОВ: Мне по-пре́жнему не совсе́м я́сно, смо́жем ли мы покры́ть ещё каки́е-то расхо́ды поми́мо уже́ ука́занных в догово́ре, но мы обсу́дим Ва́ше предложе́ние с на́шим отде́лом фина́нсов перед за́втрашней встре́чей юри́стов.

БРАУН: Что ж, Эллен, Вам бу́дет над чем потруди́ться за́втра!

СМИРНОВ: Ничего́. Я уве́рен, что на́ши юри́сты вы́работают оконча́тельную реда́кцию к на́шему взаи́мному удовлетворе́нию.

БРАУН: Мы о́чень на э́то рассчи́тываем.

Contract negotiations.

Subsequent to earlier talks on the possible formation of a joint venture with a Russian building materials company, American businessman Phil Brown and his attorney have returned to Ekaterinburg to negotiate a contract for providing new plant equipment and technical assistance to their Russian partners.

BROWN: I hope you received my letter outlining the general terms of our proposed contract.

SMIRNOV: Yes, I did. I reviewed it with my plant managers and found most of the conditions quite acceptable. All the same, there are a few points that need clarification. For example, some of the details for the shipment and payment of materials still have to be ironed out.

BROWN: Of course. That's why I've asked Ms. Butler to come with me. Ellen, can we see the draft contract?

BUTLER: Just a second. Here we are, copies in Russian and English. Do you have your copy handy, Mr. Smirnov?

SMIRNOV: Yes, right here on my desk.

BUTLER: Should we review the points that need clarification?

SMIRNOV: Fine. Let's start with the terms for payment, delivery dates, and packing. First, what are your preferred terms of payment?

BROWN: Our normal policy is to have payment made by a straight letter of credit for 80 percent of the contract value within three weeks of signing. Is that agreeable to you?

SMIRNOV: Yes, I believe we can manage that. Now, as to the delivery and shipping terms, we would like to receive the equipment and materials on a CIF basis.

BROWN: (turning to Butler) We usually ship FAS, don't we?

BUTLER: Yes, but I think we can accommodate Mr. Smirnov in view of the rather complex equipment involved.

SMIRNOV: I also assume that the equipment will be shipped on a turn-key basis.

BUTLER. That's quite correct. One other point regarding the cost. Our prices do not include the import duties, which we assume you will cover.

SMIRNOV: Yes, that would be stipulated in the section on the obligations of the contractual parties, I believe.

BROWN: There are also a few points to be clarified in the section dealing with the arbitration of any disputes or disagreements.

SMIRNOV: Yes, that's an important point. We'll ask our attorneys to meet with Ms. Butler tomorrow morning, if that's convenient for you.

BUTLER: Yes, tomorrow morning would be fine. I think we should also include a force majeure section in the final contract.

BROWN: Let's hope that we won't have to apply that provision, but still, it's probably essential to include it in the contract.

SMIRNOV: Definitely. At tomorrow's session we might also want to add some amendments to the contract, particularly regarding equipment maintenance and servicing. Although I realize that the equipment will be delivered on a turnkey basis, I don't think the draft adequately covers the training of our local personnel.

BUTLER: Actually, we might have to do some revising there, since the cost of personnel training wasn't included in the initial equipment estimates.

SMIRNOV: That could be a problem. We were counting on the present contract price to include personnel training.

BROWN: I see. Well, perhaps we can consider covering the import duties on the condition that you cover part of the training costs. (turns to Butler) What do you think?

BUTLER: I think we could look into that. We would have to get a better idea of what the import duties are.

BROWN: How would you feel about that kind of compromise, Mr. Smirnov?

SMIRNOV: I'm still not sure as to whether we would be able to cover any costs beyond the present contract level, but I'll discuss your proposal with our finance section before our attorneys meet tomorrow.

BROWN: Well, I see you have your work cut out for you tomorrow, Ellen.

SMIRNOV: No matter. I'm sure our legal teams will draw up a final contract to every one's satisfaction.

BROWN: We're counting on it.

В. ПРИМЕЧАНИЯ

1. The verb нуждáться в + a noun in the prepositional case (to require, to be in need of) is most often used in the third person. По э́тому вопрóсу, они́, действи́тельно, нужда́ются в хорóшем совéте. (They really need good advice on this matter.) Это зда́ние óчень си́льно нужда́ется в капита́льном ремóнте. (This building is in great need of capital repairs.)

2. Черновúк (rough draft) is usually understood to be a first draft. Проéкт is a draft of a formal document or legislative bill. Проéкт резолю́ции был одóбрен исполкóмом. (The draft resolution was approved by the executive committee.) Нóвый законопроéкт обсужда́ется ужé три мéсяца. (The new draft legislation has been under discussion for three months.)

3. The expression под си́лу/по си́лам (to be within one's capability) is common in business settings. Note that the person who is/isn't capable appears in the dative case. Нам не под си́лу покры́ть всю стóимость подготóвки персона́ла. (We're not able to cover the entire cost of personnel training.) Им бы́ло не по си́лам оказа́ть нам фина́нсовую пóмощь. (They were unable to give us any financial assistance.)

4. с.и.ф. (CIF, for Cost, Insurance, Freight). Russian commercial documents normally print CIF in the transliterated form rather than the actual translated form ССФ (стóимость, страхова́ние, фрахт). The

CIF method of shipping means that the price of the commodity includes insurance and freight charges.

5. ф.а.с. (FAS, for Free Alongside Ship, which translates into Russian as свобо́дно вдоль бо́рта су́дна). This method stipulates that the seller (продаве́ц) will have fulfilled his obligations (обя́занности) once the shipped product is placed alongside the ship at the pier (на прича́ле) or on lighters (на ли́хтерах). Any subsequent costs due to freight loss or damage (расхо́ды в результа́те поте́ри или поврежде́ния това́ра) must be borne by the buyer (покупа́тель).

6. Форс-мажо́р, from the French *force majeure* (act of God), also appears in Russian as непреодоли́мая си́ла (insuperable force). This is the clause in a commodity shipment contract that releases both parties from their responsibilites (сто́роны освобожда́ются от отве́тственности) for fulfilling any part of the contract in the event of an unavoidable disaster, such as a fire (пожа́р), flood (наводне́ние), earthquake (землетрясе́ние), revolution, economic blockade (экономи́ческая блока́да), governmental decrees or sanctions (са́нкции или постановле́ния прави́тельств).

C. ГРАММАТИКА И СЛОВОУПОТРЕБЛЕНИЕ

1. СТРАДАТЕЛЬНЫЕ ПРИЧАСТИЯ ПРОШЕДШЕГО ВРЕМЕНИ (PAST PASSIVE PARTICIPLES)

A) FORMATION OF LONG-FORM PAST PASSIVE PARTICIPLES

The long-form past passive participles function as adjectives and are generally formed from perfective verbs* that may take an object. For verbs ending in -ать(-ять), simply replace the infinitive ending with -нн- plus the adjectival ending -ый/-ая/-ое/-ые: написа́ть → напи́санный (written); потеря́ть → поте́рянный (lost). For second conjugation verbs ending in -ить, -ти, -чь, -зть, and -сть, replace the infinitive ending with -енн(-ённ) plus the adjectival ending -ый/-ая/-ое/-ые: получи́ть → полу́ченный (received), включи́ть → включённый (included), принести́ → принесённый (brought), укра́сть → укра́денный (stolen), оплати́ть → опла́ченный (paid). For many first conjugation verbs, especially those whose stems are monosyllabic, simply replace the infinitive ending with -т- plus the adjectival ending: уби́ть → уби́тый (killed),

---

*Past passive participles from imperfective verbs are rarely used. A few examples are ви́деть → ви́денный (seen), слы́шать → слы́шанный (heard), чита́ть → чи́танный (read), and носи́ть → но́шенный (carried, worn).

снять → сня́тый (removed), забы́ть → забы́тый (forgotten), нача́ть → на́чатый (begun), откры́ть → откры́тый (opened). Also note that the agent of action, if expressed, is in the instrumental case.

Сего́дня по́сле обе́да мы обсу́дим неда́вно полу́ченные ва́ми докуме́нты.
> This afternoon we'll discuss the documents you received recently.

За́втра вы, наве́рное, полу́чите контра́кты, подпи́санные все́ми сторона́ми.
> Tomorrow you'll probably receive the contracts signed by all the parties.

Вчера́ они́ покры́ли все расхо́ды, ука́занные в догово́ре.
> Yesterday they covered all the expenses indicated in the agreement.

B) FORMATION OF SHORT-FORM PAST PASSIVE PARTICIPLES

The short-form past passive participles are used with the verb "to be." They are formed by dropping the long-form adjectival endings and adding zero (i.e., adding nothing) to the masculine form, -o to the neuter, -a to the feminine, and -ы for plural forms. The past passive participles with the -нн- element retain only the first -н- in the short form: напи́санный → напи́сан/а/о/ы; полу́ченный → полу́чен/а/о/ы; включённый → вкючён/а/о/ы. Also note that only passive participles have short forms. Active participles have long forms only.

Не все расхо́ды на обуче́ние персона́ла бы́ли <u>вкючены́</u> в но́вый контра́кт.
> Not all the personal training expenses were included in the new contract.

На́ша фи́рма предлага́ет но́вый контра́кт, <u>включа́ющий</u> расхо́ды на обуче́ние персона́ла.
> Our company is offering a new contract that includes personal training expenses.

Notice that the formation of past passive participles frequently involves consonant mutations. Following are some examples with verbs used in this lesson:*

*See Appendix for comprehensive list of consonant mutations.

в→ вл	доста́вить	доста́влен	has been delivered
	подгото́вить	подгото́влен	has been prepared
п→ пл	купи́ть	ку́плен	has been bought
д→ жд	освободи́ть	освобождён	has been released/ liberated
з→ ж	отргузи́ть	отгру́жен	has been shippped
с→ ш	пригласи́ть	приглашён	has been invited
т→ ч	оплати́ть	опла́чен	has been paid
т→ щ	возрати́ть	возвращён	has been returned

c) LONG VERSUS SHORT FORM

The long-form past passive participles, much like active participles, can be used in place of a clause beginning with кото́рый (who, which). Note that perfective passive participles denote an action that was completed prior to the action of the verb in the main clause.

Я вчера́ получи́л пи́сьма, кото́рые написа́л мой брат.
Yesterday I received the letters that my brother wrote.

Я вчера́ получи́л пи́сьма, напи́санные мои́м бра́том. (long-form)
Yesterday I received the letters written by my brother.

As noted above, the short-form past passive participles can be used with the verb быть (to be) in the present, past, or future tense, and they agree with the noun to which they refer in case, number, and gender. This form is frequently used to denote a state or condition or the completion of an action.

Этот пункт уже включён в контра́кт.
This point has already been included into the contract.

Письмо́ подпи́сано.
The letter has been signed.

Библиоте́ка откры́та.
The library is open.

Все расхо́ды на обуче́ние бы́ли опла́чены ру́сской стороно́й.
All the training expenses had been paid for by the Russian side.

Вся сто́имость перегру́зки това́ров бу́дет покры́та на́шей стороно́й.
The entire cost of shipping the goods will be covered by our side.

Контра́кт до́лжен быть одо́брен обе́ими сторо́нами.
The contract must be approved by both sides.

Е́сли бы он прие́хал на про́шлой неде́ле, контра́кт был бы подпи́сан.
If he had arrived last week the contract would have been signed.

Past passive participles can also be used to change active voice sentences into passive voice constructions:

Мы включи́ли но́вые усло́вия в контра́кт.
We included new conditions into the contract.

Но́вые усло́вия бы́ли на́ми включены́ в контра́кт.
The new conditions were included by us into the contract.

Вчера́ наш представи́тель откры́л но́вый филиа́л на́шей фи́рмы в Москве́.
Yesterday our representative opened a new branch of our company in Moscow.

Вчера́ в Москве́ на́шим представи́телем был откры́т но́вый филиа́л на́шей фи́рмы.
Yesterday a new branch of our company was opened in Moscow by our representative.

Remember that the agent of the action must be in the Instrumental Case.

D. ИДИОМАТИКА

NEGOTIATIONS.

Here are some expressions that can be used to describe the conduct of negotiations and their results:

Куй желе́зо пока́ горячо́. (STOKE THE IRON WHILE IT'S HOT.)

Их представи́тель прие́хал всего́ на па́ру дней но, ка́жется, что за э́то вре́мя мы смо́жем с ним договори́ться о сто́имости перево́зки. —Так дава́йте, куй желе́зо пока горячо́!

Their representative will be here for just a couple of days, but while he's here I think we can come to an agreement on the cost of transportation. —Then, let's strike while the iron is hot!

Гроша́ ло́маного не сто́ит (NOT WORTH A DIME)

Так как на́ши пре́жние партнёры то́лько что обьяви́ли банкро́тство, подпи́санный и́ми контра́кт тепе́рь гроша́ ло́маного не сто́ит.

Since our erstwhile partners just declared bankruptcy, the contract they signed isn't worth a plug nickel now.

И во́лки сы́ты, и о́вцы це́лы. (EVERYONE'S HAPPY.; LIT., THE WOLVES ARE SATED, THE SHEEP ARE INTACT.)

Ну, по́сле дли́нных переговоро́в, мы наконе́ц-то пошли́ на вполне́ взаимовы́годный компроми́сс. —Да, сейча́с мо́жно сказа́ть «и во́лки сы́ты, и о́вцы це́лы».

Well, after extensive negotiations, we've finally come to a mutually beneficial compromise. —Yes, I think we now can say that we've managed to keep everyone happy.

Ти́ше е́дешь, да́льше бу́дешь. (SLOWLY, BUT SURELY.; LIT., THE SLOWER YOU GO THE FARTHER YOU'LL GET.)

Зна́ете, эти переговоро́ры стра́шно затя́гиваются! —Ничего́, ти́ше едешь, да́льше бу́дешь

You know, these negotiations are dragging on for a horribly long time! —Never mind, slowly but surely.

На пая́х (ON EQUAL FOOTING)

Ведь это совме́стное предприя́тие, на ра́вных пая́х, зна́чит, и расхо́ды должны́ быть попола́м.

This is a joint venture, after all, equally shared, so that our expenses, too, must be equally divided.

По рука́м! (LET'S SHAKE ON IT!)

Зна́чит, мы договори́лись обо всех усло́виях контра́кта, не пра́вда ли? —Соверше́нно ве́рно! По рука́м!

So, we've agreed on all the conditions of the contract, right? —Absolutely! Let's shake on it!

Nineteenth Lesson   327

Е. СТРОГО ПО ДЕЛУ

КОНТРАКТЫ И ПЕРЕГОВОРЫ
(CONTRACTS AND NEGOTIATIONS)

Since the collapse of the Soviet Union, Russian companies and entrepreneurs have been free to conclude contracts independently with foreign firms or individuals without official approval by the Ministry of Foreign Trade, with the exception of certain licensing and customs regulations. Russian laws governing domestic and foreign contracts have not been firmly established, however, and are subject to frequent change. Therefore, contracts between foreign firms and Russian parties must be largely based on mutual trust (взаимодоверие) and a clear recognition of the mutual benefit (взаимовыгодность) to be gained from a proposed partnership (партнёрство) or joint venture (совместное предприятие).*

Serious Russian entrepreneurs are very aware of the importance of a good reputation (репутация) with respect to financial commitments (финансовые обязательства), reliability (надёжность), and timely execution of contractual obligations (срочное выполнение контрактных обязательств). Consequently, considerable and careful attention should be given to rating the financial standing (оценка финансового положения/рейтинг), past performance (характеристики предыдущего исполнения обязательств), and reputation of a prospective partner. Short-term contracts (краткосрочные контракты) are usually a good way for the parties involved to test each other's abilities (способности) and strengths and weaknesses (сильные и слабые стороны). The need to proceed slowly (remember the saying, Тише едешь, дальше будешь) cannot be overemphasized in view of the complexity and relative newness of the Russian market.

The articles (статьи) of a standard sales contract normally include a preamble (предмет контракта), price and total costs (цена и общая сумма контракта), terms of payment (условия платежа), delivery dates (срок и дата поставки), quality of goods (качество товара), packaging and labeling (упаковка и маркировка), obligations of the parties (обязанности сторон), a natural disaster clause (форс-мажор), procedures for settling disputes (арбитраж), and the legal addresses of the signatories (юридические адреса сторон).

A typical contract appears on the facing page.

---

*See Урок 9 for a description of the various categories of partnerships.

КОНТРАКТ

_____ 19__ года

Настоящий контракт заключён между фирмой _____, именуемой далее Продавцом, с одной стсроны, и _____, именуемое далее Покупателем, с другой стороны, на условиях, перечисленных ниже.

1. Предмет Контракта

В соответствии с настоящим контрактом Продавец продал, а Покупатель купил на условиях _____ товары в соответствии со спецификациями, являющимися неотъемлемой частью настоящего контракта.

2. Цена и Общая Сумма Контракта

Цены на товары, указанны в прилагаемых спецификациях, устанавливаются в _____. Настоящие цены фиксированные и действительны в течение 30 дней со дня подписания контракта.

Общая сумма настоящего контракта составляет

_____

3. Условия Платежа

Оплата по настоящему контракту производится Покупателем в _____ путём _____ в банк Продавца по ниже-указанному адресу:

Все расходы, связанные с банком Покупателя, несёт Покупатель. Все расходы, связанные с банком Продавца, несёт Продавец.

4. Срок и Дата Поставки

Товар должен быть поставлен в течение _____ с момента подтверждения о получении денег банком Продавца. Досрочная или частичная поставка разрешается.

5. Качество Товара

Поставленный товар должен быть высокого качества, что подтверждается Сертификатом Качества от производителя или официальным документом о Гарантии Качества от Продавца.

6. Упаковка и Маркировка

Товар должен отгружаться в упаковке, соответствующей характеру поставляемого оборудования. Продавец несёт ответстственность перед Покупателем за всякого рода порчу товара вследствие некачественной или ненадлежащей консервации/упаковки.

7. Обязанности Сторон

Приложения к настоящему контракту действительны только в том случае, если они зафиксированы в письменной форме и подписаны обеими сторонами. Приложения являются неотъемлемыми частями контракта.

Все предыдущие соглашения и переговоры между сторонами по данному вопросу, письменные или устные, прекращают своё действие и считаются недействительными.

Ни одна из сторон не имеет права передать третьему лицу права и обязанности по настоящему контракту без письменного согласия другой стороны.

8. Форс-мажор

Стороны освобождаются от ответственности за частичное или полное неисполнение обязательств по настоящему контракту, если оно явилось следствием обстоятельств непреодолимой силы, а именно: пожара, наводнения, землятресения, революции, экономических блокад, санкций и постановлений правительств и в случае, если эти обстоятельства непосредственно повлияли на исполнение контракта.

9. Арбитраж

Продавец и Покупатель примут все меры к разрешению всех споров и разногласий, могущих возникнуть из настоящего контракта или в связи с ним, дружеским путём. В случае, если стороны не могут прийти к соглашению, то все споры и разногласия подлежат разрешению в Арбитражной Комиссии в Стокгольме. Решения Арбитражной Комиссии будут являться окончательными и обязательными для сторон.

10. Юридические адреса сторон:

Подписи сторон:
Продавец:
Покупатель:

CONTRACT

_____19

The present contract is entered into by the company_____hereafter named the Seller and the company _____hereafter named the Buyer under the conditions stipulated below

1. Contract Subject
In accordance with the present contract the Seller has sold, and the Buyer has purchased merchandise in accordance with the specifications that constitute an integral component of this contract.

2. Price and Total Value of Contract
The prices for the goods indicated in the attached specifications have been established at_____. The present prices have been fixed and are valid for a period of thirty dates from the signing of the contract.

The total value of the present contract is placed at

_____.

3. Conditions of Payment
Payment in accordance with the present contract shall be made by the Buyer at_____ by means of _____to the bank of the Seller at the address indicated below:

All expenditures connected with the Buyer's bank will be borne by the Buyer. All expenditures connected with Seller's bank will be borne by the Seller.

4. Term and Date of Delivery
The merchandise must be delivered within_____from the time the Seller's bank confirms the receipt of funds. Prepayment or partial payment is permitted.

5. Quality of Merchandise
The delivered merchandise must be of high quality as confirmed by the manufacturer's Quality Certificate or by an official Guarantee of Quality issued by the Seller.

6. Packing and Labeling
The merchandise must be shipped in packaging which is appropriate to the nature of the equipment delivered. The Seller assumes responsibility for any merchandise damage due to faulty or inappropriate storage/packaging.

7. Obligations of the Parties
The appendices to this contract are valid only if they are stipulated in written form and signed by both Parties. The appendices constitute integral components of the contract.

All previous agreements and negotiations concluded between the Parties, written or oral, are declared null and void.

Neither party has the right to transfer the rights and obligations of this contract to a third party without the written consent of the other party.

8. Force-majeure
The Parties are released from liability for any partial or full non-performance of obligations undertaken under the terms of this contract if such non-performance is caused by insuperable forces, to wit: a fire, flood, earthquake, revolution, economic blockade, governmental sanctions and decrees, and if such circumstances directly affect the execution of the contract.

9. Arbitration
The Seller and Buyer will undertake in an amicable manner all possible measures to resolve all disputes and disagreements that might arise from the present contract or that may occur in connection with it. In the event that the Parties are unable to settle their differences, then the disputes and disagreements shall be subject to settlement by the Arbitration Commission in Stockholm. The decisions of the Arbitration Commission shall be final and binding upon the Parties.

10. The Legal Addresses of the Parties:

Signatures of the Parties:
Seller:
Buyer:

Perhaps the first lesson to be learned in negotiating with potential Russian partners is that patience is indeed a virtue. Nothing should be rushed and one should expect and respect certain protocols, such as the ceremonial exchange of business cards (обмéн визи́тками), somewhat extensive preliminary speeches, and several rounds of refreshments. It is also important to keep in mind that punctuality is a rare phenomenon. Arriving on time for business appointments is more the exception than the rule. Secondly, personal contact is a must. Crucial decisions are rarely made via formulaic business letters or even by telephone, but rather in face-to-face meetings.

One must also accept a certain "conspiratorial" atmosphere in negotiations—a feeling that one side cannot gain without putting the other side to some disadvantage. In the course of negotiations your Russian counterpart may frequently refer to his "highly placed" connections (свя́зи). This partially stems from the previous importance of patronage (покрови́тельство) for any kind of upward mobility. Such connections can be helpful and should not be disregarded, although sometimes it may be difficult to verify their existence. Russians often share with Americans a desire to do "big things," and there is seldom a lack of enthusiasm for promising projects. However, many Russian businessmen exhibit a certain skepticism about ideas that seem too new or radical. Such attitudes are probably due in part to the country's turbulent political and social history.

УПРАЖНЕНИЯ

A. Замени́те предложе́ния с относи́тельными местоиме́ниями подходя́щими страда́тельными прича́стиями проше́дшего вре́мени. Не забыва́йте вста́вить предме́т де́йствия в ну́жном падеже́. (Replace the кото́рые clauses with the appropriate past passive participles. Don't forget to place the agent of the action in the required case.)

ОБРАЗЕЦ: Сего́дня мы получи́ли контра́кт, кото́рый подписа́ли ва́ши представи́тели.
Сего́дня мы получи́ли контра́кт, подпи́санный ва́шими представи́телями.

1. Вчера́ мы получи́ли това́ры, кото́рые отгрузи́ла ва́ша фи́рма три ме́сяца наза́д.
2. За́втра всту́пит в си́лу контра́кт, кото́рый мы подписа́ли на про́шлой неде́ле.
3. Управля́ющий заво́дом одо́брил попра́вки к контра́кту, кото́рые мы предложи́ли.
4. Обору́дование, кото́рое мы купи́ли в про́шлом году́, к сожале́нию, уже́ устаре́ло.
5. После́дняя статья́, кото́рую они́ включи́ли в контра́кт, отно́сится к опла́те по́шлин.
6. Я не могу́ согласи́ться с реше́нием, кото́рое при́няли ва́ши сотру́дники.
7. Но́вый магази́н, кото́рый то́лько вчера́ откры́ли, уже́ нужда́ется в капита́льном ремо́нте.
8. Вчера́ ве́чером мы нашли́ все пи́сьма, кото́рые вы потеря́ли.
9. Пода́рки, кото́рые я получи́л ко дню́ рожде́ния, доста́вили мне большо́е удово́льствие.
10. Без соотве́тствующей документа́ции, мы не смо́жем эксплуати́ровать обору́дование, кото́рое вы нам доста́вили.

B.   Замени́те сле́дующие предложе́ния действи́тельного зало́га предложе́ниями страда́тельного зало́га, испо́льзуя коро́ткую фо́рму страда́тельных прича́стий проше́дшего вре́мени. Поста́вьте предме́т де́йствия в ну́жном падеже́. (Replace the following active voice sentences with passive voice sentences by using short form past passive participles. Place the agent of the action in the required case.)

ОБРАЗЕЦ: Вчера́ мы получи́ли все необходи́мые докуме́нты.
            Вчера́ на́ми бы́ли полу́чены все необходи́мые докуме́нты.

1. Все уча́стники перегово́ров одо́брили оконча́тельную реда́кцию контра́кта.
2. Росси́йская сторона́ оплати́ла и́мпортные по́шлины.
3. То́лько сего́дня у́тром президе́нт фи́рмы подписа́л но́вый контра́кт.
4. На́ша сторона́ покры́ла все расхо́ды на обуче́ние персона́ла.
5. Позавчера́ откры́ли но́вый филиа́л на́шего ба́нка в Пи́нске.
6. Я не зна́ю, кто подписа́л это письмо́.
7. Они́ обяза́тельно включа́т в контра́кт усло́вие "форс-мажо́р."
8. О́бе сто́роны одо́брили попра́вки к прое́кту.

9. Заместитель помощника по морским делам принёс нам потрясающие документы.
10. Служащие музея закрыли его на ремонт.

C. Переведите следующие предложения на русский язык. Укажите, куда падает ударение.

1. We would like to receive the equipment on a "turnkey" basis.
2. We will assume the costs of personnel training on the condition that you cover the import duties.
3. These points will have to be included in the contract.
4. The terms of delivery and packing of equipment were discussed earlier.
5. What method of payment do you prefer for the shipment?
6. The letter of credit was approved by our bank yesterday. (use past participle)
7. Incidentally, have these changes to the contract been approved by your attorneys?
8. There are a few points in the contract that need clarification.
9. We were counting on your side paying for the installation (установка) of the equipment.
10. Of course, the final version of the contracts must be approved by both sides.

УРОК 20

А. ДИАЛОГ

Сва́дьба в Тюме́ни.[1]

В правосла́вной це́ркви, свяще́нник заключа́ет обря́д венча́ния[2] Васи́лия Степа́новича и Наде́жды Генна́дьевны.

СВЯЩЕННИК: . . . **Христо́с, кото́рый в Ка́не Галиле́йской свои́м прише́ствием освяти́л брак, поми́лует и спасёт нас по моли́твам всех святы́х и по свое́й бла́гости и человеколю́бию . . .**[3]

Предложи́в жениху́[4] и неве́сте испи́ть вина́ из о́бщей ча́ры, свяще́нник ведёт их три ра́за вокру́г алтаря́.[5]

СВЯЩЕННИК: **Поздравля́ю вас обо́их! Жела́ю вам сча́стья, здоро́вья и долголе́тия!**

Молодожёны целу́ются. По тради́ции при вы́ходе из це́ркви жени́х броса́ет гостя́м моне́ты. Пото́м молодожёны вме́сте с ро́дственниками и друзья́ми (в том числе́, америка́нцем Ма́йклом Нова́ком, деловы́м партнёром неве́стиного отца́, приезжа́ют на приём в рестора́н.

НОВАК: (подхо́дит к роди́телям новобра́чной) **Поздравля́ю вас! Обря́д венча́ния был о́чень впечатля́ющим!**

СВЁКОР: **Спаси́бо. А вам не́ было тру́дно всё вре́мя стоя́ть?**

НОВАК: **По пра́вде сказа́ть, я не́сколько раз чуть бы́ло не присе́л, но огляде́вшись круго́м, я по́нял, что в тече́ние всей церемо́нии поло́жено стоя́ть.**

ТЁЩА: (засмея́вшись) **Ну, вот. А сейча́с мо́жно присе́сть . . . Ага, вот иду́т молодожёны!**

НОВАК: (подхо́дит к новобра́чным) **Поздравля́ю вас обо́их! Пожа́луйста, прими́те от меня́ и мое́й жены́ э́тот ма́ленький пода́рок.**[6]

ВАСИ́ЛИЙ: Ах, огро́мное вам спаси́бо. Вы так добры́.

НА́ДЯ: Спаси́бо вам и жене́ ва́шей спаси́бо. Жаль, что она́ не смогла́ прису́тствовать на на́шей сва́дьбе.

НОВА́К: Да, наверняка́, ей бы́ло бы о́чень прия́тно. Но, по кра́йней ме́ре, она уви́дит сни́мки сва́дьбы, кото́рые я сде́лал. (к На́де) Кста́ти, я наде́юсь, что попо́зже вы ока́жете мне честь, позво́лив пригласи́ть вас на та́нец?

НА́ДЯ: Коне́чно. С удово́льствием!

НОВА́К: Зна́ете, я про́сто в восто́рге, что Васи́лий бу́дет рабо́тать с на́ми. По-мо́ему, мы вме́сте с ним сформиру́ем прекра́сный коллекти́в![7]

НА́ДЯ: Это очень прия́тно слы́шать. Ва́ся ча́сто мне говори́л, что он о́чень хоте́л бы рабо́тать в ва́шей фи́рме.

НОВА́К: (к Васи́лии) Причём рассчи́тываю, что не на́до будет до́лго ждать, пока́ вы не ста́нете[8] полнопра́вным партнёром, не так ли?

ВА́СИ́ЛИЙ: Ну, в конце́ концо́в . . .

НА́ДЯ: Пошли́, нас зазыва́ют к столу́!

Спустя́ не́сколько мину́т, го́сти уса́живаются за пра́здничный стол.

ТЕСТЬ:[9] Дороги́е друзья́! Вы не мо́жете себе́ предста́вить, как я сча́стлив, что на́ша дочь выхо́дит за́муж[10] за тако́го челове́ка, как Васи́лий, тепе́рь на́шего зя́тя. (аплодисме́нты) . . . поэ́тому я предлага́ю пе́рвый тост за На́дю и Васи́лия. Пусть их жизнь бу́дет по́лной сча́стья, благополу́чия, и успе́хов в рабо́те!

Го́сти встаю́т и чо́каются друг с дру́гом.

ГОСТЬ: Го́рько![11]

ВТОРО́Й ГОСТЬ: Го́рько!

В отве́т на это новобра́чные встаю́т и целу́ются.

ГОСТЬ: (пока́ молодожёны целу́ются) Раз! Два! Три![12]

СВЁКОР: Позво́льте и мне произнести́[13] тост за на́шего сы́на и неве́стку. Пусть впереди́ у них бу́дут го́ды ра́дости, здоро́вья и благополу́чия. За ва́ше здоро́вье!

ВСЕ: Ва́ше здоро́вье!

СВЕКРОВЬ: Дороги́е де́ти! За исключе́нием того́ дня, когда́ я выходи́ла за́муж, это, действи́тельно, са́мый счастли́вый день мое́й жи́зни! Я жела́ю вам всего́, что вы то́лько мо́жете пожела́ть. Я уве́рена, что ничто́[14] не омрачи́т на́ших отноше́ний, несмотря́ на то, что Надя гото́вит лу́чше, чем я! (смех) Ва́ше здоро́вье!

ТЁЩА: Да, я, коне́чно, сра́зу же соглашу́сь с Ва́ми по по́воду кулина́рных спосо́бностей мое́й до́чери, тем бо́лее что это, наве́рное, и моя́ заслу́га. Я то́же глубоко́ убеждена́, что мой но́вый зять бу́дет идеа́льным му́жем и отцо́м. Дава́йте вы́пьем за молодожёнов и за их све́тлое бу́дущее!

ВАСЯ: Спаси́бо, спаси́бо за до́брые пожела́ния. Тепе́рь я хочу́ произнести́ тост за мою́ люби́мую жену́ и спу́тницу жи́зни. Я безусло́вно, счита́ю себя́ о́чень счастли́вым челове́ком! Твоё здоро́вье, На́денька!

ВСЕ: Го́рько! Го́рько!

Молодожёны опя́ть целу́ются.

НАДЯ: Дороги́е друзья́ и родны́е! Спаси́бо за ва́ши до́брые пожела́ния в э́тот замеча́тельный день. Тепе́рь позво́льте мне предложи́ть тост за на́ших прекра́сных роди́телей, кото́рые приложи́ли[15] мно́го уси́лий для сего́дняшнего собы́тия. Спаси́бо вам за ва́шу любо́вь, понима́ние и подде́ржку в тече́ние до́лгих лет, мно́гие из кото́рых бы́ли не са́мыми просты́ми для нас. За ва́ше здоро́вье, дороги́е роди́тели!

ВСЕ: Ва́ше здоро́вье!

ТЕСТВ: А тепе́рь, дороги́е го́сти, дава́йте удели́м внима́ние пра́здничному столу́. Пото́м бу́дут му́зыка и та́нцы. Ещё раз спаси́бо вам за то, что вы пришли́ раздели́ть с на́ми э́то ра́достное собы́тие!

A wedding in Tyumen.

The officiating priest at an Orthodox church concludes the ritual at the wedding of Vasily Stepanovich and Nadezhda Gennadievna.

PRIEST: . . . Christ, who, by his presence in Cana of Galilee sanctified holy wedlock, will spare and save us through his mercy, his love of his fellow men, and through the prayers of all the saints . . .

After offering the bride and groom wine from the Common Cup, the priest leads them around the altar three times.

PRIEST: Congratulations to you both! I wish you happiness, health, and long life!

The bride and groom kiss. As they exit the church, the groom follows the tradition of casting coins to the guests. Later, the wedding party, including American businessman, Michael Novak, a partner of the bride's father, arrive at a restaurant for the reception.

NOVAK: (*walking over to the bride's parents*) Congratulations! That was a very impressive ceremony!

FATHER OF THE GROOM: Thank you. You didn't get tired standing all that time?

NOVAK: Actually, I was just about to sit down several times, until I looked around and realized that you stand throughout the ceremony.

MOTHER OF THE BRIDE: (*laughing*) Well, we can all sit now . . . Oh, here come the newlyweds!

NOVAK: (*walking up to the newlyweds*) Congratulations to you both. Please accept this gift from me and my wife.

VASILY: Thank you very much. You're very kind.

NADYA: Thank you both. I'm sorry she couldn't be here for our wedding.

NOVAK: Yes, I'm sure that she would have liked to be here very much. But at least she'll see the wedding pictures I've been taking. (*turns to Nadya*) By the way, I hope you'll do me the honor of permitting me to ask you for a dance later on?

NADYA: Of course. With pleasure!

NOVAK: You know, I'm really delighted that Vasiliy will be working with us. I think we'll make a great team!

NADYA: That's very nice to hear. Vasiya has often told me how much he would like to work in your company.

NOVAK: (*turning to Vasiliy*) And I expect it won't be long before you're a full partner, right?

VASILY: Well, eventually . . .

NADYA: Come, they're calling us to the table!

Moments later, the guests are seated.

FATHER OF THE BRIDE: Dear friends! I can't tell you how happy I am today to see our daughter marry such a fine man as Vasily, our son-in-law! (*applause*) And so I propose the first toast to Nadya and Vasily. May their lives be full of happiness, prosperity, and professional success!

The guests rise and and toast each other.

GUEST: It's bitter, make it sweet!

SECOND GUEST: It's bitter, make it sweet!

In response, the bride and groom kiss (to make it sweet).

GUEST: (*while the bridal couple is kissing*) One! Two! Three!

FATHER OF THE GROOM: Let me also propose a toast to our son and new daughter-in-law. May they have many years of health, joy, and prosperity. To your health!

ALL: To your health!

MOTHER OF THE GROOM: My dear children. Aside from the day I was married, this is truly the happiest day of my life! I wish you everything you may wish for. I am certain that nothing can taint our relationship, despite the fact that Nadya is a better cook than I am! (*laughter*) To your health!

MOTHER OF THE BRIDE: I can, of course, immediately agree with you about my daughter's culinary skills, especially since I had something to do with it. I, too, am deeply convinced that my new son-in-law will be a perfect husband and father. So here's to the newlyweds and to their bright future!

VASYA: Thank you, thank you for your good wishes. I would now like to make a toast to my lovely wife and partner for life. I consider myself a very lucky man indeed! To your health, Nadyenka!

ALL: Cheers! It's bitter, make it sweet!

The bridal couple kiss again.

NADYA: Dear friends and family! Thank you for your good wishes on this wonderful day. Now let me propose a toast to our wonderful parents, who spared no effort for today's celebration. Thank you for your love, your understanding, and your support through the years, many of which have been quite challenging for all of us. To your health, our dear parents!

ALL: To your health!

FATHER OF THE BRIDE: And now, dear guests, let's also give some attention to the feast before us. Afterward, we'll have music and dancing. Once again, thank you for sharing this joyous occasion with us.

B. ПРИМЕЧАНИЯ

1. Тюмéнь is located about 1,200 miles east of Moscow on the banks of the river Турá. Founded in 1586, it is the oldest city in Siberia. In the nineteenth century, it was an important trade center for Persia and China. Situated on the Trans-Siberian rail line, today Тюмень is a major transfer point for river and rail freight (перевáлочная бáза грýзов с воднóго путú на желéзную дорóгу). With a population of approximately 500,000, Тюмень has become a major economic and cultural center of Siberia. Its principal industries include the manufacture of machinery, metal and wood processing, chemicals, and foods. The surrounding area is rich in petroleum and natural gas.

2. Обрáд венчáния (lit., rite of coronation) is the Orthodox religious marriage ceremony in which crowns are held over the heads of the bridal pair during the entire service. The crowns symbolize their new roles as "king" and "queen" of a new line and serve as a reminder of Christ's sufferings. In general, Orthodox ceremonies tend to be very formal and symbolic. Religious ceremonies are often preceded or followed by secular ceremonies at ЗАГС (отдéл зáписи áктов

гражда́нского состоя́ния—civil registry office) where marriage licenses (бра́чные свиде́тельства) are issued.

3. The Gospel reading is that of St. John, 2:1–12, which relates the story of Christ's presence at the marriage feast in Cana, where he performed his first miracle by changing water into wine, which is commemorated by the couple's drinking from the Common Cup.

4. The terms жени́х (bridegroom) and неве́ста (bride) refer to the couple before the wedding. After the wedding the newlyweds are referred to as новобра́чный and новобра́чная.

5. The procession around the alter three times is in honor of the Holy Trinity and represents eternity and the newlyweds' pledge to preserve their marriage bond until death.

6. Russians are generous gift givers and are most appreciative of gifts received. Wedding gifts are chosen in much the same manner as in the United States, although fairly recently the presentation of envelopes with money, bonds, or securities has become an accepted custom.

7. Коллекти́в literally means a "collective" and refers to a group of coworkers, e.g., а́вторский коллекти́в (a group of authors), нау́чный коллекти́в (a team of scientists), профе́ссорско-преподава́тельский коллекти́в (university faculty).

8. Note the construction пока не + the perfective future or past to mean "until"/"until such time as." Я подожду́ здесь, пока́ она не зако́нчит разгово́р по телефо́ну. (I'll wait here until she finishes her phone conversation). Пока́ она не вы́йдёт за́муж, Кла́ра, наве́рное, бу́дет рабо́тать в больни́це. (Clara will probably be working at the hospital until she gets married.) Мы подожда́ли, пока́ новобра́чные не вы́шли из це́ркви. (We waited until the newlyweds came out of the church.)

9. The Russian in-law terminology is rather complex. Here are the principal in-laws:

wife's father	тесть	husband's father	свёкор
wife's mother	тёща	husband's mother	свекро́вь
wife's sister	своя́ченица	husband's sister	золо́вка
wife's brother	шу́рин	husband's brother	де́верь
daughter-in-law	неве́стка	son-in-law	зять

Неве́стка is also the term used for the spouse's brother's wife, i.e., sister-in-law, and зять is also the term used for the husband's sister's husband; i.e., brother-in-law. The wife's sister's husband is своя́к.

10. The verb выходи́ть/вы́йти за́муж + за + accusative case (to get married) is used only in reference to a woman, while the verb жени́ться + на + prepositional case refers to a man. Моя́ сестра́ вы́шла за́муж

за ру́сского матема́тика. (My sister got married to a Russian mathematician.) Её брат жени́лся на италья́нской певи́це. (Her brother got married to an Italian singer.)

11. It is customary at celebrations, particularly at wedding receptions, for guests to exclaim Го́рько! (It's bitter!), which is a signal for the newlyweds to sweeten the bitter taste of whatever is being drunk with their kisses.

12. In Russia, kisses are generally given in threes, symbolizing the Holy trinity. This is true on all occasions: when greeting guests, during reunions, departures, etc.

13. Other expressions that can be used to make a toast include: Предлага́ть/предложи́ть тост (to propose a toast), and провозглаша́ть/провозгласи́ть здра́вицу (lit., to proclaim a toast). Я предлага́ю тост за ва́ше здоро́вье. (I propose a toast to your health.) Тамада́ провозгласи́л здра́вицу в честь зарубе́жных госте́й. (The toastmaster proposed a toast in honor of the foreign guests.)

14. The pronoun ничто́ is generally used as the subject to verbs that take a direct object, while ничего́ is generally used with intransitive verbs. Ничто́ не беспоко́ит его́. (Nothing bothers him.) Ничто́ не интересу́ет его́. (Nothing interests him.) С ни́ми ничего́ не случи́лось. (Nothing happened to them.) Мы попро́бовали не́сколько вариа́нтов, но из э́того ничего́ не вы́шло. (We tried several versions, but nothing came of it.)

15. Приложи́ть уси́лия (to make an effort, to exert one's energy) is often used in business contexts as well. Они приложи́ли все уси́лия, чтобы зако́нчить прое́кт во́время. (They spared no effort to complete the project on time.)

C. ГРАММА́ТИКА И СЛОВОУПОТРЕБЛЕ́НИЕ

1. ПРИТЯЖА́ТЕЛЬНЫЕ ПРИЛАГА́ТЕЛЬНЫЕ (POSSESSIVE ADJECTIVES)

The possessive adjectives are very commonly used in colloquial Russian. They normally precede the noun they modify and can be used instead of placing the possessor in the Genitive Case. For example, instead of saying Куда́ ты положи́ла кни́гу бабушки? (Where did you put grandmother's book?), you can say Куда́ ты положи́ла бабушкину кни́гу? Both sentences have the same meaning, although the latter form is much more informal and is used primarily among family members. These special adjectives are formed only from nouns denoting living beings and can be grouped into two general categories. The first is primarily derived from the names of animals (во́лчий = wolf's, соба́чий = dog's, медве́жий = bear's) or from persons (рыба́чий= fisherman's, охо́тничий= hunter's). These "во́лчий" type adjectives are declined like "тре́тий" as follows:

	MASCULINE	FEMININE	NEUTER	PLURAL
NOM.	во́лчий	во́лчья	во́лчье	во́лчьи
GEN.	во́лчьего	во́лчьей	во́лчьего	во́лчьих
DAT.	во́лчьему	во́лчьей	во́лчьему	во́лчьим
ACC.	во́лчий/чьего	во́лчью	во́лчье	во́лчьи/их
INST.	во́лчьим	во́лчьей	во́лчьим	во́лчьими
PREP.	во́лчьем	во́лчьей	во́лчьем	во́лчьих

У меня́ во́лчий аппети́т.
I could eat a horse. (lit., I have a wolf's appetite.)

У него́ опя́ть соба́чья жизнь.
He's living a dog's life.

Вы чита́ли рассказ «Лошади́ная фами́лия»?
Did you read the story *A Horse's Surname*?

The second category of possessive adjectives is derived from the names of persons and is used primarily within the family. These are the ма́мин type adjectives formed by adding the suffixes -ин, -нин, or -ов to the noun stem: ма́мин (mom's), се́стрин (sister's), неве́стин (bride's), ба́бушкин (grandma's), отцо́в/па́пин (dad's). This group of adjectives is declined as follows:

	MASCULINE	FEMININE	NEUTER	PLURAL
NOM.	ма́мин	ма́мина	ма́мино	ма́мины
GEN.	ма́миного	ма́миной	ма́миного	ма́мины/ых
DAT.	ма́миному	ма́миной	ма́миному	ма́миным
ACC.	ма́мин/ого	ма́мину	ма́мино	ма́мины/ых
INST.	ма́миным	ма́миной	ма́миным	ма́миными
PREP.	ма́мином	ма́миной	ма́мином	ма́миных

Мы подошли́ к неве́стиной ма́тери и поздра́вили её.
We went up to the bride's mother and congratulated her.

Куда́ вы положи́ли отцо́ву тру́бку?
    Where did you put dad's pipe?

Мой желу́док не выно́сит тётины за́втраки.
    Auntie's breakfasts don't agree with me.

2. ИСПОЛЬЗОВАНИЕ ДЕЕПРИЧАСТИЙ В НЕКОТОРЫХ ОБЩИХ ВЫРАЖЕНИЯХ (GERUNDS USED IN SOME COMMON EXPRESSIONS)

Some gerunds are used in common expressions that function as prepositions and adverbs.

A) GERUNDS USED AS PREPOSITIONAL PHRASES

PHRASE	MEANING	CASE GOVERNED
несмотря́ на	despite	Accusative
спустя́	after	Accusative
су́дя по	judging by	Dative
благодаря́	thanks to	Dative
начина́я с	beginning with	Genitive
не счита́я	not counting	Genitive

Несмотря́ на то, что она́ гото́вит лу́чше чем я, я уве́рена, что мы с ней пола́дим.
    Despite the fact that she cooks better than I do, I'm sure we'll
    get along.

Несмотря́ на скве́рную пого́ду, мы всё же игра́ли в футбо́л.
    Despite the lousy weather, we played soccer anyway.

Спустя́* де́сять мину́т пришли́ пе́рвые го́сти.
    Ten minutes later the first guests arrived.

Три го́да спустя́ молода́я чета́ развела́сь.
    Three years later the young couple divorced.

*Спустя́ may follow or precede the noun: спустя́ три часа́ or три часа́ спустя́ = three hours later.

Неде́лю спустя́, я получи́л от него́ второ́е письмо́.
One week later I got a second letter from him.

Су́дя по всему́, на вы́борах президе́нта оде́ржит побе́ду наш кандида́т.
Judging by all acounts, our candidate will win the presidential election.

Су́дя по его хара́ктеру, я полага́ю, что он бу́дет идеа́льным му́жем и отцо́м.
Judging by his nature, I would assume that he will be an ideal husband and father.

Благодаря́ подде́ржке на́ших родителей, мы комфорта́бельно устро́ились.
Thanks to the support of our parents, we are comfortably settled.

Благодаря́ тому́, что музыка́нты пришли́ во́время, мы обе́дали под прекра́сную му́зыку.
Thanks to the fact that the musicians arrived on time, we dined to excellent music.

Начина́я с пе́рвого августа, мы бу́дем рабо́тать в но́вом зда́нии.
Starting the first of August, we'll be working in the new building.

Начина́я с пе́рвого то́ста, атмосфе́ра на приёме вдруг оживи́лась.
Starting with the first toast, the atmosphere at the reception suddenly came to life.

На сва́дьбе прису́тствовало сто челове́к, не счита́я молодожёнов и их роди́телей.
There were one hundred people at the wedding, not counting the newlyweds and their parents.

Да́же не счита́я коли́чества то́стов, предло́женных за пра́здничным столо́м, го́сти здо́рово выпива́ли.
Without even counting the number of toasts proposed at the table, the guests drank quite a lot.

B. GERUNDS USED AS ADVERBS

мо́лча	silently
скрепя́ се́рдце	(lit., clamping one's heart); reluctantly, grudgingly
стро́го говоря́	strictly speaking
не говоря́ уже́	to say nothing of
сложа́ ру́ки	(lit. with arms folded); sitting on one's hands, twiddling one's thumbs
не спеша́	unhurriedly

Го́сти мо́лча стоя́ли в продолже́ние всей церемо́нии.
> The guests stood silently throughout the entire ceremony.

По́сле дли́тельного обсужде́ния вопро́са, скрепя́ се́рдце, они́, наконе́ц, согласи́лись с на́шим предложе́нием.
> After a prolonged discussion of the problem, they at last agreed reluctantly to our proposal.

Стро́го говоря́, я о́чень сомнева́юсь в том, что она́ вы́йдет за́муж за тако́го болва́на.
> Strictly speaking, I very much doubt that she'll marry such a dumbbell.

У них бу́дет дово́льно мно́го но́вых друзе́й, не говоря́ уже́ о но́вых сосе́дях и сотру́дниках.
> They're going to have quite a few new friends, to say nothing of new neighbors and associates.

Пока́ все го́сти танцева́ли, он почему́-то сиде́л в углу́ сложа́ ру́ки.
> While all the guests were dancing, for some reason he sat in the corner twiddling his thumbs.

Свяще́нник со зво́нким го́лосом не спеша́ вёл обря́д венча́ния.
> The priest unhurriedly conducted the marriage ceremony in a resonant voice.

D. ИДИОМАТИКА

LOVE IS IN THE AIR . . .

Here are a few ways to express romantic feelings.

Влюби́ться по́ у́ши (TO FALL IN LOVE UP TO YOUR EARS)

Соверше́нно я́сно, Пе́тя влюби́лся в неё по́ уши.
It's quite obvious, Pete's head over heels in love with her.

Своди́ть/свести́ с ума́* (TO ENTHRALL, TO FALL DEEPLY IN LOVE)

Уже́ по́сле пе́рвой встре́чи с ней, она́ свела́ меня́ с ума́.
I fell for her the first time I met her.

Сде́лать предложе́ние (TO PROPOSE)

Пра́вда ли, что Ми́ша вчера́ сде́лал Ка́те предложе́ние?
Is it true that Misha proposed to Katya yesterday?

This is the formal expression for proposing marriage. A young Russian today would be much more likely to say:

Выходи́ за меня́ за́муж.
Marry me.

Дава́й поже́нимся.
Let's get married.

Кадри́ть/закадри́ть (TO COURT, TO PICK UP, TO MEET)

Ты зна́ешь де́вушку, кото́рую он закадри́л на та́нцах?
Do you know the girl he met at the dance?

This verb is derived from the word ка́дры† (personnel). In slang usage, кадр can mean an attractive man or woman.

---

*This expression can also have a negative meaning without any romantic connotations. Он чуть бы́ло не свёл меня́ с ума, дока́зывая мне, что я оши́блась. (He nearly drove me out of my mind, trying to prove that I was mistaken.)
†Ка́дры (personnel) is a term used in the Soviet era. In current business usage a personnel department is known as отде́л кадров.

Смотри, какой кадр идёт!
Take a look at that hunk!

Помешан/н/ый/ая от любви (LOVE-CRAZED, LOVE-STRUCK)

За последнее время я заметил, что Саша ведёт себя немножко странно, что с ней? — Наверное, она помешана от любви.
I noticed that Sasha has been acting a little strange lately, what's with her? —She's probably love-struck.

Любовь с первого взгляда (LOVE AT FIRST SIGHT)

Ну, смотри на неразлучников. Это очевидно любовь с первого взгляда!
Just look at those lovebirds. It was obviously love at first sight!

Любовь зла — полюбишь и козла. (LOVE IS BLIND.; LIT., LOVE IS CRUEL—YOU'LL EVEN FALL IN LOVE WITH A GOAT.)

Невероятно! Они поженились только в мае, а спустя всего два месяца уже развелись! — А я её предупредил: любовь зла—полюбишь и козла!
Incredible! They just got married in May, and only two months later they divorced! —And, I warned her: love is blind!

Брак без брака* (MARRIAGE WITHOUT FLAWS)

Очевидно, они сильно влюбились друг в друга. У них будет брак без брака.
They are obviously deeply in love. Theirs will be a perfect marriage.

E. СТРОГО ПО ДЕЛУ

СОЦИАЛЬНЫЙ СОСТАВ НАСЕЛЕНИЯ (SOCIAL COMPOSITION)

POPULATION. Approximately 150 million people live in the Russian Federation. The population of the remaining CIS states adds about another 100 million.† Sixty-six percent of the population is aged 15 to 64, 12 per-

*Брак has the dual meaning of "marriage" and "defect, flaw," so that брак без брака means a "perfect marriage."

†The remaining CIS states and their approximate populations are: Ukraine (51 million), Belarus (10 million), Uzbekistan (20 million), Kazakhstan (17 million), Azerbaijan (7 million), Georgia (5 million), Moldova (4 million), Kyrgyztan (4 million), Turkmenistan (3.5 million).

cent are over 65, and 22 percent are under 15. The rate of population growth in the Russian Federation has declined due to low birth rates (рождаемость) among ethnic Russians (approximately 9.5 births per 1,000 population, as compared to approximately 17 in the United States), and a relatively high death rate (смёртность) of 15.5 per thousand (as compared to 2.3 in the United States). The life expectancy for Russian males, in particular, has dropped alarmingly to 58 years (from approximately 64 in the pre-perestroika period), but the life expectancy for Russian women has remained stable at 74 years. This has been ascribed to much needed improvements in health care facilities, general hygiene practices, and alcoholism. Not surprisingly these conditions have also contributed to rising rates of infant mortality (дётская смёртность). Russian medical authorities, in cooperation with various Western health organizations, including the Centers for Disease Control in Atlanta, have been undertaking various measures to combat disease and improve conditions in the health sector.

On the more positive side of demographic statistics, Russians are generally well educated and well adapted to technological progress. The literacy rate (грáмотность) is 98 percent, and the population has a labor force of approximately 85 million, 83 percent of whom are engaged in production and economic services, and 16 percent in government. Such factors are certainly signficant in terms of potential industrial productivity and innovation. Although Marxist tenets and socialist principles were supposed to provide women with equal opportunities and status, Russia today remains rather conservative with respect to a woman's place in society if one considers the relatively few executive positions held by women in government, commerce, or the professions. Nevertheless, Russian women account for more than half of the students in higher education and more than a third of engineers and agronomists. In addition, the medical profession continues to be dominated by women (approximately 68 percent).

Ethnic Russians make up 82 percent of the population in the Russian Federation. Other nationals resident in the Federation include Tatars (4 percent), Ukrainians (3 percent), Chuvash (1.2 percent). Bashkirs, Byelorussians, Moldavians, and a few others comprise less than 1 percent of the population.

RELIGION. With the collapse of the Soviet Union, Russian Orthdoxy was once again granted official recognition. In contrast to the Soviet period, the number of young churchgoers has been steadily increasing. Other religious groups, too, have benefited from the collapse of the Communist state. About 20 percent of the 55 million Muslims (мусульма́не) in the former Soviet Union reside in the Russian Federation, where there has been a significant increase in the construction of mosques (мече́ти). A number of new Jewish yeshivas have opened, and several synogogues in major cities have been reopened or restored. The new religious freedom has also prompted many Western missionaries of various Christian sects to proselytize among Russians. Although small numbers of evangelical Christians (ева́нгельские христиа́не) and Baptists (бапти́сты) have existed in the former Soviet Union for some time, this has sometimes caused considerable friction and resentment, particularly on the part of the Russian Orthodox church (ру́сская правосла́вная це́рковь),

FAMILY. Most urban Russian families continue to be limited to one or two children, primarily due to economic considerations (экономи́ческие соображе́ния) and housing shortages (недоста́ток в жилпло́щади). Abortions (або́рт), which are legal and relatively inexpensive, still constitute one of the principal methods of limiting family size. Most newly married couples (молодожёны) in major Russian cities are forced initially to live with their parents. Even when a couple can afford to purchase or rent their own apartment or home, they are often joined by one or both of the in-laws, particularly if the in-law is a widow or widower. Despite the "emancipation" of women, most of the housework and shopping is still done by them, whether or not they are employed. The tension created by this inequality, in addition to overcrowding (теснота́) and overwork (переутомле́ние), particularly in urban areas, are doubtless major contributing factors to the the relatively high rate of divorce* (разво́д), although drunkenness is often cited as the primary cause in court proceedings.

Children in Russia are highly regarded and loved by the adult society, and they are the recipients of many privileges, such as adequate clothing, education, recreational facilities, and nutrition. In fact, many school administrators complain that the children are spoiled, making maintaining discipline in the school difficult. The institutional care for disadvantaged children, however, is at a low level due to poor financing and inadequate facilities. Although relatively little delinquency has occurred among the preteenage group, juvenile delinquency among teenagers has been on the rise, along with the general level of crime in the post-perestroika period.

---

*About 4.5 per thousand, which is approximately the same rate as in the United States.

A. Перепиши́те сле́дующие предложе́ния, замени́в ука́занные
жи́рным шри́фтом существи́тельные подходя́щими притяжа́тель-
ными прилага́тельными в ну́жной фо́рме. (Rewrite the following
sentences by substituting the nouns indicated in bold with the
appropriate possessive adjectives in the required form.)

ОБРАЗЕ́Ц: Я спроси́л подру́гу **ма́мы,** когда́ она́ должна́
            верну́ться домо́й.
            Я спроси́л ма́мину подру́гу, когда́ она́ должна́
            верну́ться домо́й.

1. Брат мне сказа́л, что друг **отца́,** наве́рное, опозда́ет на приём.
2. Мы подошли́ к ма́тери **неве́сты,** что́бы поздра́вить её с бра́ком
   до́чери.
3. Верну́вшись с футбо́льного ма́тча, он заяви́л, что у него́ аппети́т
   во́лка.
4. Она́ всё вре́мя говори́ла о ро́дственниках **неве́сты.**
5. Как вам понра́вилось пла́тье **ба́бушки?**
6. Куда́ вы положи́ли тру́бку **дя́ди?**
7. Почему́ они́ не хотя́т игра́ть с друзья́ми **бра́та?**
8. Вы не зна́ете, как зову́т прия́теля **сестры́?**
9. Мне ка́жется, что э́тот пода́рок от подру́ги **тёти.**
10. По всей вероя́тности, она́ вы́йдет за́муж за партнёра **па́пы.**

B. Запо́лните про́пуски, по́льзуясь подходя́щими дееприча́стиями.
(Fill in the blanks using the appropriate gerunds.)

1. _____молодожёны уе́хали на медо́вый ме́сяц.
   (Three hours later)

2. _____ все приглашённые го́сти прие́хали
   (Despite the poor weather)
   во́время.

3. Молодожёны бу́дут прожива́ть в Москве́
   _____.
   (starting at the beginning of July)

4. _____, мне совсе́м не хоте́лось танцева́ть.
   (Strictly speaking)

5. _____ за пра́здничным столо́м, я бы сказа́л,
   (Judging by his behavior)
   что он прие́хал на сва́дьбу уже́ в нетре́звом ви́де.

6. _____они́ верну́лись с да́чи с интере́сными
   (One week later)
   новостя́ми.

7. _____мне ста́ло я́сно, что это бу́дет
   (Beginning with the first toast)
   дли́нный ве́чер.

8. _____ все де́ти успе́шно зако́нчили
   (Thanks to help of their parents)
   университе́т.

9. _____ мы пригласи́ли всю их семью́, пришла́ на
   (Despite the fact that)
   сва́дьбу лишь одна́ двою́родная сестра́.

10. Так как бы́ло ещё ра́но, мы_____шли на приём.
    (leisurely)

C. Переведи́те сле́дующие предложе́ния на ру́сский язы́к.

1. I am sure that you and I will make a great team!
2. We walked up to the bride's father and congratulated him on the marriage of his daughter.
3. She walked out of the room without answering any of our questions.
4. The American guest proposed a toast to a long and successful partnership.
5. Upon exiting the church, the groom tossed coins to the guests.
6. As the guests danced, Ivan twiddled his thumbs without saying a word.
7. There were fifty people at the reception, not counting the groom's family.
8. I don't understand why nothing interests her brother.
9. Two years later the bride's sister married one of the groom's American friends.
10. I am certain that nothing will spoil our relationship, despite the fact that I am a much better cook than you.

ПРЕДЛАГАЕМЫЕ ЗАНЯТИЯ

Locate a Russian (or Greek) Orthodox church in your community and attend one of the services. The service will probably be in Old Church Slavonic, which is similar to Russian. See if you can understand any of it.

КЛЮЧ К УПРАЖНЕНИЯМ (Answer Key)

УРОК 1

A. 1. ждут 2. жела́ем 3. прошу́ 4. бои́тся 5. проверя́ем 6. де́лаете 7. иду́т 8. говори́т 9. везёт 10. наде́емся

B. 1. бра́тья (brothers) 2. гости́ницы (hotels) 3. полёты (flights) 4. мужья́ (husbands) 5. деклара́ции (declaration forms) 6. ключи́ (keys) 7. места́ (places, seats) 8. времена́ (times, seasons) 9. супру́ги (spouses) 10. города́ (cities)

C. 1. Они́ уже́ давно́ рабо́тают здесь. 2. Они́ ещё ждут в аэропорту́? 3. Где на́ши чемода́ны? 4. Этот компью́тер для со́бственного по́льзования. 5. Ско́лько вре́мени (на́до) ехать в гости́ницу? 6. Это очень до́лгий и утоми́тельный рейс. 7. Кака́я у вас пого́да в после́днее время? 8. Хорошо́. Вот свобо́дное такси́! 9. Этот пассажи́р —мой тесть. 10. Они́ сейча́с прохо́дят тамо́женный контро́ль.

УРОК 2

A. 1. два́дцать пя́того ма́я 2. три́дцать пе́рвое января́ 3. пя́того ию́ля 4. восемна́дцатое а́вгуста 5. первого декабря́

B. 1. к деся́тому ме́сяца 2. с пя́того .. по деся́тое 3. с восьми́ .. до пяти́ 4. в двадцать два часа́ 5. к семи́ часа́м

C. 1. Я ду́маю, что она́ родила́сь четвёртого апре́ля. 2. Пожа́луйста, ско́лько сейчас вре́мени? (ог: кото́рый час сейча́с?) —Сейча́с без че́тверти пять (ог без пятна́дцати пять) 3. Уже́ четы́ре два́дцать? (ог два́дцать мину́т пя́того). Я опозда́ю на самолёт! 4. Администра́тор гости́ницы сказал, что обед принесу́т в номер к шести́. 5. Вы зна́ете день рожде́ния вашей ма́тери? —Она́ родила́сь тре́тьего октября́. 6. Во ско́лько прие́хали но́вые студе́нты вчера? 7. Я ей сказа́л, что позвоню́ к оди́ннадцати утра́. 8. Я обы́чно рабо́таю с девяти́ утра́ до четырёх дня. 9. В кото́ром часу́ (ог во ско́лько)? они́ вы́писались из гости́ницы? —Ка́жется, они́ вы́писались в де́вять часо́в утра́. 10. Како́е было число́ вчера? —Вчера бы́ло два́дцать тре́тье.

УРОК 3

A. 1. За́втра я дам (переда́м) вам наш но́вый а́дрес. 2. К моему́ удивле́нию, они уже́ получи́ли наше письмо́. 3. Она́ позвони́ла мне по рекоменда́ции ва́шего колле́ги 4. К сожале́нию, у нас нет свобо́дных кварти́р. 5. Они́, наве́рное, найду́т кварти́ру к концу́ ме́сяца. 6. Вы слу́шали но́вости по ра́дио сего́дня у́тром? 7. Они́ вчера сообщи́ли ему о но́вом расписа́нии. 8. Я очень зави́дую тебе. 9. По какому а́дресу вы посла́ли письмо́? 10. Вы сказа́ли аге́нту, в какой гости́нице вы прожива́ете?

B. 1. Пожа́луйста, позови́те господи́на Петро́ва к телефо́ну. 2. Мо́жно вам позвони́ть за́втра в три часа́? 3. Я бы хоте́л снима́ть кварти́ру из двух ко́мнат в це́нтре. 4. Мы располага́ем больши́м вы́бором но́вых кварти́р. 5. Господи́н Су́слов сейча́с за́нят, говори́т по телефо́ну. Вы подождёте? 6. Вы не туда́ попа́ли. 7. Я вам сове́тую позвони́ть в аге́нтство недви́жимости. 8. Я оста́вил вам сообще́ние на автоотве́тчике. 9. Я уве́рен, что всё хорошо́ обойдётся. 10. К сожале́нию, в де́сять часо́в у господи́на Петрова назна́чена встре́ча с други́м клие́нтом. 11. Он никому́ ничего́ не говори́л по телефо́ну. 12. Они́ ничего́ не зна́ли ни о чём. 13. В том до́ме ей не понра́вилась никака́я кварти́ра. 14. Он не рекомендова́л никако́го аге́нтства недви́жимости. 15. В её кварти́ре не́ было автотве́тчика.

A. 1. За́втра они наверняка́ **пригото́вят** вку́сный обе́д, 2. Кого́ ещё они́ **пригласи́ли** на да́чу? 3. Я всегда́ **помога́ю** [or **помога́л/а**] ей гото́вить обе́д. 4. **Мы направля́лись** в лес, когда я **нашёл/нашла́** большу́ю земляни́чную поля́ну. 5. Не **звони́те** ему сейча́с! Он очень за́нят. 6. На про́шлой неде́ле, они́ **собира́ли** я́годы ка́ждый день 7. Когда́ вы вчера́ **возврати́лись** [or **верну́лись**] домо́й? 8. Как вам **понра́вился** наш обед вчера́ ве́чером? 9. Не **забыва́йте** помога́ть ему́ гото́вить обед! 10. Я очень рад, что они́ уже́ **при́няли** на́ше приглаше́ние.

B. 1. Вы верну́ли [or возврати́ли] мои кни́ги в библиоте́ку? 2. Когда я им позвони́л, они ещё гото́вили обе́д. 3. Грибы́, кото́рые вы собра́ли—про́сто изуми́тельны! 4. Их да́ча нахо́дится о́коло о́чень большо́го ле́са. 5. Я уве́рен, что они при́мут на́ше приглаше́ние. 6. Они ещё гото́вятся к экза́мену? 7. Попро́буй эту баклажа́нную икру́. Я зна́ю, что она́ вам понра́вится. 8. Мы так проголода́лись, что ждём не дождёмся обе́да! 9. Всё чже гото́во. Дава́йте сади́ться. 10. Не волну́йтесь, это блю́до очень лёгкое.

A. 1. Сади́тесь, пожа́луйста, и расскажи́те мне немно́го о себе́. 2. Запо́лните эту анке́ту, пото́м зайди́те ко мне в кабине́т. 3. Здесь нельзя́ кури́ть. 4. Пожа́луйста, говори́те погро́мче. Я вас не по́нял. 5. Оди́н экземпля́р отдади́те нам, пожа́луйста.

B. 1. К сожале́нию, по́чта не очень надёжно рабо́тает Unfortunately, the post office is not very reliable. 2. Я ду́маю, что мне бу́дет о́чень тру́дно запо́лнить анке́ту. I think it will be very hard for me to fill out the form. 3. Мы зна́ем, что вы дово́льно бе́гло говори́те по-ру́сски. We know that you speak Russian rather fluently. 4. Он ли́чно занёс запо́лненную анке́ту. He personally brought in the completed form. 5. Она сказа́ла, что они сейча́с очень акти́вно и́щут рабо́ту. She said that they are very actively looking for work.

C. 1. Я бы хоте́л(а) име́ть возмо́жность испо́льзовать зна́ния русского языка́. 2. Я зако́нчил(а) интенси́вный курс ру́сского языка́ в ма́рте. Тогда́ я поняла́, что мно́жество иностра́нных фирм акти́вно осва́ивают росси́йский ры́нок. 3. Когда вы сообщи́те мне о результа́те собесе́дования? 4. Моя́ гла́вная специа́льность была́ междунаро́дные отноше́ния, но я та́кже изуча́л(а) русский язы́к. 5. Ваш но́вый помо́щник око́нчил моско́вский университе́т? Я тоже око́нчил этот унвиерсите́т! 6. С тех пор как я встреча́лся с вами, я поменя́л а́дрес. 7. Если пона́добится, я запо́лню ещё одну анке́ту. 8. Каки́е обязанности я бу́ду исполня́ть? 9. По́сле на́шей бесе́ды, я осозна́л, что мы с ва́ми нашли́ общий язы́к. 10. Я ду́маю, что не надо нанима́ть его. У него язы́к без косте́й.

A. 1. бу́дем рабо́тать 2. покажу́ 3. Зайди́те; запо́лните 4. бу́дет опа́здывать 5. помо́жете 6. спрошу́

B. 1. каки́е-нибудь 2. когда́-нибудь 3. куда́-то 4. где-то 5. как-нибудь 6. Кто́-то 7. что́-нибудь

C. 1. Вам далеко́ прихо́дится добира́ться до рабо́ты? 2. Я наде́юсь, что она смо́жет вам как-то помо́чь. 3. На сле́дующей неде́ле ка́ждый день я бу́ду рабо́тать допоздна́. Or: Ка́ждый день на сле́дующей неде́ле я буду допоздна́ заси́живаться на рабо́те. 4. Кто-то до́лжен находи́ться в о́фисе во вре́мя обе́денного переры́ва. 5. За́втра я вам покажу́ ваш но́вый офис. 6. Вам необходи́мо заполни́ть не́сколько анкет для нало́говой инспе́кции. 7. Не беспоко́йтесь. Я знаю, что она вам всегда́ помо́жет. 8. Она что-то сказа́ла о новой до́лжности, но я её не расслы́шал. 9. Вы не смо́жете пообе́дать вме́сте с на́ми? 10. Мои ро́дственники де́ржат меня в ку́рсе ме́стных собы́тий.

УРОК 7

A. 1. В этом магазине очень богатый ассортимент продуктов This store has a very large assortment of food (products). 2. Приглашённый на чай студент, очень хорошо говорит по-русски. The student (who was) invited to tea speaks Russian very well. 3. Я абсолютно уверен(а), что новый магазин работает круглые сутки. I'm quite sure that the new store is open (operates) 24 hours a day. 4. Свежие овощи и фрукты продаются по очень доступным ценам. The fresh vegetables and fruits are sold at a very affordable (accessible) prices. 5. Я думаю, что новый рынок уже закрыт. I think the new market is closed already. 6. Широко распространённые в Америке распродажи пользуются большой популярностью. The sales that are so broadly prevalent in America enjoy considerable popularity.

B. 1. У нас редко бывают скидки на продовольственные продукты. 2. Они поехали на рынок за овощами и фруктами. 3. На прошлой неделе мы пригласили их на обед. 4. Они мне сказали, что у них перерыв на обед с часа до двух. 5. Моя сестра едет в Россию на летние курсы. 6. Когда мы ходим на рынок, мы обычно закупаемся на несколько недель. 7. Сливки прекрасно подходят к чаю или кофе. 8. Здесь есть что-нибудь по сниженным ценам? 9. За углом есть пункт обмена валюты. 10. Какой жирности это молоко в пакетах?

УРОК 8

A. 1. Какой высоты Александровская колонна? 2. Примерно какого роста ваш отец? 3. Нева какой ширины в этом месте? 4. Примерно какой длины эта улица? 5. Какого роста ваши дети? (or) Какого роста ваши сын и дочь?

B. 1. Она мне позвонила вчера вечером. 2. Я думаю, что твой отец тебя зовёт. 3. Как раньше называлась эта площадь? 4. Мне кажется, что они назвали их дочь Татьяной (or) Татьяна 5. Я забыл, как называются эти здания.

C. 1. Дворцовая площадь очень далеко отсюда? —Нет, она (находится/расположена) только в километре отсюда. Туда можно дойти пешком. 2. Екатерининский дворец расположен/находится примерно в двадцати пяти километрах от центра Санкт-Петербурга. 3. Спроси его, сколько он берёт за экскурсию по Эрмитажу. 4. Раньше она называлась Сенатской площадью. 5. Я просто не могу больше ждать. Терпение у меня лопнуло!
6. Действительно, можно назвать его очень внушительным зданием! 7. Река Нева длиной во сколько километров? 8. Эти здания построили (or были построены) по проекту итальянского архитектора Растрелли. 9. Жду с нетерпением (or мне невтерпёж) (or жду не дождусь) посмотреть экспонаты в Эрмитаже. 10. В музее есть очень большая коллекция шедевров импрессионистов.

УРОК 9

A. 1. (1) If you begin production of the new model by March, we'll be able to send our specialists to you this month. (2) Если бы вы начали производство новой модели к марту, мы смогли бы отправить к вам наших специалистов в этом месяце. (3) If you were to begin production of the new model by March, we would be able to send our specialists to you this month. (Or: If you had begun production of the new model by March, we would have been able to send our specialists to you this month.) 2. (1) If we sign the new contract they will open the new plant this year. (2) Если бы мы подписали новый контракт, они открыли бы новый завод в этом году. (3) If we were to sign the new contract, they would open the new plant this year. (Or: If we had signed the new contract, they would have opened the new plant this year.) 3. (1) If they can form a joint venture, they will increase their annual production output. (2) Если бы они смогли создать совместное предприятие, они бы увеличили годовой объём выпускаемой продýкции. (3) If they were to form a joint venture they would increase annual production output. (Or: If they had formed a joint venture they would have increased annual production output.) 4. (1) If you can meet us this evening I will show you the training program. (2) Éсли бы вы смогли́ встрéтиться с нáми сегóдня вéчером, я бы показáл вам прогрáмму обучéния. (3) If you were to meet with us this evening I could show you the training program. (Or: If you had met us this evening I would have shown you the training program.) 5. (1) If they improve product quality they will have more customers. (2) Éсли бы они́ улýчшили кáчество продýкции, у них бы́ло бы бóльше закáзчиков. (3) If they were to improve product quality they would have more customers. (Or: If they had improved product quality they would have had more customers.)

B. (1) позáвтракаем; (2) вы́делили, смогли́ бы; (3) Давáйте пообéдаем; (4) Давáйте не бýдем обсуждáть; (5) Я хотéл бы.

C. (1) Я не знáю, подписáли ли они́ контрáкт. (2) Éсли вам бýдет удóбно, мы мóжем обсуди́ть контрáкт сегóдня вéчером. (3) Мы бы хотéли увели́чить годовóй объём продýкции и разнообрáзить её ассортимéнт. (4) Мы ужé договори́лись встрéтиться зáвтра в гости́нице. (5) Я его спроси́л, рабóтает ли завóд с пóлной нагрýзкой.

УРОК 10

A. 1. Налóги, идýщие в пóльзу телестáнции, собирáются прави́тельством. 2. Прогрáммы, представля́ющие официáльные взгля́ды прави́тельства, не оплáчиваются реклáмами. 3. Стáнции, рабóтающие незави́симо, не получáют поддéржку от прави́тельства. 4. Зри́тели, лю́бящие спорт, всегдá смóтрят футбóльные мáтчи по воскресéньям. 5. Студéнты, затрудня́ющиеся отвечáть на эти вопрóсы, должны́ занимáться задáниями почáще.

B. 1. Зри́тели, óчень внимáтельно следи́вшие за новостя́ми, легкó могли́ суди́ть об объекти́вности освещéния собы́тий. 2. Мои друзья́, купи́вшие вчерá нóвые лáмпы, сказáли мне, что их реклами́ровали по телеви́дению. 3. Сосéд, согласи́вшийся с женóй, тóже считáет, что репортáж по вторóму канáлу весьмá беспристрáстен. 4. Зри́тели, посмотрéвшие вторýю прогрáмму, жáловались на коли́чество реклáм.

C. 1. Продýкты, реклами́руемые по телеви́зору, пóльзуются большóй популя́рностью. 2. Процéсс приватизáции, плани́руемый прави́тельством, навéрное, бýдет продолжáться ещё мнóго лет. 3. По-мóему, кáчество товáров, предлагáемое зарубéжными фи́рмами, óчень хорóшее. 4. Пожéртвования, получáемые стáнциями, идýт на налóги.

D. 1. Прогрáммы, оплáчиваемые реклáмами, пóльзуются большóй популя́рностью. 2. Налóги, получáемые прави́тельством, идýт в пóльзу нéскольких телестáнций. 3. Нéкоторые коммéрческие стáнции, поддéрживаемые прави́тельством, тáкже получáют пожéртвования от зри́телей. 4. Обы́чно, мы смóтрим нóвости по трéтьему канáлу в 10 часóв, потомý что репортáж беспристрáстен. 5. В нáшем гóроде есть (имéется) нéсколько незави́симо рабóтающих стáнций. 6. Большýю часть реклáмы по вторóму канáлу покáзывают в начáле прогрáммы. 7. Стáнции, получáющие финáнсовую поддéржку от зри́телей, обы́чно не представля́ют (покáзывают) реклáмы. 8. Компью́теры, кýпленные нáшим университéтом, пóльзуются большóй популя́рностью. 9. Когдá мы приéхали/пришли́ домóй, телеви́зор ужé был включён. 10. Пи́сьма, напи́санные вáшим дя́дей, бы́ли полýчены нáми вчерá. Мы вчерá получи́ли пи́сьма, напи́санные вáшим дя́дей.

УРОК 11

A. 1. Какýю сýмму вы желáете положи́ть на ваш счёт? 2. Эта óчередь к трéтьему окнý? 3. Вы мóжете получáть дéнежные перевóды в четвёртом окнé. 4. Когдá вы освободи́тесь, жди́те меня́ у вы́хода из метрó. 5. Я хотéл бы обменя́ть сто дóлларов на рубли́. 6. По́сле того́, как вы откро́ете счёт, зайди́те опя́ть ко мне, и мы займёмся аккредити́вом. 7. В како́м ба́нке они́ откры́ли бессро́чный счёт? 8. Я сове́тую вам обрати́ться к господи́ну Смирно́ву за информа́цией об откры́тии но́вого счёта. 9. Они́ стоя́т в о́череди у второ́го окна́. 10. Каки́е проце́нты мо́жно получа́ть по вкла́дам в ва́шем ба́нке?

B. 1. What sum (or how much) do you wish to put into your account? 2. Is this line for Window 3? 3. You can obtain money orders at Window 4. 4. When you get through, wait for me at the subway exit. 5. I'd like to change $100 for rubles. 6. After you open an account, come back to my office and we'll get started (or get busy) on a letter of credit. 7. At which bank did they open a demand deposit account? 8. I would advise you to see Mr. Smirnov for information about opening a new account. 9. They're standing in line at Window 2. 10. How much interest can one get on deposits at your bank?

C. 1. Я хоте́л бы получи́ть от вас (от ва́шего банка) безотзы́вный аккредити́в. 2. Мы мо́жем переводи́ть ва́шу зарпла́ту непосре́дственно на ваш счёт у нас (в на́шем ба́нке). 3. Проце́нты по сро́чному вкла́ду гора́здо вы́ше, чем по бессро́чному (вкла́ду). 4. Име́ются ли у вас и рублёвые и валю́тные счета́? 5. Составле́ние (вы́дача) аккредити́вов—это одна́ из на́ших станда́ртных услу́г. 6. Чем до́льше сро́ки вкла́да тем вы́ше проце́нты вы́плат. 7. Поско́льку я бу́ду здесь находи́ться два го́да, мне понадо́бится откры́ть персона́льный счёт. 8. Что́бы откры́ть вам счёт, мне необходи́мо уви́деть ваш па́спорт. 9. Не смотря́ на то, что у него́ нет вкла́да у нас (в на́шем ба́нке), мы (тем не ме́нее) соста́вили (вы́дали) ему́ аккредити́в по рекоменда́ции господи́на Каза́нского. 10. Что ж, всё в поря́дке (в ажу́ре). Тепе́рь займёмся де́лом!

УРОК 12

A. 1. бо́лее интере́сен 2. Лу́чшие 3. гора́здо ху́же 4. са́мыми волну́ющими 5. бо́лее драмати́чные 6. гора́здо ме́нее интере́сны 7. лу́чшее 8. са́мой смехотво́рной 9. ме́нее смехотво́рны (неле́пы) 10. лу́чше моего́

B. 1. Вы счита́ете, что ле́гче переводи́ть с ру́сского на англи́йский, чем переводи́ть с англи́йского на ру́сский? 2. Са́мые после́дние фи́льмы сложне́е ста́рых (or бо́лее сло́жные, чем ста́рые) 3. Зимо́й в Москве́ гора́здо холодне́е, чем в Вашингто́не. 4. Но́вые иностра́нные (зарубе́жные) фи́льмы интере́снее на́ших оте́чественных фи́льмов. (or бо́лее интере́сные, чем на́ши оте́чественные фи́льмы) 5. Они́ жи́ли в одно́м из са́мых краси́вых домо́в в го́роде. 6. Я не зна́ю, кака́я бу́дет там пого́да. На вся́кий слу́чай, возьми́ с собо́й зо́нтик. 7. На кра́йний слу́чай, позвони́ мне в конто́ру. Я бу́ду там до оди́ннадцати. 8. Страни́чка на интерне́те у них интере́снее на́шей. (or бо́лее интере́сная, чем на́ша) 9. Он отпусти́л себе́ таку́ю бороди́щу, что я чуть бы́ло его́ не узна́л. 10. Ну и неде́лька! Нас, действи́тельно, завали́ли рабо́той!

C. 1. Вы не ска́жете, где ближа́йшая ста́нция метро́? 2. Како́й са́мый лу́чший (наилу́чший) ру́сско-англи́йский слова́рь? 3. Его́ мла́дший сын испо́лнил роль гла́вного геро́я. 4. Кого́ вы счита́ете велича́йшим писа́телем девятна́дцатого ве́ка? (or Кто, по ва́шему, велича́йший писа́тель . . .) 5. Я жела́ю вам всего́ наилу́чшего! 6. В ху́дшем слу́чае мне придётся провести́ выходны́е одному́ (в одино́чку). 7. Фильм каса́ется нове́йших достиже́ний техноло́гии. (or фильм посвящён нове́йшим достиже́ниям техноло́гии). 8. Наилу́чшее реше́ние э́того вопро́са—па́лка о двух конца́х. 9. Э́ти фи́льмы подверга́лись строжа́йшей цензу́ре. 10. Это одна́ из на́ших старе́йших тради́ций.

УРОК 13

A. 1. Како́в 2. Каки́е 3. Каково́ 4. Тако́в 5. Каковы́ 6. Таковы́ 7. Каки́е 8. Каково́ 9. Откры́та 10. Го́лоден/Голодна́

B. 1. Интересу́емся 2. Пло́ским экра́ном 3. Каки́ми шри́фтами 4. По́льзуется большо́й популя́рностью 5. Заве́дующий магази́ном 6. Пра́вилами; э́тими компью́терами

7. Но́вой систе́мой 8. Располага́ем 9. Нас интересу́ют 10. Ознако́миться; после́дними/нове́йшими моде́лями

C. 1. Я навёл спра́вки у заве́дующего магази́ном насчёт обслу́живания и техни́ческой подде́ржки. (or: Я спроси́л заве́дующего магази́ном об обслу́живании и техни́ческой подде́ржке.) 2. Они́ интересова́лись компью́терами с большо́й операти́вной па́мятью. 3. Представи́тель воспо́льзовался слу́чаем, что́бы продемонстри́ровать (нам) компью́теры, совмести́мые со станда́ртом Ай-Би-Эм. 4. Отде́л програ́ммного обеспе́чения нахо́дится на второ́м этаже́. 5. Какова́ та́ктовая частота́ проце́ссора э́тих моде́лей? 6. Каки́ми шрифта́ми вы по́льзуетесь на э́тих компью́терах? (or Каки́е шрифты́ вы испо́льзуете . . .) 7. Вы мо́жете дать мне кра́ткую спра́вку о техни́ческих характери́стиках э́того ска́нера? 8. Вы мо́жете поменя́ть шрифты́ или язы́к с по́мощью одного́ нажа́тия горя́чей кла́виши. 9. Вы хоте́ли бы подписа́ться на на́ши катало́ги? 10. У нас ещё оста́лась у́йма вре́мени. Почему́ бы нам не верну́ться на вы́ставку и не взгляну́ть на остальны́е сте́нды?

УРОК 14

A. 1. Запо́лнив деклара́цию, мы вошли́ в рестора́н. 2. За́втракая, я обы́чно чита́ю у́треннюю газе́ту. 3. Не зна́я ру́сского языка́, она́ не поняла́, о чём мы говори́ли. 4. Возвраща́ясь с рабо́ты, я обы́чно заходи́л в кни́жный магази́н. 5. Пройдя́ тамо́женный досмо́тр, вы смо́жете подгото́виться к поса́дке. 6. Сто́я в о́череди, мы завели́ интере́сный разгово́р. 7. Вы́пив две ча́шки ко́фе, он сказа́л, что ему́ пора́ идти́ домо́й. 8. Поменя́в на́ши до́ллары на рубли́, мы купи́ли не́сколько предме́тов старины́. 9. Зайдя́ в магази́н, я уви́дел мно́го интере́сных веще́й. 10. Посмотре́в на ча́йный серви́з, я сра́зу реши́л купи́ть его́.

B. 1. заполня́я 2. не обраща́я внима́ния 3. написа́в 4. не поня́в (не понима́я) 5. верну́вшись 6. си́дя 7. прое́хав 8. принеся́ 9. прочита́в 10. возвраща́ясь

C. 1. Проходя́ че́рез тамо́жню, мои́ друзья́ спроси́ли, заполни́л ли я тамо́женную деклара́цию. 2. Я сказа́л ей, что я купи́л всё, что мне бы́ло ну́жно. 3. Пе́рвое, что вам ну́жно сде́лать, это запо́лнить тамо́женную деклара́цию. 4. Я рад (ра́да), что вы (ты) нашли́ (-шёл -шла) то, что иска́ли. 5. Что с тобо́й, ты что ли не ви́дел автобу́с о́коло остано́вки? 6. Заполня́я тамо́женную деклара́цию, мно́гие тури́сты не зна́ют, как отве́тить (отвеча́ть) на не́которые вопро́сы. 7. Поверну́вшись к продавщи́це, я спроси́л её, ско́лько сто́ит чай. 8. Приобретя́ настоя́щий самова́р, она́ реши́ла купи́ть антиква́рный подходя́щий к нему́ зава́рочный ча́йник. 9. Заплати́в за самова́р, мы отпра́вились в друго́й магази́н. 10. Зайдя́ в магази́н антиквариа́та, я уви́дел мно́го интере́сных веще́й.

УРОК 15

A. 1. мно́го ру́сских студе́нтов 2. не́скольких фе́рмеров 3. Не́которые 4. сто́лько 5. доста́точно 6. Не́сколько; прилете́ло(прие́хало) 7. о не́скольких ва́жных статья́х 8. встре́тили 9. о мно́гих пробле́мах 10. стоя́ло; ста́рых комба́йнов

B. 1. сто́лько; ско́лько 2. не́которыми (мно́гими, не́сколькими) 3. не́которые 4. доста́точно 5. мно́го (не́сколько) 6. Не́которые 7. Ско́лько 8. Наско́лько 9. сто́лько; ско́лько 10. не́сколько; не́которые

C. 1. Когда́ мы прие́хали на фе́рму, мы бы́ли встре́чены Ива́ном и его́ жено́й. (нас встре́тили Ива́н и его́ жена́) 2. На́ша фи́рма продала́ не́сколько молоти́лок прави́тельству Украи́ны. 3. Мы собра́ли о́коло двух ты́сяч тонн пшени́цы. 4. На́ши де́ти уе́хали в го́род на по́иски но́вой рабо́ты. 5. Мы вы́делили приме́рно пятна́дцать гекта́ров под ози́мую пшени́цу. 6. Указа́ния, кото́рые вы нам да́ли, бы́ли вполне́ я́сными (чёткими). 7. Мы име́ли доста́точно де́ла с сельскохозя́йственным обору́дованием. 8. Не́которые комба́йны нужда́ются в капита́льном ремо́нте. 9. Мы встре́тили не́сколько фе́рмеров из Аме́рики на встре́че вчера́ ве́чером. 10. Вот не́сколько проспе́ктов, опи́сывающих обору́дование, производи́мое на́шей фи́рмой.

УРОК 16

A. 1. удалил; с 2. забежа́ли за 3. вы́играла; со 4. допишу́ 5. заложи́ла; за 6. вы́бросил; с 7. вбро́сил; в 8. прибли́зился к 9. добежа́ли до 10. положи́ла; под

B. 1. мяч игроку́ свое́й кома́нды (мяч това́рищу по кома́нде) 2. за гру́бую игру́ 3. наруше́ние 4. к воро́там сопе́рника (проти́вника) 5. с одобре́нием (свое одобре́ние) 6. мяч (обра́тно) в игру́ 7. к медици́нскому осмо́тру 8. двух защи́тников 9. пе́рвый тайм (пе́рвую полови́ну игры́) 10. на игру́ о́чень по́здно (с больши́м опозда́нием)

C. 1. Когда́ напада́ющий удари́л по воро́там (заби́л гол), все зри́тели на стадио́не вскочи́ли на́ ноги и закрича́ли: " Гол!" 2. Он вбро́сил мяч в игру́ из-за боково́й ли́нии. 3. Обведя́ двух игроко́в, Овчи́нников отпра́вил мяч в сто́рону воро́т. 4. Игро́к "Локомоти́ва" отобра́л мяч у на́шего защи́тника. 5. На́ша кома́нда перехо́дит в контра́таку. 6. На про́шлой неде́ле уво́лили на́шего сосе́да (с рабо́ты). 7. Мы застря́ли в у́личной про́бке (у́личном движе́нии). 8. Э́тот матч уже́ бу́дет тру́дно вы́играть. 9. Судья́ реши́л отмени́ть матч (игру́). 10. Петро́в проби́л мяч в сто́рону воро́т, но мяч отскочи́л от шта́нги.

УРОК 17

A. 1. Вот врач, кото́рый 2. После́дний из тех, кто . . . приём, очеви́дно, 3. Те из нас, кото́рые . . . поликли́нику, 4. де́ти, кото́рым 5. всё, что 6. Та, кото́рая . . . у́тром, 7. Кто . . . . приви́вку, 8. Все, кто записа́лся, 9. Отделе́ние, в кото́ром . . . боле́зни, 10. Пе́рвый, кто . . . приви́вкой,

B. 1. Дава́йте начнём наш осмо́тр с отделе́ния инфекцио́нных заболева́ний. 2. Загво́здка в том, что населе́ния бы́ло вакцини́ровано недоста́точное коли́чество. 3. У вас недоста́ток (не хвата́ет) вакци́нного материа́ла? 4. Те, кто не состоя́т в на́ших спи́сках, мо́гут сде́лать приви́вку в больни́це. 5. Ста́рые шпри́цы бы́ли дово́льно ненадёжны, а вот э́ти но́вые однора́зовые шпри́цы вполне́ (весьма́) удо́бны. 6. Какой диа́гноз поста́вил до́ктор Петро́в? То́же мне до́ктор! Он осмотре́л меня́ и ничего́ не объясни́л! 7. Лишь бы то́лько де́ти записа́лись (зарегистри́ровались) на про́шлой неде́ле! 8. Что же де́лает э́та медсестра́? 9. Пожа́луйста, расскажи́ мне что́-нибудь (не́что) о де́тской поликли́нике. 10. Же́нщина, кото́рая пришла́ на повто́рный ана́лиз сли́зистой оболо́чки гло́тки, перенесла́ лёгкий слу́чай дифте́рии.

УРОК 18

A. 1. вы́учить 2. учу́/обуча́ю 3. слу́шать 4. у́чатся 5. изуча́ете 6. занима́лся 7. у́чит/ обуча́ет 8. записа́лся 9. учи́лись 10. научи́ть

B. 1. англи́йскому языку́ 2. на экза́мене 3. на́шего дя́дю неме́цкому (языку́) 4. сыновья́; в Моско́вском университе́те 5. в аспиранту́ре; на тре́тьем ку́рсе 6. на все свои́ ку́рсы 7. Кого́; ру́сскому (языку́) 8. на адвока́та (юри́ста) 9. на заня́тиях (на ле́кции) 10. на́ших друзе́й из Ло́ндона

C. 1. Мне сказа́ли, что вы сда́ли сего́дня свои́ экза́мены. 2. На́ша аудито́рия о́чень больша́я. 3. Мы о́ба у́чимся на одно́м факульте́те. 4. Ле́кция посвящена́ ру́сско-америка́нским отноше́ниям. 5. Мо́жет быть, нам лу́чше поиска́ть словари́ в кни́жных кио́сках. 6. Как прошёл экза́мен?—Профе́ссор поста́вил мне пятёрку. 7. Вы не зна́ете, когда́ открыва́ется кни́жный магази́н?—Обы́чно он открыва́ется в 9 часо́в. 8. Ско́лько вре́мени вы уже́ изуча́ете ру́сский (язы́к)? 9. На́ши друзья́ сдава́ли свой экза́мен на про́шлой неде́ле. 10. Я до́лж(ен)на́ дописа́ть курсову́ю рабо́ту к концу́ э́той неде́ли.

A. 1. Вчера́ мы получи́ли това́ры, отгру́женные ва́шей фи́рмой три ме́сяца наза́д. 2. За́втра вступи́т в си́лу контра́кт, подпи́санный на́ми на про́шлой неде́ле. 3. Управля́ющий заво́дом одо́брил предло́женные на́ми попра́вки к контра́кту. 4. Ку́пленное на́ми в про́шлом году́ обору́дование, к сожале́нию, уже́ устаре́ло. 5. После́дняя статья́, включённая и́ми в контра́кт, отно́сится к опла́те по́шлин. 6. Я не могу́ согласи́ться с реше́нием, при́нятым ва́шими сотру́дниками. 7. Откры́тый то́лько вчера́ но́вый магази́н, уже́ нужда́ется в капита́льном ремо́нте. 8. Вчера́ ве́чером мы нашли́ все пи́сьма, поте́рянные ва́ми. 9. Пода́рки, полу́ченные мной ко дню рожде́ния, доста́вили мне большо́е удово́льствие. 10. Без соотве́тствующей документа́ции, мы не смо́жем эксплуати́ровать доста́вленное нам ва́ми обору́дование.

B. 1. Оконча́тельная реда́кция контра́кта была́ одо́брена все́ми уча́стниками перегово́ров. 2. Импортные по́шлины бы́ли опла́чены росси́йской стороно́й. 3. Но́вый контра́кт был подпи́сан президе́нтом фи́рмы то́лько сего́дня у́тром. 4. Все расхо́ды на обуче́ние персона́ла бы́ли покры́ты на́шей стороно́й. 5. Позавчера́ в Пи́нске был откры́т но́вый филиа́л на́шего ба́нка. 6. Я не зна́ю, кем бы́ло подпи́сано это письмо́. 7. Усло́вие "форс-мажо́р" бу́дет обяза́тельно включено́ и́ми в контра́кт. 8. Попра́вки к прое́кту бы́ли одо́брены обе́ими сторона́ми. 9. Потряса́ющие докуме́нты бы́ли принесены́ нам вчера́ замести́телем помо́щника по морски́м дела́м. 10. Музе́й был закры́т на ремо́нт его́ слу́жащими.

C. 1. Мы хоте́ли бы получа́ть обору́дование «под ключ». 2. Мы возьмём на себя́ опла́ту переподгото́вки персона́ла, е́сли вы опла́тите тамо́женные по́шлины. 3. Эти пу́нкты должны́ быть включены́ в контра́кт. 4. Усло́вия доста́вки и упако́вки обору́дования бы́ли обсуждены́ ра́нее. 5. Како́й спо́соб опла́ты за доста́вку вы предпочита́ете? 6. Аккредити́в был заве́рен вчера́ на́шим ба́нком. 7. Кста́ти, бы́ли ли одо́брены эти измене́ния в контра́кте ва́шими юри́стами? 8. В контра́кте есть не́сколько пу́нктов, нужда́ющихся в уточне́нии. 9. Мы рассчи́тывали на то, что ва́ша сторона́ опла́тит устано́вку обору́дования. 10. Коне́чно, оконча́тельная реда́кция контра́кта должна́ быть одо́брена обе́ими сторона́ми.

A. 1. Брат мне сказа́л, что **отцо́в** друг, наве́рное, опозда́ет на приём. 2. Мы подошли́ к **неве́стиной** ма́тери, что́бы поздра́вить её с бра́ком до́чери. 3. Верну́вшись с футбо́льного ма́тча, он заяви́л, что у него́ **во́лчий** аппети́т. 4. Она́ всё вре́мя говори́ла о **неве́стиных** ро́дственниках. 5. Как вам понра́вилось **ба́бушкино** пла́тье? 6. Куда́ вы положи́ли **дя́дину** тру́бку? 7. Почему́ они́ не хотя́т игра́ть с бра́тниными друзья́ми? 8. Вы не зна́ете, как зову́т но́вого сестри́ного прия́теля? 9. Мне ка́жется, что э́тот пода́рок от **тётиной** подру́ги. 10. По всей вероя́тности, она́ вы́йдет за́муж за **па́пиного** партнёра.

B. 1. Три часа́ спустя́ молодожёны уе́хали на медо́вый ме́сяц. 2. Несмотря́ на плоху́ю пого́ду, все приглашённые го́сти прие́хали во́время. 3. Молодожёны бу́дут прожива́ть в Москве́, начина́я с нача́ла ию́ля. 4. Стро́го говоря́, мне совсе́м не хоте́лось танцева́ть. 5. Су́дя по его́ поведе́нию за пра́здничным столо́м, я бы сказа́л, что он прие́хал на сва́дьбу уже́ в нетре́звом ви́де. 6. Спустя́ неде́лю они́ верну́лись с да́чи с интере́сными но́востями. 7. Начина́я с пе́рвого то́ста, мне ста́ло я́сно, что это бу́дет дли́нный ве́чер. 8. Благодаря́ по́мощи свои́х роди́телей, все де́ти успе́шно око́нчили университе́т. 9. Несмотря́ на то, что мы пригласи́ли всю их семью́, пришла́ на сва́дьбу лишь одна́ двою́родная сестра́. 10. Так как бы́ло ещё ра́но, мы не спеша́ шли на приём.

C. 1. Я уве́рен, что мы с ва́ми сформиру́ем прекра́сный коллекти́в! 2. Мы подошли́ к свёкру и поздра́вили его́ со сва́дьбой его́ до́чери. 3. Она́ вы́шла из ко́мнаты, не отвеча́я ни на оди́н наш вопро́с. 4. Америка́нский гость предложи́л (произнёс, провозгласи́л) тост за многоле́тнее и преуспева́ющее партнёрство. 5. Выходя́ из це́ркви, новобра́чный броса́л гостя́м моне́ты. 6. Пока́ го́сти танцева́ли, Иван сиде́л сложа́ ру́ки, не говоря́ ни сло́ва. 7. На церемо́нии бы́ло пятьдеся́т челове́к, не счита́я семьи́ жени́ха. 8. Я не понима́ю, почему́ ничто́ не интересу́ет её бра́та. 9. Два го́да спустя́, неве́стина сестра́ вы́шла за́муж за одного́ из америка́нских друзе́й жени́ха. 10. Я уве́рен (-а), что ничто́ не омрачи́т на́ших отноше́ний, несмотря́ на то, что я гото́влю значи́тельно лу́чше тебя́ (чем ты).

ПРИЛОЖЕНИЯ
(Appendixes)

A. SPELLING RULES

1. After **г, к, х, ж, ч, ш,** and **щ** write **и** instead of **ы**
2. After **г, к, х, ж, ч, щ, ш,** and **ц** write **у** instead of **ю**
   and **а** instead of **я**
3. After **ж, ш, щ, ч,** and **ц** write **е** instead of unstressed **о**

B. CONSONANT MUTATIONS

Following is a list illustrating some of the most common consonant changes that occur in various verbs, comparative adverbs and adjectives:

в → вл	доста́вить	доста́влен	delivered
г → ж	до́рого	доро́же	more expensive
д → жд	освободи́ть	освобождён	released
з → ж	бли́зкий	бли́же	nearer
к → ч	восто́к	восто́чный	eastern
п → пл	купи́ть	ку́пленный	purchased
с → ш	высо́кий	вы́ше	higher
ск → щ	пло́ский	пло́ще	flatter
ст → щ	чи́стый	чи́ще	cleaner
т → ч	оплати́ть	опла́ченный	paid
т → щ	возрати́ть	возращён	returned
х → ш	тихо	ти́ше	more quietly

C. DECLENSION OF NOUNS

MASCULINE SINGULAR

	ANSWERS THE QUESTION	BASIC ENDING	HARD		SOFT -й	-ь
N	Что? Кто?	zero	стол	ма́льчик	музе́й	портфе́ль
A (Inan.)	Что?	zero	стол		музе́й	портфе́ль
A (Anim.)	Кого́?	-а		ма́льчика		
G	Чего́? Кого́?	-а	стола́	ма́льчика	музе́я	портфе́ля
P	О чём? О ком?	-е	столе́	ма́льчике	музе́е	портфе́ле
D	Чему́? Кому́?	-у	столу́	ма́льчику	музе́ю	портфе́лю
I	Чем? Кем?	-ом	столо́м	ма́льчиком	музе́ем	портфе́лем

MASCULINE PLURAL

	ANSWERS THE QUESTION	BASIC ENDING	HARD		SOFT -й	-ь
N	Что? Кто?	-ы	столы́	ма́льчики	музе́и	портфе́ли
A (Inan.)	Что?	-ы	столы́		музе́и	портфе́ли
A (Anim.)	Кого́?	-ов		ма́льчиков		
G	Чего́? Кого́?	-ов	столо́в	ма́льчиков	музе́ев	портфе́лей
P	О чём? О ком?	-ах	стола́х	ма́льчиках	музе́ях	портфе́лях
D	Чему́? Кому́?	-ам	стола́м	ма́льчикам	музе́ям	портфе́лям
I	Чем? Кем?	-ами	стола́ми	ма́льчиками	музе́ями	портфе́лями

FEMININE SINGULAR

	ANSWERS THE QUESTION	BASIC ENDING	HARD		-й	-ия	-ь
N	Что? Кто?	-а	газе́та	колле́га	неде́ля	ле́кция	вещь
A	Что? Кого́?	-у	газе́ту	колле́гу	неде́лю	ле́кцию	вещь
G	Чего́? Кого́?	-ы	газе́ты	колле́ги	неде́ли	ле́кции	ве́щи
P	О чём? О ком?	-е	газе́те	колле́ге	неде́ле	ле́кции	ве́щи
D	Чему́? Кому́?	-е	газе́те	колле́ге	неде́ле	ле́кции	ве́щи
I	Чем? Кем?	-ой	газе́той	колле́гой	неде́лей	ле́кцией	ве́щью

FEMININE PLURAL

	ANSWERS THE QUESTION	BASIC ENDING	HARD		-й	-ия	-ь
N	Что? Кто?	-ы	газе́ты	колле́ги	неде́ли	ле́кции	ве́щи
A (Inan.)	Что?	-ы	газе́ты		неде́ли	ле́кции	ве́щи
A (Anim.)	Кого́?	zero		колле́г			
G	Чего́? Кого́?	zero	газе́т	колле́г	неде́ль	ле́кций	веще́й
P	О чём? О ком?	-ах	газе́тах	колле́гах	неде́лях	ле́кциях	веща́х
D	Чему́? Кому́?	-ам	газе́там	колле́гам	неде́лям	ле́кциям	веща́м
I	Чем? Кем?	-ами	газе́тами	колле́гами	неде́лями	ле́кциями	веща́ми

NEUTER SINGULAR

	ANSWERS	BASIC ENDING	HARD	-e (SOFT)	-ие (SOFT)
N	Что?	-о	окно́	мо́ре	зда́ние
A	Что?	-о	окно́	мо́ре	зда́ние
G	Чего́?	-а	окна́	мо́ря	зда́ния
P	О чём?	-е	окне́	мо́ре	зда́нии
D	Чему́?	-у	окну́	мо́рю	зда́нию
I	Чем?	-ом	окно́м	мо́рем	зда́нием

NEUTER PLURAL

	ANSWERS	BASIC ENDING	HARD	-e (SOFT)	-ие (SOFT)
N	Что?	-а	о́кна	моря́	зда́ния
A	Что?	-а	о́кна	моря́	зда́ния
G	Чего́?	zero	око́н	море́й	зда́ний
P	О чём?	-ах	о́кнах	моря́х	зда́ниях
D	Чему́?	-ам	о́кнам	моря́м	зда́ниям
I	Чем?	-ами	о́кнами	моря́ми	зда́ниями

IRREGULAR NOUNS—SINGULAR

	MASCULINE	FEMININE		NEUTER	
N	путь	мать	дочь	и́мя	вре́мя
A	путь	мать	дочь	и́мя	вре́мя
G	пути́	ма́тери	до́чери	и́мени	вре́мени
P	(о) пути́	(о) ма́тери	(о) до́чери	(об) и́мени	(о) вре́мени
D	пути́	ма́тери	до́чери	и́мени	вре́мени
I	путём	ма́терью	до́черью	и́менем	вре́менем

IRREGULAR NOUNS—PLURAL

N	пути́	ма́тери	до́чери	имена́	времена́
A	пути́	матере́й	дочере́й	имена́	времена́
G	путе́й	матере́й	дочере́й	имён	времён
P	(о) путя́х	(о) матеря́х	(о) дочеря́х	(об) имена́х	(о) времена́х
D	путя́м	матеря́м	дочеря́м	имена́м	времена́м
I	путя́ми	матеря́ми	дочеря́ми (дочерьми́)	имена́ми	времена́ми

REGULAR NOUNS WITH IRREGULAR PLURALS

N sing.	друг	сосе́д	сын	брат	сестра́	ребёнок
N pl.	друзья́	сосе́ди	сыновья́	бра́тья	сёстры	де́ти
A pl.	друзе́й	сосе́дей	сынове́й	бра́тьев	сестёр	дете́й
G pl.	друзе́й	сосе́дей	сынове́й	бра́тьев	сестёр	дете́й
P pl.	(о) друзья́х	(о) сосе́дях	(о) сыновья́х	(о) бра́тьях	(о) сёстрах	(о) детя́х
D pl.	друзья́м	сосе́дям	сыновья́м	бра́тьям	сёстрам	детя́м
I pl.	друзья́ми	сосе́дями	сыновья́ми	бра́тьями	сёстрами	детьми́

D. DECLENSION OF ADJECTIVES

MASCULINE/NEUTER SINGULAR

	ANSWERS QUESTION	BASIC ENDING	REGULAR		END-STRESSED		SPELLING RULES	SOFT
N	Какóй?	-ый	нóвый	рýсский	вторóй	большóй	харóший	сúний
	Какóе?	-ое	нóвое	рýсское	вторóе	большóе	харóшее	сúнее
A In.	Какóй?	-ый	нóвый	рýсский	вторóй	большóй	харóший	сúний
	Какóе?	-ое	нóвое	рýсское	вторóе	большóе	харóшее	сúнее
A An.	Какóго?	-ого	нóвого	рýсского	вторóго	большóго	харóшего	сúнего
G	Какóго?	-ого	нóвого	рýсского	вторóго	большóго	харóшего	сúнего
P	О какóм?	-ом	нóвом	рýсском	вторóм	большóм	харóшем	сúнем
D	Какóму?	-ому	нóвому	рýсскому	вторóму	большóму	харóшему	сúнему
I	Какúм?	-ым	нóвым	рýсским	вторы́м	большúм	харóшим	сúним

FEMININE SINGULAR

	ANSWERS QUESTION	BASIC ENDING	REGULAR		END-STRESSED		SPELLING RULES	SOFT
N	Какáя?	-ая	нóвая	рýсская	вторáя	большáя	харóшая	сúняя
A	Какýю?	-ую	нóвую	рýсскую	вторýю	большýю	харóшую	сúнюю
G	Какóй?	-ой	нóвой	рýсской	вторóй	большóй	харóшей	сúней
P	О какóй?	-ой	нóвой	рýсской	вторóй	большóй	харóшей	сúней
D	Какóй?	-ой	нóвой	рýсской	вторóй	большóй	харóшей	сúней
I	Какóй?	-ой	нóвой	рýсской	вторóй	большóй	харóшей	сúней

PLURAL

	ANSWERS QUESTION	BASIC ENDING	REGULAR		END-STRESSED		SPELLING RULES	SOFT
N	Какúе?	-ые	нóвые	рýсские	вторы́е	большúе	харóшие	сúние
A In.	Какúе?	-ые	нóвые	рýсские	вторы́е	большúе	харóшие	сúние
A An.	Какúх?	-ых	нóвых	рýсских	вторы́х	большúх	харóших	сúних
G	Какúх?	-ых	нóвых	рýсских	вторы́х	большúх	харóших	сúних
P	О какúх?	-ых	нóвых	рýсских	вторы́х	большúх	харóших	сúних
D	Какúм?	-ым	нóвым	рýсским	вторы́м	большúм	харóшим	сúним
I	Какúми?	-ыми	нóвыми	рýсскими	вторы́ми	большúми	харóшими	сúними

E. IRREGULAR COMPARATIVE ADJECTIVES

	ADJECTIVE	COMPARATIVE	
bad	плохо́й	ху́же	worse
big	большо́й	бо́льше	bigger/more
cheap	дешёвый	деше́вле	cheaper
easy	лёгкий	ле́гче	easier
expensive/dear	дорого́й	доро́же	more expensive/dearer
fat	то́лстый	то́лще	fatter
frequent	ча́стый	ча́ще	more often
good	хоро́ший	лу́чше	better
late	по́здний	по́зже	later
loud	гро́мкий	гро́мче	louder
narrow	у́зкий	у́же	narrower
near	бли́зкий	бли́же	nearer
old	ста́рый	ста́рше	older
quiet	ти́хий	ти́ше	quieter
short	коро́ткий	коро́че	shorter
simple	просто́й	про́ще	simpler
small	ма́ленький	ме́ньше	smaller/less
tall	высо́кий	вы́ше	taller
wide	широ́кий	ши́ре	wider
young	молодо́й	мла́дше, моло́же	younger

F. CASES AND PREPOSITIONS

CASE	PREPOSITIONS	MEANING
Accusative	в	to, into
	за	for (exchange), behind (direction)
	на	to, onto
	про	about
	че́рез	through, across
Genitive	без	without
	впереди́	to the front of
	для	for (the purpose of)
	до	until, as far as, up to
	из	from (source), out of
	ми́мо	past
	о́коло	near, about
	от	from
	по́сле	after
	про́тив	against
	ра́ди	for the sake of
	с	from
	у	at, by/alongside of, at the home/office of, have"
Prepositional	в	in, at, inside of
	на	on, at, on top of
	о	about
	при	in the presence of, during the reign/administration of
Dative	благодаря́	thanks/owing to
	к	to, toward(s)
	по	according to, on (the subject of), around, along, etc.
Instrumental	за	behind (location)
	ме́жду	between
	над	above, over
	пе́ред	in front of, just before
	под	under (location), near (a city)
	с	with

G. VERB CHARTS

1. REGULAR CONJUGATION I AND II VERBS

	CONJUGATION I			CONJUGATION II	
					SHIFTING STRESS
	-атъ	-ятъ	SHIFTING STRESS	-итъ	SOFT л
PRESENT					
	де́латъ	гуля́тъ	писа́тъ	говори́тъ	люби́тъ
я	де́лаю	гуля́ю	пишу́	говорю́	люблю́
ты	де́лаешь	гуля́ешь	пи́шешь	говори́шь	лю́бишь
он/она́	де́лает	гуля́ет	пи́шет	говори́т	лю́бит
мы	де́лаем	гуля́ем	пи́шем	говори́м	лю́бим
вы	де́лаете	гуля́ете	пи́шете	говори́те	лю́бите
они́	де́лают	гуля́ют	пи́шут	говоря́т	лю́бят
PAST					
Masculine	де́лал	гуля́л	писа́л	говори́л	люби́л
Feminine	де́лала	гуля́ла	писа́ла	говори́ла	люби́ла
Plural	де́лали	гуля́ли	писа́ли	говори́ли	люби́ли
STEM	де́ла+	гуля́+	пиш+	говор+	люб+
IMPERATIVE	де́лай(те)	гуля́й(те)	пиши́(те)	говори́(те)	люби́(те)

2. CONJUGATION I VERBS WITH SPELLING CHANGES

	целова́ть	дава́ть	мыть	па́хнуть	нести́	печь
PRESENT						
я	целу́ю	даю́	мо́ю	па́хну	несу́	пеку́
ты	целу́ешь	даёшь	мо́ешь	па́хнешь	несёшь	пекёшь
он/она́	целу́ет	даёт	мо́ет	па́хнет	несёт	пекёт
мы	целу́ем	даём	мо́ем	па́хнем	несём	пекём
вы	целу́ете	даёте	мо́ете	па́хнете	несёте	пекёте
они́	целу́ют	даю́т	мо́ют	па́хнут	несу́т	пеку́т
PAST						
Masculine	целова́л	дава́л	мыл	па́хнул	нёс	пёк
Feminine	целова́ла	дава́ла	мы́ла	па́хнула	несла́	пекла́
Plural	целова́ли	дава́ли	мы́ли	па́хнули	несли́	пекли́
STEM	целу́+	да+	мо́+	па́хн+	нес+	пек+
IMPERATIVE	целу́й(те)	дава́й(те)	мо́й(те)	па́хни(те)	неси́(те)	пеки́(те)

3. IRREGULAR VERBS

	есть	хотеть	быть	дать	бежать
	PRESENT	PRESENT	FUTURE	FUTURE (Perf.)	PRESENT
я	ем	хочу́	бу́ду	дам	бегу́
ты	ешь	хо́чешь	бу́дешь	дашь	бежи́шь
он/она́	ест	хо́чет	бу́дет	даст	бежи́т
мы	еди́м	хоти́м	бу́дем	дади́м	бежи́м
вы	еди́те	хоти́те	бу́дете	дади́те	бежи́те
они́	едя́т	хотя́т	бу́дут	даду́т	бегу́т
PAST					
Masculine	ел	хоте́л	был	дал	бежа́л
Feminine	е́ла	хоте́ла	была́	дала́	бежа́ла
Neuter	бы́ло				
Plural	е́ли	хоте́ли	бы́ли	да́ли	бежа́ли
STEM	(ед+)	хо́ч+/хот+	бу́д+	(дад+)	бег+/беж+
IMPERATIVE	е́шь(те)	хоти́(те)	бу́дь(те)	да́й(те)	беги́(те)

4. VERBS OF MOTION*

IMP. MULTIDIR.	MEANING	IMP. UNIDIR.	PERF.	MEANING
ходи́ть	to go/walk	идти́	пойти́	to go (set off for) on foot
е́здить	to go/ride	е́хать	пое́хать	to go (set off for) by vehicle
носи́ть	to carry	нести́	понести́	to take (set off for) on foot
вози́ть	to convey/transport	везти́	повезти́	to transport (set off for)
води́ть	to lead	вести́	повести́	to lead (set off for)
бежа́ть	to run	бе́гать	побежа́ть	to run (set off for)
лета́ть	to fly	лете́ть	полете́ть	to fly (set off for)
пла́вать	to swim/sail	плыть	поплыть	to swim/sail (set off for)

*Unidirectional verbs can also be made perfective with any of the other prefixes used with verbs of motion just as with идти́ and е́хать. When these prefixes are added to verbs of motion, directionality is no longer an issue, and the verb is a regular imperfective/perfective pair.

H. LETTER WRITING

1. A NOTE ON LETTER WRITING

In both formal and informal writing, the addressee's name, title, and address appear only on the envelope. In formal letters, an institution's name and address often appear at the top of the document, while the date is at the bottom of the page.

Since the breakup of the Soviet Union, the form of address in formal writing has changed. Now Russians write to Mr. or Mrs. (господи́н, госпожа́), just as we do in the United States, but there is no term for Ms. The abbreviated forms are г–н or г. (Mr.) and г–жа (Mrs.). Note that they are not capitalized. In formal writing the use of a title is common, and if one wants to write to editorial offices of newspapers or journals, the phrase "Dear editorial board" (Уважа́емая реда́кция) is commonly used. Whether writing formally or informally, the initial greeting is almost always punctuated with an exclamation point rather than a comma.

The date is written with the day first, followed by the month, and then the year. The abbreviated form differs from the one used in the United States. March 12, 1999, for example, is written as 12–3–99 or as 12/III/99. The order of the address is reversed as well. Russians begin with the country, or with the city (го́род, abbreviated г.) for domestic mail, and the инде́кс (postal code) on the first line. They then write the street (usually у́лица, abbreviated ул., or проспе́кт, abbreviated пр.) and building number (дом, abbreviated д.), and perhaps the block number (кварта́л, abbreviated к–л), and then the apartment number (кварти́ра, abbreviated кв.). The company or organization name follows. The name of the addressee in the dative case, with the last name first, appears on the last line. Note also that accents are not marked, and in formal letters, the word Вы (and Ваш, Вас, Вам, and Ва́ми) is capitalized, when used as the polite form of address.

27–10–98

Дорогой Иван!

Наконец, приехал в Псков. С билетами было трудно, но, в конце концов, Ирина достала, и даже на скорый поезд. В общем, могу взяться за работу. Директор нашёл неплохую квартиру. Наверное, действительно хотят, чтобы мне было удобно. Жалко, что не успели поговорить в Москве, но в ноябре собираюсь приехать и, конечно, позвоню.

Скучаю по московским друзьям. Не забывай. Пиши!

Твой Сергей.

10–27–98

Dear Ivan,

I have finally arrived in Pskov. There was difficulty with the tickets, but in the end Irina managed to get them and even for an express train. So, I can get down to work. The director found a decent apartment. It seems they really want to make me comfortable. Too bad we didn't have time to talk in Moscow, but I plan to come in November and will call you, of course.

I miss my Moscow friends. Don't forget me. Write!

Yours,
Sergei

17–11–98

Дорогая Наташа!

Давно уже не получаю от тебя писем и очень беспокоюсь о
родителях. Как здоровье отца? Собирается мама уходить на пенсию,
или опять откладывает? Позвони мне на работу, домашний
телефон ещё не подключили.

Девочки растут, Марина пошла в первый класс и очень гордится.
Таня даёт ей советы.

Всё у нас хорошо. Миша передаёт привет. Надеюсь увидеть всех
вас на праздники.

Целую,
Ваша Галя

11–17–98

Dear Natasha,

I have not received letters from you in a while and I worry a lot
about our parents. How is father's health? Is Mom going to retire or is
she delaying again? Call me at work: our home phone hasn't been
connected yet.

The girls are growing up. Marina started first grade and is very
proud. Tanya gives her advice.

Everything is fine with us. Misha sends his regards. I hope to see
you for the holidays.

Love,
Galya

3. BUSINESS LETTERS

Business letters in Russian are written in a rather formal style that em-
ploys more participle phrases than are normally used in conversation.
However, once these conventional phrases and expressions are learned,
you will find that writing commercial correspondence is not very
difficult.

A. ADDRESSING A BUSINESS LETTER

Г-н Макаренко И. П.
Руководитель отделения сбыта
Внешнеторгового объединиеня
«Дальинторг»

ул. Лавочкина, 23
117049 Москва, Россия

Уважаемый Иван Петрович!

   В ответ на Ваш запрос сообшаем Вам, что к сожалению, мы
не можем предложить Вам приборы интересующей Вас марки
т.к. они больше не выпускаются. Мы можем сделать Вам
твёрдое предложение на аналогичные приборы новой марки.
Их цена несколько выше, но они уже пользуются большим
спросом. Мы можем поставить товар в течение 3-х месяцев с
даты получения Вашего заказа.
   Надеемся на Ваш скорый ответ.

С искренним уважением

Mr. I.P. Makarenko
Marketing Division Supervisor

"Dalintorg"
Foreign Trade Association
Lavochkina St., 23
117049 Moscow, Russia

Dear Ivan Petrovich,

   In response to your letter of inquiry, we regret to inform you that we
are unable to offer the brand of instruments you requested since they
are no longer being produced. We are able to provide you with
comparable instruments under a new brand name. The price of these
instruments is somewhat higher, but they are already in great demand.
We can deliver the instruments within three months after receiving
your order.
   We hope to hear from you soon.

Sincerely,

Уважаемые господа
Dear Sirs

Мы получили Ваше письмо от . . .
We received your letter of . . .

В ответ на Ваше письмо от . . .
In response to your letter of . . .

Вновь ссылаясь на наше письмо от . . . сообщаем, что . . .
With further reference to our letter of . . . we wish to inform you
that . . .

В связи с нашим письмом от . . .
In connection with our letter of . . .

Приносим извинение за некоторую задержку с ответом на Ваше
письмо.
We apologize for the delay in answering your letter.

Мы с сожалением узнали из Вашего письма от . . . что . . .
We are sorry to learn from your letter of . . . that . . .

К сожалению, мы не можем удовлетворить вашу просьбу о . . .
We regret that we are unable to comply with your request . . .

Вам несомненно известно, что . . .
You are doubtless aware that . . .

Просим принять во внимание, что . . .
Please note that . . .

Мы совершенно уверены . . .
　We are confident that . . .

В дополнение к вышеуказанному . . .
　In addition to the above . . .

Пользуясь возможностью напомнить, что
　We are taking the opportunity to remind you that . . .

Обращаем Ваше внимание на тот факт, что . . .
　We wish to draw your attention to the fact that . . .

Ввиду вышеизложенного . . .
　In view of the above . . .

В противном случае, мы будем вынуждены . . .
　Otherwise we shall be forced to . . .

Что касается Вашей просьбы . . .
　With regard to your request . . .

Мы испытываем затруднения с . . .
　We are having difficulty in . . .

Мы будем признательны за быстрый ответ
Your early reply will be appreciated . . .

Просим сообщить нам в ближайшем будущем
Please inform us at your earliest convenience . . .

Заверяем Вас, что мы предпримем срочные меры для исправления создавшегося положения.
We assure you that we shall take prompt measures to correct the situation.

Ждём приезда ваших представителей для дальнейших переговоров.
We look forward to the arrival of your representatives for further negotiations.

Ожидаем Вашего подтверждения.
We look forward to your confirmation.

С уважением
Respectfully yours, Truly yours, Sincerely yours, Yours sincerely

Here are some sample business letters about specific topics:

Уважаемые господа,

В ответ на Ваше письмо от 23 марта с.г., с большим сожалением сообщаем Вам, что мы не можем принять Ваше предложение об оплате кредитной части в соответсвии с графиком платежей, так как этот способ противоречит условиям межправительственного соглашения.

Что касается платежей в твердой валюте, то мы согласны с Вами, что они не будут значительными, и готовы получать их в предложенной Вами валюте.

В связи с вышеизложенным, просим Вас пересмотреть Ваши замечания по статье «Условия платежа», приняв во внимание наш проект контракта и настоящее письмо.

В ожидании скорейшего ответа,

С уважением

———————

Dear Sirs (Gentlemen),

In response to your letter of March 23 this year, we very much regret to inform you that we cannot accept your proposal with regard to the payment of the credit portion to be made against the schedule of payments, as this method runs counter to the provisions of the intergovernmental agreement.

As regards the payments in hard currency, we agree that they will not be considerable and we would be prepared to receive them in the currency of your option.

In view of the above, we would request that you reconsider your remarks with regard to the "Terms of Payment" clause, with due regard to our draft contract and the present letter.

In anticipation of your early reply, we remain

Yours faithfully,

Уважаемые господа,

В соответствии с Контрактом № 5431, поставка оборудования для строительства завода минеральных удобрений должна быть осуществлена четырьмя партиями.

Первые три партии оборудования были доставлены Вам в сроки, оговорённые контрактом, и Вы остались довольны его техническими характеристиками.

К сожалению, по вине завода-изготовителя и в связи с трудностями в обеспечении транспортных средств произошла задержка в поставке четвёртой партии. Оборудование прибыло в порт погрузки 27 октября, лишь когда срок действия вышеуказанного контракта уже истёк. Поскольку срок действия аккредитива на оплату последней партии оборудования закончился, убедительно просим Вас или продлить его до февраля 19....года, или подтвердить оплату счетов, которые будут выставлены на инкассо.

С уважением

–––––––––––

Dear Sirs,

In accordance with the conditions stipulated in Contract No. 5431 the delivery of equipment for the construction of the mineral fertilizer plant was to be carried out in four consignments.

The first three consignments were delivered to you within the period stipulated in the contract, and we understand that the technical characteristics of the equipment have met with your satisfaction.

Unfortunately, the fourth consignment was delayed because of the manufacturer's failure to produce the ordered equipment on time and, secondly, because of difficulties in securing the required transport facilities. The equipment did not arrive at the port of loading until October 27, which was already beyond the contract's expiration date. Inasmuch as the L/C for the final fourth consignment is no longer valid, we would request that you either extend its validity until February 19xx or confirm payment of invoices to be made for collection.

Sincerely,

Уважаемые господа,

Своим письмом от 18 марта с.г., Вы предложили нам услуги при размещении заказов на публикацию рекламных объявлений наших клиентов в журналах, издающихся в Российской Федерации.

Наши клиенты заинтересованы в Вашем предложении и хотели бы получить полную информацию в отношении журналов, в которых Вы намерены помещать их рекламные объявления. В частности, они хотели бы знать круг их читателей, тираж и расценки за публикацию одноразовых рекламных объявлений.

С нетерпением ждём Ваш скорейший ответ.

С уважением

Dear Sirs,

In your letter of March 18, this year, you offered your services in placing our clients' advertisements in magazines published in the Russian Federation.

Our clients are most interested in your proposal and would very much appreciate receiving more detailed information about the magazines in which you intend to place their ads. In particular, they would like to know the scope of the readership, circulation, and one-time advertising rates.

We look forward to your early reply.

Respectfully,

Addressee

Sender

г. Москва 332889
ул. Страхова, д. 5, кв. 75
Павлову Ивану Петровичу

г. Псков 32435
ул. Надеждина, д. 4, кв. 1
Сергей Суриков

Moscow 332889
5 Strakhova St, Apt. 75
Pavlov, Ivan Petrovich

Pskov 32435
4 Nadezhdina St., Apt. 1
Sergei Surikov

СЛОВАРЬ (Glossary)

ABBREVIATIONS

adj.	adjective	nom.	nominative
adv.	adverb	pej.	pejorative
attrib.	attributive	pl.	plural
f.	feminine	p.p.p.	past passive participle
imp.	impersonal	trans.	transitive verb
ind. pron.	indefinite pronoun		
joc.	jocular		
m.	masculine		
n.	neuter		

RUSSIAN-ENGLISH

A

а́вгуст August
авто́бус bus
автоотве́тчик answering machine
автостоя́нка parking lot, parking garage
аге́нтство agency
а́дрес address
аккредити́в letter of credit, L/C
а́кция share of stock
алкого́льный (adj.) alcohol
ана́лиз analysis
анги́на throat inflammation, tonsillitis
анке́та questionnaire, form, blank
антиква́рный (adj.) antique
апельси́н orange
аппети́т appetite
апре́ль April
арбитра́ж arbitration
аре́нда rent
аренда́тор lessee, tenant, renter
арендода́тель lessor
арти́ст artist; (pej.) con man
архитекту́ра architecture
аспира́нт(ка) graduate student
ассортиме́нт assortment, selection
афи́ша billboard, poster
аэропо́рт airport

Б

ба́бушка grandmother
баклажа́н eggplant
баклажа́нный (adj.) eggplant
ба́нка jar, can
банкро́тство bankruptcy
бе́дный poor

бегу́н runner
без without
    без сомне́ния without doubt
безвку́сный tasteless
безнаде́жный hopeless
безотзы́вный irrevocable
безусло́вно absolutely
бе́лый white
бесе́довать/побесе́довать to discuss
беспод о́бный incomparable, matchless
беспоко́иться worry (to)
беспристра́стный unbiased
бессро́чный without time limit
би́ржа stock exchange
благода́рность gratitude
благополу́чие welfare, well-being
благоро́дный noble
бли́зко near, close
близлежа́щий nearby
блины́ pancakes
блю́до dish; food
блю́дце saucer
бога́тый wealthy
боле́знь (f.) disease
боле́льщик fan
боле́ть (за что/кого) agonize, to grieve
    for; root for (to)
больно́й ill (adj.); patient (noun)
большинство́ majority
большо́й large
бомбарди́р bomber; ace soccer kicker
бортпроводни́(к)ца flight attendant
борщ borscht
боя́знь (f.) fear, dread
боя́ться fear (to)
брать/взять take (to)

бри́ться shave
броса́ть/бро́сить throw, cast (to)
бры́нза sheep's milk cheese
буди́ть/разбуди́ть (кого) awaken (to)
бу́дний день weekday
бу́лка small loaf
бу́лочка bun, roll
буфе́т buffet
бы́стро quickly

В

в to; in; into
   в по́льзу in favor of; on behalf of
   в тече́ние (чего) for the period of
   в ча́стности in particular, particularly
вакци́на vaccine
валю́та foreign currency
валю́тный (adj.) foreign currency
вариа́нт version, variant
варёный cooked, boiled
вбива́ть/вбить drive in; beat in; score (to)
вбра́сывать throw in (to)
ввоз import
вдвоём the two together
вдоль alongside
вози́ть/везти́ carry; convey (to)
великоле́пный splendid
венери́ческий venereal
венча́ние wedding ceremony; coronation
ве́рить/пове́рить believe (to)
ве́рсия version
весна́ spring
весно́й in the spring
весьма́ quite
ве́чер evening
ве́чером in the evening
вещь thing
взаи́мно mutually, reciprocally
взаимообя́занность (f.) mutual obligation
взве́шивать/взве́сить weigh (to)
взволно́ван(а)(ы) agitated, worried, disturbed
взгля́д view, opinion
взгля́дывать/взгляну́ть glance, look at (to)
взро́слый adult
вид view, species, type
видеока́рта video card
визи́тка business card
визи́тная ка́рточка business card
вино́ wine
винче́стер hard drive (computer)
витри́на showcase
вку́сно tasty
включа́ть/включи́ть include (to)
вкус taste
владе́ть possess, own (to)
влета́ть в копе́ечку cost a pretty penny (to)
вну́тренний (adj.) interior, internal
внима́ние attention
внима́тельно attentively
внуши́тельный impressive, imposing, striking

во́время on time
води́тельское удостовере́ние driver's license
возбужда́ться get excited/aroused (to)
вознагражде́ние, опла́та remuneration
возвраща́ться/верну́ться return (to)
возвраще́ние return
возду́шный air, aerial (adj.)
вокза́л station
волнова́ть(ся) worry, become agitated (to)
вообще́ in general
воро́та goal (sport); gates
во́семь eight
восто́рг delight, rapture
восторга́ться be delighted (to)
вперёд forward
впервы́е for the first time
впереди́ (чего/кого) ahead
впечатле́ние impression
впечатля́ющий impressive
вписа́ть inscribe, insert, enter (to)
вплотну́ю closely, in earnest
вполне́ completely, fully
впосле́дствии subsequently, afterward
впра́во on the right
впро́чем however
вре́мя time
врата́рь goalkeeper
вряд ли hardly
вса́дник horseman, rider
всегда́ always
вска́кивать/вскочи́ть jump up (to)
встава́ть/встать get up, arise (to)
встре́ча meeting
встро́енный built-in
встреча́ть/встре́тить meet (to)
вход entrance
вчера́шний (adj.) yesterday's
выбира́ть/вы́брать select, choose (to)
вы́бор selection
вы́везти export, take out (to)
вы́воз export
вы́годный beneficial, profitable
выделя́ть/вы́делить allocate (to)
вы́езд exit, departure
вы́ехать depart, drive out (to)
вы́зов call, summons
вызыва́ть/вы́звать summon, call upon (to)
выкри́кивать/вы́крикнуть shout out (to)
вы́куп repurchase, redemption
вынужда́ть/вы́нудить compel, force (to)
вы́плата payment, disbursement
выпла́чивать/вы́платить pay out (to)
выпуска́ть/вы́пустить issue, produce (to)
выра́вниваться/вы́ровняться equalize, even out (to)
выраба́тывать/вы́работать work out, develop, design (to)
выруча́ть/вы́ручить rescue, come to the help (to)
вы́севать sow (to)

выслушать hear out, listen (to)
высокоскоростной high-speed
высота height, altitude
выстраивать/выстроить arrange, draw up (to)
выучить learn (to); teach (to)
выходить/выйти exit, depart, go out (to)
выходной (день) day off
выходные days off; weekend

Г

гарантия warranty, guarantee
гарнитур complete set; suite (of furniture)
гастроном food store
гектар hectare
гибрид hybrid
главный main, principal
глагол verb
глотка pharynx
глубокий deep, profound
голодать/проголодать go hungry, starve (to)
гнездо nest
горло throat
город city
горох peas
горячий hot
господин Mr.
госпожа Mrs.
гостиница hotel
гость guest
государственный (adj) state, governmental
государство state
готовиться/приготовиться prepare oneself, get prepared (to)
гравировка engraving
градус degree (temperature)
грамматика grammar
грандиозный grandiose
граница border, boundary
    за границу abroad (direction)
    за границей abroad (location)
граф count (title)
грибы mushrooms
грубый crude, rough
грузовик truck
гулять/погулять stroll (to)

Д

дальний distant, far
дательный dative (case)
дача country house
давать/дать give (to)
давно long ago, long since
далеко far away
датироваться be dated (to)
дать подножку trip (to)
дать свисток blow a whistle (to)
двенадцать twelve
движение movement, traffic
дворец palace
дебетовая карточка debit card
девушка young woman, girl

девять nine
дежурный (adj.) on duty
    дежурный администратор duty manager, hotel manager
действительно actually
декабрь (m.) December
декларация declaration (customs form)
делать/сделать do, make (to)
деляга hustler, go-getter
денежный (adj.) money
    денежный перевод money order
десять ten
держать (кого-нибудь) в курсе keep (someone) informed (to)
деталь (f.) detail
дети children
дефицит deficit
диагностика diagnostics
диета diet
диктор announcer
динамик speaker (electronic)
дифтерия diphtheria
длинный long
добавлять/добавить add, supplement (to)
добираться/добраться reach, get to (to)
добро good
    Добро пожаловать! Welcome!
довольно enough, rather
доводить bring (to)
    доводить до кипения bring to a boil (to)
договариваться/договориться agree to (to)
договор agreement, treaty, contract
дождаться wait (as long as necessary) to
дождь (m.) rain
доклад report
долгий long
должен/должна/должны must
должность (f.) duty
должный (adj.) due, fitting, proper
долететь fly up to (to)
дом house, building, home
домой (adv.) homeward
домофон building intercom
дописывать/дописать finish writing (to)
дополнительно (adv.) additionally
дополнительный (adj.) additional, supplemental
дорабатывать/доработать put finishing touches on (to)
доработка touch up, finishing up
дорогой expensive; dear
дороже more expensive
дорожный (adj.) roadway, traveler's
доставка delivery
доставлять/доставить provide, afford, give (to)
достаточно sufficiently, rather
достигать/достигнуть reach, achieve (to)
достояние property, common property
достопримечательности sights, points of interest

досту́п(ен)(на)(ный) (short adj.)
accessible
досту́пный (adj.) accessible
дохо́дчивость (f.) lucidity, ease of
understanding
дроблёный crushed
друг (pl. друзья́) friend
дубли́рованный dubbed, duplicated
душ shower
дыха́тельные пути́ respiratory tract
дыша́ть breathe (to)
дюйм inch
дя́дя uncle

Е

европе́йский European
еда́ food, meal
еди́нственный only, singular
ежего́дный annual
ежедне́вный daily
еженеде́льный weekly
езда́ trip, drive
есть (ем, ешь, ест, еди́м, едя́т)
eat (to)
ещё still, yet

Ж

жа́реный (adj.) fried, broiled
жела́ние desire, wish
жела́ть wish, desire (to)
желу́док stomach
желу́дочно-кише́чный (adj.)
gastrointestinal
железнодоро́жный (adj.) railroad
жени́х bridegroom
жило́е помеще́ние living quarters
жи́рность (f.) fat content
жи́рный (adj.) fatty, greasy
жить live (to)
журнали́ст journalist

З

за здоро́вье! to your health!
заба́вно (adv.) amusing, funny
заби́ть drive in, score (to)
забира́ть/забра́ть pick up, collect (to)
заболева́емость (f.) disease incidence
заболева́ть/заболе́ть become ill (to)
забо́титься/позабо́титься be concerned
(to)
заброни́ровать reserve (to)
заверше́ние completion
завёртывать/заверну́ть wrap up (to) (a
gift)
зави́деть catch sight of (to)
зави́довать/позави́довать envy, be
jealous (to)
заводи́ть/завести́ bring, start, wind (to)
за́втра tomorrow
за́втрак breakfast
за́втракать/поза́втракать breakfast (to)
завяза́ть bind, tie (to)
загво́здка hitch, catch, snag, rub
за́городный suburban
заграни́ца foreign countries

зада́ние assignment
зада́ток deposit, down payment
заде́рживаться be delayed (to)
заём loan
зажа́ренный fried, broiled
зака́зчик client, customer
зака́зывать/заказа́ть order, place an
order (to)
зака́нчивать/зако́нчить complete (to)
закрыва́ть/закры́ть close (to)
закупа́ться store up, buy up (to)
закури́ть light up (a cigarette) (to)
заку́ски snacks, appetizers, hors d'oeuvre
зал hall, auditorium
зал ожида́ния waiting room
зало́жен(а) mislaid; stuffed (imp.)
зама́нчиво enticing, tempting
заменя́ть/замени́ть substitute, replace
(to)
заме́тки notes
замеча́ние remark
замеча́тельно remarkably
замеча́тельный (adj.) remarkable
замеча́ть/заме́тить remark (to)
занима́ть/заня́ть occupy (to)
занима́ться be engaged in, study (to)
за́нят(а)(ы) (short adj.) busy
заня́тия (pl.) activities, classes
занято́й (adj.) busy
за́нятый occupied
за́падный western
запа́с reserve, stock, supply
за́пах odor, smell
запи́сываться/записа́ться sign up,
register
заполня́ть/запо́лнить fill out, complete
(to)
запо́мнить remember, memorize (to)
заплани́ровать plan (to)
зараба́тывать earn (to)
зараже́ние infection
зара́нее earlier
зарубе́жный (adj.) foreign
заседа́ние session, meeting, conference
заслу́живать/заслужи́ть merit, earn
(to)
застрева́ть/застря́ть get stuck (to)
зате́м then, thereupon, next
затева́ть/зате́ять undertake, organize
(to)
зато́ on the other hand, but
затрудня́ться/затрудни́ться find
difficulty in (to)
захвати́ть grab, capture, catch (to)
заходи́ть/зайти́ drop by, drop in (to)
зачасту́ю often, frequently
заче́м what for
защи́тник defender, back (sport)
звать/позва́ть call, invite (to)
звони́ть/позвони́ть call by phone, ring
(to)
звоно́к ring (sound), bell
звукоза́пись audio recording
звукопереда́ча audio transmission
звуча́ть sound (to)

здо́рово splendily, magnificently
здоро́вье health
зелёный green
земля́ land
земляни́ка wild strawberries
земляни́чный (adj.) strawberry
знако́мить/познако́мить acquaint (to)
знамени́тый famous, celebrated
знать know (to)
зна́чит so, then, well then
значи́тельно significantly
золото́й golden
зри́тель viewer, spectator, observer
зять son-in-law; brother-in-law

И

игро́к player
идти́/пойти́ go (to)
из (чего) from, out of
избежа́ть avoid (to)
избира́ть/избра́ть choose, elect
изгото́вленный manufactured
изда́ние issue, edition
изде́лие item, article
изнача́льный initial, primordial
изображе́ние image, representation,
    portrayal
изуми́тельный (adj.) amazing
изуча́ть/изучи́ть study (to)
ико́на icon
икра́ caviar
име́ть в виду́ have in mind (to)
иммунизацио́нный (adj.) immunization
импера́тор emperor
импорти́руемый (p.p.p.) imported
иногда́ sometimes
ино́й another, different
иностра́н(ец)(ка)(цы) foreigner
интересова́ть(ся) be interested in (to)
интерко́м intercom
инфекцио́нный infectious
    инфекцио́нные боле́зни infectious
        diseases
инфля́ция inflation
информа́ция information
иска́ть/поиска́ть seek, search (to)
исключе́ние exception
исключи́ть exclude (to)
испо́льзовать utilize, use (to)
испо́ртиться be spoiled (to)
иссле́довательский (adj.) research
истече́ние expiration, outflow
исто́чник source, spring
исчеза́ть/исче́знуть disappear (to)
ию́нь June
ию́ль July

К

к to, toward, for
    к лу́чшему for the better
    к сожале́нию unfortunately
    к сча́стью fortunately
    к ху́дшему for the worse
кабине́т office, laboratory, study
ка́ждый each, every

кана́л channel (TV); canal
капиталовложе́ние capital investment
карто́фель (m.) potatoes
ка́рточка card
кассе́та cassette
ка́чество quality
ка́ша kasha, cooked cereal
квадра́тный (adj.) square
кварта́л city block, quarter, section
кварти́ра apartment
кинофестива́ль (m.) film festival
кио́ск kiosk, stall
кипяти́ть boil (to)
кири́ллица Cyrillic alphabet
клавиату́ра keyboard
класть/положи́ть place, put (to)
клие́нт client
клубни́ка strawberries (cultivated)
ключ key
ко́довый подъе́зд building entrance
ко́жаный (adj.) leather
коклю́ш whooping cough
коли́чество quantity
колле́га colleague
коллекционе́р collector
колхо́з collective farm
командиро́вка official business trip,
    assignment
комба́йн combine, harvester
комбина́ция combination
коммента́рий commentary
коммента́тор commentator
ко́мната room
компа́ния company
компроми́сс compromise
компью́тер computer
коне́чно of course
констру́кция design, structure
контра́кт contract
контрата́ка counterattack
конфере́нц-зал conference hall, room
ко́нчиться be finished, be ended (to)
копчёный smoked (food)
коридо́р corridor
корпорати́вный corporate
корреспонде́нтский (adj.)
    correspondence
кошелёк purse
кра́йность (f.) extreme
краси́вый handsome, pretty
кра́сный red
    Кра́сная пло́щадь Red Square
креди́т credit
    креди́тная ка́рта/ка́рточка credit card
кре́пость (f.) fortress; strength
кривизна́ curvature, crookedness
кро́ме besides
    кро́ме того́ in addition
кру́глый round, throughout
    кру́глые су́тки around-the-clock, all day
кры́шка lid, cover
кста́ти incidentally
кто who
кто́-нибудь anyone
кукуру́за corn

кулина́рный (adj.) culinary
культу́ры crops
купа́ться bathe, swim (to)
кури́льщик smoker
кури́ть smoke (to)
куса́ться be exorbitant, be bitten (to)
кусо́к piece
кусо́чек small piece
ку́рица chicken, hen
ку́хня kitchen
ку́шать eat (to)

Л

лату́нный (adj.) brass
лека́рство medicine
ле́кция lecture
лес forest, woods
ле́тний (adj.) summer
ле́том in the summer
лече́ние cure, treatment
ликви́дность (f.) liquidity
лимо́н lemon
лимо́нный (adj.) lemon
лифт elevator
ли́шний extra, excess
лови́ть/пойма́ть catch (to)
ло́вкий adroit, deft, clever
ло́жка tablespoon
ло́жный (adj.) false
лук onions
лук-шало́т shallots
лэпто́п laptop
любе́зный (adj.) kind
люби́ть love, like (to)
любо́й any

М

магнитофо́н tape recorder
май May
майоне́з mayonnaise
манёвр maneuver
ма́нный semolina, farina
марино́ванный marinated
ма́рка make, trade name, brand
март March
ма́сло oil; butter
маши́на machine, car
ме́бель (f.) furniture
ме́дленный (adj.) slow
ме́дный (adj.) copper
ме́жду про́чим by the way, incidentally
междунаро́дный (adj.) international
ме́лко (adv.) fine, into small pieces
ме́лочь (f.) trifle, change
ме́неджер manager
ме́сто place, location, seat
метр meter
меша́ть/помеша́ть interfere, disturb (to)
мёд honey
многокварти́рный дом apartment
    house complex
многосери́йный (adj.) serial
    (production)
многочи́сленный (adj.) numerous
моги́ла grave

моло́чный (adj.) dairy
молодожёны newlyweds
молодо́й (adj.) young
Молодчи́на!; Молоде́ц! Good chap!;
    Well done!
молоко́ milk
молоти́лка thresher
монито́р monitor (computer)
морко́вь (f.) carrots
мы́льный (adj.) soapy
мяч ball

Н

на он
    На здоро́вье! To your heart's content!
    на́ ночь for the night
набо́р set, collection
наве́рное probably
наверняка́ for sure, certainly
весно́й (adj.) hanging
наводи́ть/навести́ спра́вки make
    inquiries (to)
нагуля́ть (аппети́т) work up an appetite
    (to)
на́до necessary
наде́яться (на что-кого) rely on (to)
наеда́ться/нае́сться eat one's fill (to)
нажа́тие press
нажима́ть/нажа́ть press (to)
назнача́ть/назна́чить appoint, assign
    (to)
наилу́чший (adj.) very best
наконе́ц finally
налива́ть/нали́ть pour (to)
нали́чие presence, existence
нали́чные cash
нало́г tax
нало́говый (adj.) tax
намно́го much, far (with comparatives)
нанима́ть/наня́ть hire (to)
наоборо́т on the contrary
напада́ть/напа́сть fall upon, attack
напада́ющий striker, forward (sport)
напи́ток beverage
напомина́ть/напо́мнить remind (to)
напра́вленный (adj.) purposeful,
    directional
направля́ть/напра́вить direct, send (to)
направля́ться/напра́виться head for,
    make for (to)
напряжённый (adj.) tense, strained
нарко́тики narcotics
наруше́ние violation, disruption,
    infraction
наси́лие violence
наско́лько so far as
насле́дство inheritance
насто́льный (adj.) table, desktop
насчёт concerning, as regards
находи́ться/найти́сь be located (to)
нача́ло beginning, start
нача́льник chief, boss
начина́ние initiative, undertaking,
    project
начина́ть/нача́ть begin, initiate (to)

не no, not
    Не́ за что. Don't mention it.
    не совсе́м not quite
невероя́тно incredibly
неве́ста fiancée; bride
неве́стка daughter-in-law; sister-in-law
недви́жимость (f.) real estate
неде́ля (f.) week
недове́рие distrust
не́который certain, some
нема́ло quite a bit, a good deal
немно́го a few, a little
необходи́мо essentially
необходи́мость (f.) necessity, need
необыча́йный (adj.) extraordinary,
    exceptional
необы́чный (adj.) unusual
непосре́дственно directly, immediately
непредсказу́емо unpredictably
непреме́нно without fail
неприе́млемость (f.) unacceptability
не́сколько (adv.) several, few
несоверше́нный imperfective (aspect)
неспосо́бность (f.) inability, incapacity
неуда́ча setback, failure
неудиви́тельно (adv.) unsurprisingly
неудо́бство inconvenience
неудовлетвори́тельный (adj.)
    unsatisfactory
нехва́тка shortage
ничего́ nothing
новичо́к greenhorn, neophyte, novice
новосе́лье house-warming; new home
но́вости news
но́вый (adj.) new
но́мер number; hotel room; edition
норма́льный (adj.) normal
ночь (f.) night
ноя́брь November
нра́виться/понра́виться appeal, like
    (to)
нужда́ться be in need of (to)
ну́жный (adj.) necessary, required

О

обводи́ть/обвести́ dodge, pass (sport),
    encircle (to)
обгоня́ть/обогна́ть outstrip, outdistance
    (to)
обе́д dinner
обе́дать/пообе́дать eat supper (to)
обе́денный (adj.) supper, midday meal
облада́ть (чем) possess (to)
о́бласть (f.) region, area
облиза́ть lick clean (to)
    Па́льчики обли́жешь! Finger lickin'
    good!
обме́н (валю́ты) exchange (of currency)
обме́нивать (на что) exchange for (to)
обнима́ть(ся) embrace, hug one another
    (to)
обознача́ть signify, designate (to)
оболо́чка membrane, cover, envelope
обору́дование equipment
оборони́тельный (adj.) defensive

о́браз manner, image, mode
образе́ц sample, example
обра́тный (adj.) reverse, opposite, return
обраща́ться/обрати́ться turn to,
    address (to)
обря́д rite, ceremony
обслу́живание servicing, maintenance
обсужда́ть/обсуди́ть discuss (to)
обу́за heavy responsibility, burden
обустра́ивать/обустро́ить arrange (to)
обустро́йство arrangement
обуче́ние training
обхо́д rounds, going around
обходи́ться/обойти́сь cost, make do,
    (to)
обши́рный expansive
общепри́нятный (adj.) generally
    accepted
о́бщий general, common
объекти́вный (adj.) objective
объявля́ть/объяви́ть declare (to)
обя́занность (f.) obligation, duty,
    responsibility
обяза́тельно without fail
обяза́ться bind oneself, pledge oneself
    (to)
о́вощи vegetables
овся́ный (adj.) oat
огля́дываться look around (to)
оговорённый (adj.) specified,
    stipulated
оголода́ть go hungry, starve (to)
ого́нь (m.) fire
огорче́ние distress, chagrin
ограниче́ние limitation
огро́мный (adj.) vast, immense
одна́ко however
однора́зовый (adj.) disposable
одобре́ние approval
одобря́ть/одо́брить approve (to)
ожида́ние expectation
ози́мый (adj.) winter
ознако́мить familiarize (to)
о́коло near, about, approximately
оконча́тельный final, conclusive
окре́стность (f.) neighborhood, vicinity
окро́шка cold kvass soup; hodgepodge
октя́брь October
ола́дья (f.) fritter
оли́вковый (adj.) olive
омрачи́ть darken, cloud (to)
опа́здывать/опозда́ть be late (to)
опла́та payment
опла́чиваемый (p.p.p) paid
опозда́ние lateness, delay
определённый (adj.) definite,
    determinate, specific
организова́ть organize (to)
оруже́йный (adj.) armed
ору́жие arms, weapons
осо́бенно especially
осо́бенность (f.) peculiarity
осо́бенный (adj.) special
осо́бый (adj.) particular, peculiar
осведомлён/а (short adj.) informed

осведомля́ть/осведоми́ть inform (to)
освежа́ть/освежи́ть refresh, freshen (to)
освеще́ние собы́тий press coverage
освобожда́ться/освободи́ться be
    liberated, be freed (to)
осложне́ние complication
осмо́тр examination
основа́тельно thoroughly, soundly
основа́ть found (to)
основно́й (adj.) basic, principal
оставля́ть/оста́вить leave, abandon (to)
остально́й (adj.) remaining, the rest
остана́вливать/останови́ть halt, stop
    (to)
остана́вливаться/останови́ться stay
    over, come to a stop (to)
осторо́жный (adj.) cautious, careful
осужда́ть/осуди́ть censure, condemn,
    sentence (to)
отбива́ть/отби́ть repel (to); return a ball
    (to) (sport)
отбира́ть/отобра́ть take away, seize,
    select (to)
отведённый (p.p.p) set aside, deflected
отве́тное приглаше́ние return
    invitation
отве́тный (adj.) responsive, return
отве́тственность (f.) responsibility
отве́тственный (adj.) responsible
отвеча́ть/отве́тить respond, answer (to)
отводи́ть/отвести́ вре́мя set aside time
    (to)
отвы́кнуть break the habit, give up (to)
отдава́ть/отда́ть give back, return,
    devote (to)
отде́л department
отделе́ние division, department
отде́льный (adj.) individual, separate
отдыха́ть/отдохну́ть rest, vacation (to)
оте́чественный (adj.) domestic,
    homeland
отзывно́й revocable
отказа́ться reject, refute (to)
открыва́ть/откры́ть open (to)
отла́мывать/отломи́ть break off (to)
отли́чно excellently
отлича́ться be distinguished by (to)
отменя́ть/отмени́ть cancel, abolish (to)
отмеча́ться be noticed, be noted (to)
отноше́ния relations, attitudes
оторва́ть tear off, tear away from (to)
отправля́ть/отпра́вить dispatch, send
    (to)
отправля́ться/отпра́виться head for,
    start out, set out (to)
о́тпуск leave, vacation
    о́тпуск по боле́зни sick leave
отража́ть reflect (to)
отсве́чивание glare, light reflection
отска́кивать/отскочи́ть bounce off,
    rebound, (to)
отстреля́ться finish once and for all (to)
отходи́ть/отойти́ move away from (to)
отча́иваться/отча́яться despair (to)

отча́сти partly, in part
оштрафова́ть fine, penalize (to)
о́фис office
оформле́ние processing, design
оформля́ть(ся)/офо́рмить(ся) complete
    paperwork (to)
охо́тно willingly
очередно́й next, regularly scheduled
о́чередь line, turn

П

павильо́н pavilion
паде́ж case (grammar)
паке́т package
па́лтус halibut
па́льчики fingers
    Па́льчики обли́жешь! Finger lickin'
    good!
па́мятник monument, memorial
па́мять (f.) memory
па́ра pair, couple
партнёр partner
пас pass
пасова́ть pass (to)
пассажи́р passenger
па́спорт passport
па́хнуть (чем) smell of (to)
па́чка pack, bundle, carton
переводи́ть/перевести́ translate,
    transfer (to)
перегово́ры negotiations
передава́ть/переда́ть transmit, convey,
    pass (to)
переда́ча transmission, broadcast
передохну́ть take a break, (to)
перее́хать move, transfer, cross (to)
переи́грывать overact, overplay, replay
    (to)
перекуси́ть have a bite to eat (to)
переноси́ть/перенести́ endure, carry
    across (to)
переночева́ть overnight (to)
переодева́ться/переоде́ться change
    clothes (to)
переподгото́вка retraining
переры́в break, interval
пересека́ть/пересе́чь cut across,
    intersect (to)
пересмотре́ть reexamine (to)
перестава́ть/переста́ть stop, cease (to)
пе́рец pepper
персона́л personnel
пессими́ст pessimist
печёный (adj.) baked
пикни́к picnic
пиро́жное (noun) pastry
пита́ние nutrition, feeding, power supply
пить/вы́пить drink (to)
плани́ровать plan (to)
пла́тный (adj.) for pay, requiring
    payment
платёжеспосо́бность (f.) solvency
пло́хо poorly
пло́щадь (f.) square, area

по on, by

    по бо́льшей ча́сти for the most part

    по кра́йней ме́ре at least

    по ме́ре (чего) in proportion to, to the extent of

    по о́череди by turn, in turn

    по-пре́жнему as before

повто́рный (adj.) repeat, a second

повыше́ние increase, rise

пого́да weather

под under

    под ключ turnkey

подава́ть/пода́ть give, serve (to)

пода́рок gift

подбо́р selection

подгото́виться prepare oneself for (to)

подготови́тельный (adj.) preparatory

подде́льный (adj.) forged, counterfeit, imitation

подде́рживать/поддержа́ть support (to)

подде́ржка support

подкла́дывать/подложи́ть place under (to)

подключе́ние connection, hookup

по́длинный genuine, original

подно́жка step

    дать подно́жку trip up (to)

подно́с tray

подожда́ть wait for (to)

подозрева́ющий (adj.) suspecting

подохо́дный (adj.) income

подска́зывать/подсказа́ть prompt, suggest (to)

подсо́лнечник sunflower seed

подходи́ть/подойти́ approach, come up to (to)

подходя́щий (adj.) suitable, appropriate

подъе́зд approach, entrance

по́зже later

пожа́луйста please, you're welcome

пожа́р fire

поже́ртвование contribution

пожима́ть press, squeeze (to)

    пожима́ть ру́ки shake hands (to)

позабо́титься be concerned about (to)

позади́ behind

позаре́з extremely, very

по́иски search

пока́ for the time being; while; until

    Пока́! So long!

пока́зывать/показа́ть show, demonstrate (to)

покупа́тель customer

поку́пки shopping

пол half

    полчаса́ half-hour

    полча́шки half a cup

поле́зный useful

полёт flight

поликли́ника polyclinic

поли́тика policy

полови́на half

положи́ть place (to)

полузащи́тник halfback (sport)

получа́ть(ся)/получи́ть(ся) receive, obtain (to)

по́льзование (чем) use, utilization

по́льзоваться (чем) use, utilize (to)

поля́на glade, clearing in the woods

поме́чен(а)(о)(ы) (short adj.) marked

поменя́ть change for (to)

помеще́ния premises

помидо́р tomato

поми́мо besides, apart from

    поми́мо всего́ про́чего everything else aside

по́мниться recall, remember (to)

помога́ть/помо́чь help, assist (to)

помо́щник assistant

понима́ть/поня́ть understand (to)

поня́тие understanding, idea, concept

поня́тно (adv.) understood

попада́ть/попа́сть get to a place (to)

попра́вка correction, amendment

попро́бовать try (to)

поража́ть/порази́ть strike, amaze (to)

поре́занный (adj.) cut, sliced

поре́зать cut, slice (to)

поря́док order, sequence, procedure

поса́дка boarding, aircraft landing

посвящ(ён)(ена́)(ены́) dedicated, concerned with

посеща́ть/посети́ть visit (to)

поско́льку (adv.) inasmuch as

после́дний last

после́довательный (adj.) consecutive, successive

после́дующий next, subsequent

посошо́к staff, crook

    Пить на посошо́к! One for the road!

поста́вка delivery

поставщи́к supplier

постановле́ние decree

посыла́ть/посла́ть send (to)

посы́лка parcel, package

потерпе́ть suffer, endure, undergo (to)

потеря́ть lose (to)

потреби́тельские това́ры consumer goods

потреби́тельский (adj.) consumer

потре́бовать demand (to)

потруди́ться work for a while (to)

потряса́ющий stunning, staggering, marvelous

похо́жий (adj.) similar

почему́ why

почи́нка repair

почти́ almost

по́шлины customs

поэ́тому therefore

прав(а)(ы) (short adj.) correct, right

пра́вда truth

пра́вило rule, regulation

пра́вильно (adv.) correctly, properly

прави́тельство government

пра́во law, right

правосла́вный Orthodox faith

превосхо́дный (adj.) excellent
предло́г preposition, pretext
предлага́ть propose (to)
предложе́ние proposal, proposition, offer
предме́т subject, article, topic
предоставля́ть/предоста́вить provide, grant, give (to)
прее́мник successor
предполага́емый (adj.) presumed, planned, supposed
предполага́ть/предположи́ть presume, suppose (to)
предпочита́ть/предпоче́сть prefer (to)
представи́тельство representative office
предста́вить себе́ imagine, visualize (to)
представле́ние representation, notion
представля́ть/предста́вить present, represent, recommend
предстоя́ть lie ahead (to)
предъяви́ть present, show (to)
предыду́щий previous
преинсталли́рованный preinstalled
прекра́сно excellently, wonderfull
преподноси́ть/преподнести́ make a present of (to)
приближа́ться/прибли́зиться approach, draw near (to)
приблизи́тельно approximately
при́быль (f.) profit, gain, benefit
прибы́ть arrive (to)
приватиза́ция privatization
приве́тствовать welcome, greet (to)
приви́вка inoculation, vaccination
привлека́тельный attractive
приглаша́ть/пригласи́ть invite (to)
приглаше́ние invitation
приглашённый invited
при́город suburb
при́знак sign, symptom
призна́тельный grateful, appreciative
признава́ться confess, admit (to)
прие́зд arrival
прие́хать arrive (to)
прие́м reception, receiving, method
прийти́ arrive, come (to)
прила́вок counter, shelf
прилёт flight arrival
приме́рно approximately, exemplary
применя́ть/примени́ть apply, employ, use (to)
принадлежа́ть (кому) belong to (to)
принима́ть/приня́ть accept, receive, assume (to)
принима́ть/приня́ть во внима́ние take into consideration, keep in mind (to)
приобрета́ть/приобрести́ acquire, assume (to)
приса́живаться/присе́сть take a seat
присоедини́ться (к кому) join, be added to (to)
пристёгивать/пристегну́ть fasten, button, hook (to)
приступа́ть/приступи́ть begin, set about, proceed (to)

прису́тствовать attend (to)
приходи́ться (impersonal) have to, have occasion to (to)
прича́стие participle
причём (conj.) moreover, at that
причи́на cause, reason
прия́тный pleasant
про́бка cork, traffic jam
пробива́ться/проби́ться break through, push through (to)
проверя́ть/прове́рить check, verify, test (to)
проводи́ть/провести́ conduct, lead, guide (to)
проголода́ться
прогу́лка get hungry (to) stroll, walk, outing
прогно́з forecast, prognosis
проголода́ться get hungry, grow hungry (to)
програ́мма program
программи́ст programmer
програ́ммное обеспе́чение software
прогуля́ться go for a stroll (to)
продава́ть/прода́ть sell (to)
продаве́ц/продавщи́ца salesman (saleswoman), clerk
продвиже́ние advance, advancement
продли́ться/дли́ться last (to)
продово́льственный (adj.) food (attrib.)
продолжа́ться continue (to)
проду́кт product
проду́кты products
проду́кция production, products, output
прое́кт draft document, plan, project
прожива́ть/прожи́ть reside, live (to)
прои́грыватель lose, gamble away; perform (to)
произведе́ние work (of art or literature)
произво́дство production, manufacture, factory
прокля́тый cursed, damned
прокомпости́ровать punch a ticket, perforate (to)
происходи́ть occur, take place (to)
пропада́ть/пропа́сть disappear, be missing (to)
про́пуск pass, admission, blank, gap
проси́ть/попроси́ть request, ask for (to)
просма́тривать/посмотре́ть look over, examine (to)
проспе́кт avenue; prospectus; outline
про́сто simply, plainly
простоква́ша sour milk, yogurt
просто́рный spacious
проти́вник enemy, rival, opponent
протя́гивать/протяну́ть extend, stretch (to)
проходи́ть/пройти́ walk along, walk past, pass (to)
прохожде́ние passage, passing
процвета́ть flourish (to)
проце́нты percent interest
про́шлый (adj.) past, last
прыжо́к jump, leap

пря́мо directly, straight ahead
пункт point, station, post
пусть (particle) let
путеше́ствовать travel (to)
пу́шечный уда́р slam-kick, hit
пшени́ца wheat
пыта́ться attempt, endeavor (to)
пя́тница Friday
пя́тый fifth

Р

рабо́тать work, labor (to)
рабо́чее ме́сто workplace, job
рад(а)(ы) (short adj.) happy, glad
радиоприёмник radio receiver, radio
ра́дость joy, gladness
разбира́ть/разобра́ть analyze, examine, sort out (to)
разбира́ться/разобра́ться gain an understanding (to)
разбуди́ть awaken (to)
разгово́р conversation
раздава́ть/разда́ть hand out, distribute (to)
раздева́ться/разде́ться get undressed (to)
разде́л section, part, branch
разде́льный separate
разли́чный different, various
разнообра́зный diversified
разреша́ть/разреши́ть permit, resolve (to)
разреше́ние permission, resolution, solution
разуме́ется naturally, of course
разу́мно sensibly, rationally
разъясня́ть/разъясни́ть explain, clarify (to)
ра́ньше earlier, sooner
раскла́дка layout
расписа́ние schedule
располага́ть (чем) have available, (to)
распоря́док routine, order
распоряжа́ться (чем) handle, manage, direct (to)
распрода́жа sale, clearance
распространённый prevalent, widespread
расска́зывать/рассказа́ть relate, narrate (to)
рассла́биться relax (to)
рассчи́танный designed, intended for
расхо́ды expenses, costs
расшири́тельный expansive, broad, extended
регио́н region
региона́льный (adj.) regional
регистра́ция registration
регистри́роваться register (to)
реда́кция editorial office, edition, version
ре́дко rarely, seldom
режиссёр director (theater, film)
рейс flight, voyage
рекла́ма advertisement, publicity

рекла́мный (adj.) advertising (attrib.), promotional
рекоменда́ция recommendation
рекомендова́ть recommend (to)
реме́нь (pl. ре́мни) belt, strap
ремо́нт repair, repairs
рентгеноскопи́я X raying, X ray examination
репертуа́р repertoire
репорта́ж report, reporting
репортёр reporter
рестора́н restaurant
реце́пт recipe, prescription
речь speech
реша́ть/реши́ть decide, solve, resolve (to)
реше́ние decision, solution, judgment
ри́совый (adj.) rice
рису́нок drawing
ро́дственник relative
руби́ть chop (to)
ру́бленый (adj.) chopped
рути́на routine
руче́й stream, brook
ры́ба fish
ры́нок market
ры́ночный (adj.) market (attrib.)
ряд row, series
ря́дом (с чем/кем) next to, alongside
ря́женка baked fermented sour milk

С

с with, from
  С прие́здом! Welcome!
  с удово́льствием with pleasure
сади́ться/сесть sit down (to)
самолёт airplane
санита́рный sanitary
  санита́рный у́зел bathroom
са́харница sugar bowl
сберега́тельный (adj.) savings (attrib.)
сбор collection, gathering
сбыва́ть (кому) unload, dispose of
све́жий fresh
свеко́льник beet soup
свекро́вь mother-in-law (husband's mother)
свет light, world, society
свёкор father-in-law (husband's father)
свисте́ть whistle (to)
свисто́к whistle
свобо́дный free
своеобра́зный unique
свяще́нник priest
сда́вать экза́мен take an examination (to)
сдава́ть/сдать take, turn in, return, rent (to)
сдать экза́мен pass an examination (to)
сде́лка deal, transaction
сего́дняшний (adj.) today's
седьмо́й seventh
сейф safe
се́льский rural
  се́льское хозя́йство agriculture

сельскохозя́йственный (adj.) agricultural
семе́йный (adj.) family
семь seven
семья́ (f.) family
се́мя (n., pl. семена́) seed
сентя́брь September
серде́чно-сосу́дистый cardiovascular
середи́на middle
сере́бряный (adj.) silver
сеть (f.) network
сёмга smoked salmon, lox
сиг whitefish
сигнализа́ция alarm system
ска́нер scanner
скани́рование scanning
ски́дка discount
скла́дываться/сложи́ться take shape, develop (to)
сковорода́ frying pan
ско́лько how much
сконча́ться die (to)
ско́рость speed, velocity
скульпту́ра sculpture
следи́ть follow, watch, keep track (to)
сле́довать (кому) follow (to)
сле́дующий (adj.) next, following
сли́вки cream
сли́зистый (adj.) mucus, slimy
    сли́зистая оболо́чка mucus membrane
словоупотребле́ние word usage
сло́жно (adv.) complicated
слу́чай case, incidence, occurrence
случа́йно (adv.) by chance, by accident
слу́шатель listener, student
слы́шать/услы́шать hear (to)
смета́на sour cream
смири́ться reconcile oneself to, yield (to)
смотре́ть/посмотре́ть look at (to)
сни́женный (adj.) reduced, lowered
снижа́ться/сни́зиться come down, drop, fall (to)
снима́ть/снять take down, remove (to)
сно́ва again, anew, once again
собира́емость (f.) collection
собира́ть/собра́ть gather, assemble, harvest (to)
соблюда́ть (дие́ту) observe, keep (a diet)
собо́р cathedral
со́бственный one's own, proper
соверша́ть/соверши́ть complete, commit (to)
соверше́нно completely, entirely, utterly
    соверше́нно ве́рно absolutely correct
соверше́нный (вид) perfective (aspect)
сове́товать/посове́товать advise (to)
совме́стный joint, combined
    совместное предприя́тие joint venture
совреме́нный contemporary
совсе́м quite
    совсе́м не not at all
    не совсе́м not quite

совхо́з state-owned farm
сок juice
соль (f.) salt
сомне́ние doubt
сообще́ние communication, message
соотве́тствующий (adj.) corresponding, appropriate
сопе́рник rival
сопровожда́ть accompany, escort (to)
сопровожде́ние accompanying
сорт sort, kind, brand, quality
сосе́д neighbor
составле́ние compilation, drawing up
составля́ть/соста́вить compile, draw up, form (to)
состоя́ние status, condition, state
состоя́ть comprise, consist of (to)
сотру́дник associate
спа́льня (f.) bedroom
спад drop, fall, decline, recession
спаси́бо thank you
спекуля́нт speculator, opportunist
спи́сок list
споко́йный calm, quiet, tranquil
спра́вочный (adj.) reference, information
спра́шивать/спроси́ть ask (to)
справля́ть/спра́вить celebrate (to)
справля́ться/спра́виться cope with, handle (a task) (to)
спрос demand
спуска́ться/спусти́ться descend, go down (to)
спустя́ after
спу́тница traveling companion
сра́внивать/сравни́ть compare (to)
сравни́тельно (adv.) comparatively
срок period of time, deadline
сро́чный urgent; for a fixed period
    сро́чный вклад time-limit deposit
ста́лкиваться run into, encounter (to)
стажиро́вка practical training
станови́ться/стать become, stand, get (to)
ста́нция station
стара́ться/постара́ться try (to)
старина́ ancient times
ста́рый old
статья́ article, clause
стациона́рный stationary, permanent
стенд stand
сте́пень (f.) degree
стерилиза́ция sterilization
стиль (m.) style
стира́льный порошо́к soap powder, detergent
сто́имость (f.) cost
стоя́ть stand (to)
столбня́к tetanus
стол table
    столо́вый набо́р table setting
столо́вая dining room
сто́лько so much, so many
сторона́ side
страхо́вка insurance

стра́шный (adj.) frightful
стро́гий (adj.) strict, stern
стюарде́сса flight attendant (fem.)
суббо́та Saturday
субти́тр subtitle
суд court, trial
суди́ть judge, try, umpire (to)
судья́ (m.) judge
су́мка purse, bag
суперма́ркет supermarket
супру́га spouse, wife
су́тки twenty-four-hour period
сходи́ть/сойти́ descend, step off, go and
    come back (to)
сце́на stage
счёт account, bill
счита́ть count, consider (to)
съедо́бный (adj.) edible
сы́воротка serum
сы́гранность (f.) teamwork, harmony
сыр cheese
сюже́т plot, subject matter

Т

тайм period (of a game)
такси́ (n.) taxi
тамо́женник customs official
тамо́женный (adj.) customs
таре́лка plate
тари́ф rate, tariff
творо́г cottage cheese
теку́щий (adj.) current, present
телеви́зор television set
тележурна́л newscast
телефо́н telephone
тем не ме́нее nevertheless
темп pace, rate, tempo
тенденцио́зность biased approach,
    tendentiousness
тепе́рь now
теря́ть/потеря́ть lose (to)
тесть (m.) father-in-law (wife's father)
те́хника technology, electronic gadgets
техни́ческий technical
    техни́ческие характери́стики technical
    specifications
тёплый warm
тмин caraway
това́рищество association, company
това́ры goods
толкова́ние interpretation, commentary
то́лько only
топлёный baked (of milk)
торго́вый (adj.) commercial, trade
    (attrib.)
торт cake
тост toast
то́чка period, dot, point
   то́чка зре́ния viewpoint
то́чность accuracy, precision
тра́ктор tractor
тракто́вка interpretation, treatment
трибу́на stands (stadium)
три́ста three hundred
тропи́нка path

тру́бка tube, pipe; telephone receiver
труд labor, toil
тру́дно (adj.) difficult
туале́т toilet, rest room, vanity
тяжёлый (adj.) severe, serious, grave,
    heavy

У

убежда́ть/убеди́ть convince (to)
убива́ть/уби́ть kill (to)
убо́рочный (adj.) harvesting (attrib.)
уве́рен/а/ы (short adj.) sure, confident
увлека́тельный absorbing, fascinating
у́гол corner, angle
угоща́ть/угости́ть treat (to)
угоща́ться partake, help oneself to (to)
удава́ться/уда́ться be successful (to)
удаля́ть/удали́ть remove, take away (to)
уда́р blow, hit, stroke
удивле́ние surprise
удо́бно (adv.) conveniently, comfortably
удо́бства amenities, conveniences
удовлетворе́ние satisfaction
удосто́ить(ся) confer, award (be
    awarded) (to)
удостовере́ние certification
    води́тельское удостовере́ние driver's
    license
у́жин dinner
узнава́ть/узна́ть recognize, find out (to)
уик-э́нд weekend
указа́ние (указа́ния) indication
    (instructions)
ука́зывать/указа́ть point out, suggest,
    indicate (to)
укрепля́ть/укрепи́ть strengthen,
    reinforce (to)
ула́вливать/улови́ть catch, pick up a
    signal (to)
умира́ть/умере́ть die (to)
унесённый (p.p.p.) gone, taken away
уноси́ть/унести́ carry away, carry off
упако́вка packing, packaging
упомина́ть/упомяну́ть mention (to)
управля́ющий manager
упражне́ние exercise
упроща́ть/упрости́ть simplify,
    oversimplify (to)
урожа́й harvest
уско́ренный accelerated
ускоря́ть/уско́рить accelerate
усло́вие condition
услу́ги services
успева́ть/успе́ть have time to, manage
    (to)
успе́х success
успе́шный successful
устано́вка installation; plant; setting
устра́ивать/устро́ить(ся) arrange (to)
утоми́тельный tiring
уточне́ние clarification
утра́чивать/утра́тить lose (to)
у́тро morning
у́тром (adv.) in the morning
участко́вый (adj.) district

уче́бник textbook
учи́ть teach, learn (to)
учи́ться/научи́ться be studying, learn (to)

Ф

фа́ктор factor
фарфо́р porcelain
февра́ль February
фе́рма farm
филиа́л branch (of an institution, store)
форма́льность (f.) formality
форс-мажо́р act of God
фру́кты fruit

Х

хвата́ть seize (to)
хлеб bread
хло́пок cotton, cotton plant
хло́поты troubles; chores; worries
ходи́ть go (to), walk (to)
  ходи́ть за поку́пками go shopping (to)
холоди́льник refrigerator
холо́дный (adj.) cold
хоте́ть/захоте́ть want (to)
хране́ние storage, safekeeping
храни́ть keep, save, store (to)
хрен horseradish

Ц

ца́рский czarist, regal, fit for a king (lit. a czar)
це́лый (adj.) whole, entire
цена́ price
цензу́ра censorship
це́нность (f.) **(це́нности)** value (valuables)
центр center
центра́льный (adj.) central
це́рковь (f.) church

Ч

чаевы́е gratuity, tip
чай tea
ча́йная ло́жка teaspoon
ча́йник teapot
час hour
части́чно partially
ча́стный (adj.) private, particular
ча́сто often, frequently
ча́шечка small cup
ча́шка cup
чек check, slip, receipt
челове́к person
чемода́н suitcase
через over, across, after

чересчу́р (adv.) too, too much
чернови́к rough draft
чесно́к garlic
че́тверо four (collective)
чёрный (adj.) black
чёткий (adj.) concise, clear, distinct
число́ number, date, day
что-нибудь anything, something
что-то something
чтобы in order to
чу́вствовать себя́ feel (in a certain way)
  Как вы себя́ чу́вствуете? How do you feel?
чуть hardly, scarcely

Ш

шве́йный (adj.) sewing
шеде́вр masterpiece
шесть six
шкату́лка small box
шко́льни(к)(ца) schoolboy (schoolgirl)
шля́па hat
шнурки́ shoelaces
шпиль spire, steeple
шприц syringe
шрифт font, typeface
шта́нга crossbar (sport)
штрафно́й (adj.) fine, penalty (attrib.)

Э

экза́мен examination
экземпля́р copy, specimen
эконо́мика ecnomics, economy
экску́рсия excursion
экспози́ция display, exhibit
экстренный (adj.) emergency, urgent
электро́нный electronic
  электро́нная по́чта electronic mail, e-mail
электроприбо́ры electric appliances
эмули́ровать emulate (to)
эта́ж floor, story

Ю

юри́ст attorney, lawyer
юриди́ческий (adj.) juridical, legal, judicial
юрисконсу́льт legal adviser

Я

я́блоко apple
я́блочный (adj.) apple
я́годы berries
яйцо́ egg
я́сность clarity

ENGLISH-RUSSIAN

A

a few, a little немно́го (adv.)
about около
abroad (location) за грани́цей
abroad (direction) за грани́цу
absolutely безусло́вно
   absolutely correct соверше́нно ве́рно
absorbing увлека́тельный
accelerate (to) ускоря́ть/уско́рить
accelerated уско́ренный
accept (to) принима́ть/приня́ть
accessible досту́п(ен)(на)(ный) (short adj.)
accessible досту́пный
accompany, escort (to) сопровожда́ть
accompanying сопровожде́ние
account счёт
accuracy то́чность
acquaint (to) знако́мить/познако́мить
acquire (to) приобрета́ть/приобрести́
activities заня́тия (pl.)
actually действи́тельно
add (to) добавля́ть/доба́вить
additional дополни́тельный (adj.)
additionally дополни́тельно
address адрес
address (to) обраща́ться/обрати́ться
adult взро́слый
advance продвиже́ние
advertisement рекла́ма
advertising рекла́мный (adj.)
advise (to) сове́товать/посове́товать
after спустя́
after через
afterward впосле́дствии
again сно́ва
agency аге́нтство
agonize (to) боле́ть (за что/кого)
agree to договариваться/договори́ться
agreement догово́р
agriculture се́льское хозя́йство
agricultural сельскохозя́йственный
ahead впереди́ (чего/кого)
air (adj.) возду́шный
airplane самолёт
airport аэропорт
alarm сигнализа́ция
alcoholic (adj.) алкого́льный
all весь, кру́глый
all day кру́глые су́тки
allocate (to) выделять/вы́делить
almost почти́
alongside вдоль
always всегда́
amazing изуми́тельный
amenities удо́бства
amusing (adv.) заба́вно
analysis ана́лиз
analyze (to) разбира́ть/разобрать

announcer ди́ктор
annual ежего́дный
another ино́й
answer отве́т
   answering machine автоотве́тчик
antique (adj.) антиква́рный
any любо́й
anyone кто́-нибудь
anything что-нибудь (indef. pron.)
apartment кварти́ра
   apartment house complex бло́чный дом
   apartment house intercom домофо́н
appetite аппети́т
appetizers заку́ски
apple я́блоко
appoint (to) назнача́ть/назна́чить
approach подъе́зд
approach (to) подхо́дить/подойти́ (come up to); приближа́ться/прибли́зиться (draw near)
approval одобре́ние
approve (to) одобря́ть/одо́брить
approximately приблизи́тельно; приме́рно
arbitration арбитра́ж
architecture архитекту́ра
armed оруже́йный (adj.)
arrange (to) обустра́ивать/обустро́ить; устра́ивать/устро́ить(ся); выстра́ивать/вы́строить
arrangement обустро́йство
arrival прие́зд
arrive (to) прие́хать; прибы́ть; прийти́
artist арти́ст
as before по-пре́жнему
as far as наско́лько
ask (to) спра́шивать/спроси́ть
assignment зада́ние
assignment (business trip) командиро́вка
assistant помо́щник
associate сотру́дник
association това́рищество
assortment ассортиме́нт
at по; на; в
   at least по кра́йней ме́ре
attack (to) напада́ть/напа́сть
attempt (to) пыта́ться
attend (to) прису́тствовать
attention внима́ние
attentively внима́тельно
attorney юри́ст
attractive привлека́тельный
audio звуко-
   audio recording звукоза́пись
   audio transmission звукопереда́ча
avenue проспе́кт
avoid (to) избежа́ть
awaken (to) буди́ть/разбуди́ть (кого)
award (to) удосто́ить

B

baked печёный (adj.)
ball мяч
bankruptcy банкро́тство
basic, principal основно́й (adj.)
bathe (to) купа́ться
bathroom санита́рный узел, ванная
be (to) быть
  be concerned (to)
    забо́титься/позабо́титься
  be concerned about (to) позабо́титься
  be dated (to) дати́роваться
  be delayed (to) заде́рживаться
  be delighted (to) восторга́ться
  be distinguished by (to) отлича́ться
  be engaged in (to) занима́ться
  be exhorbitant (to) куса́ться
  be finished (to) ко́нчиться
  be in need of (to) нужда́ться
  be interested in (to) интересова́ть(ся)
  be late (to) опа́здывать/опозда́ть
  be liberated (to)
    освобожда́ться/освободи́ться
  be located (to) находи́ться/найти́сь
  be noticed (to) отмеча́ться
  be spoiled (to) испо́ртиться
  be studying (to) учи́ться/научи́ться
  be successful (to) удава́ться/уда́ться
become ill (to) заболева́ть/заболе́ть
become, stand, get (to)
  станови́ться/стать
bedroom спа́льня (f.)
begin (to) начина́ть/нача́ть;
  приступа́ть/приступи́ть
beginning нача́ло
behind позади́ (adv.)
believe (to) ве́рить/пове́рить
bell звоно́к
belong to (to) принадлежа́ть (кому)
belt реме́нь (pl. ре́мни)
beneficial вы́годный
berries ягоды
besides кро́ме
beverage напи́ток
bind, tie (to) завяза́ть
black чёрный (adj.)
blow a whistle (to) дать свисто́к
boil (to) кипяти́ть
boss нача́льник
bottle буты́лка
branch филиа́л (of an institution, store);
  ветвь (of a tree)
brass лату́нный (adj.)
bread хлеб
break переры́в
break (to) лома́ть/слома́ть
break off (to) отла́мывать/отломи́ть
  break the habit (to) отвы́кнуть
  break through (to)
    пробива́ться/проби́ться
breakfast за́втрак
breakfast (to) за́втракать/поза́втракать
bride неве́ста

bridegroom жени́х
bring (to) заводи́ть/завести́
  bring to a boil (to) доводи́ть до кипе́ния
brother-in-law зять
budget бюдже́т
buffet буфе́т
building зда́ние
  building entrance подъе́зд здания
built-in встро́енный
bun бу́лочка
bundle па́чка
burden обу́за
bus авто́бус
business бизнес; дело
  business card визи́тка; визи́тная
    ка́рточка
  businessman/woman бизнесме́н/ка
busy за́нят(а)(ы) (short adj.); за́нятый;
  занято́й (adj.)
but зато́
butter ма́сло
by по; к
  by chance случа́йно
  by the way, ме́жду про́чим
  by turn по о́череди

C

cake торт, пиро́жное
call (to) звать/позва́ть
  call by phone (to) звони́ть/позвони́ть
calm (adj.) споко́йный
can ба́нка
cancel, abolish (to) отменя́ть/отмени́ть
capital investment капиталовложе́ние
cardiovascular серде́чно-сосу́дистый
careful осторо́жный
carrots морко́вь (f.)
carry (to) вози́ть/везти́
  carry away (to) уноси́ть/унести́
case слу́чай (occurrence); паде́ж
  (grammar)
cash нали́чные де́ньги
cassette кассе́та
catch (to) лови́ть/пойма́ть; захвати́ть
  catch a signal (to) ула́вливать/улови́ть
  catch sight of (to) уви́деть, заме́тить
cathedral собо́р
cause причи́на
caviar икра́
celebrate (to) справля́ть/спра́вить;
  пра́здновать
censorship цензу́ра
censure (to) осужда́ть/осуди́ть
center центр
central центра́льный
certainly наверняка́
change (to) меня́ть/поменять
change clothes (to)
  переодева́ться/переоде́ться
channel кана́л
check чек
check (to) проверя́ть/прове́рить
cheese сыр
chicken ку́рица

children де́ти
choose (to) избира́ть/избра́ть
chop (to) руби́ть
chopped ру́бленый (adj.)
church це́рковь (f.)
city го́род
   city block кварта́л
clarification уточне́ние
clarity я́сность
clear чёткий
clever ло́вкий
client клие́нт; зака́зчик
close (to) закрыва́ть/закры́ть
closely вплотну́ю
cold (adj.) холо́дный
colleague колле́га
collector коллекционе́р
combination комбина́ция
combine (noun) комба́йн (agriculture)
commentary коммента́рий
commentator коммента́тор
commercial (adj.) торго́вый
communication сообще́ние
companion спу́тник(ца)
company компа́ния
comparatively сравни́тельно (adv.)
compare (to) сра́внивать/сравни́ть
compel (to) вынужда́ть, вы́нудить
compilation составле́ние
compile (to) составля́ть/соста́вить
complete (to) зака́нчивать/зако́нчить;
   соверша́ть/соверши́ть
   complete paperwork (to)
   оформля́ть(ся)/офо́рмить(ся)
completely соверше́нно; вполне́ (adv.)
completion заверше́ние
complicated сло́жно (adv.)
complication осложне́ние
compromise компроми́сс
computer компью́тер
concerning насчёт
condition усло́вие
conduct (to) проводи́ть/провести́
conference hall конфере́нц-зал
confess (to) призна́ться
connection подключе́ние
consecutive после́довательный (adj.)
consist (to) состоя́ть
consumer потреби́тельский (adj.)
   consumer goods потреби́тельские
   това́ры
contemporary совреме́нный
continue (to) продолжа́ться
contract контра́кт
contribution поже́ртвование
conveniently удо́бно (adv.)
conversation разгово́р
convince (to) убежда́ть/убеди́ть
cooked варёный
cope with (to) справля́ться/спра́виться
copper ме́дный (adj.)
copy экземпля́р
corn кукуру́за
corner у́гол

corporate корпорати́вный
correct прав(а́)(ы́) (short adj.)
correction попра́вка
correctly пра́вильно
correspondence (adj.)
   корреспонде́нтский
corresponding соотве́тствующий
corridor коридо́р
cost сто́имость (f.)
cost (to) обходи́ться/обойти́сь
   cost a pretty penny (to) влета́ть в
   копе́ечку
cotton хло́пок
   cotton plant хлопча́тник
count (to) счита́ть
counterattack контрата́ка
counterfeit подде́льный
court суд
cream сли́вки
credit card креди́тная ка́рта/ка́рточка
crops культу́ры
crushed дроблёный
culinary кулина́рный
cup ча́шка
current теку́щий
cursed прокля́тый
curvature кривизна́
customer покупа́тель
customs по́шлины
customs (adj.) тамо́женный
   customs official тамо́женник
cut (to) поре́зать
cut (adj.) поре́занный (sliced)
Cyrillic alphabet кири́ллица

D

daily ежедне́вный
dairy моло́чный (adj.)
darken (to) омрачи́ть
date число́
daughter дочь
   daughter-in-law неве́стка
day день
   day off выходно́й (день)
   days off (weekend) выходны́е
deal сде́лка
dear дорого́й, уважа́емый
decide (to) реша́ть/реши́ть
decision, solution, judgment реше́ние
declaration деклара́ция (customs form)
declare (to) объявля́ть/объяви́ть
decline спад
decree постановле́ние
dedicated посвящ(ён)(ена́)(ены́)
deep глубо́кий
defensive оборони́тельный
deficit дефици́т
definite определённый
degree сте́пень (f.); гра́дус (temperature)
delay опозда́ние
delight восто́рг
delivery доста́вка; поста́вка
demand спрос
demand (to) потре́бовать

depart (to) вы́ехать
department отде́л
departure вы́езд
deposit зада́ток
descend (to) спуска́ться/спусти́ться; сходи́ть/сойти́
designed for рассчи́танный
despair (to) отча́иваться/отча́яться
detail дета́ль (f.)
detergent стира́льный порошо́к
diagnostics диагно́стика
die (to) умира́ть/умере́ть; сконча́ться
diet дие́та
different разли́чный
difficult тру́дно
dining room столо́вая
dinner ужин
diphtheria дифтери́я
direct (to) направля́ть/напра́вить; распоряжа́ться (чем)
director режиссёр (theater, film)
disappear (to) исчеза́ть/исче́знуть; пропада́ть/пропа́сть
discount ски́дка
discuss (to) бесе́довать/побесе́довать; обсужда́ть/обсуди́ть
disease боле́знь (f.)
dish блю́до
display экспози́ция
disposable однора́зовый
disruption наруше́ние
distant да́льний
distress огорче́ние
distribute (to) раздава́ть/разда́ть
district участко́вый (adj.)
distrust недове́рие
diversified разнообра́зный
division отделе́ние
do (to) де́лать/сде́лать
domestic оте́чественный
Don't mention it. Не́ за что.
doubt сомне́ние
drawing рису́нок
drink (to) пить/вы́пить
driver води́тель; шофёр
driver's license води́тельское удостовере́ние
drop by (to) заходи́ть/зайти́
dubbed, duplicated дубли́рование
duty до́лжность (f.)
duty manager дежу́рный администра́тор

E

each ка́ждый
earlier зара́нее; ра́ньше (sooner)
earn (to) зараба́тывать
eat (to) есть (ем, ешь, ест, еди́м, едя́т); ку́шать
eat one's fill (to) наеда́ться/нае́сться
eat supper (to) обе́дать/пообе́дать
economics эконо́мика
editorial office реда́кция
egg яйцо́
eggplant баклажа́н

eggplant (adj.) баклажа́нный
eight во́семь
electric электри́ческий
electric appliances электроприбо́ры
electronic mail, e-mail электро́нная по́чта
elevator лифт
embrace (to) обнима́ться
emperor импера́тор
emulate (to) эмули́ровать
endure (to) переноси́ть/перенести́
enemy проти́вник
engraving гравиро́вка
enough дово́льно
enter (to) вписа́ть
entrance вход
envelope оболо́чка
envy (to) зави́довать/позави́довать
equalize (to) выра́вниваться/вы́ровняться
equipment обору́дование
erotica эро́тика
especially осо́бенно
essentially необходи́мо
European европе́йский
evening ве́чер
everything всё
everything else aside поми́мо всего́ про́чего
examination осмо́тр; экза́мен
example образе́ц
excellent превосхо́дный
excellently отли́чно прекра́сно
exception исключе́ние
exchange of currency обме́н
exchange for (to) обме́нивать (на что)
exclude (to) исключи́ть
excursion экску́рсия
exercise упражне́ние
exit вы́езд
exit (to) выходи́ть/вы́йти
expansive обши́рный
expectation ожида́ние
expenses расхо́ды
expensive дорого́й
expiration истече́ние
explain (to) разъясня́ть/ разъясни́ть
export вы́воз
export (to) вывози́ть/вы́везти
extend (to) протя́гивать/протяну́ть
extra ли́шний
extraordinary необыча́йный
extreme кра́йность (f.)
extremely позаре́з

F

factor фа́ктор
fall (to) снижа́ться/сни́зиться
false ло́жный
familiarize (to) ознако́мить
family семья́ (f.)
family (adj.) семе́йный
famous знамени́тый

fan боле́льщик
far далеко́
farm фе́рма
fasten (to) пристёгивать/
　пристегну́ть
father оте́ц
　father-in-law свёкор (husband's father);
　　тесть (m.) (wife's father)
fear боя́знь (f.)
fear (to) боя́ться
feel (in a certain way) (to) чу́вствовать
　себя́
fill out (to) заполня́ть/запо́лнить
film фильм (movie); плёнка (photog.)
　film festival кинофестива́ль (m.)
final оконча́тельный
finally наконе́ц
find out (to) узнава́ть/узна́ть
fine (adj.) штрафно́й
fine (to) оштрафова́ть
fingers па́льчики
finish (to) конча́ть/ко́нчить
　finish writing (to) допи́сывать/дописа́ть
fire ого́нь (m.); пожа́р
fish ры́ба
flight полёт; рейс
　flight arrival прилёт
　flight attendant бортпроводни́(к)ца;
　　стюарде́сса (f.)
floor эта́ж (story)
flourish (to) процвета́ть
fly up to (to) долете́ть
follow (to) сле́довать (someone); следи́ть
　(keep track)
font шрифт
food (noun) еда́
food (adj.) продово́льственный
　food store гастроно́м
for для; по; на; к; за
　for the better к лу́чшему
　for the first time впервы́е
　for the most part по бо́льшей ча́сти
　for the night на́ ночь
　for the period of в тече́ние (чего)
　for the time being, пока́
　for the worse к ху́дшему
foreign (adj.) зарубе́жный; иностра́нный
foreign currency валю́та (n.); валю́тный
　(adj.)
foreigner иностра́н(ец)(ка))(цы)
forest лес
form анке́та
formality форма́льность (f.)
fortunately к сча́стью
forward вперёд
found (to) основа́ть
four че́тверо (collective)
free свобо́дный
fresh све́жий
Friday пя́тница
fried жа́реный, зажа́ренный (adj.)
friend друг (pl. друзья́)
frightful стра́шный (adj.)
fritter ола́дья (f.)
from из (чего)

fruit фру́кт(ы)
furniture ме́бель (f.)

G

gain an understanding (to)
　разбира́ться/разобра́ться
gap про́пуск
Garden Ring (Boulevard Ring) Садо́вое
　кольцо́
garlic чесно́к
gastrointestinal желу́дочно-кише́чый
gates воро́та
gather (to) собира́ть/собра́ть
gathering сбор
general о́бщий
　generally accepted общепри́нятый
genuine по́длинный
get (to) достава́ть/доста́ть;
　получа́ть/получи́ть
　get excited, aroused (to) возбужда́ться
　get hungry (to) проголода́ться
　get stuck (to) застрева́ть/застря́ть
　get to a place (to) попада́ть/попа́сть
　get undressed (to)
　　раздева́ться/разде́ться
　get up (to) встава́ть/встать
gift пода́рок
give (to) дава́ть/дать
give (to) подава́ть/пода́ть
glare отсве́чивание
go (to) идти́/пойти́
　go for a stroll (to) прогуля́ться
　go hungry (to) проголода́ться
　go shopping (to) ходи́ть за поку́пками
goalkeeper врата́рь
golden золото́й
gone унесённый (p.p.p.)
goods това́ры
government прави́тельство
grammar грамма́тика
grandiose грандио́зный
grandmother ба́бушка
grateful призна́тельный
gratitude благода́рность
grave моги́ла
greasy жи́рный
green зелёный
greenhorn новичо́к
guarantee гара́нтия
guest гость

H

half полови́на
　half a cup полча́шки
　half-hour полчаса́
halibut па́лтус
hall зал
handsome краси́вый
hanging навесно́й (adj.)
happy рад(а)(ы) (short adj.)
hard твёрдый (not soft); тру́дный
　(difficult)
　hard drive (computer) винче́стер
　hard-boiled egg яйцо́ вкруту́ю
hardly вряд ли; чуть

harvest урожа́й
harvesting (adj.) убо́рочный
hat шля́па
have (to) име́ть
    have a bite to eat (to) перекуси́ть
    have available, (to) располага́ть (чем)
    have in mind (to) име́ть в виду́
    have time to (to) успева́ть/успе́ть
have to (to) приходи́ться (impersonal)
head for (to) направля́ться/
    напра́виться
health здоро́вье
hear (to) слы́шать/услы́шать
    hear out (to) вы́слушать
height, altitude высота́
help (to) помога́ть/помо́чь
high высо́кий
    high-speed (adj.) высокоскоростно́й
hire (to) нанима́ть/наня́ть
hit уда́р
home дом
homeward домо́й (adv.)
honey мёд
hopeless безнадёжный
horse ло́шадь (f.)
hot горя́чий
hotel гости́ница
hour час
how как
    how much ско́лько
however впро́чем;
hustler деля́га
hybrid гибри́д

I

icon ико́на
ill больно́й
image изображе́ние
imagine (to) предста́вить себе́
immediately непосре́дственно
immunization (adj.)
    иммунизацио́нный
import (noun) ввоз
imported импорти́руемый (p.p.p.)
impression впечатле́ние
impressive впечатля́ющий
in в, на
    in addition кро́ме того́
    in favor of в по́льзу
    in general в о́бщем, вообще́
    in order to чтобы
    in particular в ча́стности
    in perfect order в ажу́ре
    in proportion to по ме́ре (чего)
    in the evening ве́чером
    in the morning у́тром (adv.)
    in the spring весно́й
    in the summer ле́том
inability неспосо́бность (f.)
inasmuch as (adv.) поско́льку
inch дюйм
incidentally кста́ти
include (to) включа́ть/включи́ть
income подохо́дный (adj.); дохо́д (noun)
incomparable бесподо́бный

inconvenience неудо́бство
increase повыше́ние
incredibly невероя́тно
indicate (to) ука́зывать/указа́ть
individual отде́льный (adj.)
infection зараже́ние
infectious инфекцио́нный
    infectious diseases инфекцио́нные
    боле́зни
inflation инфля́ция
inform (to) осведомля́ть/осведоми́ть
information информа́ция
informed осведомлён/а (short adj.)
inheritance насле́дство
initial изнача́льный
install (to) устана́вливать/установи́ть
installation устано́вка
instructions указа́ния
insurance страхо́вка
intercom интерко́м
interfere (to) меша́ть/помеша́ть
interior (adj.) вну́тренний
international междунаро́дный
interpretation толкова́ние; тракто́вка
intersect (to) пересека́ть/пересе́чь
invitation приглаше́ние
invite (to) приглаша́ть/пригласи́ть
invited приглашённый
irrevocable безотзы́вный
issue изда́ние
issue (to) выпуска́ть/вы́пустить
item изде́лие

J

jar ба́нка
join (to) присоедини́ться (к кому)
joint (adj.) совме́стный
    joint venture совместное предприя́тие
journalist журнали́ст
joy ра́дость
judge судья́ (m.)
judge (to) суди́ть
judicial юриди́ческий (adj.)
juice сок
jump прыжо́к
jump (to) вска́кивать/вскочи́ть

K

keep (to) храни́ть
keep (to) соблюда́ть (диету)
keep informed (to) держа́ть в ку́рсе
key ключ
keyboard клавиату́ра
kill (to) убива́ть/уби́ть
kind любе́зный (adj.)
kitchen ку́хня
know (to) знать

L

labor труд
land земля́
laptop лэпто́п, ла́птоп
large большо́й
last после́дний
last (to) дли́ться/продли́ться

later по́зже
law пра́во
lawyer юри́ст
layout раскла́дка
learn (to) вы́учить
leather (adj.) ко́жаный
leave (to) оставля́ть/оста́вить
lecture ле́кция
lemon лимо́н (noun.); лимо́нный (adj.)
lessor арендода́тель
let пусть (particle)
letter письмо́; бу́ква (of alphabet)
　letter of credit, L/C аккредити́в
lid кры́шка
lie (to) лежа́ть (to position); врать лгать
　(to make a false statement)
lie ahead (to) предстоя́ть
light (a cigarette) (to) закури́ть
like (to) нра́виться/понра́виться
limitation ограниче́ние
line о́чередь
liquidity ликви́дность (f.)
list спи́сок
listener слу́шатель
live (to) прожива́ть/прожи́ть
loan заём
long до́лгий; дли́нный
　long ago давно́
look (to) смотре́ть/посмотре́ть
　look around (to) огля́дываться
　look at (to) взгля́дывать/взгляну́ть
　look over (to)
　　просма́тривать/просмотре́ть
lose (to) теря́ть/потеря́ть;
　утра́чивать/утра́тить; прои́грывать
　(gambling)
love (to) люби́ть
lowered сни́женный
lucidity дохо́дчивость (f.)

M

machine маши́на
main гла́вный
maintenance обслу́живание
majority большинство́
make (noun) ма́рка (trade name)
make (to) делать
　make a present of (to)
　　преподноси́ть/преподнести́
　make inquiries (to) наводи́ть/навести́
　　спра́вки
manager ме́неджер; управля́ющий
maneuver манёвр
manner о́браз
manufactured изгото́вленный
marinated марино́ванный
marked поме́чен(а)(о)(ы) (short adj.)
market ры́нок; ры́ночный (adj.)
masterpiece шеде́вр
mayonnaise майоне́з
medicine лека́рство
meet (to) встреча́ть/встре́тить
meeting встре́ча
memorize (to) запо́мнить
memory па́мять (f.)

mention (to) упомина́ть/упомяну́ть
merit (to) заслу́живать/заслужи́ть
meter метр
middle середи́на
milk молоко́
mislaid зало́жен(а) (imp.)
money де́ньги
　money order де́нежный перево́д
monitor монито́р (computer)
monument па́мятник
moreover причём (conj.)
morning утро
mother мать
　mother-in-law свекро́вь (husband's
　　mother); тёща (wife's mother)
move (to) перее́хать
　move away from (to) отхо́дить/отойти́
movement, traffic движе́ние
Mrs. госпожа́
Mr. господи́н
much намно́го
mushrooms грибы́
must до́лжен/должна́/должны́
mutual obligation взаимообя́занность
　(f.)
mutually взаи́мно

N

narcotics нарко́тики
naturally разуме́ется
near бли́зко
nearby (adj.) близлежа́щий
nearest ближа́йший
necessary на́до (adv.); ну́жный (adj.)
necessity, need необходи́мость (f.)
negotiations перегово́ры
neighbor сосе́д
nest гнездо́
network сеть (f.)
nevertheless тем не ме́нее
new но́вый
　new home новосе́лье
newlyweds молодожёны
news но́вости
next ря́дом (с чем/кем) (adv.); сле́дующий
　(adj.); очередно́й; после́дующий
night ночь (f.)
nine де́вять
noble благоро́дный
normal норма́льный (adj.)
notes заме́тки
nothing ничего́
now тепе́рь
number число́; но́мер (of a hotel room,
　edition)
numerous многочи́сленный
nutrition пита́ние

O

oat (adj.) овся́ный
objective (adj.) объекти́вный
obligation обя́занность (f.)
occupy (to) занима́ть/заня́ть
occur (to) происходи́ть/произойти́
odor, smell за́пах

of course коне́чно
office офис; кабине́т
often ча́сто; зачасту́ю
oil ма́сло
old ста́рый
olive (adj.) оли́вковый
on на, над
    on the contrary наоборо́т
    on the right впра́во
    on time во́время
one's own со́бственный
onions лук
only то́лько; еди́нственный
open (to) открыва́ть/откры́ть
opportunist спекуля́нт
orange (noun) апельси́н
order поря́док
order распоря́док
order (to) зака́зывать/заказа́ть
organize (to) организова́ть
Orthodox faith правосла́вный
outdistance (to) обгоня́ть/обогна́ть
overact (to) переи́грывать
overnight (to) переночева́ть

P

pace темп
package паке́т; посы́лка
packaging упако́вка
paid опла́чиваемый (p.p.p)
pair па́ра
palace дворе́ц
parking lot автостоя́нка
partake (to) угоща́ться
partially части́чно (adv.)
participle прича́стие
particular осо́бый (adj.)
partly отча́сти
partner партнёр
pass (sports, cards) пас
pass (admission) про́пуск
pass (to) пасова́ть (trans.);
    проходи́ть/пройти́
    pass an exam (to) сдать экза́мен
passage прохо́д
passenger пассажи́р
passport па́спорт
past (adj.) про́шлый
pastry пиро́жное
path тропи́нка
patient (noun) больно́й
pavilion павильо́н
pay (to) выпла́чивать/вы́платить
paying пла́тный
payment опла́та; вы́плата
peas горо́х
peculiarity осо́бенность (f.)
pepper пе́рец
percent interest проце́нты
perfective (aspect) соверше́нный (вид)
period тайм (of a game); срок (of time)
permission разреше́ние
permit (to) разреша́ть/разреши́ть
person челове́к

personnel персона́л
pessimist пессими́ст
pick up, collect (to) забира́ть/забра́ть
picnic пикни́к
piece кусо́к
place (to) класть/положи́ть
    place under (to)
    подкла́дывать/подложи́ть
place ме́сто
plan (to) плани́ровать/ заплани́ровать
plate таре́лка
player игро́к
pleasant прия́тный
please пожа́луйста
pledge oneself (to) обяза́ться
plot сюже́т
point пункт
policy поли́тика
poor бе́дный
poorly пло́хо
porcelain фарфо́р
possess (to) владе́ть; облада́ть
poster афи́ша
potato карто́фель (m.); карто́шка
pour (to) налива́ть/нали́ть
practical training стажиро́вка
preinstalled преинсталли́рованный
prefer (to) предпочита́ть/предпоче́сть
premises помеще́ния
preparatory подготови́тельный (adj.)
prepare oneself (to)
    гото́виться/пригото́виться
preposition предло́г
prescription реце́пт
presence нали́чие
present (to) предъяви́ть
press (to) нажима́ть/нажа́ть
press coverage освеще́ние собы́тий
pressing нажа́тие
presume (to)
    предполага́ть/предположи́ть
presumed (adj.) предполага́емый
previous предыду́щий
price цена́
priest свяще́нник
private ча́стный (adj.)
privatization приватиза́ция
probably наве́рное
processing оформле́ние
product проду́кт
production, произво́дство (process);
    проду́кция (output)
products проду́кты
profit при́быль (f.)
prognosis прогно́з
program програ́мма
programmer программи́ст
project прое́кт
proper до́лжный
property достоя́ние
proposal предложе́ние
propose (to) предлага́ть
provide (to) доставля́ть/доста́вить;
    предоставля́ть/предоста́вить

punch (to) прокомпости́ровать (a ticket)
purposeful напра́вленный (adj.)
purse кошелёк; су́мка
put (to) класть/положи́ть;
    ста́вить/поста́вить
  put finishing touches on (to)
    дораба́тывать/дорабо́тать

Q

quality ка́чество
quantity коли́чество
quickly бы́стро
quite весьма́
  quite a bit нема́ло

R

radio радиоприёмник
railroad (adj.) железнодоро́жный
rain дождь (m.)
rarely ре́дко
reach (to) достига́ть/дости́гнуть
  (achieve); добира́ться/добра́ться (get
  to)
real действи́тельный, реа́льный
real estate недви́жимость (f.)
rebound (to) отска́кивать/отскочи́ть
receive (to) получа́ть(ся)/получи́ть(ся)
reception приём
recipe реце́пт
recommend (to) рекомендова́ть
recommendation рекоменда́ция
reexamine (to) пересмотре́ть
reflect (to) отража́ть
refresh (to) освежа́ть/освежи́ть
refrigerator холоди́льник
regal ца́рский
region о́бласть (f.) (territorial); регио́н
  (local)
regional региона́льный
register (to) регистри́роваться;
  запи́сываться/записа́ться
registration регистра́ция
reject (to) отказа́ться
relate (to) расска́зывать/рассказа́ть
relations отноше́ния
relative ро́дственник
relax (to) рассла́биться
rely on (to) наде́яться (на что-кого)
remaining (adj.) остально́й (adj.)
remark замеча́ние
remark (to) замеча́ть/заме́тить
remarkable замеча́тельный
remarkably замеча́тельно
remember (to) по́мниться (imp.)
remind (to) напомина́ть/напо́мнить
remove (to) удаля́ть/удали́ть
remuneration вознагражде́ние, опла́та
rent аре́нда
repair почи́нка; ремо́нт
repeat (adj.) повто́рный
repel (to) отбива́ть/отби́ть
repertoire репертуа́р
report докла́д; репорта́ж
reporter репортёр

represent (to)
  представля́ть/предста́вить
representation представле́ние
request (to) проси́ть/попроси́ть
rescue (to) выруча́ть/вы́ручить
research (adj.) иссле́довательский
reserve (to) заброни́ровать
resolution разреше́ние
resolve (to) реша́ть/реши́ть
respond (to) отвеча́ть/отве́тить
responsibility отве́тственность (f.)
responsible отве́тственный (adj.)
responsive отве́тный (adj.)
rest (to) отдыха́ть/отдохну́ть
restaurant рестора́н
retraining переподгото́вка
return возвраще́ние
return (to) возвраща́ться/ верну́ться;
  сдава́ть/сдать (trans.)
return invitation отве́тное приглаше́ние
return, devote (to) отдава́ть/отда́ть
reverse обра́тный (adj.)
revocable отзывно́й
rice ри́совый (adj.)
right пра́во
ring звоно́к
rite обра́д
rival сопе́рник
road доро́жный (adj.)
room ко́мната
rough гру́бый
rough draft черпови́к
rounds, going around обхо́д
routine рути́на
row ряд
rule пра́вило
run (to) бе́гать/бежа́ть
  run into (to) ста́лкиваться
runner бегу́н
rural се́льский

S

safe сейф
sale распрода́жа
salesman продаве́ц
saleswoman продавщи́ца
salt соль (f.)
satisfaction удовлетворе́ние
Saturday суббо́та
saucer блю́дце
savings (adj.) сберега́тельный
scanner ска́нер
scanning скани́рование
schedule расписа́ние
schoolboy шко́льник
schoolgirl шко́льница
score (to) заби́ть
sculpture скульпту́ра
search по́иски
section разде́л
seed се́мя (nom. pl. семена́)
seek (to) иска́ть/поиска́ть
seize (to) хвата́ть
select (to) выбира́ть/выбрать

selection вы́бор; подбо́р
sell (to) продава́ть/прода́ть
semolina ма́нный
send (to) отправля́ть/отпра́вить
    (dispatch someone or thing);
    посыла́ть/посла́ть (something)
sensibly разу́мно (adv.)
separate разде́льный
serial (adj.) многосери́йный (production)
serum сы́воротка
services услу́ги
session заседа́ние
set набо́р
set aside отведённый (p.p.p)
set aside time (to) отводи́ть/отвести́
    вре́мя
set out (to) отправля́ться/отпра́виться
setback неуда́ча
seven семь
seventh седьмо́й
several не́сколько (adv.)
severe тяжёлый
sew (to) шить (шью, шьёшь)
shake (to) (agitate) трясти́
    shake hands (to) пожима́ть ру́ки
share а́кция (stock)
share (to) дели́ть, разделя́ть
shave (to) бри́ться
shelf прила́вок
shoe боти́нок
    shoelaces шнурки́
shopping поку́пки
shortage нехва́тка
show (to) пока́зывать/показа́ть
showcase витри́на
shower душ
sick leave о́тпуск по боле́зни
side сторона́
sights достопримеча́тельности
sign при́знак
significantly значи́тельно
signify (to) обознача́ть
silver (adj.) сере́бряный
similar похо́жий
simplify (to) упроща́ть/упрости́ть
simply про́сто
sit down (to) сади́ться/сесть
six шесть
slow ме́дленный
small ма́ленький
    small box шкату́лка
    small loaf бу́лка
    small piece кусо́чек
    small table сто́лик
smell of (to) па́хнуть (чем)
smoke (to) кури́ть
smoked копчёный
smoker кури́льщик
snag загво́здка
so так
so much сто́лько
software програ́ммное обеспече́ние
solution разреше́ние
solve (to) реша́ть/реши́ть
solvency платёжеспосо́бность (f.)

some не́который
something что-то (indef. pron.)
sometimes иногда́
son-in-law зять
soon ско́ро
sort сорт
sound (to) звуча́ть
source, spring исто́чник
sow (to) вы́севать
spacious просто́рный
speaker дина́мик (electronic); ора́тор,
    докла́дчик (person)
special осо́бенный (adj.)
specifications техни́ческие
    характери́стики
specified оговорённый (adj.)
speech речь
speed ско́рость
splendid великоле́пный
splendidly здо́рово (adv.)
spouse супру́га (fem); супру́г (m.)
spring весна́
square (adj.) квадра́тный
stage сце́на
stand кио́ск
stand стенд
stand (to) стоя́ть
state госуда́рство (noun);
    госуда́рственный (adj.)
state-owned farm совхо́з
station вокза́л, ста́нция
stationary стациона́рный
status состоя́ние
stay (to) остава́ться/оста́ться
stay over (to)
    остана́вливаться/останови́ться
steeple шпиль
step подно́жка
sterilization стерилиза́ция
still ещё
stock а́кции
    stock exchange би́ржа
stomach желу́док
stop (to) остана́вливать/останови́ть
    (trans.); перестава́ть/переста́ть
storage хране́ние
straight ahead пря́мо (adv.)
strawberry (adj.) земляни́чный
    cultivated strawberries клубни́ка
stream руче́й
strength кре́пость (f.)
strengthen (to) укрепля́ть/укрепи́ть
strict стро́гий (adj.)
strike (to) поража́ть/порази́ть
stroll прогу́лка
stroll (to) гуля́ть/погуля́ть
structure констру́кция
student слу́шатель, студе́нт, уча́щийся
study (to) изуча́ть/изучи́ть
stunning потряса́ющий
style стиль (m.)
subject предме́т
substitute (to) заменя́ть/замени́ть
subtitle субти́тр, подзаголо́вок
suburb при́город

suburban за́городный
success успе́х
successful успе́шный
successor прее́мник
suffer (to) потерпе́ть
sufficiently доста́точно
sugar са́хар
   sugar bowl са́харница
suggest (to) подска́зывать/подсказа́ть
suitable подходя́щий (adj.)
suitcase чемода́н
summer ле́тний (adj.)
summon (to) вызыва́ть/вы́звать
summons вы́зов
supermarket суперма́ркет
supper обе́д (noun.); обе́денный (adj.)
supplier поста́вщик
supply запа́с
support подде́ржка
support (to) подде́рживать/поддержа́ть
suppose (to) полага́ть
sure уве́рен/а/ы (short adj.)
surprise удивле́ние
suspecting подозрева́ющий
swim (to) купа́ться; пла́вать
syringe шприц

T

table (adj.) насто́льный
   table setting столо́вый набо́р
tablespoon ло́жка
take (to) брать/взять
   take a break, (to) передохну́ть
   take a seat (to)
      приса́живаться/присе́сть
   take an examination (to) сда́вать
      экза́мен
   take away (to) отбира́ть/отобра́ть
   take down (to) снима́ть/снять
   take into consideration (to)
      принима́ть/приня́ть во внима́ние
   take shape (to)
      скла́дываться/сложи́ться
tape ле́нта
   tape recorder магнитофо́н
tariff тари́ф
taste вкус
tasteless безвку́сный
tasty вку́сно
tax нало́г (noun); нало́говый (adj.)
taxi такси́ (n.)
tea чай
   tea set ча́йный серви́з
   teapot ча́йник
   teaspoon ча́йная ло́жка
teach (to) учи́ть/научи́ть
teamwork сы́гранность (f.)
tear (to) рвать; разрыва́ть
tear off (to) оторва́ть
technical техни́ческий
technology те́хника
telephone телефо́н
   telephone receiver тру́бка
television телеви́зор
   television newscast тележурна́л

tempting зама́нчиво
ten де́сять
tenant аренда́тор
tense напряжённый (adj.)
textbook уче́бник
thank (to) благодари́ть/поблагодари́ть
   Thank you. Спаси́бо.
then зате́м
therefore поэ́тому
thing вещь
thoroughly основа́тельно (adv.)
three hundred три́ста
thresher молоти́лка
throat го́рло
   throat inflammation анги́на
throw in (to) вбра́сывать/вбро́сить
throw, cast (to) броса́ть/бро́сить
time вре́мя
   time-limit deposit сро́чный вклад
tiring утоми́тельный
to на, за
   To your health! За здоро́вье!
   To your heart's content! На здоро́вье!
toast тост
today's сего́дняшний (adj.)
toilet туале́т
tomato помидо́р
tomorrow за́втра
too чересчу́р (adv.)
touch-up дорабо́тка
tractor тра́ктор
traffic jam про́бка
training обуче́ние
translate (to) переводи́ть/перевести́
transmission переда́ча
transmit (to) передава́ть/переда́ть
travel (to) путеше́ствовать
tray подно́с
treat (to) угоща́ть/угости́ть
treatment лече́ние
trifle ме́лочь (f.)
trip езда́
trip (to) дать подно́жку
troubles хло́поты
truck грузови́к
truth пра́вда
try (to) попро́бовать;
   стара́ться/постара́ться
twelve двена́дцать

U

unacceptability неприе́млемость (f.)
unbiased беспристра́стный
uncle дя́дя
understand (to) понима́ть/поня́ть
understanding поня́тие
understood поня́тно (adv.)
undertake (to) затева́ть/зате́ять
undertaking начина́ние
unfortunately к сожале́нию
unique своеобра́зный
unload (to) сбыва́ть (кому)
unpredictably непредсказу́емо
unsatisfactory неудовлетвори́тельный
unsurprisingly неудиви́тельно

unusual необы́чный
urgent экстренный
use по́льзование (чем)
use (to) применя́ть/примени́ть
use (to) по́льзоваться (чем);
    испо́льзовать (что)
useful поле́зный

V

vacation о́тпуск
vaccination приви́вка
vaccine вакци́на
value це́нность (f.); це́нности (pl.)
vast огро́мный (adj.)
vegetables о́вощи
verb глаго́л
version ве́рсия; вариа́нт
vicinity окре́стность (f.)
view взгля́д (opinion); вид (type)
viewer зри́тель
viewpoint то́чка зре́ния
violence наси́лие
visit (to) посеща́ть/посети́ть

W

wait (to) дожда́ться; подожда́ть
waiting room зал ожида́ния
want (to) хоте́ть/захоте́ть
warm тёплый
wealthy бога́тый
weapons ору́жие
weather пого́да
wedding венча́ние
week неде́ля (f.)
weekday бу́дний день
weekend уик-энд
weekly еженеде́льный
weigh (to) взве́шивать/взве́сить
welcome (to) приве́тствовать
Welcome! Добро́ пожа́ловать!; С
    прие́здом!
well-being благополу́чие
Western за́падный
what for заче́м

wheat пшени́ца
whistle свисто́к
whistle (to) свисте́ть
white бе́лый
whitefish сиг
whole це́лый (adj.)
why почему́
widespread распространённый
wild ди́кий
    wild strawberries земляни́ка
willingly охо́тно
wine вино́
winter ози́мый (adj.)
wish жела́ние
wish (to) жела́ть (чего-кому)
with с
with pleasure с удово́льствием
without без
    without doubt без сомне́ния
    without fail непреме́нно; обяза́тельно
    without time limit бессро́чный
work произведе́ние (of art or
    literature)
work (to) рабо́тать
    work for a while (to) потруди́ться
    work out, develop, design (to)
        выраба́тывать/вы́работать
    work up an appetite (to) нагуля́ть
        (аппети́т)
workplace, job рабо́чее ме́сто
world мир, свет
worried взволно́ван(а)(ы)
worry (to) беспоко́иться (to be troubled);
    волнова́ть(ся) (to become agitated)
wrap up (to) завёртывать/заверну́ть

X

X raying рентгеноскопи́я

Y

yesterday's вчера́шний (adj.)
yield (to) смири́ться
young молодо́й (adj.)
    young woman де́вушка

INDEX

NOTES

NOTES

NOTES

NOTES

NOTES

NOTES

NOTES